CW01186937

THE PRINTING AND THE PRINTERS
OF *THE BOOK OF COMMON PRAYER*, 1549–1561

Bibliographers have been notoriously 'hesitant to deal with liturgies', and this volume bridges an important gap with its authoritative examination of how *The Book of Common Prayer* came into being. The first edition of 1549, the first Grafton edition of 1552 and the first quarto edition of 1559 are now correctly identified, while Peter Blayney shows that the first two editions of 1559 were probably finished on the same day. Through relentless scrutiny of the evidence, he reveals that the contents of the 1549 version continued to evolve both during and after the printing of the first edition, and that changes were still being made to the Elizabethan revision weeks after the Act of Uniformity was passed. His bold reconstruction is transformative for the early Anglican liturgy, and thus for the wider history of the Church of England. This major, revisionist work is a remarkable book about a remarkable book.

PETER W. M. BLAYNEY is an independent scholar widely considered to be the leading expert on the book trade in Tudor and early Stuart London. His publications include *The Texts of King Lear and their Origins* (1982), which reconstructed the printing of the First Quarto in unprecedented detail; his ground-breaking monograph, *The Bookshops in Paul's Cross Churchyard* (1990), which pioneered the field of book-trade topography; and *The Stationers' Company and the Printers of London, 1501–1557* (2013), one of the most important contributions to the history of the book trade and printing for several generations. He has been awarded fellowships by Trinity College, Cambridge, the National Endowment for the Humanities, the Folger Shakespeare Library, the Guggenheim Foundation, and the Bibliographical Society.

THE PRINTING AND THE PRINTERS OF *THE BOOK OF COMMON PRAYER*, 1549–1561

PETER W. M. BLAYNEY

CAMBRIDGE
UNIVERSITY PRESS

CAMBRIDGE
UNIVERSITY PRESS

University Printing House, Cambridge CB2 8BS, United Kingdom

One Liberty Plaza, 20th Floor, New York, NY 10006, USA

477 Williamstown Road, Port Melbourne, VIC 3207, Australia

314–321, 3rd Floor, Plot 3, Splendor Forum, Jasola District Centre,
New Delhi – 110025, India

103 Penang Road, #05–06/07, Visioncrest Commercial, Singapore 238467

Cambridge University Press is part of the University of Cambridge.

It furthers the University's mission by disseminating knowledge in the pursuit of education, learning, and research at the highest international levels of excellence.

www.cambridge.org
Information on this title: www.cambridge.org/9781108837415
DOI: 10.1017/9781108939713

© Peter W.M. Blayney 2022

This publication is in copyright. Subject to statutory exception and to the provisions of relevant collective licensing agreements, no reproduction of any part may take place without the written permission of Cambridge University Press.

First published 2022

Printed in the United Kingdom by TJ Books Limited, Padstow Cornwall

A catalogue record for this publication is available from the British Library.

Library of Congress Cataloging-in-Publication Data
NAMES: Blayney, Peter W. M., 1944– author.
TITLE: The printing and the printers of the Book of common prayer, 1549–1561 / Peter W.M. Blayney.
DESCRIPTION: Cambridge, United Kingdom ; New York, NY, USA : Cambridge University Press, 2022. | Includes bibliographical references and index.
IDENTIFIERS: LCCN 2021024760 (print) | LCCN 2021024761 (ebook) | ISBN 9781108837415 (hardback) | ISBN 9781108940597 (paperback) | ISBN 9781108939713 (ebook)
SUBJECTS: LCSH: Church of England. Book of common prayer. | Church of England – Publishing. | Printing – England – History – 16th century. | BISAC: LANGUAGE ARTS & DISCIPLINES / Publishers & Publishing Industry
CLASSIFICATION: LCC BX5145 .B59 2022 (print) | LCC BX5145 (ebook) | DDC 264/.03–dc23
LC record available at https://lccn.loc.gov/2021024760
LC ebook record available at https://lccn.loc.gov/2021024761

ISBN 978-1-108-83741-5 Hardback

Cambridge University Press has no responsibility for the persistence or accuracy of URLs for external or third-party internet websites referred to in this publication and does not guarantee that any content on such websites is, or will remain, accurate or appropriate.

*To the memory of Elizabeth A. ('Betsy') Walsh:
for 35 years one of the great treasures of
the Folger Shakespeare Library*

Contents

List of Figures and Plates	page x
Preface: The Archaeology of a Printed Book	xiii
Acknowledgements	xix
Permissions	xxi
Conventions	xxii
List of Abbreviations	xxvi

1 From Henry VIII to the First Edwardian Prayer Book   1
   The Book of the Common Prayer, 1549   3
   How the Books were Printed   5
   The Preliminaries   7
   The Main Text, Part 1   9
   An Introduction to Shared Printing   12
   The Main Text, Part 2   14
   Three Remarkable Volumes   15
   Corroboration from the Past   21
   The Reprints of 1549   24
   The End of Demand   27

2 The Second Edwardian Prayer Book   29
   Inflation and the Collation   34

3 Mary's Reign and Elizabeth's First Parliament   44
   Mary's Counter-Reformation   44
   Elizabeth's First Parliament   46

4 Richard Grafton's Edition (STC 16291)   52
   The Collation   52
   The Required Revisions   54
   The Benefits of Recycling   58
   The Grouping of the Recycled Sheets   60

5 The First Jugge-and-Cawood Edition (STC 16292)   62
   The Printers   62

	Quires A–F: Reyner Wolfe and Edward Whitchurch	65
	Quire G: John Cawood	72
	Quires H, M, and the Outer Sheets of Quire I: Owen Rogers	73
	Quires K, L, and the Inner Sheets of Quire I: Thomas Marshe	78
	Six Sheets of Quires N and O: Richard Payne	80
	Two Sheets of Quire O: John Kingston	81
	Quire P, Sheet N3:6, and Some Cancels: Richard Jugge	82
	Productivity and Chronology	84
6	**The Preliminaries: Collaboration and Cancels**	90
	The Lectionary Errors of 1552	90
	The Grafton/Kingston Calendar of 1559	93
	The Jugge-and-Cawood Calendar and Sheets ᵀA5–8: Reyner Wolfe	94
	The New Act of Uniformity and Table of Proper Lessons: John Kingston	97
	Title-page, Contents, and Almanack: Jugge and Kingston	102
	The 'Grafton' Title-page and Almanack	105
	Summary	111
7	**The Orphaned Ordinal**	113
	History and Name	113
	The Corpus Christi Copy	117
	The Printers of the Jugge Ordinal	125
	The Revisions	126
	Whatever Happened to Sheet BB5:6?	128
8	**The Third and Fourth Editions**	134
	Disentangling Some Facts	134
	Quires A–E: Richard Jugge	137
	Quires F–G: John Cawood	138
	The Return of Owen Rogers	138
	Quires L–P	140
	A Brief Summary	142
	The Preliminaries	143
	Richard Grafton Gives Up Printing	143
	Which Edition is the 'Best'?	148
9	**The Quarto and Octavo Editions**	152
	The Two Quartos	153
	The Psalter	155
	The Extant Octavo	160
	The Newcastle Fragment	160
10	**The 1561 Revision of the Calendar**	164
	The Lectionary from 1549 to 1560	164
	Elizabeth Intervenes	165
	The Folio Miscellaneous Column before 1561	171

Printing the Cancel Calendars (1)	174
The Survival of the Biggest	179
The Edwardian Quartos and Octavos	181
Other Pre-Elizabethan Calendars	185
The Last Calendars before the Revision	187
Printing the Cancel Calendars (2)	190

11 Concluding Summary 196

Appendixes 209
  A The Etymology of 'Black Rubric' 209
  B The Missing Act of 1559 213
  C The Recycled Calendar of 1560 220
  D The Editions of 1559 (and the Cancels of 1561–62) 224
Bibliography 234
Index 238

A colour plate section will be found between pages 164 and 165.

Figures and Plates

1	The colophons of March 1549.	*page* 18
2	Title-page of the first edition of 1549, with annotations *c.* 1600.	22
3	Title-page of Grafton's first edition of 1552 (STC 16286.5).	36
4	Title-page of Whitchurch's last edition of 1552 (STC 16282.7).	37
5	Ornamental initials and display type.	64
6	The stop-press correction of page D4^v, lines 27–34.	69
7	Richard Jugge's great primer w's.	70
8	Owen Rogers and his I shortage.	75
9	Thomas Marshe's press figures, 1557 and 1559.	79
10	Third page of the table of proper lessons.	99
11	Kingston's title-page for Fabyan's *Chronicle*, 1559 (STC 10663).	108
12	Privy Council signatures in the Grafton prayer book.	118
13	The last extant page of the Grafton ordinal (with colophon).	120
14	Prices as printed in the second Jugge-and-Cawood edition.	122
15	The title-page of the Jugge ordinal.	124
16	John Kingston's original sheet BB5:6, 1559.	130
17	Thomas Dawson's replacement sheet BB5:6, 1580.	131
18	Thomas Purfoot's replacement sheet BB5:6, *c.* 1581.	132
19	Title-page of the fourth edition (JC3 = STC 16292a).	136
20	Owen Rogers initials in JC2–3.	139
21	Some initials of Grafton, Jugge, and Payne.	144
22	The cancel slip formerly pasted over Grafton's imprint.	146
23	Title-page and colophon of the Seres psalter.	156
24	Title-page and colophon of the complete octavo edition (STC 16293.5).	161
25	The use of red ink in almanack columns 4–10, editions 1 and 2 of 1561.	191

List of Figures and Plates

26	The Black Rubric, 1663.	210
27	Jugge's January in Cawood's Bible, 1560 (STC 2094).	222
28	January reimposed in Jugge's own prayer book, 1560 (STC 16294).	223

Plates (after p. 164)

1*a* 20 April 1559. The Act of Uniformity is passed by the Commons.
1*b* 21–22 March 1559. The (lost) Act for Collating Bishops is read.
2 The Grafton first edition of 1559 (STC 16291).
3 The Jugge-and-Cawood first edition of 1559 (STC 16292).
4 Kingston's calendar for the Grafton edition (STC 16291).
5 Wolfe's calendar for Jugge and Cawood (STC 16292).
6 The first edition of Jugge's cancel calendar, 1561.
7 The third edition of Jugge's cancel calendar, 1562.
8 The first edition in quarto (STC 16293.3).

Preface: The Archaeology of a Printed Book

This book began as a detailed investigation into both how and why a surprisingly large number of printers collaborated on transforming the second Edwardian prayer book of 1552 into the Elizabethan *Book of Common Prayer* – a process that was not really completed until the end of 1561.

More than twenty years ago at the British Library I first opened one of the two earliest folio editions of the 1559 version, whose imprint names Elizabeth's two Queen's Printers, Richard Jugge and John Cawood. I was already aware that they were not partners in a single business and that each ran his own independent printing house, so I wanted to know which part or parts of the book each had printed. What I found, however, was so extraordinary and unexpected that far more time would be needed to unravel its complexity – especially since I was already working on a large and time-consuming project. After a brief look at the Library's other 1559 editions, therefore, I arranged to have all six of them microfilmed so that I could excavate them at leisure.

I cannot claim to be a liturgiologist, and the Elizabethan Settlement is a topic that has preoccupied many historians and scholars far more expert in the relevant disciplines than I am. But what has made me step into this dauntingly crowded arena is that the prayer books of 1559 have never been examined really closely by analytical bibliographers. Never before has anyone realized how extraordinary the editions of that year are as printed books. It was not possible to limit the study to the single edition that first drew my attention. To begin with, two substantially different editions were printed soon after Elizabeth's Act of Uniformity prescribed what the book should contain, and the relationship between them (not limited to the question of which came first) needed clarification. Each was a reprint, with most of the required revisions, of an edition of the second Edwardian prayer book, and the reasons why those 1552 editions were themselves so differently structured needed to be explained. And when that investigation led back to the first Edwardian prayer books of 1549, examining the seemingly settled question of which of *those* editions was the first to be printed and published opened a new can of worms.

Many years ago, in an essay on the revised *Short-Title Catalogue*, I drew attention to some examples of the wry wit of Katharine F. Pantzer, including her memorable note that 'Most bibliographers are hesitant to deal with liturgies from the period before, during, and after the Reformation' – which of course means all liturgies, past, present, and future.[A] I must confess that I had long been a member of the hesitant majority in this (dis)regard, because none of the printers who most interested me were known to have printed liturgies. The category 'liturgical books' is therefore one that I had usually been content to leave to those more interested in the liturgy itself.

But at the same time I have long accepted what many now consider to be an obsolete definition of *bibliography*, namely the study of books as material objects without regard to their contents. As a bibliographer in that sense, I am most interested in books that tell stories. Not books *of* stories, but material objects that tell their own stories: books that contain evidence of one kind or another that their progress through the printing house may have been neither routine nor regular. Rather than 'The History of the Book' (whatever 'the Book' may mean in the capitalized singular) – or the history of *a* book, or of books collectively – I have always thought of what I do as more akin to the archaeology of books.

Since the early 1970s I have made something of a speciality of identifying the printers of books printed anonymously in England, and, in particular, of determining whether a book was printed throughout by a single printer, or whether one or more parts of it were printed by one or more others (as is not uncommon in and after Elizabeth's reign). This is a field of study that is not exactly crowded, and while three of the revisers of the *Short-Title Catalogue* were very good at it, the sheer magnitude of their task did not allow them to devote as much time to individual Edwardian or Elizabethan liturgies as their unsuspected complexity required. So although the contents of the prayer books of 1549–59 have been minutely examined and copiously discussed over the centuries by numerous scholars whose learning I cannot hope to emulate, they have hardly ever been closely scrutinized by any expert in the kind of detective work in which I specialize. Nobody, for example, has noticed (or, at least, mentioned) that one sheet in the first of Edward Whitchurch's editions of March 1549 was printed by Nicholas

---

[A] Blayney, 'The Numbers Game', 381, citing STC, II, 68, col. 2.

Hill, who also contributed more extensively to three of Whitchurch's next four editions. Nobody seems to have observed (in either sense) that in the same year Robert Wyer printed parts of three 'Grafton' editions, that in 1552 Steven Mierdman printed parts of two 'Whitchurch' editions, or that one 'Grafton' edition of that year includes sheets from both Nicholas Hill and John Day. Nor, indeed, has it even been realized that the edition listed by STC as Grafton's last of 1552 is in fact his first of that year.[A]

When I focused on 1559, however, I discovered that the first 'Jugge and Cawood' folio edition of *The Book of Common Prayer* (STC 16292) was the collaborative work of a completely unprecedented number of printers – several of whom subsequently also worked on both the third and fourth editions. Meanwhile all known copies of the rival first edition (printed mostly by Richard Grafton but partly by one of his former apprentices) contain one or more sheets (in two cases more than twenty) recycled from the last 'Grafton' edition of 1552. The folios were followed by two quarto editions, of which at least the first is the work of four printers, and not until one of the last editions of the year (an octavo) do we find one certifiably printed by a single printer from beginning to end (although he was neither of the two men named in both the imprint and the colophon).

I reported an early version of those parts of this study as the twenty-fourth George Kiddell Memorial Lecture, given in 2018 at the Thomas Fisher Rare Book Library, Toronto, under the title 'How Many Printers Does It Take to Change a Liturgy?'. Later that year I gave a substantially revised version at the Annual General Meeting of the Friends of Lambeth Palace Library, and rewrote it as 'Printing the 1559 *Book of Common Prayer*: Events Without Precedent' in the *Lambeth Palace Library Annual Review 2018*, pp. 106–34. And more recently I reported some of the conclusions reached in the present Chapter 1 to *New College Notes* as 'The First Issue of the First Edition of the First Edwardian Prayer Book: New College Library, Oxford, BT1.131.19'.

Unlike those papers, this book does not always travel in a straight line towards a single conclusion. Its principal focus remains the first two 1559 editions of *The Book of Common Prayer*. But the physical form of those books had already been essentially determined by the reprinting history of the editions of 1552, which in turn owed much to lessons learned by their printers in 1549. The first three chapters are therefore essentially

---

[A] David N. Griffiths, whose *Bibliography of the Book of Common Prayer* was published in 2002, apparently relied almost exclusively on the revised STC for all editions before 1641. All STC's errors about the Tudor editions are reproduced, augmented by additional errors of Griffiths's own.

introductory, but each in a different way. After a brief sketch of the historical background from Henry VIII's break with Rome to the accession of Edward VI, Chapter 1 offers a radically revised history of the earliest editions of the 1549 *Book of the Common Praye*r, and attempts to explain why each of the printers changed the structure of his later editions in different ways. Chapter 2 outlines the similarly varied reprinting histories of the replacement book of 1552, which explain why the physical structures of the two first editions of the Elizabethan book are so different. And Chapter 3 outlines the difficulties in which the reign of Mary Tudor left the London printing trade, and describes how Elizabeth's first parliament made it possible for the 1552 liturgy to be both revived and revised.

The text of the 1559 book would shape the religion of a nation for centuries, but those who printed it were not the men who wrote it. As this study will show again and again, the process of printing a book could be unpredictably complicated, and sometimes seemingly irrational. The London book trade of 1559 was no longer what it had been under Edward VI – and even then it had been more remarkable for energy and commitment than for high-quality workmanship. Mary's reign had seriously compromised the productivity of one of the houses that had printed the Edwardian prayer books, and had imposed conditions that led to the closure of the other. Elizabeth's first Queen's Printer had never before been a printer, had no printing house, and took several months to find and equip one. She therefore appointed a partner for him: *Mary's* Queen's Printer, who had himself never been a printer until Mary chose him, and had owed his royal appointment to his Catholic faith.

Of those who worked on the 1559 books, four were men who (under the terms of the charter that Mary had granted the Stationers' Company in 1557) had no legal right to print at all because they were not Stationers. Two of the Stationers who worked on the folio editions of 1559 had barely four years' experience as master printers, and one of them had recently been in trouble for his involvement (together with one of the four non-Stationers) in the carelessly printed piracy of a book of sermons by one of Mary's bishops. These were among the men who, at or soon after the end of April 1559, were given the impossible task of supplying every parish in England with enough books to allow the new service to be introduced on 24 June, when it was supposed to become compulsory. And among the additional difficulties was that even after the printing began, further revisions to the 1552 service book were still being devised by the authorities (though no longer with parliamentary sanction).

Chapters 4–7 focus on the first two folio editions of 1559. They depend, however, on the interpretation of a variety of kinds of evidence, some of which will be unfamiliar to many readers, and cannot easily be presented in strict order, either chronological or bibliographical. One of those editions reprinted (with the necessary revisions) a Grafton edition of 1552, while the other likewise reprinted a Whitchurch edition. It has been implausibly suggested that the Grafton example (which accurately quotes the Act of Supremacy and reprints the Act of Uniformity verbatim) had been finished before Parliament assembled on 23 January. In reality there is reason to believe that the other edition, printed in the names of the Queen's Printers, was the first to be started. But the preliminaries show clear signs of cooperation between the two teams of printers, and there is evidence strongly suggesting that the rival title-pages were printed on the same day.

Although the Jugge and Cawood edition was probably started first, in Chapter 4 I begin with the main text of the Grafton edition. I do so partly because the question of its date needs to be cleared up, and partly because the most obvious bibliographical complication of that edition is fairly simple to describe and explain – but chiefly because the edition by the Queen's Printers is the principal ancestor of all subsequent editions. Chapter 5 then focuses on the distinctly more complicated progress of the main text in that edition. In Chapter 6, however, the partly collaborative preliminaries of both editions (the first quires in the books but the last to be printed) are examined side by side. Chronology is then violated again when Chapter 7 considers the ordinal that each team had printed before they turned to the preliminaries – and also before they were informed that it was not to be included after all, but marketed separately (or in one case perhaps suppressed).

The next two chapters examine the subsequent editions of the same year. Chapter 8 looks at the two folio reprints (each shared by five of the former printers but not divided in quite the same way); Chapter 9 examines the two known editions in quarto (one with an appended psalter that reveals an unexpected conflict between royal patents) and the two known octavos (one of which survives only as a fragment whose precise location is at present unknown).

The lengthy Chapter 10 examines the second stage of the Elizabethan revision. In 1561 the queen commanded that changes be made to the liturgical calendar, claiming that some of the prescribed Old Testament readings in the lectionary could usefully be replaced by more edifying ones. The lectionary did need attention, but the real problems were consequences of the 1559 revision of the table of proper lessons – and what the reforms of 1561 actually accomplished fell far short of what Elizabeth intended. Editions printed in and after 1562 with the new calendar are no concern of this study, but many of the several thousand owners of 1559 folio editions (most of them clergy) urgently needed the new information. So Richard Jugge was given the task of printing cancel calendars to be inserted into copies from which the obsolete leaves had been removed. The most important changes were in the lectionary columns, but the most noticeable were a substantially increased number of saints' days, feasts, and fasts added to the column once reserved only for red-letter holy days. At first sight these additions could suggest a revival of Catholic traditions, but investigation shows that more than three-quarters of them had also been anticipated in 1552–53 by the unquestionably Protestant Whitchurch and Grafton in their small-format editions, and that others could be found in the calendars of Edwardian bibles and New Testaments, seemingly added at the discretion and choice of their printers. Not until 1562 was a complete edition of the Elizabethan book printed (in quarto) that actually incorporated the changes of 1561, and can claim to be the first fully revised edition of *The Book of Common Prayer* as it would endure throughout Elizabeth's reign until revised again under James I.

It seems likely that some readers (perhaps many) would prefer to find out where the journey is going before choosing to focus on the many and varied steps along the way. Chapter 11 therefore attempts to summarize the whole story, from the first Edwardian edition to Elizabeth's cancel calendars, as a single narrative.

Acknowledgements

Most of those who have materially helped with the research for this book are on the staff of libraries or archives holding one or more of the early books mentioned in it. One of the most significantly valuable events in that respect was the acquisition in 2017, by the Thomas Fisher Rare Book Library, University of Toronto, of what thus became the only 1559 *Book of Common Prayer* in Canada (bound with one of the only two copies of the 1559 ordinal outside England), for which I am deeply grateful in alphabetical order to Pearce Carefoote (Head of the Department of Rare Books and Special Collections), Loryl MacDonald (Director), and Philip Oldfield (retired librarian).

The following list is alphabetical by library or archive, where I have particular reasons to be grateful to the following: at the Bodleian Library, Oxford (Jo Maddocks, Dunja Sharif, and Sarah Wheale); Boston Public Library (Jay Moschella); Brasenose College, Oxford (Liz Kay); British Library (Karen Limper-Herz and Christian Algar); Cambridge University Library (William Hale); Christ Church, Oxford (David Stumpp and Gabriel Sewell); Corpus Christi College, Cambridge (Alexander Devine); Corpus Christi College, Oxford (Joanna Snelling and Julie Blyth); Durham Cathedral Library (Gary Butler and Sarah-Jane Raymond); Eton College Library (Lucy Gwynn); General Theological Seminary, New York (Patrick Cates); Houghton Library, Harvard (Leslie A. Morris and William P. Stoneman); Huntington Library (Steven Tabor); Jesus College, Oxford (Owen McKnight); Keble College, Oxford (Yvonne Murphy); Lambeth Palace Library (Giles Mandelbrote, Ken Gibb, and Hugh Cahill); Lincoln Cathedral Library (Claire Arrand); Lincoln's Inn (Dunstan Speght); The Morgan Library & Museum (John Bidwell); New College, Oxford (Christopher Skelton-Foord, William Poole, and Anna-Nadine Pike); Oxford University Press Archives (Martin Maw); Pembroke College, Cambridge (Pat Aske); St John's College, Cambridge (Kathryn McKee); Westminster Abbey (Matthew Payne); and York Minster (Steven Newman).

In addition, a very special thanks to Sophie Floate for taking the photographs used in Figures 1 and 2.

Stephen Tabor has also earned my gratitude as one of two sources of information about (and recipients of criticisms of) entries in the ESTC; the other (to whom I am equally grateful) being John Lancaster. Ben Higgins deserves particular thanks for examining and photographing books in Oxford for me, and for going above and beyond when reporting on them in detail, while Simon Healy's expertise in matters parliamentary saved me from a couple of embarrassing oversights.

Despite being a practitioner of bibliography 'without regard to [a book's] contents', I have sometimes needed to ask questions about the text itself and to discuss its historical context. I thank both Paul Edmondson and Diarmaid MacCulloch for having responded to uninvited questions, and Pearce Carefoote for always being willing to answer others. My principal gratitude in this respect, however, is owed to Brian Cummings. In 2007 I was able to give him some (now partly obsolete) information about the 1559 books, since when I have often turned to him with questions about their contents. It was he who suggested that I expand my fairly cursory discussion of the 1549 editions, not realizing where that would lead. And once it had led there, G. Thomas Tanselle kindly agreed to read an early version of the result, and offered some valuable criticisms. Meanwhile, for advice and answers of many kinds, I must as usual thank my fellow-student in 1970 (and friend ever since), David McKitterick.

I am also grateful to Brian Cummings and Henry Woudhuysen for reading my original typescript for the Press in 2019. Their valuable suggestions led to very extensive revision, and if I occasionally chose not to follow a suggested additional path it was not because I doubted the potential value of doing so. My gratitude is also due to those at Cambridge University Press who patiently awaited the final revisions and pandemic-delayed illustrations (Emily Hockley and George Laver), and to Bethany Johnson and copy-editor Deborah Hey for making the endgame far less stressful than it could have been.

During the years when I wrestled with the printer-identifications, revising them, and constantly correcting the details – when I was wondering if, when, and how this could ever become a coherent book – my wife Leslie Thomson must often have wished that she had never heard the terms *BCP* and *lectionary*. But once I started writing in earnest she patiently read my drafts and always steered them (and me) towards greater clarity. It may be a long time before either of us can look casually at a calendar again, but without her this book would not exist.

Permissions

I should like to express my gratitude for the permission that has been granted for the reproduction of the illustrations here listed, by and for the following:

Boston Public Library: Figure 6*a*.
Bridwell Library Special Collections, Perkins School of Theology, Southern Methodist University: Figure 26.
The British Library Board: Figures 5*a–e*, 6*b*, 8*a–d*, 9*d–f*, 10, 18, 20*h*, 21*a*, 21*c–d*, 23*a–b*, 27, 28, and Plates 3, 5, and 8.
Cambridge University Library: Figure 22.
The Chapter of York: Figures 7, 14, 21*b*, 21*f*, and Plate 6.
The Folger Shakespeare Library: Figure 20*g*.
Lambeth Palace Library: Cover image, Figures 3, 4, 9*a–c*, 11, 20*b*, 20*f*, 20*i*, and Plate 7.
The Master and Fellows of St John's College, Cambridge: Plate 4.
The Parliamentary Archives: Plate 1.
The Morgan Library & Museum, New York: Figure 24.
The President and Fellows of Corpus Christi College, Oxford: Figures 12, 13, and Plate 2.
The Principal and Fellows of Jesus College, Oxford: Figure 17.
The Principal and Fellows of Brasenose College, Oxford: Figures 1–2.
The Thomas Fisher Rare Book Library, Toronto: Figures 15, 16, 19, 20*d–e*, and 21e.
The Warden, Fellows, and Scholars of Keble College, Oxford: Figure 20*a* and c.

Conventions

Bibliographical References

Readers unfamiliar with the conventions used by bibliographers when citing the pages of early printed books will find them simpler than they may seem at first sight, and Chapter 1 includes a brief introduction to the way in which books in folio were printed and to the accepted way of referring to the quires, leaves, and pages in them. The following notes add a few details not covered there.

Two books discussed in Chapter 9 were printed in quarto, which means that each sheet of paper was folded twice to make four leaves half the size of those of a folio (joined in pairs at the top, and needing to be cut open). To be more precise, each edition is a 'quarto in eights', in which each quire contains two sheets quired together (the outer sheet forms leaves 1–2 and 7–8; the inner sheet leaves 3–6). The last two editions of 1559 were in octavo, each sheet having been folded three times to make eight leaves half the size of those of a quarto. But in each case the printer's way of signing the first few leaves of each quire, and the way of referring to quire, leaf, and page, is exactly the same as for folios.

References are made in roman letters and arabic numerals, no matter what kind of type or numerals are used in the originals. Virtually all the signatures in the prayer books discussed here are in textura (blackletter, or 'gothic'), but although the ninth textura capital resembles a roman J rather than an I, and the twentieth looks more like a roman U than a V, their roman equivalents are I and V rather than J or U. For unstated reasons, while the revisers of the *Short-Title Catalogue* followed the accepted usage with textura I, when referring to quires signed with textura V they printed it as U. That practice has become common, but is not followed here.

When teaching literary students how to refer to the pages of early printed books, McKerrow explained that 'When the signature of a leaf consists of two or more similar letters, as BB, bbb, &c. (not Bb), it is usual and convenient to give these as 2B, 3b, &c'.[A] Usual it may have been, but it is difficult to argue seriously that 2B is substantially more convenient than BB, and while it may be fractionally easier to write two characters (3b) than three (bbb), the claim of convenience really only applies to higher numbers. But at least McKerrow made no pretence that Bb – two *dissimilar* letters – was in any way analogous. Six years later, however, Greg showed less common sense in addressing what he called the 'slight complication' of books whose signatures exceed a single alphabet. The italics are mine.

> If the signatures are in lower case, a becomes aa and aaa, &c. and all is straightforward. But when an upper-case alphabet is doubled, A may become either AA or Aa – usually the latter. It is possible that printers occasionally distinguished between AA and Aa; *but if so the instances are too few to deserve recognition, and in practice we ignore them.* This enables us to write 2a in place of aa, and 2A in place either of AA or of Aa. The convention is important, since, if our formulas are to be manageable and our references convenient, we must endeavour to avoid such clumsy terms as Aaaaaaa^4 (=7A^4) or DDDDDD7^v (=6D7^v) which would otherwise occur.[B]

Here Greg inserted a footnote to the effect that 'I am assured by my incunabulist friends that in the fifteenth century printers did, sometimes at any rate, distinguish between AA and Aa, using both in the same book', but defended his practice by declaring himself willing to 'go a long way to avoid unwieldy terms' – though evidently not an inch to avoid ambiguity. Twenty-five years later he appeared to have forgotten his 'incunabulist friends', and baldly asserted that 'the alternative forms [*that is, AA and Aa, etc.*] are never, so far as I am aware, used for purposes of differentiation and therefore need not be distinguished'.[C] A decade earlier, in fact, Fredson Bowers had rather reluctantly allowed the possibility of making an exception for doubled letters (though not for triples), saying that 'There can be no absolute objection to this partial expansion [*more accurately a refusal to contract*] ... but in Greg's view it is illogical'.[D] He was mistaken: Greg's 'rule' was based not on logic but aesthetics.

Although an aversion to clumsiness could reasonably support a convention of condensing signatures either containing or exceeding *four* letters, to pretend that there is never a need to distinguish AAA from AAa or Aaa (all of which can be found in sixteenth-century

---

[A] McKerrow, *An Introduction to Bibliography*, 161.　[B] Greg, 'A Formulary of Collation', 373.
[C] Greg, *A Bibliography of the English Printed Drama*, iv, clii. But STC 11275, printed in 1598 by Thomas Creede (a year and a printer Greg knew well), collates 2°: A–Z^6 AA–CC^6 Aa–Aaa^6 Bbb^4.
[D] Bowers, *Principles of Bibliographical Description*, 205–6. On pp. 457–8, however, he appears to accept 'Long form' formulae as an allowable alternative to his preferred 'Shorthand' versions.

London outside Greg's comparatively narrow literary focus) is myopic and perverse. Clumsiness cannot always be avoided when writing collations for bibles, chronicles, dictionaries, collected statutes, or editions of Foxe's *Acts and Monuments*. But Greg never had to wonder whether a quotation from '3A2ʳ' in Foxe's 1563 edition was on AAa2ʳ or 264 pages away on AAA2ʳ.

In this book, no signatures are condensed, and I shall note in Chapter 1 that a false distinction between the collations of the first and second Grafton prayer books of 1549 was a direct consequence of Greg's ambiguous convention.

In another departure from standard practice, I indicate conjugacy with a colon. In references to leaves that are not conjugate, their numbers are separated by commas, as in 'leaves A5,6 and P2,3,5,8'. But if two of them are conjugate, convention separates them with a period, as in 'A4.5 and M2,4.7,9'. To my mind, the difference between conjugate and separate is bigger than the tiny quantity of ink that makes a comma bigger than a period. Moreover, a period separates wholes; a colon joins parts into a whole. And because what lies between conjugate leaves is a vertical fold perforated with stitching, the colons I prefer in 'A4:5' and 'M2,4:7,9' can also claim to be illustrative.

Transcription

When transcribing printed text I here use roman and ignore long s and ligatures, although I do not modernize spelling or punctuation. When transcribing from manuscript I expand most contractions by supplying missing letters in italic, but otherwise follow the original as closely as feasible.

Dating

All dates follow the calendar year, with the numbered year beginning on New Year's Day (a name that was never applied to any day other than 1 January). The liturgical year likewise begins with the Feast of Circumcision (1 January), so even though the Year of the Incarnation was considered to begin on 25 March, liturgical almanacks and calendars typically identified a year by the number of the Year of Grace that began *during* it. (The very different distinction between Old Style and New Style did not exist before the Gregorian reforms of 1582.)

STC and ESTC

In volume 2 of the revised STC (1976), the twelve 'known' editions and issues of *The Book of the Common Prayer* dated 1549 are catalogued under the numbers 16267–76.[A] The order is determined by a combination of assumed chronology, the printer named on the title-page, and the format ($2°$ precedes $4°$). The series is in the 16000s because the books are in the alphabetical class 'Liturgies' (15791–16607) and sub-class 'Church of England' (16267–16559). In the online ESTC, the same twelve records in the same order are as follows: S109513, S93744, S113625, S93745, S113633, S112894, S108244, S112062, S112066, S93746, S121500, S93747.[B] In each case the 'S' identifies them as belonging to the STC period (1475–1640), but the numbers are determined not by any fact about the authorship, content, date, or format of the books themselves, but by when and where the online record was created.

Neither reference work at present includes an entry for either of the first two issues of the first edition, and neither recognizes that what are listed as mere reissues of two later editions are in fact distinct editions. Eventually, ESTC will presumably emend several of the existing records and add at least two new ones. Any STC entry here described as erroneous will always be there to be examined, but what I write today about an ESTC record may no longer be either true or verifiable if (or when) that record is emended or cancelled.

With a few exceptions in Appendix D, therefore, I have not used ESTC numbers in this study. The relevant records can all be found in an advanced search of ESTC by entering 'STC', a space, and the STC number in the 'Citation note' field.

Footnotes

Because there are so many references to one or more of the quires in numerous books, and because each quire is identified with a superior number denoting how many leaves it contains, to reduce the chances of confusion I have used capital letters to identify footnotes.

[A] Only ten numbers, but the series includes 16269.5 and 16270a.
[B] That is (in numerical order without the 'S'): 93744–7, 108244, 109513, 112062, 112066, 113625, 113633, 121500, and 122894.

Abbreviations

Book-titles whose abbreviations also serve as elements of standard reference numbers (DMH, STC, TRP) are here abbreviated in roman rather than italic. Place of publication is London unless otherwise specified.

APC	*Acts of the Privy Council of England. New Series. A.D. 1542–1558*. Ed. John Roche Dasent. 6 vols. 1890–93.
Arber	Edward Arber, ed. *A Transcript of the Registers of the Company of Stationers of London; 1554–1640 A.D.* 5 vols. 1875–7, Birmingham 1894.
BCP	*Book of (the) Common Prayer*
BL	British Library.
CJ	*Journals of the House of Commons. From November the 8th 1547 . . . to March the 2d 1628.* 1802.
cm	centimetre(s).
col.	column.
ed.	edition, edited by.
EEBO	Early English Books Online (https://search.proquest.com/eebo).
ESTC	English Short-Title Catalogue (http://estc.bl.uk).
Graf.1	STC 16286.5 (ESTC S93760).
Graf.2a	STC 16285 (ESTC S93754).
Graf.2b	STC 16285.5 (ESTC S93755).
Graf.3	STC 16285.7 (ESTC S93756).
Graf.4	STC 16285a (ESTC S93757).
Graf.5	STC 16286 (ESTC S93758).
Graf.6a	STC 16286.2 (ESTC S93759).
Graf.6b	STC 16286.3 (ESTC S122910).
JC1	STC 16292 (ESTC S111841).
JC2	'STC 16292+'.
JC3	STC 16292a (ESTC S93764).

List of Abbreviations

LJ	*Journals of the House of Lords, Beginning Anno Primo Henrici Octavi*. Vol. 1: 1509–1577. 1846.
LMA	London Metropolitan Archives.
McKerrow	Ronald B. McKerrow. *Printers' & Publishers' Devices in England & Scotland, 1485–1640*. 1913.
McK & F	Ronald B. McKerrow and F. S. Ferguson. *Title-Page Borders Used in England & Scotland, 1485–1640*. 1932.
m(m).	membrane(s).
mm	millimetre(s).
n(n).	note(s).
OED	*The Oxford English Dictionary*. Second edition, prepared by J. A. Simpson and E. S. C. Weiner. 20 vols. Oxford, 1989.
p(p).	page(s).
PArch.	Parliamentary Archives (formerly House of Lords Record Office).
PBSA	*Papers of the Bibliographical Society of America*.
r	recto.
Stationers and Printers	Peter W. M. Blayney. *The Stationers' Company and the Printers of London, 1501–1557*. 2 vols. Cambridge, 2013.
Statutes	*Statutes of the Realm*. Volume IV, part 1 (1547–1585). 1819.
STC	*A Short-Title Catalogue of Books Printed in England, Scotland, and Ireland, and of English Books Printed Abroad, 1475–1640*. Compiled by A. W. Pollard and G. R. Redgrave. Second edition, revised by W. A. Jackson, F. S. Ferguson, and Katharine F. Pantzer. 3 vols. 1976–91.
TNA: PRO	The National Archives: Public Record Office.
TRP	*Tudor Royal Proclamations*. Ed. Paul L. Hughes and James F. Larkin. 3 vols. New Haven, 1964–69.
UMI	University Microfilms International.
Whit.1a	STC 16279 (ESTC S93749).
Whit.1b	STC 16280–80.5 (ESTC S93750, S93751).
Whit.2	STC 16281 (ESTC S93752).
Whit.3	STC 16281.5 (ESTC S123430).
Whit.4	STC 16282.3 (ESTC S123381).
Whit.5	STC 16282.7 (ESTC S93753).
v	verso.

Wing — Wing, Donald, ed. *Short-Title Catalogue of Books Printed in England, Scotland, Ireland, Wales, and British America and of English Books Printed in Other Countries, 1641–1700*. Second edition, revised and edited by Timothy J. Crist, John J. Morrison, Carolyn W. Nelson, and Matthew Seccombe. 4 vols. New York, 1982–89.

CHAPTER I

From Henry VIII to the First Edwardian Prayer Book

In 1534, the marital plans of Henry VIII led him to break with Rome, to deny the authority of the pope who would not grant him a divorce, and to declare himself the Supreme Head of the Church in England. But although he thereby ceased to be a *Roman* Catholic, the comparatively few reforms he allowed in the conduct of religion were more political than doctrinal. Those such as Thomas Cromwell (Henry's vicar general and vicegerent in spirituals) and Thomas Cranmer (archbishop of Canterbury) who wanted to steer the church in directions inspired by European reformers had to move slowly and warily, because by no stretch of the imagination could Henry himself be described as a Protestant.

On 3 March 1542, the Convocation of Canterbury decreed (probably at the suggestion of the Supreme Head) that from henceforth all church services in England should be ordered according to 'Sarum use':[A] that is, the version of the liturgy and rites associated since Norman times with the diocese of Salisbury, and already far more widespread throughout the kingdom than the uses of York, Hereford, and a few less influential sees. To ensure uniformity (and to hasten the demise of rival uses), the following January the king granted a joint patent to the former partners Richard Grafton and Edward Whitchurch, giving them a lifetime monopoly of printing all Sarum liturgies, namely

> The masse booke/ the Graill, the Antyphoner, The Himptnall, The portaus, and the prymer bothe in Latyn and in Englishe of Sarum vse for the province of Canterbury ... And ... that they and their assignes oonly and none other person nor persons ... haue libertie to printe the bookes abouesaid.[B]

[A] Bray, *Records of Convocation*, 267. The name 'Sarum' derives from the habit of contracting Latin *Sarisburia* to *Sa* followed by the symbol usually reserved for terminal *-rum*.
[B] TNA: PRO, C 66/716, m. 34 (28 January), quoted from the warrant, C 82/804/[14] (23 January).

Grafton and Whitchurch, who would become the most important printers of Edwardian prayer books and would also contribute to those of 1559, had begun their careers as merchants with no intention of becoming printers.[A] Grafton served as an apprentice in the Grocers' Company, and was made a freeman in December 1534 while in his early twenties. Whitchurch, probably a year or two Grafton's junior, was freed from his apprenticehip in the Haberdashers' Company in June 1536. After their first mercantile venture with another young Haberdasher ended in litigation, the partners' shared zeal for religious reform led them to finance the printing in Antwerp of the translation that became known as the 'Matthew' Bible of 1537.[B] They followed that success with an even more ambitious project: a substantial revision by Miles Coverdale of that translation, to be printed in an unusually large format and destined to become known as the 'Great Bible'. No press of the required size had ever been constructed or used in England, so the job was given to François Regnault in Paris.

About three-fifths of the printed sheets had already been shipped to England, and Regnault had almost finished the remainder, when the Inquisition summoned him and seized all the sheets still in his hands. But although the French authorities never released the confiscated sheets and eventually burned them, they not only allowed the publishers to acquire one of Regnault's presses and some of his types, ornaments, and even employees, but were apparently the first to suggest that solution. And so Grafton and Whitchurch set up a printing house in the Greyfriars' former precinct in London, and rapidly learned how to run it. By November 1539 they had replaced all the confiscated sheets and begun selling the Great Bible, and because Henry's injunctions of 1538 had required every parish church in the land to acquire a copy, they proceeded to reprint the whole book six times with extensive financial assistance from another Haberdasher.[C]

By the time they had finished supplying the nation's churches with bibles, their printing house had become the largest and most productive yet seen in England. There is no obvious sign of dissension between them, and

---

[A] The following brief account of their Henrician careers is condensed from *Stationers and Printers*, 1, 357–74, 378–85.
[B] This was the second English translation to be printed, preceded by the Coverdale Bible of 1535 (itself reprinted in 1537). Cyndia Susan Clegg's claim that it was printed in Amsterdam ('The 1559 Books of Common Prayer', 106) is mistaken.
[C] For the injunctions, see *Stationers and Printers*, 1, 377–8. The Haberdasher was Anthony Marler, who was probably related to the man sued by the partners over their earlier trading venture (1, 379–80).

they continued to collaborate for many years, but sometime around the turn of 1542–43 Whitchurch took a share of the materials and set up a printing house of his own. Whether he did so before or after the two were jointly granted the patent for Sarum liturgies is uncertain. In late 1544 Grafton (alone) was appointed printer to the young Prince Edward, and the following May he and Whitchurch were given another joint patent, this time for a royally approved primer.[A] Meanwhile, whichever of them had custody of the actual patent for liturgies had apparently lost it, and in January 1546 they paid for an inspeximus exemplification of it.[B] Had they known that Henry had only a year left to live, and that Catholic service books would not be needed during the next reign, they could have avoided that expense.

The Book of the Common Prayer, 1549

The accession of Edward VI in January 1547 brought promotion for Grafton, who replaced Thomas Berthelet as King's Printer in April.[C] On the same day he and Whitchurch received a new patent for any and all

> bookes concerning dyvyne seruice or conteyning any kinde of sermons or exhortacions that shalbe vsed suffred or Aucthorised in our Churches of Englande and Irelande ... being in the Englysshe or Lattyn tongue.[D]

Archbishop Cranmer had been working towards a vernacular form of the liturgy since the 1530s, and as early as 1544 had persuaded Henry to allow the publication of an English litany that could be included in the Sarum service. Under Edward he began anew, and (with the aid of other like-minded divines) by late 1548 he and his collaborators had prepared what would be published in March 1549 as *The Book of the Common Prayer*.[E] The Act of Uniformity that both authorized and imposed it (2 & 3 Edw. VI, c. 1) was introduced in the Commons by a bill that was read on 19 December

---

[A] Ibid., 1, 557; STC 16034, LL2^r.
[B] TNA: PRO, C 66/769, m. 16: a certified copy under the Great Seal, probably costing nearly as much as the original grant. It is possible (though I think unlikely) that the copy was procured because one of them doubted the motives of the other who had custody of the original. But I can see no obvious signs of mutual distrust at any date, and a year later they were jointly granted another patent.
[C] TNA: PRO, C 82/868/[4] (warrant of 20 April); C 66/805, m. 1 (enrolled patent, 22 April).
[D] TNA: PRO, C 66/802, m. 7 (quoted from the warrant of 20 April, C 82/868/[19]).
[E] Note the second '*the*'. As author of *The Bibliography of the Book of Common Prayer, 1549–1999* (2002), David N. Griffiths was entitled to devise his own conventions, so his unvarying '*The book of common prayer*' for all pertinent entries from 1552 (regardless of the original spelling, capitalization, or line-division) can be defended. But using the same rubber stamp instead of Cranmer's own wording for the editions of 1549–51 suggests inattention.

1548, but was redelivered to Secretary Smith rather than proceeding. It reappeared and was read in the Lords on 7 January, where after two more readings it passed on the 15th – but while both archbishops supported it, eight of the eighteen bishops present dissented. After three readings in the Commons it passed without division on the 21st.[A]

Both Whitchurch and Grafton must have begun printing the book as soon as (or even before) the Lords had voted, because although the Act would not become law until it received the royal assent on 14 March, their colophons are dated the 7th and 8th of that month respectively.[B] The new form of service was to become compulsory at Pentecost next (9 June), so the printers still had three more months to make progress towards the ideal of providing at least one copy for every parish. How close they came to that goal, however, is unknown. Each produced at least four more editions dated 1549 (a date that probably became a mere formula before they had finished), but the exact order of those reprints is not completely clear. Whitchurch's STC 16270 and 16270a are both dated May on the title-page and 4 May in the colophon, while his 16272 and 16273 are dated June on the title-page and 16 June in the colophon. In each case one of those colophon dates is merely reprinted from its copy, and it is quite likely that at least one edition was really finished as late as 1550. The precise dates of the Grafton editions are equally uncertain, because all have title-pages that claim the month as March 1549. The two that are probably latest (16274–5) have colophons dated June, but it is unclear which is the earlier. Meanwhile John Oswen of Worcester, who had been granted a patent to print books for church use in Wales and the Marches,[C] printed the only known edition in quarto (16271, dated 24 May) and a folio dated 30 July (16276). Although Humphrey Powell had no comparable patent, he printed a folio edition in Dublin in 1551 (16277),[D] apparently unaware that it was shortly to be replaced by a substantially revised version.

In Chapters 4 and 5 I shall discuss the physical structure of the first two folio editions of 1559 in some detail. In each case that structure was inherited from an edition of 1552, and how those earlier editions evolved will be examined in Chapter 2. Those editions in turn were shaped by lessons the printers learned while mass-producing the first Edwardian

---

[A] *CJ*, 1, 5–6; *LJ*, 1, 331, 354.
[B] Both title-pages were printed later than the colophons, and are dated simply '*Mense Martij*'.
[C] *Stationers and Printers*, 11, 604, 649–50.
[D] On 15 July 1550 Powell was paid £20 by a royal warrant 'towards the setting vp of a printe in Ireland' (TNA: PRO, E 315/259, 114ᵛ), and in the colophon of his prayer book he describes himself as 'Printer to the | Kynges Maiestie', but the patent rolls contain no record of the grant of a royal office.

version in 1549.[A] But when I looked closely at the 1549 editions I realized that despite the historical importance of their contents they had never been studied really carefully as physical objects. Even the basic question of which edition was the first had never been properly investigated, and will here be answered for the first time.

In order to explain how I reached some of the conclusions here offered – how one can tell which parts of a book were printed first, or who printed them – it will be necessary to spell out in some detail how books were printed and, perhaps even more significantly, how they were not. The next section is therefore of particular importance, for unless it is read attentively some of the deductions offered later may not be properly understood. Sixteenth-century printed books (and this may be the single most noteworthy fact to learn and remember about them) were not manufactured one at a time, and did not emerge from the press one after another as if on a conveyor belt.

How the Books were Printed

Until Chapter 9, almost all the books mentioned in this one will be *folio* editions. All that means is that each pair of leaves (each *bifolium*) is a single sheet folded in half, so each leaf is half the size of a sheet of the paper used (which in the case of the prayer books measured approximately 38 × 28 cm, or 15 × 11 inches). A folio book consists of a series of *quires* (or *gatherings*), which occasionally consist of only a single folded sheet but are usually made up of multiple sheets (though seldom more than six) folded together, and therefore contain between four and twelve leaves (between eight and twenty-four pages). Each quire is eventually sewn through the fold to a series of cords that lie across the spine and will secure the boards to the finished book.

Each folio sheet has two pages printed on each side, and the pair of pages for one side of each sheet is called a *forme*.[B] Because very few printers had really large supplies of type, folios were usually printed *by formes*. If we use a quire *in sixes* as an example (three sheets, six leaves, twelve pages), the usual method of printing it was to *cast off* the text for the first five of those pages: to mark up the copy and indicate where each page should begin, and to begin setting with pages six and seven (the innermost forme of the quire).

[A] The pun inherent in mass-producing Protestant communion books has been noticed at least a few times during the past century, and should not be claimed as original if noticed again.
[B] The two formes of a folded sheet are rather obviously distinguished as the *outer forme* and the *inner forme*.

While that forme was being printed the *compositors* (type-setters) would set pages five and eight to be printed on the other side of all those sheets (to *perfect* them) – and after distributing the type from pages six and seven back into the type-cases, would set pages four and nine to print on the first side of the next heap of sheets.

Few printers could afford to keep supplies of type large enough to print more than a few folio pages before an earlier forme of type had to be scrubbed, rinsed, dried, and distributed back into the cases. If a thousand copies of a book were being printed, what existed halfway through the process was not five hundred copies of the book but a thousand copies of half of it, and no copy could be completed and sold until the very last forme was being printed.

To inform the eventual binder of the order in which the quires should be bound, each quire was identified by a *signature* (a letter or other character) printed below the text on its first page. To explain the order of the other sheets in the quire, below the text on the first page of each (a right-hand page, or *recto*) the relevant number would follow the signature. In a three-sheet quire designated D, therefore, below the text on the first three rectos would appear D (or D1), D2, and D3 respectively (or D.i., D.ii., and D.iii.).

Because the pages were seldom set or printed in text order, page-numbers were very easy to get wrong and comparatively seldom used. Numbering leaves (*foliation*) was more common (although also prone to error), but frequently done without. In a bibliographical study such as this one, leaves or pages are usually cited by the more reliable signatures (although they too can be misprinted), and referred to as (for example) leaf A5, page $E3^r$ (for *recto*, or front), page $G1^v$ (for *verso*, or back), and so on.[A]

An unsigned quire in a book's *preliminaries* (quires of prefatory material, dedications, contents lists, or anything else preceding the main text) is conventionally identified by bibliographers as π (Greek *p* for preliminary), and a second such quire would be called ππ or 2π. Sometimes preliminary quires are lettered, and if the letter is one *also* used in the signatures of the main text it is cited with a superior π prefixed (^{π}A). But a letter *not* used to sign the main text (as lower-case a in the preliminaries of a book otherwise signed only in capitals) does not need a prefix.[B]

[A] The signatures are always cited in roman, no matter what kind of face is used in the original; the numbers are always cited in arabic, and references to versos (or other pages with no *printed* signature) are not bracketed.

[B] An unsigned quire whose position obviously implies a letter (for example, between quires signed D and F respectively) is cited with the inferred letter (in this case *E*) in italic.

A book's signatures can also be used to describe its overall structure (or *collation*) by means of a formula. At this point I should perhaps reassure any reader whose reactions to the word *formula* include an aversion to anything suggesting either calculation or any branch of mathematics or science. A collational formula is no more than a compact, step-by-step description of how the book is made up: how many quires, how many leaves in each, and how they are signed. And while the complete formula for any of the earliest editions may look a little intimidating at first sight, to begin what I think of as the 'archaeological' approach, I intend to divide each formula up into sections: the preliminaries; what I shall call parts 1 and 2 of the main text (each part subdivided); and two belated afterthoughts.

The Preliminaries

Each of the earliest editions of 1549 has a *colophon* (a statement of who printed it, where, and when, but not on the title-page where that would be called an *imprint*) dated in early March. Edward Whitchurch's colophon (at the end of the book) is dated 7 March and Richard Grafton's (at the end of the Communion service) a day later, so the common (and careless) assumption has long been that Whitchurch's edition beat Grafton's into the shops by a day and is therefore the *editio princeps*. I shall reexamine that conclusion later in the chapter, but since each title-page is dated simply '*Mense Martij*' with no day specified (Figure 2), and since their preliminaries are identical in structure, I need record the formula for them only once:

2°: ❦^{2} $^\pi A^8$,

The '2°' (which I shall not repeat for the other sections) simply indicates that the book is a folio, in which each sheet contains two leaves (a quarto would be '4°'); the comma after $^\pi A^8$ merely separates the preliminaries from the main text. The first 'quire' is a single sheet: a bifolium whose first leaf has the title-page on the recto and a list of contents on the verso. Title-pages are almost never signed, but leaf ❦2 is signed with an 'Aldine leaf' rather than a letter. At its right extremity the tip of Whitchurch's leaf bends downwards and Grafton's upwards, but that is not important. What *is* significant is that both printers misprint the leaf number as 'i.' instead of 'ii.'.

It could hardly be clearer that one of these sheets was printed from the other, rather than each independently from manuscript copy. It is unsurprising that the wording of the title is identical, and the minor differences of line-division are easily accounted for by the differences in size and proportion of the central spaces in the two woodcut compartments. More dramatic is the resemblance between the two lists of contents, in which although the spelling of individual words differs quite freely, each line-division in the entries that exceed one line is in exactly the same place (including the redundant double hyphen in 'Communion of the=|same' in item ix). The first paragraph of the Preface on ❧2ʳ is necessarily divided differently because Whitchurch had to fit the text around a larger ornamental initial, but in the second paragraph and the whole of the second page all lines divide at the same point in both. It is also reasonably clear that whichever printer was the first to set and print this, it was the *last* sheet of his edition to be printed, as is often true of title-sheets.[A]

The second preliminary quire ($^\pi A^8$, prefixed by π to distinguish it from the first quire of the main text) was also used as copy by whichever printer was the second to print it. But whoever printed it first may have done so at almost any time during the proceedings. The first page ($^\pi A1^r$) has only a section title that introduces the next three pages; they contain an explanation of the order in which the Psalms are to be read throughout each month ($^\pi A1^v$), a table illustrating that order ($^\pi A2^r$), and an explanation of the order in which the rest of the Bible is to be read ($^\pi A2^v$). The remaining twelve pages of the quire contain a liturgical calendar, with each month filling a page.

The calendar quire presented special challenges, and in each printing house would have been assigned to experienced workmen with specific skills. Thirteen of the sixteen pages needed to be set by compositors capable of handling tabular material: the table of Psalms ($^\pi A2^r$) and the more difficult nine-column calendar pages (similar to those of 1561 reproduced in Plates 6 and 7). One of the difficulties is that in such tables the vertical and horizontal rules, which are printed from thin strips of brass, cannot cross each other. In those tables, therefore, most of the vertical lines are really made up of short, line-high rules, each set in approximately the right place according to a mark scratched on the setting rule on which the compositor assembled the type.[B]

Moreover, each forme of the calendar quire is printed in two colours, and not all pressmen had the necessary skills or experience for that. When set, the whole forme was first printed in red on a sheet of parchment. The words to be printed in red were then carefully cut out so that when the cut

---

[A] Had the Preface (which is essentially an introduction to the calendar's lectionary) been available when the calendar quire itself was printed, it would have made better sense to print the preliminaries as a single ten-leaf quire (as each printer would subsequently do in later editions).

[B] Numerous examples are illustrated in Figures 27–28 and Plates 4, 6, and 7.

parchment was placed (as a *frisket*) between the type and a clean sheet of paper, only the selected words actually touched the paper. When all the sheets had been printed with those words in red the frisket was removed, and the forme was cleaned. The red words were taken out and replaced by spaces and quads so that the rest of the text and the rules could be printed in black.[A] Because of this extra difficulty, the Grafton calendar quire was printed in sufficiently large numbers to supply at least two editions (perhaps as many as 3,000 copies; perhaps more), and the preliminaries in at least his first two editions are essentially identical. Whitchurch, however, apparently printed only enough for a single edition, and arranged the preliminaries slightly differently for his next edition.

The Main Text, Part 1

Whitchurch (STC 16267) A^8 $B–I^6$ K^8 $L–X^6$ Y^8
Grafton (STC 16268) $A–I^6$ K^8 $L–T^6$ V^8 X^6 Y^8

At this point we meet parts of two collational formulae that are much simpler than they may seem at first sight. Here I have followed tradition by listing Whitchurch first, so let us begin by walking through his formula. His main text begins with an eight-leaf quire A, but continues with a series of eight six-leaf quires signed B–I. Another eight-leaf quire signed K is followed by eleven more six-leaf quires (L–X), and the section finishes with a third eight-leaf quire (Y). At first sight Grafton's formula may look very different, but in fact it contains exactly the same number of leaves (138). The 'major' differences are that while both printers have eight leaves in quires K and Y, Whitchurch also does so in quire A but Grafton in quire V.

What I have here called part 1 of the prayer book deals with the 'usual' services for the whole year. Section 1a presents the order for Matins and Evensong, which are essentially the same for every day of the year (although a few special variants are indicated in those sections). Section 1b then prints all the special Introits, Collects, Epistles, and Gospels prescribed for use during the Communion services held on ninety special days thoughout the year, while Section 1c presents the 'basic' Communion service itself. If we divide the collational formulae by those sections the two

---

[A] Quads were extra-wide spaces, usually ranging in width from half the body-height of the type (one *en*) to three times the body-height (three *ems*). Because the whole quire was printed in two colours, each of the non-tabular pages also took advantage of the opportunity to include some red emphasis.

editions appear even less different. In this case I have placed Grafton first, because there is clear evidence that he was the first to *print* part 1.

	1a	1b	1c
Grafton	A⁶ |	B–I⁶ K⁸ L–T⁶ V⁸ |	X⁶ Y⁸
Whitchurch	A⁸ |	B–I⁶ K⁸ L–V⁶ |	X⁶ Y⁸

Grafton began, in fact, with section 1b (the Introits etc.), whose running titles throughout are 'At the Communion'. He correctly predicted that section 1a would need no more than a single quire, and so began setting the texts for the first Sunday in Advent on the first page of a quire he signed B (numbering the recto page 'Fol. vii.' on the correct assumption that quire A would probably contain only six leaves). The work apparently proceeded regularly as a series of six-leaf quires until at least part of the way through quire L (whose leaves are numbered in roman numerals Lxi–Lxvi) and perhaps beyond, until a problem arose. Either part of the manuscript copy had been misplaced or the authorities decided only belatedly to add special texts for Easter Monday, but one way or another it became necessary to scrap K⁶ and to replace it with a quire with two more leaves (K⁸, each of whose last three leaves is therefore numbered 'Fol.Lx.'). The work then proceeded without visible problems until quire T, whose completion left too much text remaining to fit into twelve pages. The copy for section 1c may not yet have been available, so rather than leave section 1b incomplete Grafton chose to use another eight-leaf quire (V⁸) whose last leaf was left blank.

It was probably at this point that he went back to the beginning of part 1 and began to work on quire A, containing the orders for Matins and Evensong. The compositor cast off the first five pages so he knew where to start setting the sixth page (A3ᵛ), readied his galley by heading it with a running title from a recently distributed verso page, and began to set. When he finished that page he began the next (A4ʳ), using a running title from a recent recto but remembering to change the folio number in the top right corner to 'iiij'. Once that forme was imposed and ready for the press he moved on to the next (A3ʳ:4ᵛ), and then another. Since he had started from the middle of the quire one might expect inner forme A2ᵛ:5ʳ to be next – and it may indeed have been the next to be *set*, although outer forme A2ʳ:5ᵛ was the first to be *printed*. But it was not until the press had started printing inner forme A2ᵛ:5ʳ that someone realized that although the folio numbers had been corrected, the actual running titles still read 'At the Communion' as throughout section 1b.[A] The press was stopped and

---

[A] As the first page of the order for Evensong, page A4ʳ should not have had a running title at all.

the headlines were belatedly corrected to 'Matins' and 'Euensong' before the remaining copies were perfected, although sheets A3:4 and A2:5 were then apparently set aside, reprinted with the correct running titles, and not included in the first edition. But someone subsequently printed the words 'Mattins' and 'Euensong' many times on one or more sheets of paper, covered up the erroneous headlines with paste-on cancels (blank, in the case of A4^r), and added the modified sheets to the heaps from which one or more later editions were gathered.[A] Finally, after finishing section 1a, Grafton apparently returned to the other end of part 1 and printed the Communion service on quires X^6 and Y^8, leaving the final page Y8^v blank.

I have as yet offered no evidence that Grafton printed part 1 before Whitchurch did – but it is plentiful. Section 1a differs quite substantially between the two versions, but in quires B–M of section 1b the two settings agree page for page and indeed usually line for line, and any occasional departure is brought back into agreement within a very few lines. While that close agreement (especially as regards the anomalous quire K^8) makes it clear that one printer was using the other's sheets as copy, it does not show which was which, but after quire M that becomes obvious. In quire N the two versions begin to diverge, with each of Whitchurch's quires containing a little more text than Grafton's. When Grafton finished the last page of quire T he still had enough text left to fill fourteen pages: too much for a six-leaf quire but not quite enough to fill the sixteen pages of V^8. Whitchurch's carefully calculated casting off left his section 1b finishing neatly on V6^r, leaving only a single final blank to focus attention on X1^r and the beginning of the Communion service. So not only can we deduce that Whitchurch was using Grafton's sheets as copy: we can also be reasonably certain that Grafton had finished quire V some time before Whitchurch reached quire N. The casting off required the whole contents of Grafton's N–V (twenty-five printed sheets) to be available for marking up. There is no sign here of two printers racing to finish only a day apart: the distance between them would take a single press more than three weeks to close.

[A] Cambridge University Library has a copy identified as STC 16269.5 (Young.239, which contains sheets from several editions) that includes sheet A2:5 with all four cancels. Also in Cambridge, the Parker Library copy at Corpus Christi College identified as 16269 (EP.V.11) has that sheet with the inner forme corrected but cancels on A2^r:5^v, and also A3:4 with all four cancels. Those cancels are unconnected with a larger paste-on found on A4^r in some other copies of 16269. In that edition and 16269.5, a passage at the beginning of Evensong in which the Lord's Prayer is abbreviated to 'OVRE FATHER &c.' was revised, with the prayer printed in full but the following versicles and responses abbreviated instead. A setting of the original text (which was restored in 16274–5) is pasted over the revised version in at least the Huntington and Eton College copies of 16269.

There is, moreover, one important difference between the two printers' versions of section 1a (Matins and Evensong). Grafton was quite right when he assumed that a single six-leaf quire A⁶ would be all he needed to allow before beginning section 1b on B1ʳ. Indeed, when he finally printed it the text filled only ten of the twelve available pages, so A6ʳ was used for a completely unnecessary *explicit* ('THVS EN=| deth the order of Matyns and | Euensong, through | the hole yere.') and A6ᵛ remained blank. Whitchurch, however, used an eight-leaf quire A⁸, filled thirteen of its pages with text, reprinted the *explicit* on A7ᵛ, and left the whole leaf A8 blank.[A]

In Matins on A2ʳ, both printers begin the page with the same three rubrics, set as ten lines by Grafton but as twelve by Whitchurch. The third rubric calls for the recitation of the canticle *Te deum laudamus* in English, except in Lent when it is to be replaced by *Benedicite omnia opera*, also in English. Either Grafton or whoever wrote out his manuscript copy apparently assumed that *Te deum* in English was too familiar to need repeating, and so supplied only *Benedicite* in full,[B] but Whitchurch printed the whole text of both canticles. On A3ʳ (Grafton) or A3ᵛ (Whitchurch) another canticle is called for, namely *Benedictus* – and once again Grafton omits it but Whitchurch includes it. Likewise in Evensong, rubrics call for the English recitation of both *Magnificat* and *Nunc dimittis*, both of which Grafton omits but Whitchurch includes. And that is why Whitchurch's section 1a fills five more pages than Grafton's.

An Introduction to Shared Printing

Before I turn to the shorter part 2 it is necessary to add a rider to my statements about Whitchurch and his printing of section 1b, because as the section stands in all the extant copies I have seen he did not print quite all of it. Paging through quire X one might notice that while four of the six folio numbers are in lower case with no internal punctuation (Fol.cxxj.), leaves X3 and X4 both use a capital C followed by a period (Fol.C.xxiii.). And although few readers would be in a position to recognize it as not belonging to Whitchurch, the 28-mm capital D on page X3ʳ is part of an alphabet of brass initials I have written about elsewhere, and which in 1549

[A] It is also likely that Whitchurch originally reprinted Grafton's A⁶ more or less verbatim, though perhaps without the rather unnecessary *explicit*. This will be discussed in more detail below.
[B] Both printers had produced primers in English during Henry's reign. In Grafton's first of 1545 (STC 16034) *Te deum* is on B3ʳ–4ʳ, *Benedictus* on C4ʳ⁻ᵛ, *Magnificat* on G3ᵛ–4ʳ, and *Nunc dimittis* on H3ʳ.

belonged to the printer Nicholas Hill (originally vanden Berghe).[A] Hill had come to England from the Low Countries in about 1519, had taken out letters of denization in July 1544, and in 1548–49 he collaborated with Whitchurch on several books, including one reprint of the Great Bible and five editions of Erasmus's New Testament *Paraphrases*.[B] In this case his printing of a single sheet hardly rises to the level of 'sharing', and may indicate that Whitchurch discovered something seriously wrong with his own sheet X3:4 but was too busy to print the necessary *cancel* (replacement) himself. If there was indeed a problem, its nature is beyond discovery, and Hill's replacement for the most part follows Grafton line for line.[C] But because shared printing would play an increasingly important role in the Tudor prayer books, now is a good time to outline its history.

What could perhaps be considered the first English example was the three-volume *Graunde Abbregement de le Ley* of 1516 (STC 10954), of which John Rastell printed the first volume and Wynkyn de Worde the second and third. But while that *project* was shared, each volume is the work of one printer throughout. The beginnings of 'real' shared printing in England appear in the 1520s, when de Worde occasionally shared a book with one of his ex-apprentices, either to find him a small task to do (in 1521 John Skot printed the first quire of 10631.5 for him, but it is de Worde whose name appears in the colophon) or perhaps to help him meet a deadline (in 1524 de Worde contributed sheets D3:4 and E2:3 to 15050, otherwise printed by Robert Copland). Later in the 1520s John Rastell in London rather surprisingly shared at least four books with Peter Treveris across the river in Southwark, and in 1532 Treveris shared another with Robert Wyer in London.[D] From the mid-'30s to the mid-'40s about a dozen examples are known (not counting the Great Bible, mostly printed by François Regnault in Paris but completed by Grafton and Whitchurch in London after Regnault's arrest). But during the Edwardian Reformation the book trade went into overdrive, and I know of more than thirty examples from those years. (Mary's less bookish reign would apparently produce only half a dozen.) Moreover, while each of the earlier examples was the work of two printers only, three of the Edwardian examples each involved *three* printers. Motives for the practice could vary, but in one way

---

[A] *Stationers and Printers*, 1, 498–9; 'Initials within Initials', 446–7.
[B] Westminster Abbey, WAM 12261, m.26+3 (Page, *Letters of Denization*, 124 'Hilles'); STC 2079, 2854–54.6.
[C] Using a five-line capital D where Grafton had used a smaller one, Hill is out of sync for lines X3^{r}11–19, but otherwise the only departure is at line X3^{v}23.
[D] Rastell and Treveris STC 9363.6, 18084, 23148.8, 23664; Wyer and Treveris 23961.

or another the question of speed usually came into it, because two printers could always produce completed sheets more quickly than one. So the printers who were tasked with producing the books on which the Edwardian Reformation relied – bibles, the *Paraphrases* of Erasmus, and the successive English prayer books – often needed to enlist others to assist them.

The Main Text, Part 2

Whitchurch (STC 16267)   ¶a–¶e⁶ ¶f⁸
Grafton (STC 16268)[A]   Aa–Ee⁶ f⁸

Here it seems unnecessary to add a separate presentation formally divided into the two sections of the text, because section 2b occupies only the last eight-leaf quire in each edition. Section 2a contains what one could describe as the 'occasional' services whose celebration is completely independent of the calendar: Baptism, Confirmation, Marriage, Visitation of the Sick, Burial, and the Purification ('Churching') of Women after childbirth.

Section 2b, however, begins with a ceremony that does depend on the Easter calendar, and is headed on its first page as 'The firste daie of lente commonly called Ashe-wednesday' (Whitchurch, ¶f1ʳ). In the contents list that is elaborated to 'A declaration of scripture, with certein prayers to bee vsed the firste daye of Lent, commonlye called Ashwednesdaie' (☙1ᵛ), and in 1552 and all subsequent versions of the prayer book that ceremony is known as the Commination. It finishes on ¶f4ᵛ, and is followed on ¶f5ʳ by a four-page essay 'Of Ceremonies: why some be abolished and some retayned'. That in turn is followed on ¶f7ʳ by 'Certayne notes' (five in number), 'Finis.', and Whitchurch's colophon of 7 March (Figure 1a).

In the formula above and the foregoing paragraph it will be noticed that this time I have given Whitchurch's edition priority – because here the evidence points in that direction almost as clearly as in part 1 it pointed towards Grafton. Whitchurch's use of the capitulum (¶) in his signatures suggests that when he began to print he was unsure exactly what sequence

---

[A] Under Series 2/2 the 'Chart of Editions' in STC (II, p. xxiii) misdescribes part 2 of the first Grafton edition as collating AA–EE⁶ f⁸. This is a consequence of Greg's ill-advised rule that both AA and Aa should condense to an ambiguous 2A (see above, pp. xxiii–xxiv). That part of the collation was evidently reported as '2A–2E⁶' to someone who guessed wrongly when uncondensing it. What STC lists as the first three Grafton editions all belong to Series 2/3.

of signatures would precede this section,[A] whereas Grafton's two-letter signatures clearly follow his almost-completed single-letter alphabet.[B] And while Whitchurch foliated part 2 separately from i to xxxvii, when Grafton reprinted it he was able to continue the foliation from the end of his completed part 1 (C.xxxv–C.lxx, leaving the page of 'Certain notes' unnumbered).

At first sight there seem to be more differences than similarities between the two versions, although in most of the services Grafton's first page ends with the same catchword as Whitchurch's. But the drop capitals with which Grafton begins most prose passages of any length are seldom the same size as Whitchurch's, so his line-breaks do not commonly match Whitchurch's. Nor, indeed, do the page divisions, although each service occupies exactly the same number of pages in each edition. But Grafton was able to spread the text more evenly through the pages than had Whitchurch, whose layouts sometimes seem quite eccentric.[C] Before his compositors started work Grafton must have done some very careful casting off, but his dependence on the Whitchurch setting is perhaps best indicated by the folio number on Aa6^r. That page's 'Fol. v.' in fact misprints Whitchurch's 'Fol. vi.' – but in Grafton's numbering it should have read 'Fol. C.xl.'

Three Remarkable Volumes

It is now useful to examine the seemingly unrelated question of how many copies of the earliest editions of 1549 survive. When searched in March 2020 the relevant ESTC entries listed seventeen copies of Whitchurch's STC 16267 (ESTC S109513), but only seven copies of Grafton's 16268 (ESTC S93744). Given that Whitchurch's colophon is dated a day before Grafton's, its status as the apparent first edition might perhaps be enough to have skewed the figures – but those numbers are not the end of the story. Of the seven Grafton 'copies', one is an isolated specimen of his colophon

---

[A] The *capitulum* originated as a filled-in or decorated capital C to indicate a new chapter. The modern pilcrow (¶) may simply be a tailed form, or may have been intended to suggest a P for paragraph (see also *OED*, paraph, *n*, 2). The word *pilcrow* originally applied equally to either form, but in bibliographical contexts it can be useful to distinguish between them.

[B] The absence of Z is no impediment: curtailed signature-alphabets ending in Y (22 letters) or V (20 letters) are quite common in books long enough to go into multiple alphabets, probably because even numbers made estimating costs much simpler.

[C] For example, there are five rubrics on Whitchurch's ¶c2^r, containing respectively 1, 1, 4, 2, and 8 lines (total 16). Measuring from the left margin they are indented respectively 21, 18, 34, 37, and 50 mm. Grafton indents them respectively 14, 15, 6, 7, and 6 mm, and thus saves a total of four lines.

leaf, bound into a privately owned copy of a later edition. And the one listed as at Keble College, Oxford, is really a copy of 16269 wanting everything before B1, misreported some years ago to SOLO (Search Oxford Libraries Online) as 16268. Which apparently leaves the score at Whitchurch 17, Grafton 5.

But those numbers are not final either, because three extant volumes appear in *both* lists.[A] Each of those three has part 1 of Grafton's edition (⁊ꝰ ᵖᵢA⁸, A–I⁶ K⁸ L–T⁶ V⁸ X⁶ Y⁸) followed by part 2 of Whitchurch's (¶a–¶e⁶ ¶f⁸). Each library has evidently treated its volume as two distinct items bound together, and in two of them the Grafton part has '(1)' after the call number while the Whitchurch part has '(2)'. Each has clearly been believed to be a 'made-up' copy, cobbled together by a comparatively modern bookseller or collector from parts of two defective books. Moreover, because none of the three includes either Grafton's Litany (in the final quire of his STC 16268, presumed lost with his part 2) or Whitchurch's (the quire immediately preceding part 2 in his STC 16267, presumed lost with his part 1), each has been considered not only 'made-up' but also textually incomplete.

To accept that, however, we would have to imagine three copies of Grafton's edition, each perfect at the beginning but seriously defective after part 1, each coming into the hands of a bookseller or collector who owned a more seriously defective (though more desirable) Whitchurch first edition whose part 2 was the only salvageable fragment. Some such explanation could have seemed plausible if the British Library copy (acquired in 1859) had been the only exemplar.[B] But the volume containing the Brasenose copy was catalogued there in the 1660s, and at least two of the early annotators of the New College copy practised their handwriting in both printers' shares. All three are in good condition, and they outnumber the only two recorded copies of Grafton's 16268, neither of which is quite perfect.[C]

When examining part 1 I pointed out that for Whitchurch to have been able to cast off and re-divide the text of Grafton's printed sheets N–T⁶ and V⁸ he would have needed access to at least twenty-five of the sheets that

---

[A] The three in question are British Library, C.25.l.12; New College, Oxford, BT1.131.19; and Brasenose College, Oxford, Lath. R.3.18(2).
[B] It was once owned by Humphrey Dyson, whose title-page signature was enthusiastically crossed out by a later owner. In 2006 part 1 was filmed by University Microfilms as if a defective copy of STC 16268 (reel 2287, item 8) and then digitized by EEBO, but part 2 was not filmed.
[C] The Durham Cathedral copy of 16268 reportedly has A5 supplied from another copy; in the one at Christ Church, Oxford, both A3 and A4 are defective while Bb5 has been supplied from another copy and ✠4 from another edition.

Grafton had already printed (and if Grafton had already finished section 1c, at least thirty-two sheets). But Grafton's colophon dated 8 March is on Y8^r, so unless that date is a fiction Whitchurch's part 1 could not have been finished much before the end of the month (if indeed in March at all). And since his reprint of the Grafton preliminaries is slavishly precise even down to the misprinted signature '⁊.i.', his repetition of Grafton's '*Mense Martij*' on the title-page is hardly trustworthy. But in much the same way, Grafton's edition of part 2 is manifestly later than his own part 1 (whose foliation it continues), and cannot have been finished before the date of either colophon.

Rather than made-up copies constructed decades or centuries later, therefore, the three hybrid volumes are evidently copies of the prayer book as it was originally issued in early March 1549. They are complete copies of a book that was shared by the two printers: part 1 by Grafton with his dated colophon on his final page (Y8^r) and part 2 by Whitchurch with his dated colophon on *his* final page (¶f7^r). Neither of the pioneers of the formulary of collation had any idea how commonplace a practice shared printing was in the period on which their attention was focused, so neither Greg nor Bowers imagined that a convention was needed to indicate its presence. So let me propose that in comparatively simple cases such as this, a semicolon might usefully mark a division between printing houses.[A] This, then, is the collation of the true first edition of the 1549 prayer book:

2°: ⁊² π A^8, A–I^6 K^8 L–T^6 V^8 X^6 Y^8; ¶a–¶e^6 ¶f^8.

But the Litany is not the only thing 'missing' from the three supposedly made-up copies, none of which has the note on retail prices found on Whitchurch's ¶f7^v in all copies of STC 16267 that I have seen. This is an official order from King Edward (ostensibly 'by the aduyse of', but really *by*, Protector Somerset and the Privy Council), limiting the maximum retail price for an unbound copy to 2*s.* (24 pence), or for a copy 'bounde in paste or in boordes', 3*s.* 4*d.* (40 pence). Exactly when this was calculated is unrecorded (the extant registers of the Edwardian Privy Council seldom mention matters of this kind), but it may have been based on the printers' original estimate, which would not have included the unexpected extra sheet in quire K^8 or any other belated additions.[B] The British Library and New College copies each contain 186 leaves, or ninety-three printed sheets,

---

[A] But when a *quire* is the work of two or more printers (as is the Whitchurch-and-Hill quire X^6), the most practical way to record the facts is by adding an explanation.

[B] Whitchurch's ¶f5^r–7^r ('Of Ceremonies' and 'Certayne Notes'), which might more appropriately belong in the preliminaries, could themselves have been afterthoughts too late to place there.

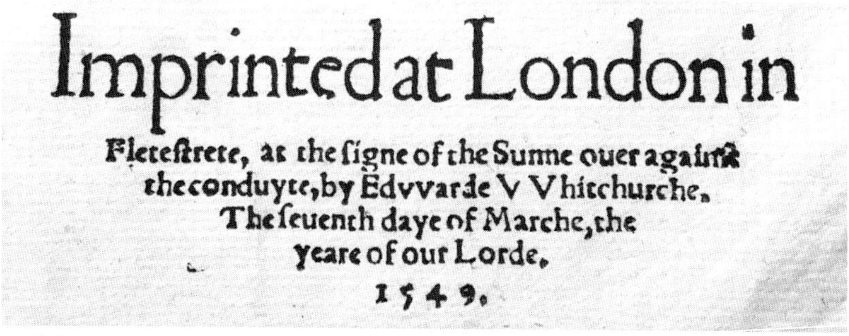

Imprinted at London in

Fleteſtrete, at the ſigne of the Sunne ouer againſt
the conduyte, by Edvvarde V Vhitchurche.
The ſeuenth daye of Marche, the
yeare of our Lorde.
1549.

(a)

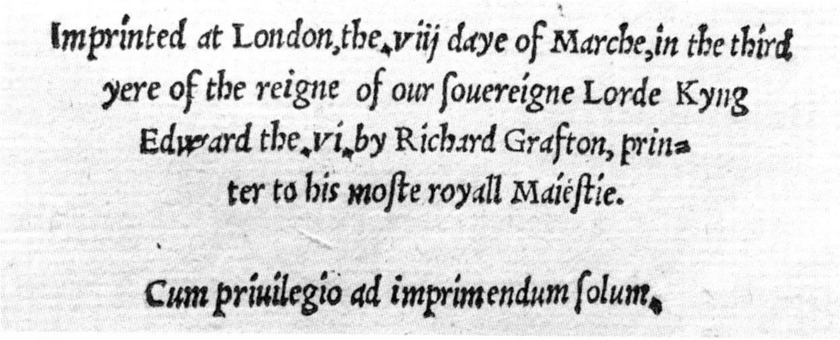

Imprinted at London, the viij daye of Marche, in the third
yere of the reigne of our ſouereigne Lorde Kyng
Edward the vi, by Richard Grafton, prin=
ter to his moſte royall Maieſtie.

Cum priuilegio ad imprimendum ſolum.

(b)

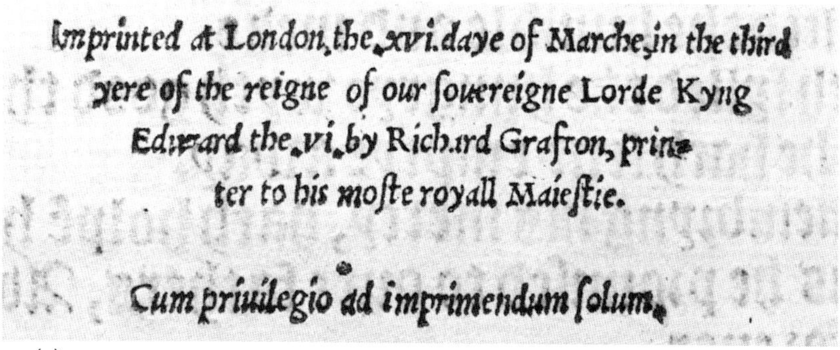

Imprinted at London, the xvi. daye of Marche, in the third
yere of the reigne of our ſouereigne Lorde Kyng
Edward the vi, by Richard Grafton, prin=
ter to his moſte royall Maieſtie.

Cum priuilegio ad imprimendum ſolum.

(c)

Figure 1 The colophons of March 1549.
(a) Whitchurch's colophon for part 2 (7 March).
(b) Grafton's colophon for part 1 (8 March).
(c) Grafton's colophon updated and reimposed for the appended canticles (16 March).
(Brasenose College, Oxford, Lath. R.3.18(2): (a) ¶f7[r], (b) Y8[r], (c) ✠2[v].)

so for 2s. unbound a retail purchaser would obtain 3.875 sheets for each penny.

There is, however, yet another layer to the story, revealed by a unique bifolium now bound between the two parts in the Brasenose copy. Signed with a Maltese cross (✠²), it contains the four canticles that Grafton had not included in section 1a but which Whitchurch inserted when he printed his enlarged version of quire A. As presently bound it follows immediately after the leaf with Grafton's original colophon on its recto, although that is not where it was intended to be placed. It ends on its own final verso with a *second* Grafton colophon, printed from exactly the same lines of italic type used for his first, but with the date altered from '*the.viij daye of Marche*' to '*the.xvi.daye of Marche*' (Figures 1*b* and 1*c*). And between the end of the canticles and that colophon appears Grafton's setting of what I shall now call the *original* note of those same prices: 2s. unbound or 3s. 4d. in paste or boards.

Whitchurch was evidently planning to reissue his part 2 with a reprint of Grafton's part 1, and I suspect that he had already reprinted a substantial part of it, including the six-leaf quire A that lacked the canticles. His extant leaf A1 reprints Grafton's more or less line for line and with the same catchwords on each page. In Grafton's quire the conjugate leaf A6 contains nothing of significance: only the unnecessary *explicit* on A6ʳ that Whitchurch might well have decided to do without. I therefore believe that at some date after 16 March Whitchurch cancelled his own A2–5, reprinted those eight pages as eleven new pages that included the canticles, and reinstated the *explicit* on his A7ᵛ only to avoid a completely blank opening. What had been blank A6 thus became the present blank A8.[A]

The Grafton sheet ✠² that Whitchurch probably used as copy for the added canticles also included the note about retail prices that clearly belongs at the end of the book. So Whitchurch evidently put his remaining copies of sheet ¶f2:7 through the press again to add the note to page ¶f7ᵛ. But he should have waited a little longer before doing so, because the four canticles were not the last of the belated additions.

At this point I need to confess that what STC classifies as each printer's first edition of the book contains a two-sheet quire that I have not included in the partial collations I have presented above. In Whitchurch's edition it is signed with a capitulum (¶⁴) and placed between parts 1 and 2; in

---

[A] This suggestion seems supported by Whitchurch's numbering of B1ʳ as 'Fol.vii' (A7ʳ has the same but with an added period; blank A8 is unfoliated), although he could perhaps have chosen simply to follow Grafton's foliation without having to add 2 every time.

Grafton's it is signed with a Maltese cross and placed at the very end (✠4). Each was added sometime after 16 March, when the compilers realized that although the first of the rubrics following the Communion service (on Y7^r in each printer's edition) prescribes when the Litany should be said or sung, the Litany itself had been omitted from the book. In Whitchurch's quire the Litany fills leaves ¶1–3 (the blank fourth leaf is usually missing). But Grafton reprints the canticles first, ignoring the verse structure that had filled three and a quarter pages in bifolium ✠2 and cramming them as prose into two pages and twelve lines. The Litany, too cramped to be allowed a heading but implicitly identified by the running titles, follows immediately after *Nunc dimittis*, and ends on ✠4^v leaving just enough space for the note about retail prices and yet another Grafton colophon (this time undated).

On at least three detectable occasions the printers had either to add new sheets or replace ones already printed: Grafton had to replace his original quire K^6 with K^8, to add ✠2, and later to replace it with ✠4; Whitchurch had to replace A2–5 with A2–7 and insert quire ¶4. I suspect that Grafton may have reminded either Cranmer or some other Privy Councillor of these incidents – because on ✠4^v the prices had been revised upwards: from 2*s*. to 2*s*. 2*d*. unbound, and from 3*s*. 4*d*. to 3*s*. 8*d*. when bound in paste or boards. The retail purchaser of an unbound copy would now get only 3.655 sheets for each penny (although Whitchurch had to wait until his next edition before he too could print the revised prices).[A]

To summarize the early history in print of the 1549 *Booke of the Common Praier*, then, let me resort to collational formulae, with the quires of the first edition underlined:

2°: ⁂² π A^8, A–I^6 K^8 L–T^6 V^8 X^6 Y^8; ¶a–¶e^6 ¶f^8.

Of the first issue of that edition, only two copies are currently known, at the British Library (C.25.l.12) and New College, Oxford (BT1.131.19).

In the second issue of the first edition Grafton added the omitted canticles at the end, in a new bifolium now surviving (misplaced after Y8 by a later owner) only in the copy at Brasenose College, Oxford (Lath. R.3.18(2)):

2°: ⁂² π A^8, A–I^6 K^8 L–T^6 V^8 X^6 Y^8; ¶a–¶e^6 ¶f^8; ✠².

[A] In Worcester, John Oswen evidently thought he could get away with printing those revised prices in his quarto edition (STC 16271), which contained only 58 sheets. It is very unlikely that he had official permission either to do that or to raise each price by fourpence when emending the note for his folio edition (16276, 66 sheets).

For the third issue of the first edition (STC 16268), now known only from slightly defective copies at Durham Cathedral (F.IV.56) and Christ Church, Oxford (Gibbs.1), Grafton reprinted Whitchurch's part 2 and for the first time added the Litany (following the canticles in a new quire that replaced ✠²):^A

2°: ❦² πA⁸, A–I⁶ K⁸ L–T⁶ V⁸ X⁶ Y⁸, Aa–Ee⁶ f⁸ ✠⁴.

Meanwhile Whitchurch had been busy reprinting Grafton's preliminaries and part 1 (with a little assistance from Nicholas Hill), inserting the omitted canticles where they belonged in part 1a and adding the Litany in a new quire ¶⁴ at the end of his reprinted section:

2°: ❦² πA⁸, A⁸ B–I⁶ K⁸ L–V⁶ X⁶(±X3:4) Y⁸, ¶⁴, ¶a–¶e⁶ ¶f⁸.

Because 80 per cent of this fourth version (STC 16267, the *editio* formerly known as *princeps*) is newly printed, it is most realistically defined as the second edition, with part 2 reissued from the first.

But although 16267 can no longer claim priority, it is arguably the *best* of the early editions. It is the first to incorporate each of the four omitted canticles where it belongs in the daily services, and while the Litany more obviously 'ought' to be between sections 1a and 1b (where it would appear in and after 1552), Whitchurch's position for it between parts 1 and 2 (not followed by Grafton until his fourth edition) is certainly better than at the very end as the second of two afterthoughts.

Corroboration from the Past

I had already worked out most of the above after first seeing the contents of bifolium ✠², when cataloguer Sophie Floate sent me a photograph of the Brasenose title-page. And once I read the anonymous annotations below the woodcut border I realized that the essential facts had already been documented some four centuries ago. Sometime in or soon after the late sixteenth century, the book's then owner reported as follows (as shown in Figure 2).

> This former Service book of ₍K Edwᵈ, was printed 4 times in one yeare 1549: the first inpression was this by Grafton & Whitchurch; in wᶜʰ, the Litanie wᵗʰ the following praiers, was omitted, & Te Deũ, Benedictus, Magnificat, and nũc Dimittis were added to the later end.

[A] Each of Grafton's successive addenda, ✠² and ✠⁴, has the price note and colophon on its final verso and so was clearly intended to be bound at the end of the book. Liturgically, however, placing each of them in part 1 between quires A and B would have made better sense.

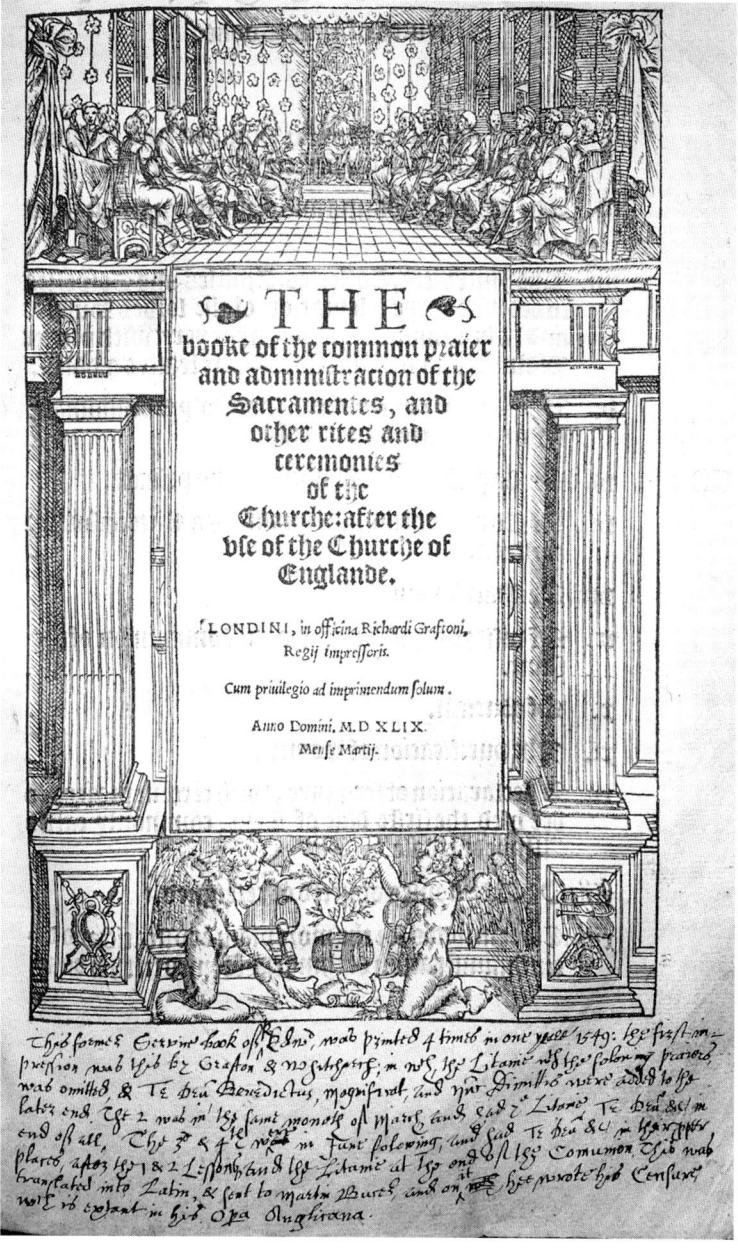

Figure 2 Title-page of the first edition of 1549, with annotations c. 1600.
(Brasenose College, Oxford, Lath. R.3.18(2), ❧1ʳ.)

The two most important details here are the writer's unconcerned acceptance of the fact that the volume was the work of both printers whose colophons appear in it, and the observation that the canticles bifolium was at that time the last quire in the book, where Grafton would later place its successor, quire ✠4. The writer then tells us about Grafton's next editions:

> The 2 [*impression*] was in the same moneth of March, and had ye Litanie, Te Deū &c/ in end of all.

That may not have been STC 16268, because the description would fit one of Grafton's next two editions equally well, but it certainly shows that the annotator was a competent and interested observer.

> The 3d & 4th [*impressions*] was^{ere} in Iune folowing, and had Te Deū &c/ in their *pro*per places, after the 1 & 2 Lessons [*in Matins and Evensong*], and the Litanie at the end of the Comunion.

I suspect that those two 'impressions' were one copy of either 16272 or 16273 (Whitchurch) and a second of either 16274 or 16275 (Grafton). All four have June colophons, the canticles embedded where they belong, and the Litany between parts 1 and 2, and the writer would have had to examine them very closely to distinguish the members of either pair from each other.

It was probably a subsequent owner of the Brasenose copy who moved bifolium ✠2 to its present position between Grafton's Y8 and Whitchurch's ❡a1: probably the same owner who appended the volume to the 1637 first edition of the prayer book 'for the use of the Church of Scotland' (STC 16606) and had them bound together. The writer of the title-page notes would have known better than to assume that the canticles *without* the Litany belonged after the Communion, despite the similarity of the two Grafton colophons. The only clue to the date of the notes is the final sentence, in which it is observed that the 1549 book

> was translated into Latin, & sent to Martin Bucer, and on ^^{it}wch hee wrote his Censure, wch is extant in his O*pe*ra Anglicana.

The correct title is *Martini Buceri Scripta Anglicana*, and it was printed in Basel by Pietro Perna in 1577.

Exactly how the events of 1549 played out is beyond recovery, but what I believe to be a fairly plausible reconstruction can be built around some completely imaginary numbers. Let us therefore hypothesize that soon after the passage of the Act on 21 January, Grafton (the King's Printer) and Whitchurch (his partner in the patent for 'bookes concerning dyvyne ser*u*ice') are told that the immediate need is for a few hundred advance copies so that the clergy in the parishes of the capital (and a few other important cities and dioceses) can all prepare to introduce the new services simultaneously (while copies will necessarily reach some parts of the country rather later). Grafton decides on a speedy initial edition of 600 (except of the preliminaries, of which he will print many hundreds more); Whitchurch calculates that he can print 1,200 copies of the substantially shorter part 2 (which contains only nineteen sheets beside Grafton's seventy-four) by the same deadline. When they finish their shares in early March, the authorities decide to begin by distributing 300 of those copies, which are duly assembled and bound.[A]

With 300 copies of part 1 still in his warehouse, Grafton is advised that the canticles should have been included in part 1. He therefore prints enough copies of bifolium ℞² to update both those copies and any of the first 300 that have not yet been bound. Whitchurch withholds his 900 copies of part 2 so he can add the note of prices to ¶f7ᵛ; Grafton begins to reprint 300 copies of part 2, and when the omitted Litany is supplied he reprints it with the canticles as quire ℞⁴ of the first all-Grafton edition (with a revised list of prices). Whitchurch meanwhile prints 900 copies of part 1 (with the canticles included where they belong) and appends the Litany to complete the first all-Whitchurch edition. If documentary evidence for the numbers and dates were suddenly to be discovered, nobody would be more surprised than I if they were really close to my guesses. But the observed facts do appear to indicate something on those lines.

The Reprints of 1549

We have already seen Whitchurch taking advantage of setting from printed copy, and rearranging part of the text for no apparent reason beyond saving a sheet by reducing Grafton's quire V⁸ to his own V⁶. The capped retail price gave him an even better motive. He probably sold comparatively few copies to retail customers: a printing house was a factory rather than a bookshop, and while his premises probably *included* a shop, most of what he printed was sold at wholesale prices to retail booksellers. But whatever he demanded as a fair price from a shopkeeper who could not resell above the official price limit, reducing

---

[A] It should be remembered that until Edward gave it his assent on 14 March, the Act of Uniformity (and consequently *The Book of the Common Prayer*) had no status in law.

the number of sheets in the book would increase his profit margin. So it need come as no surprise that his *next* edition and its successors packed a little more text into every page, reduced the number of blank pages from eight to three, and (with a collation of πA^{10}, A–P^8 Q^4 R–T^8 V^{10}) reduced the number of sheets in each copy from ninety-five to eighty-four. While the price for an unbound copy thereafter remained constant, the maximum price of a *bound* copy was raised again after two more editions, from 'bounde in past or in bordes' not above 3*s*. 8*d*. to 'bounde in paste or in boordes couered with calues leather' not above 4*s*.[A]

Grafton's reprinting strategy was rather different, and his next two editions were essentially page-for-page reprints, with the same collational formulae and the same number of leaves as his first. But while that may seem to waste an obvious opportunity, there are some potential advantages in reprinting page for page, and Grafton was evidently aware of them. For example, however many copies of a given sheet are wanted, in practice some sheets might be damaged or spoiled. The number of *usable* sheets therefore sometimes falls short of the number actually printed, and pressmen were anyway quite capable of miscounting when assembling the heap of clean sheets to be dampened and readied for the press run. The maximum number of complete copies that could be gathered from the ninety-five heaps of printed sheets was the number present in the smallest heap, after which all the sheets left in all ninety-four of the other heaps were unusable. But if the book were to be reprinted page for page, those leftover sheets could be used in the next edition, and commensurately fewer *new* copies of each relevant sheet printed.

It is, moreover, easier (and consequently more efficient) for compositors to reprint text line for line and page for page than to rearrange it. So while Whitchurch decided to incorporate the 'missing' canticles in his quire A^8, Grafton twice chose to reprint his original quire A^6 without them, leaving them cramped in quire ⊞^{4}.

Grafton, indeed, sometimes seems content to mingle the sheets from different print-runs without much regard for the order in which they were printed. No matter how small his original edition of part 1, he seems to

---

[A] That price is apparently found on only two Whitchurch editions (STC 16272–3), but there are grounds for doubt. If we subtract the three copies of the real first edition, ESTC records the following number of copies of the Whitchurch editions: 16267 (14), 16270 (10), 16270a (13), 16272 (14), and 16273 (32). I have not attempted the task, but the numbers suggest that careful comparison might reveal that '16273' includes two editions.

have printed far more copies of his first setting of the preliminaries, which reappear in most copies of STC 16269 and some copies of 16269.5.[A] Not until his fourth edition did he follow Whitchurch's lead and print them as a single five-sheet quire, thus allowing himself to use some red ink on the title-page. Most copies of what STC distinguishes as 16269 and 16269.5 appear to include at least a few sheets that may really 'belong' to the other, and as I have already noted, his original sheets A3:4 and A2:5 (with the incorrect running titles corrected by slip cancels) are found only in copies of one or other of those later editions.

Quire ✠4 is another puzzle. The only extant copy of STC 16268 with what I presume to be the original setting is the copy at Durham Cathedral, with ✠1ʳ signed '✠.j.' and line ✠4ᵛ1 reading 'here' in the outer forme of the outer sheet. The same setting of both formes is found in the copy of 16269.5 that EEBO mistakenly attributes to Cambridge University Library (really British Library C.25.l.2). But while the Huntington Library copy of 16269 apparently has the same setting of the inner forme, its outer forme has '✠.i.' and 'heare' respectively. Sheet ✠2:3, however, has the same inner forme in all three copies, but parts of the outer forme differ – most notably where the shoulder-note identifying *Nunc dimittis*, correctly beside the first line of that canticle in 16268 and 16269, is several lines lower beside the beginning of the Litany in 16269.5.[B] Meanwhile the other copy of 16268 (Christ Church, Oxford, Gibbs.1), which lacked quire ✠4 when Kenneth Gibbs acquired it, was later supplied by Quaritch with a copy from an otherwise unknown edition printed after the next change in the note about prices.[C]

Grafton did eventually take advantage of the opportunity to reduce the size (and consequently the cost) of reprints, and having taken rather more time over it than Whitchurch had, he did a better job. By eliminating *all* blank pages, and by being prepared to begin a new section on a verso (or even mid-page) rather than necessarily on a new recto, Grafton was able to print each of his last two editions (collating ⁂¹⁰, A–R⁸ S–T⁶) in only seventy-nine sheets, instead of Whitchurch's eighty-four.

[A] In the other copies of 16269.5 the first sheet is signed A (and is therefore ᵖA²) rather than ⁂.

[B] But in the same forme at ✠3ᵛ6 those copies of 16268 and 16269.5 (sycke) agree against 16269 (sicke), and both have the catchword 'Lord' that is missing from 16269.

[C] That quire must have been printed before Grafton printed his next *known* edition after 16269.5, because none of his subsequent editions had a quire ✠4. Unlike the other settings, ✠4ᵛ has 'God saue the kyng.' between the note of prices and the colophon. It appears there in his subsequent editions 16274–5, but on page T6ᵛ, where it follows the end of 'Certain notes' rather than the Litany.

There had been, however, a different advantage to be gained from Grafton's earlier preference for repeating an existing structure. It is easier for a compositor to reset a forme page for page and line for line than to start at a mark somewhere in one page of copy (even printed copy) and finish precisely at a similar mark on another page. That advantage applies especially when the printer of the earlier edition asks a second printer to help out with the reprint, because he can simply hand over copies of whatever sheets are needed and request exact copies of them. Both Whitchurch and Grafton did indeed seek such help. Nicholas Hill, who had provided Whitchurch with the presumed cancel X3:4 in the first edition, was also asked to contribute twelve sheets to STC 16270 (K^8; R^8; N4:5; S1–3:6–8), twenty to 16270a (A1,2:7,8; C4:5; G^8; I^8; N^8; R1,2:7,8; S1–3:6–8), and fifteen to 16273 (G1–3:6–8; I^8; N^8; R1,2:7,8; S2,3:6,7). Less expected is the presence in three of Grafton's editions of quires printed by Robert Wyer (a freeman of the Salters' Company who specialized in small pamphlets: often illustrated, rarely larger than octavo, and averaging fewer than four sheets each). Despite his usual habits, though, he was evidently asked by Grafton to contribute six folio sheets to STC 16269.5 (L^6; Cc^6), four to 16274 (C^8), and twelve to 16275 (C^8; H^8; N^8).

The End of Demand

Ideally, of course, the combined efforts of all the printers actively involved should have produced enough copies to supply at least one to each of England's parishes, between 8,500 and 9,000 in number. Many parishes, of course, would need more than one copy, and parish clergy were by no means the only parties interested in both reading the book at home (a practice actively encouraged during the Reformation) and following the services while in church. We do not know the size of any of the extant editions, and it is quite possible that one or more small-format editions have completely perished.

Meanwhile, however, there was no shortage of conservative critics for whom the 1549 book had gone far too far – or on the opposite side, of champions of reform who felt that the new liturgy retained too many traces of popery. In particular, while the Communion service could hardly be said either to preach transubstantiation or to require belief in it, those most convinced that the ceremony merely *commemorates* the Last Supper found the rubric and the accompanying words much too easy to interpret as implying a corporal Real Presence.

> And when he deliuereth the Sacrament of the body of Christ he shall saie to euery one these wordes.
>
> The body of our Lorde Iesus Christe whiche was geuen for thee, preserue thy body and soule vnto euerlastyng lyfe.[A]

In his Edwardian writings on the Eucharist both before and after 1549 Cranmer repeatedly makes it clear that while Christ is really present during Communion, his presence is spiritual as distinct from corporal, and that the bread and wine remain unchanged in substance both during and after the event. As expressed, however, the 1549 words of administration allowed even diehard conservatives to accept the new ritual by interpreting it (or as its author would have insisted, *mis*interpreting it) in their own way. This was by no means the only part of the first Edwardian prayer book that failed to satisfy the most ardent reformers, so by the end of 1551 the authorities had decided that it should be replaced by a substantially revised version.

[A] STC 16268, Y4ᵛ. When 'the Sacrament of the bloud' is then delivered, the words 'body' and 'geuen' are replaced by 'bloud' and 'shed'.

CHAPTER 2

The Second Edwardian Prayer Book

Throughout this chapter I shall often need to refer to one or other of the London editions of 1552. For the 1549 editions I have hitherto used the numbering of the revised *Short-Title Catalogue* (STC), and any reader wanting more detailed information about a particular edition can easily consult either the printed STC or the online ESTC.[A] For the 1552 editions, what will usually matter most are the answers to two questions. Was it printed (wholly or mostly) by Whitchurch or by Grafton? And is it an early edition or a later one? I can hardly expect many readers to be so familiar with this very specialized field that any number from 16279 to 16286 (with or without added letters or decimals) will immediately answer both questions. I shall therefore identify each edition in the text as either 'Whit.' or 'Graf.' followed by an edition-number (from 1 to 5 for Whitchurch and 1 to 6 for Grafton).[B] Three of those editions are found in more than one 'issue' – which can here be interpreted as meaning that most of the sheets are found in a single setting, but that some copies have a number of sheets (always fewer than half) in a different setting. If I need to refer to a specific issue of one of those editions (Whit.1, Graf.2, or Graf.6) I shall append the letter a or b to the number; when no such letter is present the statement applies to the whole edition. The relevant STC and ESTC numbers can be found in the Abbreviations on pp. xxvi–xxvii.

What appears to be the first parliamentary mention of the revised liturgy is a bill 'for an vniformitie in Religion' that received its first reading in the Lords on 9 March 1552. But it was not until 6 April that the extant Journal

---

[A] The printed STC has the considerable advantage of showing each edition or issue in context, usually with more detailed information available in the headnote and Chart of Editions (11, 87–91) – and, for the 1552 editions, two additional columns of notes (needing revision, but nevertheless helpful) on pp. 91–2. Each ESTC record has to be viewed in isolation, and while its list of holdings is often longer, the additions are not always verified. Moreover, copy-specific information is often either limited or absent. To find a particular edition or issue, use 'Advanced Search', select 'Citation note', and enter 'STC', a space, and the number.
[B] I shall, however, use the STC number and a signature reference in any footnote that includes a quotation.

recorded the passage on its third reading of a bill 'for the vniformitie of Service, and administracōn of the Sacrament*es* through owt the Realme'. Since the Journal demonstrably fails to mention a second reading, this might possibly have been a revised bill superseding that of 9 March, and whose first reading also escaped record. Once passed, that bill was sent down to the Commons, 'and therw*i*thall a booke of the saide Service drawen owt by certaine p*er*sons appointed by the King*es* Ma*ie*stie for that purpose'.[A] In the Commons the bill was read once on 7 April, a second time on the 11th (now described as 'for confirmacōn of the booke of cōen prayer'), and a third time on the 13th – but it was not passed until after a fourth reading on the 14th, the day before the acts of that session each received the royal assent.[B] Among the many important changes from 1549, the words spoken at the delivery of the Communion were now to be firmly memorialist. When the minister 'delyuereth the bread [to the communicants] in theyr handes kneling', he should say:

> Take and eate this, in remembraunce that Christe died for the, and fede on him in thy heart by faith, with thankes geuyng.[C]

It was perhaps the experience of 1549, when only three months were allowed for the books to be printed and distributed, that led the second Act of Uniformity (5 & 6 Edw. VI, c. 1) to allow six and a half months before the new liturgy became compulsory on 1 November 1552. The title was now *The Book of Common Prayer* (no longer *of the Common Prayer*, although it is unclear whether that change was considered important). It is difficult to be precise about the number of editions that were printed, for several reasons. On average, the various editions and issues have survived in rather smaller numbers than their 1549 counterparts, so side-by-side comparison with other copies can be more difficult to arrange. And the efforts of both collectors and booksellers to 'perfect' defective copies have sometimes made it difficult to distinguish between genuine reissues and nonce hybrids.[D] But we can be

---

[A] *LJ*, 1, 409, 421; *CJ*, 1, 22–3. Quoted respectively from the Parliamentary Archives (hereafter PArch), HL/PO/JO/1/2, pp. 235, 255; HC/CL/JO/1/1, fol. 48ᵛ.
[B] *CJ*, 1, 22–3.
[C] Whit.1, N7ʳ. When the minister then 'delyuereth the cuppe', he should say 'Drinke this in remembraunce that Christes bloud was shed for thee, and be thankfull'.
[D] For example, 'STC 16284.5' is a copy of Whit.1 whose missing prelims have been supplied from a copy of Graf.1, and whose CC3–6 have been wrapped in the two outermost sheets of Cc⁸ also from Graf.1 (a quire wrongly described as Cc¹⁰ by STC, 11, 88, Series 2/16). And as I have noted elsewhere, the Bodleian volume described by STC as 16287 is a defective Whit.2, partly completed by 22 leaves from a copy of the real 16287, of which Worcester Cathedral has a more nearly complete copy lacking N⁸ and having only the colophon of the ordinal (*Stationers and Printers*, 11, 649, n.B, where I failed to mention the ordinal).

reasonably certain that by 27 September Whitchurch and Grafton had each completed at least three editions and John Oswen one.[A]

A few days earlier, John Knox had preached a sermon before Edward in which he strongly attacked the revised liturgy for having the communicants kneel to receive Communion. So influential was his criticism that on the 27th the Privy Council (who evidently had little or no idea how many editions had already been printed and distributed, or which of the printers had the manuscript copy) ordered Grafton not to distribute or sell any copies 'vntill certaine faultes therein be corrected'.[B] Cranmer had not been present at that Council meeting, and on 7 October he wrote to his fellow councillors, pointing out that the question of kneeling had been carefully considered by all the bishops and other divines who helped compile it, and that the text had already been approved by Parliament.[C]

Cranmer refused to alter the rubric that required the Communion to be delivered 'to the people in theyr handes kneling'. Instead, 'an article to be added to the booke of cōmon prayer declaring the right meaning of kneling at the receyving of the cōmunion' was written, and on 22 October it was approved and signed by the king.[D] MacCulloch claims that what happened on that day was that 'the Council took the decision to add [that article] to the final version of the Prayer Book' and that the declaration itself 'was issued on Council authority alone',[E] but that is significantly inaccurate. It was not until five days later (four days before the new book was supposed to come into use) that the Council instructed the lord chancellor to cause 'a certaine declaracion signed by *the* king*es* ma*i*estie and sent vnto his lordship touching the kneling att the receyving of the Communion' to be added to the book,[F] so Edward had clearly seen and

---

[A] For John Oswen's Worcester edition, STC 16287, see previous note.
[B] TNA: PRO, PC 2/4, 611 (*APC*, IV, 131). The principal 'fault' was the insistence on kneeling to receive Communion, and only three of the errata in the lists *perhaps* inspired by this order are mentioned by both printers. Corrections 1, 6, and 13 in Whitchurch's 'errata 1' (printed after Whit.2: nos. 1, 3, and 7 in his later 'errata 2') are corrections 1, 11, and 19 in Grafton's 'errata 4' (his only list, printed after Graf.5): for details see STC, II, 91–2. Grafton's 'errata 5' is as imaginary as the leaf Cc10 on which it was supposedly printed, but Whitchurch's corrections 5 and 6 (only) are also listed on sig. BB12[r] of Oswen's 16287. All the others listed by Whitchurch are corrected in Oswen's text.
[C] TNA: PRO, SP 10/15, 34[r]–5[r]. Clegg misreads the letter as 'responding to the privy council's request' ('The 1559 Books of Common Prayer', 116), but the councillors had neither 'recall[ed]' the book nor requested anything. They had told Grafton to stop printing it, but without consulting Cranmer.
[D] Whit.1, N7[r]; BL, MS Royal 18.C.xxiv, 262[v] (22 October). At an unknown date it was also entered on the Close Rolls: TNA: PRO, C 54/485/47.
[E] MacCulloch, *Thomas Cranmer*, 527. [F] TNA: PRO, PC 2/4, 630 (*APC*, IV, 154).

approved what is now called the Black Rubric days before the Council even knew it existed.

There are two common myths concerning that declaration, one of them noticed but the other perpetuated by MacCulloch. For the first, he observes that

> The idea that [it] was a victory for Knox and a defeat for Cranmer started very early[,] Dr Hugh Weston already promulgating the legend [in] April 1554 ... However, it is mysterious why any less partisan observer has ever regarded this text as symbolizing a defeat for Cranmer. The rubric exactly represents his eucharistic theology as it had been openly expressed since 1548, particularly in his detestation of adoration of the elements. (*Thomas Cranmer*, 528.)

That notion has, however, been widely held, even in modern times by historians less biased than Dr Weston. J. E. Neale considered the requirement for kneeling to have been 'so obnoxious to the Puritans of the time that they had obtained the last-minute insertion ... of the so-called "Black Rubric"', while A. G. Dickens called the Rubric itself 'Knoxian'. Jennifer Loach described it as 'added to the 1552 Prayer book at the insistence of John Knox, explaining that kneeling ... did not imply adoration' (although Knox wanted the kneeling eliminated, not explained), and Brian Cummings has suggested that it was Knox (rather than the Council) who on 27 October asked the lord chancellor to have the declaration inserted, whereupon Cranmer 'intervened' with the letter that he had in fact written twenty days earlier.[A]

It may therefore be useful to recapitulate the who, the why, and the when. Without consulting the Primate of their Church, the rest of the Privy Council reacted to Knox's sermon by suspending the printing of the prayer books mandated by Parliament. Ten days later Cranmer politely but firmly told his fellow councillors that they had acted out of turn, and during the next two weeks someone wrote an *anti*-Knoxian defence of the kneeling required by those books. The king signed it, and a few days later the Council told the lord chancellor to have the printers insert it. How much closer to obvious could it be that the Black Rubric was written by Cranmer himself?

Having tried to explode the 'Knoxian' myth, though, MacCulloch unfortunately espoused another, suggesting that the Black Rubric is

---

[A] Neale, *Elizabeth I and Her Parliaments*, 63; Dickens, *The English Reformation*, 359; Loach, *Parliament under the Tudors*, 164, n.4; Cummings, *The Book of Common Prayer*, 793–4.

so called because time was now rushing on so fast towards the All Saints' Day deadline that at first the rubric appeared only on slips tipped into the already printed volumes, rather than taking its place in red ink in the text like conventional rubrics. (527)

There were no 'slips': the inserts and cancels were printed on complete leaves. But more importantly, *all* the rubrics in *all* Edwardian prayer books were printed in black, and this avoidance of the standard practice of Catholic liturgies (whence the name 'rubric') was probably a deliberate policy rather than a mere convenience. In Cranmer's prayer books, red ink was used only in the preliminaries: it was confined to the calendar quire and (except in the earliest editions of 1549) the forme containing the title-page.[A] And while the instruction that the bread and wine were to be delivered to the communicants 'in theyr handes kneling' qualifies as a rubric no matter what its colour, the 'article' or declaration that defends the required kneeling is not a rubric in any accepted sense.

According to *The Oxford Dictionary of the Christian Church*, the nickname

> dates only from the 19th cent. when the practice of printing the BCP with the rubrics in red was introduced and the fact that the 'Declaration' was really not a rubric at all was marked by printing it in black'. (214)

But whatever nineteenth-century printers may have done, that explanation is no more credible than MacCulloch's – because in 1688 Abraham Woodhead reported that 'the *Puritans* at the *Savoy-Conference* 1661 … inserted the restoring of the *Black Rubrick* into favour'.[B] In Appendix B I have offered what I believe to be a more plausible explanation for the name.

As soon as the text of the 'article' reached them in late October 1552, Grafton and Whitchurch began to print it on leaves to be distributed to as many as possible of those to whom copies had already been sold, and on cancels to insert in as-yet-undistributed copies of the existing editions.[C] And in all subsequent '1552' editions, the Black Rubric was included where it belonged. Before King Edward died Grafton had printed the equivalent

---

[A] Inexplicably, in John E. Booty's 1976 edition of the 1559 book (which uses STC 16292 as copy-text), while anachronistically using red for every rubric in pages 48–322, he declines to reproduce any of the original red on the title-page (1) or in the almanack and calendar (35–47).

[B] Woodhead, *A Compendious Discourse* (Wing W3440A), 157. The term was also used by Thomas Ward (d. 1708) in *Englands Reformation*, 1710 (ESTC T132416), 79.

[C] Oswen's 16287 includes a Black Rubric insert not listed in STC, II: 91. In the copy at Worcester Cathedral it is on the second recto of an otherwise blank bifolium bound before O1 (i.e. inserted after the now-missing quire N^8), has a 4-line inverted V serving as initial A, and the last full line ends 'then in'.

of four more editions in folio and one in octavo, and Whitchurch two folios, two quartos, and an octavo.[A]

Size, however, was not the only difference between the folios and copies in smaller formats. As will be discussed in greater detail in Chapter 7, appended to each folio edition was an ordinal: a brief manual prescribing the procedures for ordaining deacons, priests, bishops, and archbishops. But the folio editions were designed primarily for use by the clergy when officiating in church services. The smaller editions were aimed more towards members of the congregation, who would seldom if ever need to consult an ordinal. And so what was appended to the quarto and octavo editions instead was a psalter with a few additional 'Godly Prayers'. The psalms themselves were in the Great Bible translation, which was still the verson authorized (and indeed prescribed) for use in church. Instead of either a generic running title naming the work simply as 'The Psalms of David' or a specific heading identifying the particular psalm(s) on each page, each headline indicates instead the day of the month to which its contents are assigned by the 'Table for the Order of the Psalmes' in the prayer-book preliminaries. While an occasional copy of such a psalter has survived as a separate item, they were clearly intended to accompany the prayer books with which they are usually bound.

Inflation and the Collation

Before the history of the 1552 editions can be outlined, it needs to be recognized that the STC treatment of what is presented as the last of Grafton's editions is seriously wrong, and that the errors go beyond the mistakes in the collational formula of Series 2/16 in the Chart of Editions (II, p. 88). The final quire of the ordinal should not be Cc^{10} as indicated, but Cc^{8}, while the appended note ('C10 lacking, prob. had errata and prices') should obviously be deleted. What the Chart presents in the main sequence as $A–Y^6$ should read (as John Lancaster first pointed out to me) $A–Q^6 R^8 S–Y^6$. But the biggest mistake was listing this edition as Grafton's *last* of 1552, when it was really his first (Figure 3).

[A] Grafton: Graf.4 (which STC implies is merely a reissue of Graf.3, but about two-thirds of the sheets are in new settings), Graf.5, and Graf.6, all in folio and formulaically dated August 1552, and STC 16290 in octavo with the psalter dated 1553. Whitchurch: Whit.4 and Whit.5 in folio, STC 16288 and 16288a in quarto, and 16290.5 in octavo dated 1553. Whit.4 and Whit.5 each include sheets printed by Steven Mierdman; each issue of Graf.6 includes some sheets printed by John Day and some by Nicholas Hill.

Inflation and the Collation

As the lengthiest Grafton edition of the revised text, what I here call Graf.1 ought to have been suspected of priority for that reason alone, but there are other clues as well. In the order for Evening Prayer both printers defy expectation by *adding* to the text when reprinting. In each first edition Evening Prayer fills six pages, and the *Magnificat* is followed by the rubric, 'Or the .xcviii. Psalm. *Cantate Domino canticum nouum, quia mirabilia fecit.*'[A] In their next editions both printers actually print that psalm rather than merely referring to it. Whitchurch thus lengthens his section to seven pages and Grafton to six and a half, at which point the latter begins his Litany mid-page instead of starting a new page. Moreover, the copy of Graf.1 in Christ Church, Oxford, has the original leaf T6 without the Black Rubric (and must therefore have been printed before that declaration was written in October), while the other three known copies have a cancel leaf that includes it.[B] And although one last clue fails to confirm it as necessarily the first of Grafton's editions, it proves that it cannot be the last. The 1552 preliminaries include a nineteen-year almanack on a8^v, covering 1552–70. In all the Whitchurch editions and most of Grafton's, whoever calculated the dates of Easter did so only for the first ten of those years – but Grafton filled in the remaining nine blanks in Graf.5 and Graf.6. He evidently printed Graf.1 before doing so, because it is one of the editions that show Easter dates only through 1561.

To begin the discussion of the 1552 editions it will be useful to compare the collational formulae, making them perhaps a little easier to interpret by aligning the three parts.

Whit.1 (STC 16279) 2°: a^8 b^6 ^{2}a^2, ¶^{6} ¶¶^{8} A–Q^8 R^6, AA–BB^6 CC^8
Graf.1 (STC 16286.5) 2°: a^8 b^6 π A^2, A–Q^6 R^8 S–Y^6 z^6 &^{4}, Aa–Bb^6 Cc^8

While the structure is very different *between* the commas, the preliminaries before the first comma are very similar, as are the ordinals that follow the second comma. Those ordinals will be separately discussed in Chapter 7, so I shall begin here with the preliminaries.

All folio editions of the 1552 *Book of Common Prayer* begin with a preliminary quire of four sheets (eight leaves) signed with lower-case a, followed by a calendar quire of three sheets (six leaves) signed b. With the exception of the capitula in the first Whitchurch edition, all the quires of the main text in all editions are signed with capitals, so no 'π' needs to be

---

[A] Thus Whitchurch's ¶¶1^v. Grafton's B1^v misprints the psalm number as 'xvi', and omits the last three words.

[B] One of those three copies, formerly in the Zion Research Library, Brookline, Massachusetts (BO^6 in STC), was apparently sold privately when the library was dispersed in 1998, and has not been traced.

Figure 3 Title-page of Grafton's first edition of 1552 (STC 16286.5).
(Lambeth Palace Library, [**] H5415.A4G7 1552, a1^r.)

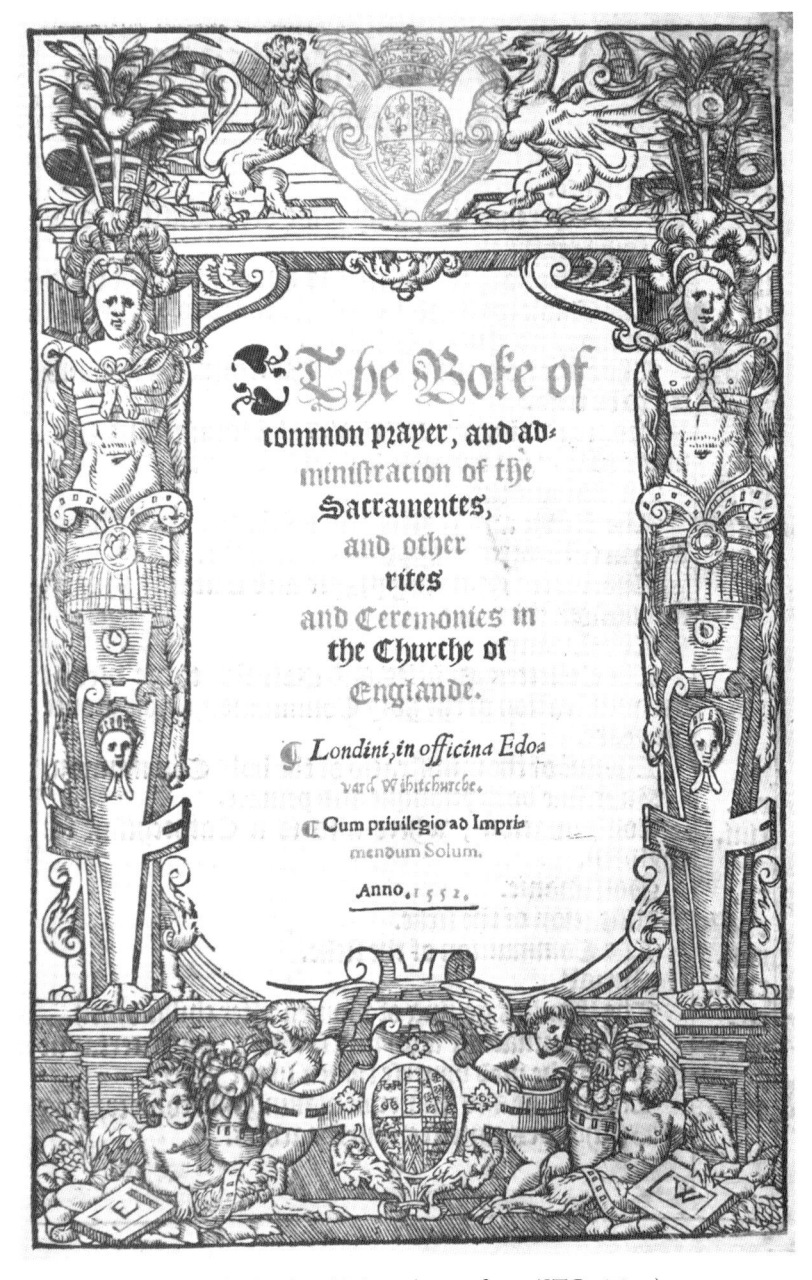

Figure 4 Title-page of Whitchurch's last edition of 1552 (STC 16282.7).
(Lambeth Palace Library, [**] H5415.A4W4 1552, a1^r.)

included when describing those two preliminary quires as a^8 b^6. Between them and the main text, however, is usually found a single bifolium signed with lower-case a in the Whitchurch editions (whose preliminaries therefore collate a^8 b^6 $^2a^2$) and capital A in Grafton's (a^8 b^6 $^\pi A^2$). That bifolium contains only the 1552 Act of Uniformity that required the new book to replace its predecessor of 1549. Why neither printer gave that quire the signature c is a mystery, but it is clear that including the Act was a belated afterthought (though perhaps a little less belated than the addition of the Black Rubric). It is not mentioned in the list of contents that had already been printed on the verso of the title-page.[A]

The afterthought responsible for the Act's inclusion may have been Parliament's own, whose members seem to have had some difficulty deciding exactly what the legislation was supposed to be for. The new prayer book itself is not mentioned at all until nearly halfway through the text of the Act. Section I begins by implicitly praising the qualities of the *previous* book, lamenting the fact that many people have refused to participate in its services, and ordering that all the king's subjects should hereafter (in the absence of any lawful or reasonable excuse) attend church service on every Sunday and holy day throughout the year on pain of punishment. Sections II and III explain how that punishment should be imposed by the clergy. One could be forgiven for suspecting that these sections, which take up almost half of the original Act (twenty-seven of the fifty-eight manuscript lines),[B] may have originated separately as a mysterious bill 'for the appointing of an ordre to coom to Devyne Servyce' that disappeared after a single reading in the Lords on 23 January 1552 (and which may or may not have been the same as an equally elusive 'bille for comyng to dyune [*sic*] seruice' that vanished after a first reading in the Commons three days later).[C] The completely distinct business of introducing and mandating the new service book does not begin until line twenty-eight of the Act, and occupies just over sixteen lines as Section IV, to which Section V appends eight lines that specify the penalties for taking part in any other form of service or rite on or after the coming 1 November.

[A] The absence of the Act from some copies of the early editions may often reflect no more than the ravages of time, but when such copies still preserve part or all of quire b it is reasonable to doubt that the Act was ever present.
[B] PArch, HO/PO/PU/1/1551/5&6E6n1 (*Statutes*, IV, i, 130–1).
[C] *LJ*, I, 394; *CJ*, 1,16 (respectively quoted from PArch, HL/PO/JO/1/2, p. 209, and HC/CL/JO/1/1, fol. 33ʳ).

In 1549 it had evidently been considered unnecessary to reprint the first Act of Uniformity in the service book itself. What probably made the difference in 1552 was the closing Section VI of the new Act, whose seven lines required each incumbent to read out the whole Act 'in the Churche at the tyme of the moste assemblie', once a quarter during the first year of the new service and once a year thereafter. The only practical way of ensuring that the clergy had a text to read from was to include it in the service book itself. In this case it was probably Grafton rather than Whitchurch who worked from manuscript copy, because as King's Printer it was his responsibility and prerogative to print the acts of each Parliament. He would therefore have been supplied with careful copies of the originals as soon as possible after the session had ended.

Placing the Act between the calendar and the beginning of Morning Prayer was hardly ideal, but with quire a^8 already printed the only realistic alternative for each first edition would have required binders to be somehow instructed to insert it after either a1 or a4. The printers could presumably have chosen to begin later editions with a^8 replaced by a quire a^{10} in which the Act occupied either $a2^r$–3^v or $a5^r$–6^v.[A] But both men chose instead to keep printing it as a bifolium belonging between quires b and A. For his fifth edition Grafton decided to insert 'An Acte for the vniformitie of common praier' into the contents list as the first item before 'A Preface', after which he reprinted the revised list in both Graf.6 and his octavo of 1552–53 (STC 16290). In Graf.6 that could perhaps be interpreted as an instruction for binders – although the Act is still printed as πA^2, and all copies I have seen have it in the usual position after the calendar. But doubt is cast on Grafton's intentions by the contents list of his octavo edition, in which the Act is listed as the first item although it is nevertheless placed between the calendar and the main text. In that edition the collation and signing are not at all ambiguous: the preliminaries collate a–c^8, and the Act occupies pages $c6^r$–7^v.

If we divide the main text of the prayer book into parts as before, the units are not quite the same as in the 1549 version. The Litany now follows Morning Prayer and Evening Prayer (formerly Matins and Evensong) as part of section 1a, and in each edition the Commination begins on the

---

[A] This is perhaps what Clegg means when claiming that 'In all the 1552 Prayer Books, the preliminaries in an ideal collation would be a^{10} b^{6}' (107). But her discussion on pp. 107–10 (especially such sentences as 'The representation, then, of the preliminaries as A^{10} works only in an ideal collation.') suggests uncertainty about both printing-house practice and the bibliographical meaning of 'ideal copy'.

verso of the last page of the Churching of Women, essentially eliminating any distinction between parts 2a and 2b.

	1a	1b	1c	2a–b
Whit.1	¶⁶ ¶¶⁸	| A–L⁸ M1^{r}–5^{v}	| M6^{r-v} N⁸ O1^{r-v}	| O2^{r}–8^{v} P–Q⁸ R⁶
Graf.1	A–B⁶ C1^{r}–2^{r}	| C2^{v}–6^{v} D–Q⁶ R⁸ |	S–T⁶	| V–Y⁶ z⁶ &⁴

In Chapter 1, dividing the collations according to the parts of the text had the effect of reducing the apparent differences between the formulae (p. 10), but here the differences are emphasized.

The first point to note is that Whitchurch's use of capitula instead of letters for section 1a may suggest one of two things. If it was the first section he set, it might simply mean that he did not yet know whereabouts it was to be placed, but that seems rather unlikely. The more probable alternative is that he began work on section 1b without giving much thought to what might precede it, and had to resort to non-alphabetic signatures when the copy for section 1a finally arrived.

The latter scenario is, I think, the correct one, because there is reason to suppose that Whitchurch started work some time before Grafton did. In 1549 the first edition of section 1b originally filled 234 pages when set by Grafton and 231 pages when trimmed down by Whitchurch. In the 1552 version all the Introits were omitted, as were the first Communion for Christmas Day, the second for Easter, and the whole service for St Mary Magdalene's Day. What was left would fill fewer than 200 pages, and the only other substantive change was that the short Collect for St Andrew's Day was rewritten. It would therefore have been easy enough to mark up a printed edition of 1549 so that Whitchurch could start work on that section while manuscript copy was prepared for the more sensitive revisions. That in turn suggests that Grafton started work rather later, after Whitchurch had received and printed the copy for section 1a.[A] Not only was Grafton able to start his first signature alphabet with A, but in setting sections 1a and 1b in text order from Whitchurch's printed sheets he was able to cast off the copy for his own convenience. He had no need, real or imagined, to begin section 1b on the first page of a quire, or even on a recto page at all. So with very little effort he could trim sections 1a and 1b from

---

[A] In early October Archbishop Cranmer needed a reliable source from which to compile an errata list, but in the absence of the clerk of Parliaments he was unable to access the manuscript bearing the Great Seal and kept with the original Act of Uniformity. On the 7th he wrote to the Council that he had, however, been able to obtain 'the copy which m^r Spilman [the clerk] deliuered to the printers to printe by' (TNA: PRO, SP 10/15, 34^r). If the printers had only one manuscript copy (as seems to be implied), that would help to explain the order of events.

Whitchurch's 28+185 pages (two of them blank) to 27+181 (only one blank). Both printers set the Communion service as twenty-four pages (Grafton more neatly as two whole quires), after which Grafton reduced part 2 from fifty-eight pages to fifty-six. His overall saving of eight pages was comparatively trivial: if one includes the preliminaries and ordinal (each of which is the same size in both editions), Whitchurch's book contains ninety-two sheets and Grafton's exactly ninety. But the best time for serious compression would be after the revised maximum prices were set.

Neither Whit.1 nor Graf.1 has a note about prices, but it is safe to assume that the limits were set after inspection of one of the first copies to be completed, and that seems likely to have been one of Whitchurch's. But while each contained slightly fewer sheets than the first editions of 1549, the inflation initiated by Henry VIII's debasements of the coinage was still rampant – so when the Privy Council set the new maximum retail price for an unbound copy in 1552 they raised it to 2s. 6d. (30 pence).[A] This time the prices for bound copies were spelled out in rather more detail: a copy bound in parchment or forel should not exceed 3s. 4d. (40 pence), and one 'bound in leather, in paper boordes or claspes' should not exceed 4s. (48 pence). The same order applied to all subsequent editions and was not revised. Even John Oswen of Worcester followed suit in his close reprint of Whit.2.

Once again, each printer proceeded to lower his production costs by decreasing the size of the book. For his second and third editions Whitchurch reduced the main text from seventy-four sheets to seventy, retaining an initial three-sheet quire at the beginning for Morning Prayer, but then switching to his favoured four-sheet quires until what was left at the end required only another of three sheets (A^6 $B-R^8$ S^6). Grafton chose instead to take an even bigger step, to a format he would be happy to repeat indefinitely thereafter. On the one hand he wanted to use as little paper as possible; on the other he needed to use type of a size from which a minister with less than perfect eyesight could comfortably read aloud (at least until he had memorized the most frequently repeated sections).[B] So he reduced the seventy-two sheets of the main text to sixty-four ($A-V^6$ X^8) and the appended ordinal from ten sheets to nine ($Aa-Cc^6$). The preliminaries, however, remained an essentially irreducible eight sheets.

[A] The prices set for copies without the ordinal are discussed in Chapter 7 (p. 123).
[B] It is noticeable that smaller type is typically reserved for the rubrics that have to be obeyed but not recited, and for the responses of the congregation who are not reading from the same volume.

As explained in the previous chapter, if the sheets of successive editions are essentially interchangeable, leftovers from one edition can be used up in the next, or shortages can be made up by printing extra copies of the next edition. A second advantage is that if a printer needs assistance to meet a deadline, he can ask a colleague for help and give him any selection of sheets – either specially or randomly chosen – to reprint page for page as best suits either his own or his subcontractor's convenience. Grafton managed to print the first five of his 1552 editions without assistance, but when he needed help with Graf.6 (which became one of the first three English books known to have been shared by *three* printers),[A] he was able to give whatever quires or sheets he chose to John Day (quires A, G, Q, L, and S for Graf.6a; sheets F2–5 and quire K for Graf.6b) and to Nicholas Hill (sheets I3:4 and X3:6 for Graf.6a; H1:6 and X3:6 for Graf.6b), and simply ask to have them reprinted. We should beware of assuming that there must have been a single, rational, or discoverable reason why those particular sheets were the ones chosen.

Having seen Grafton compact the text down to sixty-four sheets and the ordinal to nine, Whitchurch once again decided to do better with his fourth edition. Grafton's section 1a now occupied twenty-five pages followed by a blank (A–B^6, C1); Whitchurch was content to fill the same number of leaves with twenty-six pages (A1^r–B5^v). Grafton's section 1b took up 155 pages (C2^r–Q1^r), so to match him Whitchurch would have to lose at least twenty pages from his existing 175, which would have required every eight new pages to hold the text from nine old pages. But by the time he began work on his new quire H he knew that he would miss that target by several pages.

Whether or not that is why he then subcontracted part of the work to the immigrant printer Steven Mierdman is beyond discovery – but it is a fact that Whitchurch's next contribution to this prayer book was to begin the Communion section with a new quire M, giving Mierdman the job of fitting sixty-three old pages of Collects, Epistles, and Gospels into quires I, K, and L. Cramming them into a mere forty-eight new pages was hardly feasible, but Mierdman was better at compressing than was Whitchurch, and got them down to fifty-two by a variety of methods that included the rather obvious one of setting to a wider measure. As a consequence, quire L had to contain ten leaves rather than eight – which is why the structure of Whitchurch's last two editions is less regular than

---

[A] The others are folio bibles, each involving Whitchurch and Nicholas Hill: STC 2079 (1548? with an unidentified printer) and 2091 (1553 with Steven Mierdman).

Grafton's.^A Whitchurch's M and N were both eight-leaf quires, but left twenty leaves still to be printed. He could have chosen to print them as two eights and a four, but having one ten-leaf quire in the book already, he printed them as two more tens. The final collation of the main text, then, is A–K^8 L^{10} M–N^8 O–P^{10}, and the total of sixty-three sheets is one less than in Grafton's editions. The appended ordinal, occupying ten sheets collating AA^8 BB^{12}, was also given to Mierdman to compress, and emerged as nine sheets with a collation of AA^8 BB^{10}. When that was reprinted as what would be Whitchurch's last edition (Figure 4), both Whitchurch and Mierdman reprinted their previous sections.

The structure of the first editions of 1552 owed comparatively little to the 1549 editions they replaced. But the first two Elizabethan editions would be directly reprinted (albeit with some small but important revisions) by Grafton from Graf.6 and by Whitchurch and others from either Whit.4 or Whit.5 (or perhaps both), so I shall close this chapter with the collations and the textual divisions of the main text of those last editions. The preliminaries of 1559 would differ considerably, and the ordinals will require a chapter of their own, but the main sections of the prayer books of 1559 would be very close descendants of the last ones of 1552.

Graf.2–6b (STC 16285–86.3)   2°: a^8 b^6 ^{π}A^2, A–V^6 X^8, Aa–Cc^6
Whit.4–5 (STC 16282.3–82.7)   2°: a^8 b^6 ^{2}a^2, A–K^8 L^{10} M–N^8 P^{10}, AA^8 BB^{10}

	1a	1b–c	2a–b	
Graf.2–6b	A–B^6 C1^{r-v}	C2^r–6^v D–R^6	S–V^6 X^8	(256 pages)
Whit.4–5	A^6 B1^r–5^v	B6^r–8^v C–K^8 L^{10}	M–N^8 O–P^{10}	(252 pages)

^A Whit.4 and Whit.5.

CHAPTER 3

Mary's Reign and Elizabeth's First Parliament

Mary's Counter-Reformation

King Edward died less than a year after the crisis that inspired the Black Rubric, and soon afterwards Mary I began to undo his Reformation and steer the Church of England back towards Rome. On 12 August 1553 she declared to the mayor and recorder of London that

> albeit her graces conscience is stayed in matters of religion: Yet she meaneth graciousely, not to compell or constreyne other mennes consciences, other wise then god shall (as she trusteth) putte in their harts, a persuasion of the truthe that she is in, thorough thopeninge of his wurde unto them by godlye, vertuouse and lerned preachers.[A]

But six days later a proclamation made it clear that her tolerance would last only until

> suche tyme as further ordre by common assent maye be taken therein. Forbyddinge neuerthelesse, all her subiectes of all degrees, at theyr perylles, to moue sedicions, or to styrre vnquietnes in her people by interpretyng the lawes of this realme after theyr braynes and fansies, but quietly to continue for the tyme, tyl as before is sayde further order maye be taken.[B]

As the text went on to make obvious, 'interpretyng the lawes of this realme after theyr braynes and fansies' included any public practice, expression, or discussion of the religious orthodoxy of the previous reign. Before the year ended there were two sessions of Parliament. The only public act of the first session returned the legal definitions of *treason* and *praemunire* to those in force before the reign of Henry VIII; a few weeks later the second act of the second session repealed all the acts that had enabled the Edwardian Reformation.[C]

[A] TNA: PRO, PC 2/5, 66 (*APC*, IV, 317).   [B] STC 7849, 1ʳ (TRP 390, p. 6).
[C] 1 Mar. I, st. 1, c. 1; 1 Mar. I, st. 2, c. 2 (*Statutes*, II, i, 198, 202).

But even before Parliament met, the new regime had carried out a purge of the book trade, whose most influential members were men who had profited from the Reformation.[A] No formal record survives to indicate who planned and executed it, but the most likely leaders were Bishops Stephen Gardiner (Winchester) and Edmund Bonner (London), newly released from their Edwardian imprisonment in early August. Richard Grafton had already lost his position as Royal Printer by late July for having printed a proclamation on the 10th announcing the accession of Queen Jane. He was quickly replaced by the Stationer John Cawood, from whom the Privy Council commissioned a proclamation on the 28th, although his appointment did not become official until December.[B] His main qualification must have been his Catholicism: during and since his apprenticeship with John Reynes (a bookbinder and occasional publisher) he had never even published a book, let alone printed one. But among the printers who had actively contributed to the Edwardian Reformation, and whose careers in England suddenly ended in the autumn of 1553, were two Protestant immigrants who hastily returned to Europe: Nicholas Hill and Steven Mierdman. And while there is no evidence that the takeover was anything more forced than an amicable purchase, Cawood acquired the presses, types, and ornament stock that had been Mierdman's. It is likely that he also hired some of Mierdman's former employees.

Under Edward, the printing houses of Grafton and Whitchurch had been the most productive in England, so rather than destroy potentially useful resources, the Marian authorities seem to have devised another way of preventing those presses from being used against them. Each man was apparently allowed to remain the tenant of his premises and the owner of his equipment, but had to accept a Catholic informer chosen by the regime as manager of the business – probably in return for a percentage of any profits, although I have found no evidence of that. Until Mary died, the books printed with Grafton's materials were printed in the name of Robert Caly, a native of Norwich who had worked for a Catholic printer in Rouen until his employer died in 1552. Under Caly the productivity slumped to no more than one-third of Grafton's level, either because Caly was less successful in attracting customers or because Grafton's best employees simply refused to work for the unpopular pursuivant nicknamed 'Robin Papist'.

The story of the Whitchurch business is less straightforward, but until early 1556 its products appeared in the name of John Wayland, a Scrivener

---

[A] For a more detailed discussion, see *Stationers and Printers*, II, 753–63.
[B] TNA: PRO, PC 2/6, 10 (*APC*, 4: 421); C 82/978/51 (warrant, 18 Dec.); C 66/865, mm. 22–3 (patent, 29 Dec.).

who had had a brief but unsuccessful career as a printer in the 1530s. The evidence suggests that in 1556 Whitchurch and Wayland quarrelled, and that Whitchurch decided to sell his lease, move to Camberwell, and put his equipment in storage rather than continue. The authorities would have had no obvious reason to object if Whitchurch had made it impossible for his presses to be used illegally – so while Wayland continued to publish, he had to hire other printers to manufacture the books for him. Even if the regime's plan had been to preserve the two businesses as valuable assets, the result was that one was seriously diminished and the other shut down.

When Mary took the throne from Edward's chosen successor in 1553, even most Protestants seem to have accepted that right (as defined by the will of Henry VIII) had triumphed over wrong – although the many who believed that Mary would preserve or perhaps even advance her brother's religious agenda were soon to be disillusioned. But while her Catholic subjects were doubtless pleased when England and Rome were reconciled in late 1554, even among them Mary's initial popularity significantly eroded over the years. Her marriage to Philip of Spain, the burning of Protestants, the loss of Calais, and the phantom pregnancies that twice raised the fear that the half-Spanish queen would produce a three-quarters-Spanish heir: all those events took their toll, and it is unlikely that her death was mourned quite as widely and deeply as Edward's had been.

Elizabeth's First Parliament

Elizabeth became queen on 17 November 1558. Doubtless at the suggestion of William Cecil, who had already become her closest adviser, the man she chose as the printer of the proclamation that announced her accession was the Stationer Richard Jugge – who, like his predecessor Cawood, had never been a printer before being appointed Queen's Printer.[A] But unlike Cawood, he was unable simply to take over an existing printing house, because no printers had reacted to Elizabeth's accession by fleeing the country. Jugge's first official products, therefore, were really printed for him by John Day, and not until the following May did a printed sheet appear that can be credibly attributed to a press actually owned by Jugge himself.[B]

During the reign of her Catholic half-sister, Elizabeth had outwardly conformed in religious observance, although it was widely rumoured that

---

[A] Nor had he even been an apprentice before purchasing the freedom of the Stationers' Company in 1541 (*Stationers and Printers*, 1, 513–14). He had, however, been a publisher during Edward's reign.

[B] The proclamation STC 7897, dated 16 May.

her real sympathies lay closer to those of their late half-brother. But while her choice of advisers clearly pointed in that direction, she made no unambiguous declaration of intent before her first parliament assembled. Very early in 1559 she had Jugge publish a small pamphlet containing a revised form of Cranmer's 1544 English Litany that was being used in her private chapel. But even this was equivocal, because while the original had been approved by Henry to be incorporated in the use of Sarum, Elizabeth's version omitted the words in which Henrician and Edwardian congregations had asked to be delivered from 'the tyranny of the byshop of Rome, and all his detestable enormities'.[A]

Whenever (and by whomever) the final decision was formally made, it was hardly a major surprise that 'the Elizabethan Settlement' would be for the most part a return to the church of the Edwardian Reformation, albeit with a few small but very significant alterations to the prayer book of 1552. But no matter what the queen and her councillors planned, the anti-Reformation acts of Mary's parliaments would remain the law until an Elizabethan parliament could repeal or replace them. That would not be easy, because all the lords spiritual in the upper house had been appointed by either Mary or her father, and there were enough Catholics among the lords temporal to make the successful passage of reforms an uncertain prospect. No significant changes could be made unless Parliament first accepted Elizabeth as the supreme ruler of the English Church.[B]

The original supremacy bill was first read in the Commons on 9 February 1559, and after a second reading on the 13th and two days of 'Argument*es*' it was sent to committee on the 15th. Evidently encouraged, on that day someone introduced a bill 'for order of Servyce and mynysters in the churche', but after a second reading on the 16th it disappeared without trace.[C] During the next two months a second supremacy bill with

---

[A] STC 10620, B5ᵛ.
[B] Henry VIII and Edward VI had each been Supreme 'Head'; Elizabeth tactfully preferred 'supreme gou*er*nour' (PArch., HL/PO/PU/1/1558/1Eliz1n1, line 123).
[C] PArch, HC/CL/JO/1/1, fols. 189ʳ–90ʳ (*CJ*, 1, 54). The full entry for February 15th reads '1 The bill for order of Servyce and mynysters in the churche' (189ᵛ), and that for the 16th, '1 The boke for cōmon prayer and mynystrac*ion* of sacramentes' (190ʳ). Jones suggests that if the figure preceding the second entry is a '1' for a first reading, the first entry 'would have legalized the Edwardian ordinal or something similar' (*Faith by Statute*, 92) – but Edwardian ordinals deal with ordaining ministers, not ordering services. If that figure is a '2', however, both entries refer to the same bill. Jones's suggestion (p. 93) that it really is a '2' is certainly mistaken, for while the clerk's '1' usually begins and often ends with a light uptick, his '2' is markedly curved and ends with a clear stroke which, when not horizontal, usually curves or slopes downwards. It nevertheless remains likely that this was a second reading that *should* have been numbered '2'. Jones also suggests that the first supremacy bill and the service-book bill (or bills) 'were fused together in ... committee', and that an incident recorded on 4 March '*proves* that the new bill for supremacy contained a service book' (ibid., my emphasis). But that incident proves only that the 1552 prayer book was not universally admired, and the imagined 'fusing' is unsupported by the record.

a growing series of provisos and addenda moved back and forth between the two houses. Not until that bill seemed reasonably certain to survive a few last stages of revision (after a total of nine readings in the Commons and six in the Lords) was a new bill concerning the prayer book introduced on 18 April, read three times, and passed by the Commons on the 20th.[A]

'The bill for the vnytie of seruyce in the churche and admynystracon of the Sacramentes' was the third bill that the Commons passed that day. Whether or not they considered it of particular urgency is uncertain, but before continuing with the day's business they arranged for Secretary Cecil to deliver all three (together with three they had passed on Saturday the 15th and another from Monday the 17th) to the Lords. Exactly when the manuscript Journal was compiled is equally uncertain, but the record of sending up those seven bills – 'the vij last billes ∧past sent to | the L by m^r Secretarye' – was written in before the second reading of a bill concerning watermen was added. So when Cecil's errand failed (or at least, when the clerk discovered the fact) the entry had to be crossed out.[B] The only business conducted by the Lords that Thursday was adjourning until Saturday morning, and on Saturday morning they adjourned again until Tuesday the 25th. So on *that* day, having meanwhile worked on the 21st and 22nd, and having passed two more bills on the 24th, the Commons sent Sir Anthony Cooke to deliver *nine* passed bills to the Lords.

The Act of Uniformity was eventually passed by the Lords on the 28th with a majority of only three – at which date the Act of Supremacy was still one proviso and one day short of its own final passage.[C]

I think it unlikely that the queen's advisers waited until the end of April before at least planning to have the revised prayer book printed. When Elizabeth gave her formal assent to the acts of her first parliament on 8 May 1559, the Act of Uniformity required the clergy to begin using the new liturgy less than seven weeks later on 24 June.[D] An experienced

---

[A] Jones reports that it was passed on the 19th (*Faith by Statute*, 145), but this is clearly just a slip: that was the day on which it was engrossed.
[B] HC/CL/JO/1/1, fol. 210^v: see Plate 1a. Note that the deleted entry is neither transcribed nor mentioned in the published *Journals* (*CJ*, 1, 60). For the marginal 'assent' beside the prayer-book entry (also ignored by *CJ*), see Appendix B, pp. 217–18.
[C] *CJ*, 1, 54–5, 58–60; *LJ*, 1, 555, 563–5, 568, 574; Davis, 'An Unpublished Manuscript', 536–9.
[D] 1 Eliz. I, c. 2. The date was altered when the act was engrossed on 19 April. In the first two occurrences 'the feast of' is followed by an erasure overwritten with 'the natyvytye', followed by a caret pointing to the interlined 'of saynt Iohn baptist' (PArch., HL/PO/PU/1/1558/1Eliz1n2, lines 11 and 13–14. The St John's date (24 June) appears without alteration in lines 19, 25–6, 54–5, 81–2, 101–2, 115, and 117). The deleted feast was probably that of St Barnabas (11 June).

printer with two presses could probably have produced a single edition of 1,200–1,500 copies in those weeks, but there were more than 8,500 parishes in England. Many of them could make do for a while by using some of the numerous Edwardian books that had illegally survived Mary's proclamation of 1555,[A] but the authorities could hardly have been unaware that beyond the metropolitan area the official deadline was utterly unrealistic. In the event, by the end of the year only four editions in folio, two in quarto, and two in octavo had yet been printed. It is hardly possible that any printer could have started work before the first bill was introduced in early February, but by then the Privy Council must at least have begun to consider the problem of who was going to print the new books. During other reigns, in other circumstances, the obvious first choice would have been the Royal Printer. Since at least the beginning of February Elizabeth officially had two of those to choose from, having appointed her sister's printer as Jugge's partner. But Jugge had still not yet actually become a printer, and John Cawood's annual output had never even approached that of the Edwardian prayer-book printers.[B]

The only units in which the productivity of an early modern printer can easily be measured are edition-sheets – the number of which is determined very simply by counting how many sheets of paper were required to make up a single copy of each item he printed during the period in question. Since we almost never have any reliable information about how many copies of any of those books were printed, what the number really signifies is so many sheets of paper multiplied by an unknown *average* edition-size – an average at which we can only guess, and which undoubtedly varied from house to house and year to year. But unless we assume that in most houses the annual averages usually differed from each other by less than an order of magnitude, we cannot even begin to discuss output at all. Edition-sheets are therefore the only units available.

With an average annual production of a little over 480 (extant) edition-sheets, Richard Tottell was the only printer in Mary's reign who came close

---

[A] STC 7865, 1^r–2^r (TRP 422, p. 59).

[B] Clegg considers it 'significant that the patent that appointed Jugge and Cawood to the office ... was dated 24 March 1559, the same day that parliament was adjourned until after Easter' ('The 1559 Books of Common Prayer', 111). But they were identified as partners in that office on a proclamation dated 7 February, and the warrant for their patent is dated 20 March. The adjournment could not have been foreseen on either of those dates, so it is difficult to see any real significance in the date on which the warrant was delivered to the Office of the Six Clerks to await fair-copying and sealing. (That delivery, not the signing or sealing, is what the date of a patent records.)

to the Edwardian averages of Grafton (nearly 530) or Whitchurch (just over 600), and Tottell's closest Marian competitor was the Queen's Printer, John Cawood (about 215). Because the lawbooks for which Tottell held a monopoly accounted for more than two-thirds of his output, the legal profession would not have wanted him to divert his efforts into liturgical printing. And if Cawood were to devote himself to mass-producing prayer books it might seriously affect his ability to drop everything when he was needed in his capacity as the only one of Elizabeth's own printers who really was a printer.

The seemingly 'obvious' candidates for the job were the two men who had already proved themselves able to produce enough prayer books to satisfy the nation's immediate need in a matter of months, and who had done so twice. Whether or not the Privy Council knew it, Grafton had already evicted Robert Caly and reclaimed his printing house, although he had probably not yet started using it.[A] Whitchurch was less ready, having given up his Fleet Street premises in 1556 – but his equipment was in storage somewhere, and as events would show, it could be accessed when needed. An obstacle had been raised during Mary's reign, because on 4 May 1557 she had granted a monopolistic charter to the Company of Stationers. One important clause restricted printing itself to two groups of people: freemen of the Stationers' Company and anyone expressly permitted by royal letters patent. If necessary, of course, Elizabeth could easily have eliminated that obstacle by granting patents to Grafton the Grocer and Whitchurch the Haberdasher. That she did not do so suggests that it was not found necessary, and that if Elizabeth wanted the new book to be printed by those best qualified, the Stationers were unlikely to challenge her decision.

What the evidence suggests, then, is that the Privy Council decided to begin by commissioning *two* editions. One team involving Edward Whitchurch (though probably headed by Richard Jugge) would reprint

---

[A] Misled by Grant Ferguson ('Richard Grafton', 167), Clegg believes that Richard Tottell had been using Grafton's presses and type during Mary's reign ('The 1559 Books of Common Prayer', 107, 118). But although Tottell did borrow some title-page borders from the Grafton stock (McK & F nos. 46, 48, 54, 59, and 67), the presses and type were used by Robert Caly at Grafton's address throughout the reign. The equipment was not dispersed until after Grafton's 1559 prayer book was finished, and Tottell (who did not become Grafton's son-in-law until January 1558) was not the only printer who acquired some. In his edition of *Typographical Antiquities* (1, 538), William Herbert lists 'Philip Gerard his inuective' as printed by Grafton in 1559. But Herbert's source was Maunsell's *Catalogue* (STC 17669, E3ʳ, col. 2), where no date is given. The real date is 1547 (STC 11797).

the last of Whitchurch's 1552 editions with the revisions required by the new Act of Uniformity incorporated. Meanwhile Richard Grafton would reprint his last edition of the 1552 book but with the same revisions. Exactly when either team started work is unknown, but before late April it was impossible to be certain exactly what revisions the final Act of Uniformity would require.[A] So if either team started work before the Act achieved its slender majority in the Lords on 28 April, they would have risked needing to cancel and reprint passages they did not yet know were to be revised. The presence of cancels in the main text of the 'Jugge and Cawood' edition (and the absence of any detectable examples in the Grafton edition except in the preliminaries) suggests that the former was put in hand first. But I shall nevertheless begin the investigation with the Grafton edition, for which an implausibly early date has recently been suggested.

[A] It might appear that a last-minute change was indeed made in the Lords, because in the original act the words 'and the forme of the letanye altered and corrected' are interlined above a caret (PArch., HL/PO/PU/1/1558/1Eliz1n2, m. 1, line 23). But the revised Litany had already appeared in early 1559 as the last of the four items printed by John Day as if 'by Rychard Iugge, Printer vnto the Quenes Maiestie' (STC 16454, C4^v). Until Jugge became a printer in reality, all subsequent royal publications (beginning with a proclamation of 7 February: STC 7890) were printed by Cawood as if 'by Rychard Iugge, and Ihon Cawodde, Prynters to the Quenes Maiestie'. So the Litany must have been revised before 7 February, long before the Act was introduced on 18 April.

CHAPTER 4

Richard Grafton's Edition (STC 16291)

The Collation

The edition of 1559 printed by Richard Grafton (see Plate 2) has usually been treated as the first, but not because of any valid or compelling evidence. One of the few foundations on which an argument for priority could be erected is an item in the preliminaries of the rival edition whose absence from the Grafton preliminaries could perhaps be taken as a sign of incompleteness. The rival edition has 'A briefe declaration when every Terme beginneth and endeth' on page $^{\pi}$A11^{v} – a total of seventeen lines including the heading, between two woodcut ornaments that serve to fill what would otherwise be quite a lot of empty space. Grafton's $^{\pi}$A11^{v} is blank – and because the facing page $^{\pi}$A12^{r} is blank in both editions, Grafton's rather unsightly empty opening might perhaps suggest that he was too impatient to wait for the final piece of copy. But it could equally be argued that because the dates of the law terms are hardly an essential component of the preliminaries to a prayer book, the rival printer simply foisted them in rather than leave a complete opening blank. The real reason why the Grafton edition is usually listed first is probably nothing more complicated than that it was never reprinted. The rival edition is the direct ancestor of all subsequent editions, so it would be inappropriate to list them as if they descended from Grafton's.

Each of the folio editions of 1559 begins with a twelve-leaf quire of miscellaneous preliminary matter followed by a six-leaf calendar.[A] The two first editions of those quires are sufficiently similar to be discussed together in Chapter 6, but the structure of the main text differs significantly between editions. Each follows the edition of 1552 of which it is a revised

---

[A] The unique copy of the third edition lacks the preliminaries, but there is no reason to doubt that they shared the same collation as the other three.

reprint, and whose collation evolved during that year as described in Chapter 2. Grafton's consists of a series of twenty six-leaf quires followed by a final quire of eight leaves: sixty-four sheets to add to the nine sheets of preliminaries for a total of seventy-three.

In her 2016 article, 'The 1559 Books of Common Prayer', Cyndia Susan Clegg's discussion of the collations is both confused and misleading. It is simply not true that 'Like Whitchurch's, all of Grafton's Prayer Books [of 1552] have the same collation (though different from Whitchurch's) in the body of the service book'.[A] As discussed in Chapter 2, Grafton used two quite distinct collations and Whitchurch three. Nor is it true that 'both printers had the text cast off in such a way that the content units of the Prayer Book could be printed separately, which accounts for the varied length of the gatherings' (108).

> Morning Prayer, Evening Prayer, and the Litany comprise one unit beginning at A1^r and ending at C1^r, with the verso of C1 left blank. The Collects, Epistles, and Gospels begin at C2^r and end at Q1^r, with the verso of Q1 left blank. While beginning at C2 seems to contradict the idea that sections of the prayer book were discrete printings, the number of sheets still make the gatherings consistent. What Grafton appears to be doing here is using signatures somewhat arbitrarily.[B]

But beginning at C2^r does not merely 'seem' to contradict that notion – it flatly disproves it. Leaf C1 (with the end of the Litany and a blank) is part of the same sheet of paper as C6 (the ninth and tenth pages of the Collects section), while leaf Q1 (the end of the Collects and a blank) is conjugate with the ninth and tenth pages of the Communion. Printers work in units of formes, sheets, and quires, so exactly how 'separately' could these 'content units' have been printed? And the only 'varied length' in the gatherings of either Graf.2–6 or their successor of 1559 is found when (after an unbroken series of six-leaf, twelve-page quires A–V) he has to use a quire of eight leaves to accommodate the final fifteen pages of text.

In 1549, each separate section (or 'content unit') was probably set from a separately delivered sheaf of manuscript copy. Each began on

---

[A] The claim that 'In one Whitchurch Prayer Book … the A gathering in 8 contains Morning Prayer' (108–9) implies that it fills that quire, but it occupies only ¶1^r–6^v in Whit.1, only A1^r–6^v in Whit.2 and Whit.3, and one page less (ending on A6^r) in Whit.4 and Whit.5. Clegg also implies that Grafton's Series 2/15 editions all include the Act of Uniformity in the list of contents, but that is true only of Graf.5 and Graf.6.

[B] Clegg, 'The 1559 Books of Common Prayer', 109. For clarity I have corrected Clegg's signature-references to conform with the accepted bibliographical conventions: C2^r instead of Cii^r, etc. Exactly what 'the number of sheets still make the gatherings consistent' means is uncertain.

the first recto of a new quire, and the presence or absence of blanks following it (not preceding it) was determined by how many pages were left empty in its final quire. Blank pages were not deliberately inserted in pursuance of some imaginary scheme to reprint the section 'separately'. Neither printing house owned enough type to be able to keep even the twelve pages of a single six-leaf quire as standing type for later reprinting – as can easily be seen by the frequent occasions on which an ornamental initial appears twice (or occasionally thrice) in the same quire. The second appearance is only possible because the page of type in which it first appeared no longer existed, having been washed, dried, and taken apart, with all its types distributed back into the cases.

Once each printer chose to compress his next edition into fewer pages, the desire to conserve paper led many of the original blanks to disappear, because there was seldom any need to begin any section (except the first) on the first leaf of a new quire. The only blanks that survived that process, including C1^v and Q1^v in Grafton's condensed editions (series 2/15 and 2/20) are a consequence of a different tradition. It has long been customary to begin a new major section of a text on a recto page, whether or not the previous section ended on a verso.

There is nothing 'arbitrary' about Grafton's use of signatures in any of his editions: he uses them to distinguish quire from quire, and sheet from sheet within a quire. They identify physical units within the book's structure, without regard to the textual contents. And when he enlisted the aid of John Day and Nicholas Hill in late 1552, their shares of Graf.6 were determined not by content but by signatures. One quire contributed by Day begins in mid-sentence on the final page of the Collects section (Q1^r) and ends in mid-sentence on Q6^v in the Communion service; one sheet contributed by Hill (I3:4) begins in the middle of the word 'Bap= | ptisme' and ends in the middle of 'spi= | rite'.

The Required Revisions

The Elizabethan revisions prescribed for the 1552 *Book of Common Prayer* can be considered as falling into three groups. The first group consists of three changes which are announced near the beginning of the Act of Uniformity. As the clerk who wrote out the surviving manuscript of the original Act first recorded them there were only two, the first being 'one alteracion or addicion of certen lessons to be vsed on euery Sunday in the yere'.[A] Because every day of the year had four 'lessons' assigned to it in the lectionary, to describe a revision that could potentially alter more than two hundred Sunday lessons as 'one alteraci*on* or addici*on*' is something of an understatement, although the changes of that nature actually made in 1559 were considerably less numerous. But they were changes to the preliminaries and calendar rather than to the text of the service book itself, and will be discussed in Chapter 6.

The second revision specified is 'ij sentences onely added in the delyu*er*ey of the sacrament to the com*mu*nycantes & none oth*er* or otherwise'.[B] The two sentences are, famously, those spoken in 1549 at the delivery of the Communion, each importing its Real Presence into the otherwise unaltered memorialism of 1552. In each case the two versions are duct-taped together with a hopelessly inadequate 'and', as if the incompatible utterances could actually combine into a single sentence.[C] In the following quotation from Grafton's rendition, the interpolations from 1549 are in italics.

> Then shall the minister fyrste receyue the Communion in bothe kyndes him selfe, and next deliuer it . . . to the people in their handes kneling. And when he deliuereth the breade, he shall saye.
> *The bodie of our lord Iesu Christ which was geuen for the, preserue thy body & soule into euerlastinge life, and* take, and eate this, in remembraunce that Christ died for thee, feede on him in thine heart by faith with thankes geuynge.
> And the minister that deliuereth the cuppe shall saye.
> *The bloude of our lorde Iesu Christ which was shedd for the, preserue thy body and soule into euerlasting life. And* drinke this in remembraunce that Christes bloude was shedde for thee, and be thankeful.[D]

After recording those two required revisions, the parliamentary clerk who was penning the original act went back and inserted a caret between them, interlining a third instruction above. It is unfortunately impossible to know when he did so: whether the new instruction was something he had simply omitted or a later amendment made during debate in one or

---

[A] PArch., HL/PO/PU/1/1558/1Eliz1n2, m. 1, lines 22–3.   [B] Ibid., lines 23–4.
[C] Note that when the 'and' is present, it makes the imperative verbs 'take' and 'eate' (or 'drinke') appear to parallel the optative 'preserue' as additional actions that 'The bodie' (or 'The bloude') is enjoined to perform. In 1662 the overstrained conjunctions were mercifully removed.
[D] STC 16291, R4^r. Cranmer's 1549 sentences expressed a view of the sacrament that he chose not to emphasize in 1552, so they were rejected and replaced. I cannot imagine that so gifted a writer would have condoned this clumsy cobbling together of the two versions. The twofold replacement of 'vnto' by 'into' avoided everlasting life, but persisted until 1660 (Wing B3618A, B9v). The original word was restored in 1662 (B3622, X4v).6.

other of the houses. The latter would make for a more interesting history, but the former is more probable. The interlined addition reads, 'and the forme of the letanye altered and corrected'. It seems rather unlikely that this could have been a belated afterthought, because Elizabeth's preferred form of the Litany had already been published by Jugge 'according to the tenor of the Proclamation' (of 27 December 1558),[A] probably before Parliament even assembled and certainly before it first discussed revising the prayer book. Grafton duly printed the revised Litany from copy deriving from pages A2^r–B6^v of the Jugge booklet, easily fitting its slightly expanded text into the available space because in the 1552 edition he was otherwise reproducing, the Litany had ended on C1^v and was followed by a blank page.

In addition to that group of three revisions, the Act also explicitly sanctions changes (without actually prescribing them) to the second of the two rubrics that begin the main text of the service book: what is usually called the 'ornaments rubric'. It does so, however, near the end of its text, a long way from the three instructions already discussed.

In 1552 the first of those two rubrics (at the head of A1^r) required Morning Prayer and Evening Prayer to be 'vsed in suche place of the Churche, chapell, or Chauncell, and the minister shall so turne hym, as the people maie best here',[B] and referred any controversy to the ordinary of the diocese. The 1559 version merely requires the services to be 'vsed in the accustomed place of the churche, chapel, or chauncell, except it shalbe otherwise determined by the ordinarie of the place', which can be defended as not really being a change at all. The catch, of course, is that 'accustomed' fails to specify whether the customs are those of 1549–51, 1552–53, or 1553–58.

The second (or 'ornaments') rubric is less equivocal. In 1549 the vestments to be worn when celebrating Communion were prescribed in the third rubric at the beginning of the relevant section:[C] a white alb and a cope (or when only assisting at Communion, an alb and a tunicle). Meanwhile the notes that followed the essay 'Of Ceremonies' required a surplice to be worn during Matins, Evensong, and the services for baptism or burial.[D] In 1552 'Of Ceremonies' was moved into the preliminaries and its notes omitted, while the second rubric on A1^r ordered that

---

[A] STC 16454, A1^r. The proclamation referred to was STC 7889 (TRP 451). [B] Graf.1, A1^r.
[C] In STC 16267–9.5, sig. X1^r; in 16270–73, O6^r; in 16274–5, O1^v.
[D] At the end of the book (except in Grafton's STC 16268–9.5, in which the Litany quire ✠4 follows the notes).

The Required Revisions

> the minister at the tyme of the cōmunion, & at all other tymes in his ministracion, shall vse neither Albe, Vestement, nor Cope: but beyng Archebishop, or Bishop, he shall haue and weare a rochet, and beyng a priest, or Deacon, he shall haue and weare a surplus onely.[A]

Under Elizabeth, however, the usage was quite explicitly returned to that of 1549, as sanctioned by Edward's first Act of Uniformity (2 & 3 Edw. VI, c. 1).

> And here is to be noted, that the Minister ... shall vse suche ornamentes in the church, as were in vse by aucthoritie of parliament in the second yere of the reygne of king Edward the .vi. according to the acte of parliament set in the beginnyng of thys booke.[B]

The 'acte of parliament' here referred to is not Edward's but Elizabeth's Act of Uniformity, 'set in the beginnyng' of the 1559 preliminaries (πA2^r–4^v), whose last proviso begins:

> Prouided alwaies & be it enacted that suche ornamentes of the churche & of the ministers thereof shalbe reteyned and be in vse as was in this churche of Englond by auctoritie of parliament in the seconde yere of the reign of king Edwarde the vjth vntill other order shalbe therein taken by thauctoritie of the quenes maiestie with the advise of her comyssioners appointed and auctorized vnder the grete zeale of Englond for causes ecclesiasticall/ or of the metropollytan of this realme.[C]

In other words, 1559 revived the usage of 1549. But what is seldom mentioned when these changes are discussed is that nowhere in the 1559 book is there any explicit indication of what those contentious 'ornaments' actually were – because neither the notes that had followed 'Of Ceremonies' in 1549 nor the vestment instructions in the third rubric before the 1549 Communion service were ever restored. It is legitimate to wonder whether the revised book would have been accepted quite as easily had the 'ornaments rubric' more openly explained what it meant.

The most significant change that does *not* appear to be sanctioned by the Act is the omission of the Black Rubric. The Rubric itself begins with a defence of kneeling while the Communion is received, and explains that it is a gesture of humble gratitude and respect, not adoration or idolatry. But while the removal of that defence sends a clear signal to anyone aware of its former presence that kneeling requires no defence, it is difficult to argue

---

[A] Graf.1, A1^r. [B] STC 16291, A1^r.
[C] Ibid., πA4^{v}22–9, here quoted from PArch., HL/PO/PU/1/1558/1Eliz1n2, lines 144–9.

that its unsanctioned absence makes any material difference to either the performance or the meaning of the Communion service itself.

Although discussions of the Black Rubric usually and understandably focus on the issue of kneeling, its last three sentences are perhaps even more important.

> Lest yet the same kneelynge myght be thought or taken otherwyse, we dooe declare that it is not mente thereby, that any adoracion is doone, or oughte to bee doone, eyther vnto the Sacramentall bread or wyne there bodelye receyued, or vnto anye reall and essenciall presence there beeyng of Chrystes naturall fleshe and bloude. For as concernynge the Sacramentall bread and wyne, they remayne styll in theyr verye naturall substaunces, and therfore may not bee adored, for that were Idolatrye to be abhorred of all faythfull christians. And as concernynge the naturall bodye and bloud of our sauiour Christ, they are in heauen and not here: for it is agaynst the trueth of Christes true naturall bodye, to be in moe places then in one at one tyme.[A]

Had Cranmer written such an explicit and emphatic denial of both the (corporal) Real Presence and transubstantiation before 1547, he would have been sent to the stake by Henry VIII rather than by Mary. And while the Elizabethan Act of Uniformity did not formally permit it to be deleted, once the 1549 Communion wording was reintroduced the Black Rubric could obviously not be allowed to stand.[B]

The Benefits of Recycling

Four years before Grafton began printing his 1559 edition, on 13 June 1555 Mary had issued a proclamation that included the names of two dozen authors whose books were considered heretical and consequently banned. Not only was Cranmer's name prominent amongst them, but the prohibition specifically included

> any book, or bookes, wrytten or prynted ... concernyng the common seruyce and mynystration, set forth in englyshe, to be vsed in the churches of this realme, in the tyme of Kyng Edwarde the sixt, commonly called the communion booke, or bookes, of common seruyce and orderyng of ministers, otherwyse called the booke set forth by aucthoritie of parliament, for common prayer and admynystratiō of the Sacramentes, to be vsed in the mother toungue, within the churche of Englande.[C]

[A] Quoted from 'Rubric Insert 1' in the Huntington Library copy of Whit.3 (call no. 62282).
[B] 'Obviously', at least, under Elizabeth. A little over a century later a revised version of it was reinstated in *The Book of Common-Prayer* (Wing B3622), 1662, Y1^r, and is still there (Standard edition, 2016, p. 262).
[C] STC 7865 (TRP 422).

The Benefits of Recycling

All Edwardian prayer books were to be surrendered to the ordinary of the diocese within fifteen days, and by him to be burnt or otherwise lawfully disposed of. Provision was made for searching the premises of anyone suspected of being likely to conceal such books, and because his 'chaperon' Robert Caly was a well-known informer, Grafton would have had to be very careful if he wanted to hide any substantial stock of unsold copies or the printed sheets from which to assemble them. But careful he evidently was, and when he came to print the 1559 edition he had a large supply of 1552 sheets left. He was therefore able to print fewer new copies of those sheets than the whole edition demanded.

The old preliminary sheets were of course useless, but if we consider only the calendar and quires A–X, no more than thirteen of the sixty-seven sheets contained readings that would be significantly revised – and even some of those sheets could be used with only a word or two needing correction by a fastidious purchaser.[A] I have been able to verify the existence of, and to examine, five surviving copies of the Grafton edition, and each contains at least one leftover sheet from Graf.6. Two of them contain only one example each (sheet F1:6 in St John's College, Cambridge, and John Day's sheet Q1:6 in Cambridge University Library), while the British Library copy has eight recycled sheets (including Nicholas Hill's I3:4). But the Bodleian Library copy includes twenty-three leftovers (almost one-third of the book), while the uniquely important copy at Corpus Christi College, Oxford, contains no fewer than twenty-nine (plus another in the associated ordinal).[B] Both the British Library and Corpus Christi copies have the whole calendar quire from 1552; the Bodleian copy lacks the calendar, but both that and the Corpus Christi copy have an Edwardian printing of sheet A2:5, with 'O Lorde saue the Kyng' on A5^v.[C]

[A] The thirteen sheets are b1–6; A1,2:5,6; B1,3:4,6; C1:6; Q2–5; R1,3:4,6; T3:4.
[B] Most of the Corpus Christi recycling was first noticed by Clegg, including b^6, A2–5, F1:6, I^6, L1,2:5,6, N1:6, O^6, T^6, and V1,3:4,6 ('The 1559 Books of Common Prayer', 113). But Clegg mistakenly includes V2:5, fails to clarify her conclusions about quires E (all recycled), H (all but H3:4 recycled), and X (only X3:6 recycled), and overlooks G1:6 and M1:6.

Four of the Corpus Christi leftovers were printed by Nicholas Hill (H1:6, I3:4, N1:6, and X3:6) and two by John Day (L1,2:5,6), while one of Grafton's own comes from a slightly earlier 1552 edition, namely Graf.5 (L3:4 – the Bodleian copy has the Day setting from Graf.6a). The Corpus Christi volume also includes the only extant copy of Grafton's ordinal (see Chapter 7). Its only recycled sheet (Bb2:5) makes reference to 'the Othe concernyng the Kynges Supremacie' on Bb5^v.
[C] The 1552 mention of 'the Kyng, and his mynysters' on leftover T3^r in the Bodleian and Corpus Christi copies was also left unrevised in 1559 by both Grafton and his rivals (in the Jugge-and-Cawood edition it is on O3^v).

Grafton did not have enough copies of any 1552 sheet to free him completely from the need to reprint it, so he did set and print every sheet of the main text in 1559. Moreover, he may also have miscalculated more than once, printing so few copies of a sheet that he had to reset and reprint enough replacements to make up the total. At least two sheets appear to exist in *two* Grafton settings of 1559. In the case of sheet X1:8 I cannot completely discount the possibility that what the Cambridge University Library copy has is a 1552 setting not found in any copy I have yet seen.[A] But there can be no comparable doubt about sheet R3:4 in that same copy, because both settings of that sheet have the 1559 revision of the Communion.[B] In this case the pressmen may have mistakenly printed too few copies because there was a good supply of 1552 sheets, only to realize too late that because of the Communion revisions the leftovers could not be used.

The Grouping of the Recycled Sheets

It is a commonplace of bibliography that because books are not manufactured one complete copy after another, it is rarely if ever possible to define an individual copy of a sizeable book as being either an early or a late *copy*. As Charlton Hinman pointed out, the pressmen who worked on the Shakespeare First Folio did not always turn a printed heap over so that the first sheets printed on one side were also the first to be perfected. Thus, while some of the sheets with both formes variant have early states on both sides, in other sheets the early states are usually backed by late states.[C] As Moxon explains in some detail,[D] after the sheets had been printed on both sides they were hung up to dry, then taken down and stacked, and eventually laid out in heaps so that individual copies (either of a whole book or, in the case of a large one, of part of it) could be *gathered* (assembled) one after another. At each stage in that process the 'original' order of the sheets in each heap could be reversed or scrambled, so no one copy of the book could be considered either early or late *as a copy*. When Grafton laid out the freshly printed sheets of his 1559 prayer book in

---

[A] On X1ᵛ, the second line of the third rubric begins 'Chap. to'. In the British Library, Bodleian, and Corpus Christi copies it begins 'the Corin.', and the copy at St John's College, Cambridge, lacks sheet X1:8.
[B] In the first rubric on R4ʳ, the first line in the Cambridge University Library copy ends 'both kin='; in the other copies it ends 'bothe kyn='.
[C] Hinman, *Printing and Proof-Reading*, 1, 231–3.   [D] Moxon, *Mechanick Exercises*, 311–17.

preparation for gathering, therefore, we cannot tell whereabouts in each heap the first-printed copies (or if different, those first perfected) would have been.

But as I have explained elsewhere, ink 'dries' considerably more slowly than dampened paper – indeed, since its fluid component is oil varnish rather than water, 'dries' is a somewhat misleading word to describe what it does.[A] And although the process of pressing the gathered copies before sale rarely caused significant set-off from page to facing page, booksellers and binders were aware that the printed text retained its ability to set off under favourable conditions for weeks or even months. When the heaps were first laid out in 1559, therefore, it would have made sense to put any 1552 leftovers that were to be included on top of each heap, so that any sheet whose ink had already had six or seven years to dry would be among the first to be bound.

As will be discussed in greater detail in Chapter 7, the Corpus Christi copy must have been one of the first (perhaps *the* first of those extant) to be assembled, and was delivered to the Privy Council before marketing began so that an official maximum retail price could be decided. At the other chronological extreme, the copy in Cambridge University Library is the only copy with two sheets in a second 1559 setting, presumably printed after the last copies of the first setting had been used up.[B]

Each of the twenty-three leftovers in the Bodleian copy is a sheet also found in the Corpus Christi copy, except that while Bodleian sheet L3:4 comes from Graf.6, the Corpus Christi copy is from Graf.5. Moreover, five of the eight leftovers in the British Library copy are also found in both those copies, while the remaining three are the calendar quire, recycled in the Corpus Christi copy but missing from the Bodleian copy.[C] And when the only leftover sheet in the copy in St John's College, Cambridge, is a sheet also found in those three copies, the facts irresistibly suggest the gradual shrinking of a supply of leftover sheets of which varying numbers had been placed on the top of each relevant heap. A sample of only five copies is obviously far too small for any kind of statistical analysis – but I think that the facts allow them to be placed with considerable confidence in the order in which they were gathered before leaving Grafton's premises.

[A] Blayney, 'Dry Discourse', 391–2; Gaskell, *New Introduction*, 125.
[B] There is also reason to suppose that it was not wholesaled until after Grafton finally gave up the book trade: see Chapter 8, pp. 145–6. The only recycled sheet in that copy is John Day's Q1:6 from Graf.6, not found in any of the other copies.
[C] Apart from the missing calendar quire, the only recycled sheets found in the Corpus Christi copy but *not* in the Bodleian copy are E1:6, E3:4, and X3:6.

CHAPTER 5

The First Jugge-and-Cawood Edition (STC 16292)

The Printers

Up to now I have usually referred to the printers of 'the other first edition' of 1559 as Grafton's 'rivals' rather than by name – because had I named either Jugge or Cawood, or both, most of those statements would have been false. It is true that the title-page identifies the book as coming from 'Londini, in officina Richardi Iugge, & Iohannis Cawode' (Plate 3), but it does not explicitly claim that they *printed* it, and in fact neither of them printed very much of it at all. Cawood supplied only a single quire of four sheets, and before the preliminaries (which were printed last) Richard Jugge had contributed only one five-sheet quire, a single sheet, at least one cancel sheet, and two cancel leaves.

The first thing that needs to be clearly understood about Jugge and Cawood is that while they were partners in the jointly held office of the Queen's Printers, they were never joint owners or users of a single printing house. Cawood had a retail bookshop at the sign of the Holy Ghost in the range of buildings along the north side of Paul's Cross Churchyard, but what was probably his first Marian printing house was a few doors east of that shop, at the west side of the gate leading into Cheapside.[A] By 1558, however, he had almost certainly already moved his printing materials into a larger building at the east end of the precinct, between the 'new' Paul's School on the north and the site of the previous school on the south.[B] Neither printing house is known to have used a sign during Cawood's occupancy. Jugge too had a retail bookshop in the churchyard, at the sign

---

[A] See Blayney, *Bookshops*, 39; *Stationers and Printers*, II, 999–1000, nos 14 and 18 (shown in Map 3, p. 996). If Cawood began his printing career in Mierdman's old premises in the parish of St Mary at Hill (which is possible), it was not long before he moved the equipment into Paul's.

[B] *Stationers and Printers*, II, 990 (Map 2). While the limits of the building are not there shown, both school sites are indicated.

of the Bible on the end of the north transept and east of the great north door.[A] But that shop was probably not big enough to house a printing business the size of the one he set up in the early months of 1559 and ran until his death in 1577. After 1558, however, he never mentioned either a sign or a specific address until the 1570s. It was quite common for publishers and booksellers who had more than one address to decline to mention any of them, so exactly where Jugge did his printing in the first few years of the reign is unknown.

Most of the books and other items printed under the auspices of the joint office describe themselves (in various spellings and languages) as 'Imprinted ... by Richard Iugge and Iohn Cawood, Printers to the Queen's Majesty', and in some cases that is really true, because each man printed part of them. But the majority (especially, of course, proclamations and other single-sided items) were printed by either one or the other but not both.[B] The few surviving warrants for payment for royal publications were all issued as if to a single, jointly owned business,[C] even though the first (which covers the beginning of the reign until sometime after 17 May 1559) includes three proclamations printed for Jugge by John Day in late 1558 and only one printed by Jugge himself.

As I explained in Chapter 1 (p. 13), there was nothing inherently new about the printing of a book being shared by more than one printing house (although it was exceptionally rare for an imprint or colophon to name more than one of a book's printers). But in the Jugge-and-Cawood prayer book of 1559 we are not just dealing with a pair of partners, and the number of printers who collaborated on the volume was completely without precedent.

No matter who really printed which parts of it, I can devise no completely satisfactory name for it. With no way of knowing which of the two original 1559 editions reached the clergy first, I am reluctant to call it either the 'first' or the 'second' of them. All but one of the editions of that year whose title-pages survive implicitly claim to have been printed by both the Queen's Printers – and as we shall see in Chapter 8, even some copies of the Grafton edition were marketed under their names. But none was printed by *only* those two men, neither of whom contributed to all of them. Once Grafton had given up printing and begun disposing of his equipment, however, Jugge and Cawood were certainly the principal or exclusive

---

[A] Ibid., II, 1000, being part of the building in cathedral bays E–F (for which see Map 3, p. 996).
[B] There are very few contexts in which it is appropriate to liken Jugge and Cawood to Lennon and McCartney, but this appears to be one of them.
[C] Arber, I, 564, 570.

(a)

𝕷𝖔𝖗𝖉𝖊, now lettest thou thy seruai
parte in peace: accordyng to thy w
For mine eies haue seen: thy sa
whiche thou hast prepared: bef
face of all people.
  To be a light to lighten the Ge
and to be the glory of thy people Israel.
Glory be to the father, and to the sonne, and, &c.
As it was in the beginning, and is now, &c. A

Or els thys Psalme.

God be merciful vnto vs, and blesse vs: an
vs the light of his countenaunce, and bee
full vnto vs.

(b) ¶ Oure father whiche arte. &c.

(c) ¶ An Ordre for Euenynge

(d) O God, vnifest merci (e) The Epiphanie.

Figure 5 Ornamental initials and display type.
(a) Wolfe's L, Whitchurch's G. (b) 230 textura. (c) Wolfe Fraktur. (d–e) 'Bible Fraktur'.
(© The British Library Board, C.25.m.7: (a) A7^v, (b–c) A6^v; (d–e) C.25.l.9, D3^v.)

wholesalers of Elizabethan prayer books, so I can see no real need to put their names in scare quotes for each edition.

Quires A–F: Reyner Wolfe and Edward Whitchurch

The first six quires of the main text mark the first reappearance since 1556 of the Whitchurch ornament stock,[A] here represented by forty-four of his display capitals of various sizes, making a total of eighty-six appearances. Whitchurch had freed his last known Edwardian apprentice in September 1556, and by June 1557 was recorded as living in Camberwell,[B] so he must have given up the lease of his former printing house when he and John Wayland parted ways. It is therefore of considerable significance that the ornamental initials in quires A–C also include three that belonged at Reyner Wolfe (Figure 5*a*), and that thirteen of the pages in those quires also make use of cast capitals from a distinctive 230-mm Fraktur fount first found in Wolfe's books in 1544 and not known to have been used by anyone else in England before 1559 (Figure 5*c*).[C] Most London printers who used Fraktur at all had supplies of a 270-mm fount widely used in Europe from at least the 1530s. English readers would have encountered it first in the Coverdale Bible (Cologne, 1535), and in 1549 it arrived in England with the unknown printer (probably German) of an edition of the Great Bible that was completed by Nicholas Hill and Edward Whitchurch.[D] I shall hereafter distinguish between the 230-mm 'Wolfe Fraktur' and the 270-mm 'Bible Fraktur' (Figure 5*d*–*e*). The absence of Wolfe Fraktur from quires D–F does not, I think, indicate any significant difference in the printing arrangements, because ten of the Whitchurch initials found in those three quires also appear at least once in quires A–C.

[A] Clegg claims that 'Late in 1558 Edward Whitchurch ... printed one of the earliest Elizabethan proclamations for Richard Jugge', and cites the authority of STC, III, 181 ('The 1559 Books of Common Prayer', 107). This is untrue: the STC page in question merely cites (for Whitchurch under the year 1559) a note appended to the main entry for STC 9459, which is neither a proclamation nor dated 1558. The note reports that several sheets in that statute-book 'are by a different pr[inter] or compositor, who uses some Whitchurch/Grafton init[ial]s and a few ... belonging to J. Kingston' (1, 430). The printer using Whitchurch and Kingston initials was Jugge himself (see p. 83 below), who printed most of the book; Cawood printed only sheets A1:6 and B1:6.

[B] Guildhall Library, CLC/L/HA/C/007/MS15857/001, 95^r (apprentice); TNA: PRO, E 159/338, Recorda, Trinity, 63^v (Byrom, 'Some Exchequer Cases', 414–15).

[C] The first known occurrence is on the title-page of Wolfe's STC 22270 (1544). Whole lines are found in the prayer book on A6^v, B1^v, B2^r, and B6^r; odd capitals on sigs. A5^v, B7^v, B8^v, C1^v, C3^r–4^r, C6^v, and C8^r.

[D] *Stationers and Printers*, II, 639–41; STC 2079. Some of its English users seem to have had only the regular capitals and/or an associated set of 'Kanzlei' titling capitals, and used them only as drop capitals.

Wolfe had been appointed King's Typographer and Bookseller in Latin, Greek, and Hebrew by Edward VI in April 1547,[A] although the title was rather more grandiose than the reality. He did print a little Greek, but there is no evidence that he ever owned any Hebrew type, and in reality the position was not much more than a monopoly of Lily's Grammar. Unusually, after Edward's death Wolfe was retained in office first by Mary and then by Elizabeth. I know of no documented association of any kind between him and Whitchurch in the reigns of either Henry or Edward, but under Mary they acquired a common interest. In June 1557, Wolfe and a former servant of Cranmer's named John Gawyn were granted some of the late Archbishop's property that had been forfeited to the Crown when he was burned in 1556. Later evidence shows that their motive was not to profit from Cranmer's death, but to hold the property until they could legally restore it to his widow and children.[B] It therefore seems only appropriate that in reprinting Cranmer's book, Wolfe should collaborate with Margaret Cranmer's second husband, Edward Whitchurch. Exactly how they collaborated can only be conjectured, but perhaps the most likely scenario is that Whitchurch retrieved his types and ornaments from wherever he had stored them and set up a largely self-contained typesetting operation (and perhaps one of his own presses) somewhere in Wolfe's sizeable printing house, which was a few yards northeast of Richard Jugge's bookshop in Paul's Churchyard.[C]

Between them, Wolfe and Whitchurch printed more than a third of the book.[D] Somehow, though, in quire B they managed to make the most serious textual mistake in the whole two-edition project. The Act explicitly required the Litany to be 'altered and corrected', and in its first four pages ($B2^r$–$B3^v$) the comparatively few necessary changes were duly made. On $B2^v$ the list of evils from which the congregation asked to be delivered no longer includes 'the Bisshop of Rome, and all hys detestable enormities'; in the State Prayer 'Edwarde the sixth … our Kynge' is replaced by 'Elizabeth our most gracious Queene', and God is asked not only to keep her but to keep and strengthen her in the true worshipping of Him, in righteousness and holiness of life. More simply, the gender of the pronouns in the next two versicles is changed, including two examples in the first line of $B3^r$. After that, no more alteration was required until $B4^v$. What was needed on

---

[A] TNA: PRO, C 82/868/[5] (warrant of 17 April); C 66/805, m. 1 (enrolment of 19 April).
[B] TNA: PRO, C 66/918, mm. 13–14; C 3/191/68. See also MacCulloch, *Thomas Cranmer*, 609–10.
[C] See *Stationers and Printers*, II, 996 (Map 3) and 997–8 (nos. 6–7).
[D] Twenty-four sheets of the main text. Five sheets of the preliminaries that will be examined later are probably the work of Wolfe alone.

that page was the insertion of a completely new prayer for Elizabeth herself, after which one of the remaining Edwardian prayers should have been omitted and three new ones added. But for some reason sheet B4:5 is simply reprinted page for page from the 1552 edition with none of the required changes.

As the revised STC reports (though without expressing agreement), 'Mr. [John R.] Hetherington suggests that the official printers were temporarily denied access to this part of the new revisions' (II, 93, note to entry for 16292). That, however, makes little sense, because the required revisions had already been published in octavo by the first of 'the official printers' in January (Jugge's STC 16454). Slightly more plausibly, one could argue that because all the changes *correctly* made in the prayer book are found in quire A of the January octavo but all the overlooked corrections in quire B, Wolfe and Whitchurch may have been mistakenly given only the first quire of the octavo to work from. But tempting as that suggestion might seem, the prayer that ends on line A8^{v}7 of the octavo has a closing 'Amen' there. Since neither Wolfe-and-Whitchurch nor Grafton printed that 'Amen', it is unlikely that either of them used the printed octavo itself as copy.[A]

In the normal course of events, the 'routine' order in which the formes of a folio quire were set and printed was from the middle outwards: beginning with the inner forme of the innermost sheet and ending with the outer forme of the outermost. In a first (or heavily revised) edition this minimized the amount of text that needed to be carefully cast off for setting, because it was never necessary to estimate how much text would fill more pages than half a quire minus one. In a page-for-page reprint, of course, the formes within a quire (and the quires themselves) can be printed in any order at all, but in the absence of any compelling reason to depart from custom, sheet B4:5 was probably the first sheet of quire B to be printed. We can therefore speculate that it was printed before the compositors had been warned that the Litany was to be altered, and that when the revised text (in whatever physical form) was made available, nobody thought to check whether or not any changes ought to have been made in what had already been printed. It seems difficult to believe that such an elementary oversight could have been made – but whatever the exact cause, the blunder nevertheless happened.

The one credible excuse I can imagine depends on the imprecise wording of the Act, in which what was to be altered and corrected was

---

[A] In 16292, the prayer ends at B4^{r}25 with no room in the line for an 'Amen'; in Grafton's 16291 it ends at B5^{v}31 with enough room for three of them.

called simply 'the letanye'. But the ritual that is usually so called (as I have usually called it in this book) is more precisely 'the Litany and Suffrages', in which the Litany proper (rather more than half the text) is followed by a series of longer suffrages or petitions, some of which are spoken only if circumstances require: for example, prayers for either more rain or (if appropriate) for considerably less, or in time of famine, war, or plague. The revisions that were not performed in the Jugge edition are all in the 'Suffrages' section, beginning with the new prayer for Elizabeth. As an excuse that would be rather flimsy, but it is nevertheless a fact that in the January octavo edition, the first running title that identifies 'Suffrages' as distinct from 'The Letany' is on B2^r – immediately above the heading for the new 'prayer for the Quenes Maiestie' with which the folio's omissions begin.

There are several reasons why it is hard to understand this oversight. One is the care that was taken to correct a considerably smaller lapse. Near the foot of D4^v, the Epistle whose first eight lines end the page ought to have begun with an ornamental W: 'WE as helpers exhorte you'. The compositor, however, mistakenly used a 21-mm Y as a four-line drop capital instead. When this comparatively minor slip was noticed, it seems that the combined ornament stock of Whitchurch and Wolfe contained no W of quite the right size, so the W chosen for the correction was only 16 mm square. When the press was stopped, the compositor took the trouble to re-space and re-divide the first six lines of text so that the W could be used as a *three*-line drop capital without leaving unsightly gaps. In addition, rather than casually following the well-established practice of simply leaving the 'YE' copies to be used in their uncorrected state, the printers had the W hand-stamped in the centre of a sufficient number of 21-mm squares of otherwise blank paper to paste over the Y – as in the Benton copy now in the Boston Public Library (see Figure 6*a*).[A] But page D4^v is not the only place in the Wolfe-and-Whitchurch section where errors were first committed and subsequently corrected, and what happened in quires A and C adds to the difficulty of explaining how sheet B4:5 escaped replacement.

Quire C contains two bibliographical peculiarities, one major and one (probably) minor. The minor one is that page C5^r is signed 'E.v.'. The only essential difference between textura capitals C and E is that the latter has a small middle arm, so the two letters are as easily mistaken for each other as

---

[A] I am grateful to Jay Moschella of the Boston Public Library for photographing the recto lit from behind so I could identify the initial under the patch.

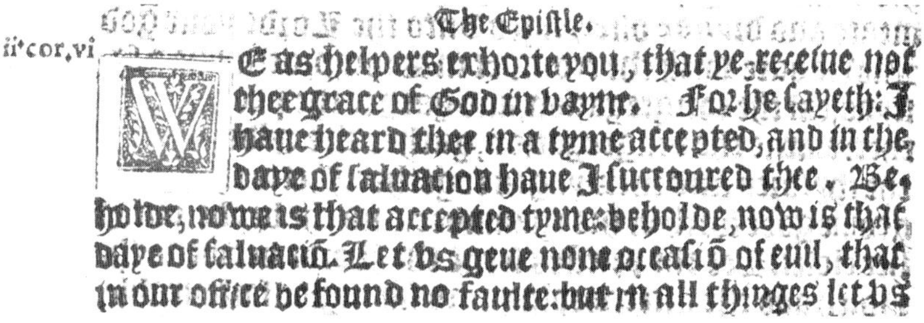

Quires A–F: Reyner Wolfe and Edward Whitchurch

ii. cor. vi

(a)

ii. cor. vi

(b)

Figure 6 The stop-press correction of page D4^v, lines 27–34.
(a) State 1: 3-line W pasted over erroneous 4-line initial Y.
(b) State 2: initial corrected, lines 28–30 respaced and lines 31–3 redivided.
  (a Boston Public Library, Benton 1.95; b © The British Library Board, C.25.m.7.)

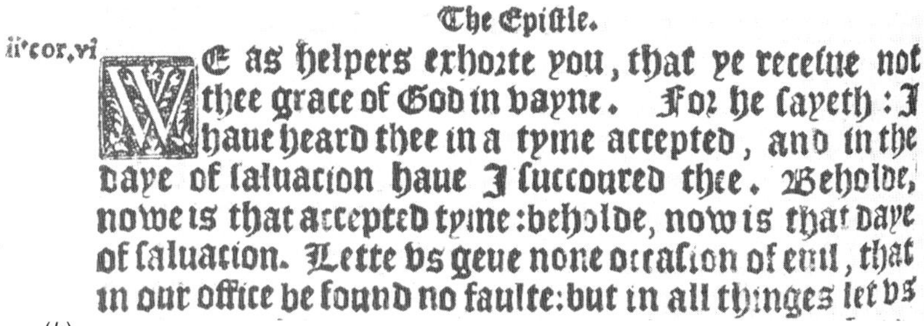

are roman C and G. It would therefore be easy to dismiss the erroneous signature as a simple typographical error were it not for the fact that the only other quires in the book in which the fifth recto is signed at all are those containing more than eight leaves: quires $^{\pi}$A^{12}, M^{10}, O^{10}, and P^{10}. In a printing house where several jobs were in progress at once, a compositor working alternately on pages for more than one book might mistakenly set a signature in one that 'belonged' in the other – but no other book dated 1559 from Wolfe's printing house is known, and none of those dated 1558 or 1560 is in folio. There was, moreover, no signature of any kind on the printed page of 1552 from which the compositor was setting.

  To explain the more important anomaly in quire C (and also that in quire A) it is necessary to jump ahead to what happened after quires A–F were first completed. While they were in progress, Richard Jugge had been finding suitable premises in which to set up a printing house fit for a

70 The First Jugge-and-Cawood Edition (STC 16292)

w⁵ᶜ **waye** **with** **word**

w²⁺ **waye** **with** **word**

Figure 7 Richard Jugge's great primer w's.
(York Minster Library, XI.F.19(1): w⁵ᶜ from L8ᵛ; w²⁺ from L4ᵛ.)

Queen's Printer. He had also acquired at least small quantities of type and ornamental material from various sources, including the estate of the late John Mychell, who had printed in Canterbury until he died in 1556. But not long after quire F was finished Jugge evidently bought most of the Whitchurch ornament stock. At the same time he acquired some great primer type closely resembling (and I believe the same as) the fount of that size used in quires A–F, which presumably belonged to either Wolfe or (more likely) Whitchurch.

There were, however, few varieties of great primer available from London type-founders at this date, which makes certain identification difficult. Like most textura used in England, the founts were of French origin and had no original w (lower-case or capital). Some suppliers either found a suitable lower-case example elsewhere or commissioned one, and most of the printers who used that size with any frequency fall into three groups. In the Wolfe-Whitchurch lower-case version of w (also used by Grafton) the third minim is the shortest, and rises only to the x-height. The second is slightly taller, while the first is not only tallest but, after first bending to the left, turns to the right as it rises and tapers off. If we follow the classifications in the key-plate at the beginning of Isaac's *English & Scottish Printing Types, 1535–58*, this letter belongs to the family numbered w⁵, and most closely resembles w⁵ᶜ. In the version preferred by two of the other printers in this book (Cawood and Marshe) the first and second minims are essentially identical. Both are considerably taller than the third, and at the top they both curl over to the left. This design falls halfway between Isaac's w² and w³: in the former the left 'counter' (the white space between the first two minims) is straight, but in Isaac's w³ the upper half bends more to the left than does the version shown in Figure 7, which I therefore call w²⁺.[A] A third

---

[A] Richard Payne has an essentially similar fount, but with the real w³ rather than w²⁺.

group of printers (represented in this book only by John Kingston) used a mixture of both designs.[A]

To return to Richard Jugge: towards the end of the first Jugge-and-Cawood prayer book (in sheets N3:6 and quire P), in the single sheet that he contributed to the ordinal at about this time (AA3:6), and in the opening quire of the next edition, he used a fount of great primer that either was or closely resembled the w^{5c} fount used by Wolfe and Whitchurch. But in most of his later quires in the next two editions he used a w^{2+} fount, and although he continued to make sporadic use of the w^{5c} fount, he apparently kept the two separate and unmixed.

The reason why any of this matters to the Wolfe and Whitchurch quires A–F is that Jugge's extant leaf N3 is a cancel, and while N6 uses w^{5c} (as presumably did the original N3), the only lower-case great primer w in the cancel leaf (most of which is printed in smaller type) is a w^{2+}. And in quires A–F there are three leaves that use both w^{2+} and Whitchurch initials, and must therefore be cancels belatedly printed by Jugge: leaf A1 (which is visibly a cancel pasted to the stub of the original leaf) and sheet C2:7.

The contents of sheet C are wholly uncontroversial passages in the section devoted to Collects, Epistles, and Gospels. The text on the pages of C2:7 differs in no substantive way from either the 1552 editions or the others of 1559, so I suspect that the sheet had to be cancelled for purely bibliographical reasons. (Perhaps one forme of the cancelled setting had its pages imposed in the wrong halves of the chase, or a few lines were imposed upside down, so the whole sheet had to be discarded.) But each of Jugge's other two cancels is a single leaf, evidently replacing an original leaf in which a required revision had been either incorrectly made or overlooked. His cancel N3 replaces a leaf originally printed by Jugge himself (with his first fount), and since the recto of that leaf is where the Black Rubric had appeared in 1552 editions, it can hardly be doubted that this leaf was cancelled because Jugge had failed to omit that declaration. And it seems equally probable that leaf A1 was cancelled because one or both of the two rubrics that precede Morning Prayer on A1^r had been either wrongly revised or not revised at all.

What the revisions on A1^r and N3^r have in common is that neither was clearly mandated by the Act of Uniformity. As I explained in Chapter 4 (p. 56), the question of 'ornaments' is raised only in the very last proviso included in the Act, and no explicit instructions are given about where or

---

[A] Owen Rogers is an exception, with a lower-case w that Isaac defines as capital w^7 (and which is, despite its size, used as a capital by Grafton).

how the 1552 text should be revised accordingly. Moreover, nothing anywhere in the Act requires (or even allows) the Black Rubric to be omitted. What those two cancellations obviously imply, therefore, is that the printers were set to work before the authorities had finished deciding exactly what should be revised and where. That, however, raises questions about Richard Grafton. Did he, perhaps, make those same corrections in his own edition by reprinting complete sheets (in his case A1:6 and R1:6) rather than single leaves? If so, they would be all but impossible to detect, because unlike Jugge he used the same founts of type throughout his edition. Or could he have been given access to the revisions before the queen's own official printers? And if so, why and by whom?

It is perhaps more likely that Wolfe and Whitchurch printed at least quire A and sheet B4:5 before Grafton began work at all, and before the extent of the revisions had been finally decided. As will be shown in the next chapter, in the preliminaries at least the Act of Uniformity was printed first by the Jugge-and-Cawood team and reprinted by Grafton. But in their surviving form the two editions were almost certainly completed on the same day and must have been issued more or less simultaneously.

Quire G: John Cawood

Whitchurch's closure of his Fleet Street printing house in 1556 left Grafton's as the biggest in London. And although its Marian output under Robert Caly's management was nowhere near what it had been under Grafton himself, there is no reason to suppose that Caly had seriously compromised its potential (although he would certainly have lost Grafton's best Edwardian employees and retained a substantially smaller workforce). Grafton, therefore, probably had not only the equipment, but also the ability and experience to outperform most or all of his 1559 rivals if he could hire enough adequately skilled workmen. In which case it can hardly be doubted that the reason why so many printers collaborated on the Jugge edition was that none of them on his own could match Grafton's potential productivity.

As the non-printer chosen by Mary to be Queen's Printer because he was a trustworthy Catholic, John Cawood may have been the least enthusiastic participant in creating a new Protestant liturgy. It is likely that he was essentially a Henrician Catholic rather than an admirer of the papacy, and it is probably no coincidence that in later years the Elizabethan Bishops' Bible was usually printed by Jugge alone while editions of the Henrician Great Bible translation were usually printed by Cawood alone. The single quire Cawood printed for the new prayer book was part of the long section of Collects, Epistles, and Gospels, and while some of the Collects may not have been entirely to his taste, the Epistles and Gospels followed the Great Bible. But his limited participation may anyway have little or nothing to do with his own religious politics, because until Jugge's own printing house was up and running, Cawood was the one who had to do most of the work of printing proclamations, the new statutes, and other official publications.

Quires H, M, and the Outer Sheets of Quire I: Owen Rogers

The youngest of the printers who contributed to the Jugge edition was the Welshman Owen Rogers, who completed his apprenticeship in the Stationers' Company and paid the fee for his freedom on 8 October 1555.[A] He may perhaps have paid it rather late, because he had already set up a printing house and completed at least his first dated book before the end of that year.[B] When he equipped the house in which he produced it he acquired only a single alphabet of small ornamental initials, not quite 15 mm in height. Three major subdivisions of that first book called for something more prominent, so he borrowed three 18-mm initials from the printer (John King), who also lent him the woodcut border for the title-page, and then returned them. During the next few years he acquired a few extra initials of that size and larger from a variety of sources – perhaps while working for others as a journeyman, because his surviving output is too small to suggest that his own press was in full-time use.[C]

His 15-mm alphabet was probably 'complete' at twenty-three letters. I have not seen the Q (his one sizeable Latin book was not the kind of text that required it), the X (the rarest initial in English printing), or the Z (usually found only when rotated a quarter turn if N was in short supply).[D] But the absence of a W, which was one of the four most commonly used initials in England,[E] almost certainly means that the set was of French origin. By the time he began working on the prayer book, Rogers had also acquired at least a large A and B (42 mm and 45 mm respectively), a 38-mm W that had once been Grafton's, a 27-mm D that had once belonged to either Whitchurch or Thomas Gaultier, a 25-mm crude woodcut copy of

---

[A] Arber, 1, 34. [B] STC 16246.
[C] From the seven years during which he is known to have printed (1555–61), fewer than 150 of his edition-sheets are known to survive: an annual average of just over 21 edition-sheets.
[D] The first word spoken in *A Midsummer Night's Dream* is 'Now'. Richard Bradock (in Q1, 1600) and William Jaggard (in Q2, 1619) each chose a rotated Z as its drop capital.
[E] The others were A, I, and T.

a common design of W, and three 18-mm initials that had last belonged successively to John, Katherine, and William Herford: N, T, and V. The large A and B and the smaller W were woodcut; all the rest, including the 15-mm alphabet, were metal, and that would matter. So would the fact that his supply of the four most frequently needed initials was limited to one small A and a second one rather too large for ordinary contexts, one large and one medium W, two small T's and only a single small I.

If we assume that Rogers began work with the innermost forme of quire H and worked outwards, the third forme he encountered needed an A in each of its pages, so one page had to make do with a disproportionately large one. But when he reached his seventh forme (pages H1^v and H8^r) he found that each page needed an I – and he owned only one.

A printing type is a letter cast in relief on the end of a stick of metal about an inch tall. While all the types in a given fount had to be the same height, not every fount in every printing house was exactly the same height as all others. An ornamental initial was therefore usually made a little shorter than most types, and the printer had to glue or paste layers of paper or thin card on the foot to bring the printing surface up to type height. If the initial was too short, the edges next to the letterpress text would not print properly. So Rogers took his 18-mm T, rotated it half a turn to put the crossbar at the bottom, and peeled a layer or two off the foot so that the crossbar failed to print and the stem looked like an I (Figure 8*a*) . But he still needed to use the T as a T, so after bringing it back to type height he decided to try a different trick next time. Meanwhile he chose to follow a tried-and-true tradition for coping with a shortage of A's, and on I7^v he used his 18-mm V upside down.[A]

Rogers's 18-mm T first came to England in 1539, when Grafton and Whitchurch bought a large supply of new French metal initials to add to those they had acquired from the stock of François Regnault, and the T was among the first they used when they began work by printing the end of Regnault's unfinished Great Bible.[B] When Whitchurch later set up alone it was included in his share of the ornament stock, and he used it until 1545 (STC 24720, B3^v; 15204, G8^v and L8^r). In 1540 the ex-printer Richard Bankes had ventured on a second printing career, using a selection of mismatched initials begged or borrowed from several printers, and he acquired the T and used it once in or soon after 1545. But before long he

---

[A] See Figure 8*c*. For eight examples in John Day's own sheets of his 1549 bible (STC 2077), see G1^v, I4^r, K6^r, M4^r, O2^v, P6^v, Q6^r, and Iii5^r. For a lone example by his collaborator Steven Mierdman see Gg5^v.

[B] STC 2068, on Mm6^r, 6^v, 7^v, and 8^v; they subsequently used it forty-six times in pages that appear much earlier in the book.

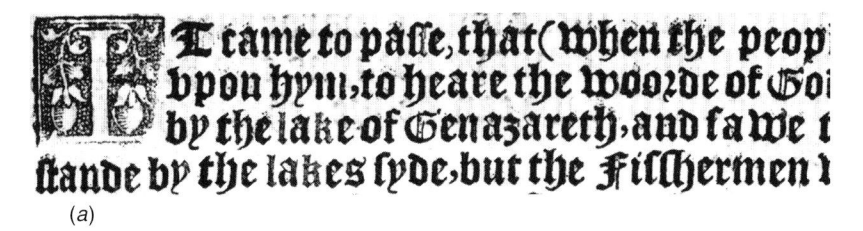

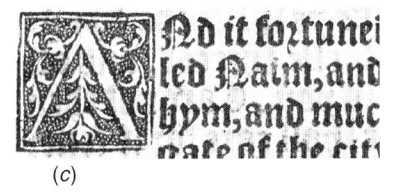

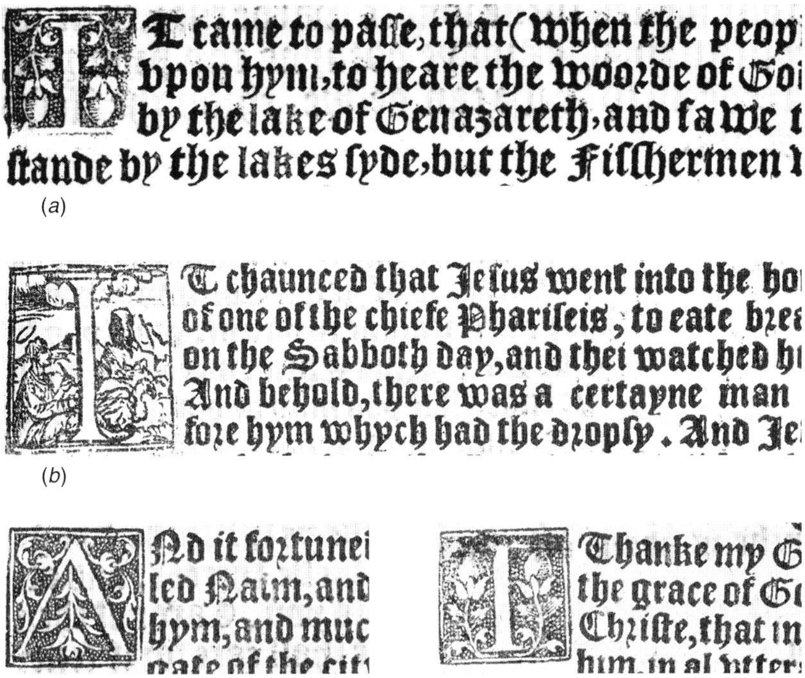

Figure 8 Owen Rogers and his I shortage.
(*a*) 18-mm T inverted and lowered (set with great primer type).
(*b*) 26-mm I borrowed from Whitchurch (set with large english type).
(*c*) 18-mm V inverted for use as A. (*d*) 18-mm T with crossbar packed.
(© The British Library Board, C.25.m.7: (a) H8^r, (b) I8^r, (c) I7^v, (d) I8^v.)

retired again, and when the initials he had borrowed from John Herford were returned to their owner, several others including the T went with them (20423 and 20424, in each case A6^r, B1^r, and B5^v). Rogers presumably acquired it (together with his 18-mm N and V) from John's son William Herford. And the reason why that history seems worth recounting is that the only time Richard Bankes is known to have used it, he 'packed' its crossbar and used it as an I (STC 2968.7, D3^r).

Like the types they accompanied, ornamental initials printed in relief: the ink was transferred from the high areas – the peaks, ridges, and plateaus – while the white areas (in this case including the letter T itself) were the grooves and valleys between them. What Bankes did was to pack the arms of the T with some substance sticky enough to remain in the groove both while the ink was applied and when the inked paper was lifted away, but not so sticky that it was pulled out by either the inkball or the paper. I cannot say what the substance was, because I have found no account, early or modern, of a 'botch' that writers such as Le Roy, Plantin, or Moxon would surely have considered too deplorable even to mention. My guess would be beeswax, either dripped into place from a candle or packed into position as shavings before heating the (metal) initial and then allowing it to cool.

The Bankes example is the earliest I have noticed,[A] although others certainly knew of the practice in the late 1540s. Steven Mierdman, for example, twice packed the bottom arm of an E to create an F in John Day's 1549 bible (STC 2077, Cc2^v, ^{2}Q3^r), and did the same to the crossbar of an A when using it upside-down as a V in the same book (^{2}H5^r). But I cannot help wondering whether the T which began this digression could have been acquired from Bankes by a journeyman compositor subsequently hired first by Herford and then by Rogers. Because on the next two occasions when Rogers used it as an I (on both I8^r and I8^v) he used it as Bankes had done: the right way up but with both arms packed (Figure 8*d*).

Forme I1^v:8^r, however, was still problematic, because two I's were needed in each of its two pages. So in addition to improvising, Rogers went to Wolfe's printing house and borrowed two rather larger woodcut examples, which he appears to have returned quite quickly. Both had been used in sheet H of the Whitchurch edition from which Rogers may have been working:[B] one was 38 mm in height, and depicted Jacob's ladder, while the other was only 26 mm tall and depicted St John on the isle of Patmos. That smaller one (Figure 8*b*), which can also be seen in the Wolfe and Whitchurch section on D5^v, would eventually pass to yet another of the collaborators, and thus become the only initial used by three different printers in the same book.

Rogers's final quire (M) caused him fewer problems, except that when forme M2^v:7^r needed three A's he had to invert his 18-mm V (though he had anyway done the same thing on I7^v and M4^r without visible need). The 64-mm calligraphic S on M1^r, which closely resembles the one used by Grafton at the same point in the text but is certainly not the same,[C] must

---

[A] Although I may well have overlooked earlier examples. I did, after all, have the initial filed as an I for a year or two in the 1990s before recognizing it as a doctored T.
[B] Whit.5, H1^v; H7^r and 8^r. The evidence suggests, however, that at least the preliminaries of the Jugge-and-Cawood edition followed a copy of Whit.4.
[C] STC 16291, Q2^r.

have been borrowed – probably from Cawood, who owned other letters of the same style. Rogers would, however, have the opportunity to display even more ingenuity when contributing to subsequent editions of *The Book of Common Prayer* later in the year.

But it is not just his games with initials that sets Rogers's share of the book apart from the others. In all the Edwardian folio editions the main text is set in type of the size known as great primer.[A] The name indicates a range of sizes rather than a completely standardized measurement: twenty lines can measure approximately 115 (Rogers), 116 (Cawood), 117 (Payne), or 118 mm (Jugge). Major headings usually begin with a line approximately twice that size (such as the 230 textura shown in Figure 5*b*), and various smaller sizes are used for rubrics, minor headings, and the congregation's responses – but on most pages great primer predominates.

As I noted in Chapter 3 (p. 42), when Whitchurch was printing Whit.4 in 1552, having finished quire H he jumped ahead to quire M while Steven Mierdman compressed sixty-three pages of the previous edition into the fifty-two pages of quires I–L. Whitchurch's pages of quire H were set to a measure (line-length) of approximately 123 mm, and one of the ways in which Mierdman squeezed more text into each page was to use a slightly wider measure of 127 mm. Whichever Whitchurch edition he was setting from (Whit.5 was a close reprint of Whit.4 in which both Whitchurch and Mierdman repeated their previous shares), Rogers had no obvious difficulty in reprinting Whitchurch's quire H in his own great primer at a measure of approximately 133 mm (Figure 8*a*). But when he began to reprint the two outer sheets of Mierdman's quire I he seems to have expected problems. Perhaps he had been warned by Thomas Marshe, if Marshe had already started work on the two inner sheets of that quire, in which even a measure of almost 140 mm did not always let him follow Mierdman's line-division exactly. So Rogers chose to switch from great primer to the size known as large english (of which twenty lines measured approximately 104 mm) and a measure of 121 mm (*Figure 8b–d*). He then used the same type and measure for most of quire M, with the exception of the outer sheet. The first page of that sheet consists of a series of rubrics set in 94-mm type to approximately the measure he had used in sheet I (132 mm). On the verso he used the same measure, but with the large english type, and for some reason he chose a measure of almost 124 mm for both pages of the conjugate leaf M8.

[A] In typographical contexts, *primer* rhymes with *swimmer*, not *climber*.

Quires K, L, and the Inner Sheets of Quire I: Thomas Marshe

The second youngest of the printers, Thomas Marshe, was probably about three years older than Rogers, but had spent a year or two as a bookseller and publisher before likewise setting up as a printer in 1555. It is rather unexpected to find Marshe working as part of a team that also included Reyner Wolfe. As Typographer in Latin, Greek, and Hebrew to his third successive monarch, Wolfe enjoyed a very lucrative monopoly of the standard introductory Latin text now usually known as Lily's Grammar, and during Mary's reign a group of London book-traders had arranged to have a series of pirate editions printed overseas. Two of the ringleaders were Marshe and a Draper named Abraham Veale, against whom Wolfe had already taken legal action at least once and would shortly do so again.[A]

What is most notable about Marshe's sheets of the prayer book is a practice he had pioneered two years earlier, and which he now implemented in a slightly more irregular fashion for what appears to be the last time. In the ESTC record for this book as it stood in early 2018 (record S111841), the collational formula was interrupted by a parenthetical note reporting that quire L^{10} has '(L6,8,9 signed "M")'. As I have noted elsewhere, this note was 'not only inappropriately placed but also both inaccurate and incomplete. The roman M's found in the direction lines of those pages are not signatures at all.'[B] Like the similar M's in the direction lines of pages $I3^v$, $I4^v$, $K1^v$, $K2^r$, and $L4^v$, their nearest bibliographical equivalents are what are called 'press figures', although those were not invented until the 1620s. The M's are the initial of Marshe's surname, each placed on a single page of eight of the eleven sheets he printed (Figure 9d–f) presumably to identify them as his work. Why three of his sheets are left without figures is uncertain, especially because when he pioneered this practice (in 1557, in his rather larger contribution to John Kingston's Latin missal, STC 16219) he figured every sheet he printed, and always below the first column of text on the page whose signature was under the second column (Figure 9a–c). One example in the prayer book (on $K1^v$) is partly obscured by 'frisket-bite',[C] so it is possible that one or more of the three

---

[A] See my 'Two Tales of Piracy', forthcoming in *The Library*, 7th ser., 23 (2022).
[B] Blayney, 'Thomas Marshe', 465–6.
[C] The *frisket* was a sheet of parchment in which holes were cut to allow the inked type to poke through, while masking all other inky areas from making contact with the sheet being printed. If carelessly cut, the edge of a hole could mask or 'bite' part of the type and prevent it from printing.

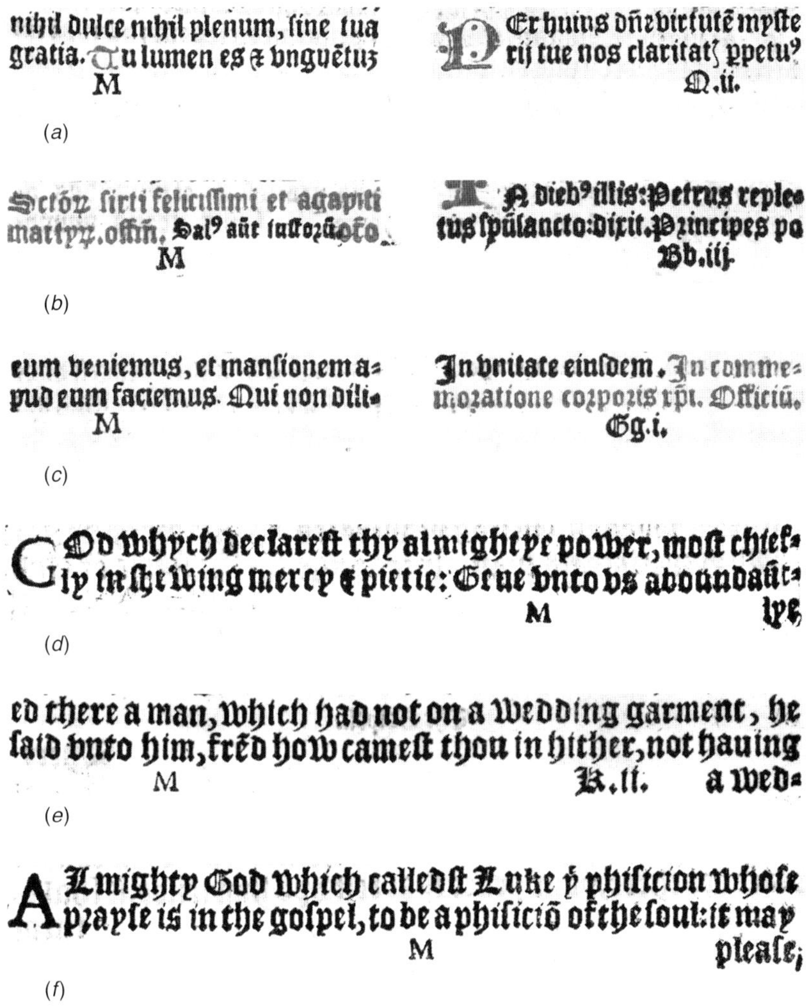

Figure 9 Thomas Marshe's press figures, 1557 and 1559.
(*a–c*) Examples from the missal of 1557 (STC 16219).
(Lambeth Palace Library, [**] H5412.M5 1557, Q2^r, Bb3^r, Gg1^r.)
(*d–f*) Examples from the 1559 prayer book (STC 16292).
(© The British Library Board, C.25.m.7, I3^v, K2^r, L8^r.)

'missing' M's were accidentally masked. But in the later age of the press figure, irregularity and inconsistency seem to be the norm – so perhaps Marshe pioneered that as well.

Six Sheets of Quires N and O: Richard Payne

Richard Payne, gentleman, was never a member of the Stationers' Company or even a freeman of London, and none of the books he printed ever bore his name. But despite his anonymity, for about eight years he was the de facto owner and master of the substantial printing house – the sign of Lucrece in Fleet Street – that had previously belonged to Thomas Berthelet, King's Printer to Henry VIII.[A] When Payne married Berthelet's young widow Margery in early 1556 it would have been perfectly legal for him to have taken over the business in his own name. But the Stationers' Company was then actively seeking a charter of incorporation (a quest of which Berthelet had been one of the main instigators) in which the right to print would be restricted to freemen of that company, so Payne remained tactfully anonymous. When reprinting Berthelet books he usually reproduced the original imprint (including the date); other books claimed simply to have been printed 'in the house late Thomas Berthelettes', while still others claimed to have been printed by the Stationer Thomas Powell – Berthelet's nephew and also (as the husband of Margery Payne's sister) his brother-in-law.[B] But depositions given in a Chancery action of 1564 make it clear that although Powell was 'chief Seruante vnto' Payne and 'as gouernoure vnder' him,[C] he was only an employee and not the master. I know of no obvious reason why the Stationers would have refused to accept Payne as a freeman if he had purchased the freedom of the City 'by redemption', yet in both February 1556 and March 1559 he promised the Court of Aldermen that he would indeed become a freeman by a specified date but then failed to do so.[D]

It is not clear why neither of the quires on which Payne worked is his throughout. In the case of quire N, leaf N6 is part of the first full sheet known to have been contributed by Richard Jugge himself, using what I have called his w^{5c} fount of great primer. But as already discussed, the present leaf N3 is a cancel also printed by Jugge, and the only great primer

---

[A] The following brief account of Payne is partly derived from *Stationers and Printers*, II, 788–93, but with a few additions and corrections.
[B] STC 7649, N8^r. After Powell died intestate in 1563, the administration of his goods was granted to Margery Payne, the legitimate and natural aunt of his daughter Elizabeth (LMA, DL/C/B/001/MS09168/012, 126^v). Berthelet's nephew cannot have been Margery's brother, so he must have married her sister.
[C] TNA: PRO, C 24/67/Trinity 6 Eliz/26: *Wolfe v. Payne*, depositions of Dyonisius Insbroeck and Lenard Adriaensen.
[D] LMA, COL/CA/01/01/015, 368^r, COL/CA/01/01/016, 142^r.

w used in it (on N3^{v}4) is his later w^{2+} design.[A] In the Lincoln Cathedral copy the stub of N6 is clearly visible before N3, and the stub of N3 before N6.[B] Moreover, the distance between the chainlines in that copy varies between 19 and 21 mm in N3, but between 25 and 28 mm in N6. Both pages of leaf N6 are printed with Jugge's w^{sc} fount, so it was certainly Jugge who printed the original N3, presumably including the Black Rubric. But why it was Jugge and not Payne who printed the original sheet N3:6 is a question that remains unanswered.

It is no easier to understand why Payne printed only three sheets of quire O (leaves O2–4 and 7–9). In this case the innermost sheet (O5:6) and the outermost (O1:10) were both printed by John Kingston, but neither seems likely to be a cancel because there was only one place in the quire where the text needed to be revised – and on O3^v Payne, like Richard Grafton in his edition, failed to notice and update the reference to 'the king and his ministers' in the catechism that precedes the service of Confirmation. If the sheets of quire O were worked in the 'usual' order, perhaps when Payne finished quire N he found that John Kingston had already begun work on the innermost sheet of quire O. But Kingston also printed the outermost sheet, so it may well be that the precise reasons for (and the mechanics of) the sharing are beyond recovery.

Two Sheets of Quire O: John Kingston

Apprenticed to Richard Grafton in October 1536, more than two years before Grafton became a printer, John Kingston had presumably been trained in his master's new profession by the time he was freed in 1545.[C] It may be doubted, however, that he was quite as firmly committed to religious reform as was his master. He did not set up as a printer until 1553, when the immigrant Nicholas Hill wisely reacted to Mary's accession by returning to the Low Countries. Kingston promptly took over Hill's premises and equipment in partnership with the Stationer Henry Sutton, and for much of Mary's reign they became the principal printers in England of Catholic liturgical books (a field otherwise dominated by Continental imports). Sutton left the partnership in 1556 or 1557, and set up a printing house of his own.

[A] Note that the great primer w used by Richard Payne, who printed the rest of quire N, really is Isaac's w^3.
[B] In the copies at the British Library, Boston Public Library, and the Huntington Library, leaf N3 is simply glued or pasted to the stub of N6.
[C] Guildhall Library, CLC/L/GH/D/001/MS11571/005, 71^r, 248^r.

As a freeman of the Grocers' Company Kingston had no more legal right to run a printing house in 1559 than did Grafton, Whitchurch, or Payne. But whether it was because he had once been Sutton's partner, and was perhaps related to the Stationer Anthony Kingston (with whom he jointly published a book in 1551),[A] for some reason the Stationers appear to have accepted him as a special case. He continued to enter books in the Stationers' Register and to print quite openly until he died in 1584, and there is no evidence that the Stationers ever objected. As I have noted elsewhere, Kingston was the principal printer of the 1557 missal in which Marshe first used press figures, and another book of uncertain date either had seen or would soon see the two of them working together with Richard Payne.[B] And less than a year before work began on the prayer books, Kingston had come to the attention of the Marian authorities when the pirates Thomas Marshe and Abraham Veale hired him to print an illicit edition of a collection of sermons by the bishop of Lincoln.[C]

The only sheets Kingston printed in the body of the Jugge-and-Cawood prayer book are the innermost and outermost of quire O: sheets O5:6 and O1:10. As we shall see, however, he did print four sheets of the ordinal before the authorities detached it from the prayer book. He also printed at least three sheets of the preliminaries – or more probably four, since there is reason to believe that the present sheet $^\pi$A4:9 is a cancel.

Quire P, Sheet N3:6, and Some Cancels: Richard Jugge

Educated at Eton and at King's College, Cambridge (although not known to have taken a degree), Richard Jugge became a Stationer by purchasing the freedom of London in 1541.[D] He began to publish in 1547, but although his books usually claimed to have been printed 'by' him they were really printed *for* him, usually by Steven Mierdman. Under Mary he kept a low profile until 1558, when he had two books printed by John Day and one by John Kingston.

Jugge probably owed his Elizabethan appointment to Sir William Cecil, who was Elizabeth's principal adviser in the first few days of her reign. In

---

[A] STC 15545 was printed with Grafton's equipment 'by Ihon Kyngston ... And are to be sold at the West doore of Poules, by Anthony Kyngston' (a7^v).
[B] Blayney, 'Thomas Marshe', 459–61, 466–7.
[C] On 17 July 1558 the Privy Council ordered the Lord Mayor of London to have the houses of Kingston and Marshe searched for copies of STC 25113 (TNA: PRO, PC 2/8, p. 17; *APC*, vi, 346); see also my 'Two Tales of Piracy'.
[D] *Stationers and Printers*, I, 513–14.

1552 Jugge had published a revised version of the Tyndale translation of the New Testament (STC 2867–70) for which he had been granted a royal patent the previous year, and for which a price was formally set by the Privy Council. The revisers are not named in the book, but within the Stationers' Company this version apparently became traditionally known as 'm*aste*r Cheekes translation', and the only person to whom that could plausibly refer is Cecil's former brother-in-law Sir John Cheke.[A]

It is perhaps not immediately apparent that Jugge was the printer of quire P. The final verso admittedly uses a large device that incorporates a monogram of his name, and which had been cut for use in his 1552 New Testament. But the only actual printer who had used it in Jugge's publications had been Steven Mierdman, so its presence hardly proves that page P10^v was printed by Jugge himself. Also used in that quire are twenty-two ornamental initials (three of which appear twice each). All but one of them came from the stock of Edward Whitchurch, and eleven of those can also be found in the Whitchurch-and-Wolfe quires A–F. They include the I depicting St John on Patmos (Figure 8*b*, previously used by Owen Rogers in page I8^r and now found in Jugge's P1^v). The one non-Whitchurch initial present is an N (on P7^v) previously owned by the late John Mychell of Canterbury.

At first sight that does not appear to be very strong evidence that the quire was printed by Jugge. But if we look at the other books dated 1559 and attributed to him (or at least, the parts of the books attributed to Jugge-and-Cawood that were not printed by Cawood) what we find is an extraordinary mixture: more than seventy initials formerly belonging to Whitchurch, at least fourteen from the estate of John Mychell plus about the same number of similar age and style that I have not found in Mychell's extant books, and (a little later in the year) nine or more from Richard Grafton. There are also ten borrowed from John Kingston but given back to him by 1560, seven borrowed or acquired from Reyner Wolfe, five from Richard Payne, and at least two from John Cawood. Not until the turn of 1559–60 did Jugge first acquire some new initials of his own, when he became one of the first printers in England to introduce an alphabet of a new design of which copies were almost immediately acquired by several other printers and remained commonplace for several decades.[B] But although he then returned what he had borrowed from Kingston and

---

[A] Ibid., II, 732–3.
[B] First found in quire T of the second quarto prayer-book dated 1559 (STC 16293), they are between 20 and 22 mm tall, approximately square, unframed (although framed copies and analogues were soon introduced). Letters D, O, and V include a bird, while L has a face on a shield and R stands astride a

made less frequent use of the rest, for several years some of his favourites from the stocks of Whitchurch, Grafton, and Mychell reappear from time to time.

Leaves N3 and N6 perhaps best typify the first few months of his career as an actual printer. They contain three ornamental initials: an I from Reyner Wolfe, a W from Edward Whitchurch, and another W from John Mychell. These are the consequences of being unable to take over an existing printing house, and having to assemble a business piece by piece.

Productivity and Chronology

I have so far considered the printers of quires A–P in order of first appearance. But even if each of them printed his sheets in what we could consider the 'obvious' order, the overall production cannot have proceeded likewise. The only credible motive for dividing the work among so many printers can have been to save time – and employing them one after another would have made no sense at all.

If we assume that the two preliminary quires ($^{\pi}A^{12}\ ^{\pi}B^{6}$) were printed last, the text of the prayer book itself required the printing of sixty-five sheets (if we include the original A1, C2:7, and N3, and credit Jugge with two sheets for cancelling them). Of those, the 'first' twenty-four were printed by Whitchurch and Wolfe, the next twenty-five by Cawood, Rogers, and Marshe, and the last sixteen by Payne, Kingston, and Jugge. But here I need to anticipate Chapter 7 and observe that before the preliminaries were tackled, the last group also printed the nine sheets of the ordinal that they believed was to form part of the book: Kingston four sheets, Payne three, Jugge one, and unexpected newcomer William Copland one (BB4:7). Adding those nine sheets brings the total to seventy-four sheets, dividing into three almost exactly equal sections: twenty-four, twenty-five, and twenty-five.

Precisely how the work was divided up within those sections is probably beyond reconstruction, but there are a number of facts that can help both to guide and control speculation, and one of those is comparative productivity. Some years ago, in a study of a printing house operating early in James's reign, I presented evidence suggesting that 'while a single press *could* produce 300 [edition-]sheets a year, the annual production of a continuously-operated printing house would in practice be more like 200

---

flower, but most of the decoration consists of rather untidy vines and foliage. (Katharine F. Pantzer used to describe them informally as 'weedy'.)

[edition-]sheets per press'.[A] An approximation like that, of course, has to be treated with extreme caution. For one thing, any printer whose annual output is known or suspected to have been close to 300 edition-sheets may have been either using only a single press but at close to maximum efficiency, or using two presses but having trouble attracting customers. Moreover, while it is sometimes permissible to assume that most of the output of a seventeenth-century printer is represented by surviving copies (or fragments, or documentary evidence of items no longer extant), the farther back one reaches into the sixteenth century the more pessimistic it is necessary to be. In a more recent study I argued (and then assumed) that what survives from 1551–59 may represent somewhere in the region of two-thirds of what was actually printed during those years, and I still consider that to be a plausible approximation.[B] It should not, however, be mistaken for a claim that two-thirds of the copies of *any* book or books from that period still survive. It means little more than that the books that have disappeared without trace are likely to have been substantially outnumbered by those that survive or are known to have existed.[C]

To begin with the most complex case, I have already noted that under Edward VI, Whitchurch's annual surviving average (and hereafter the word *surviving* is implicit in all such statistics) was a little over 600 edition-sheets. It therefore seems likely that he both owned and used at least three presses and probably four – but in 1556 he either stored them out of harm's way or sold them. He did not, however, sell his ornament stock, and if he was keeping alive the possibility of using it again it seems likely that he would have preserved at least one press.

Wolfe's known Edwardian average was a little over 150 edition-sheets, although his monopoly of Lily's Grammar (whose twenty-nine sheets were typically used to destruction rather than preserved) probably means that his real productivity was considerably higher, and in the two-press range. Mary allowed him to remain her Typographer in Latin, Greek, and Hebrew, but as a sometime protégé of Anne Boleyn he cannot have been high on Mary's list of favourites, and when she replaced Edward's injunction at the beginning of Lily's Grammar she omitted her brother's reference to Wolfe's monopoly. Perhaps coincidentally, it was during her reign

---

[A] Blayney, *The Texts of 'King Lear'*, 42–3.   [B] *Stationers and Printers*, 1, 101.
[C] Perhaps more controversially, in the present study I also assume that the printers most likely to be hired for a project such as the new prayer book were printers best known for their book-printing, and that in most cases the jobbing work they also undoubtedly did was a comparatively small percentage of their business. Owen Rogers was almost certainly an exception – as were both Queen's Printers, though in a very different way.

that the first known pirated editions began to appear,[A] which presumably reduced the demand for his official editions. His known annual average in 1554–58 (which includes only one extant edition of the Grammar) is below thirty sheets, so during Mary's reign he is unlikely to have needed more than a single press. Apart from the prayer book itself he is not known to have printed anything in 1559, but his annual average in 1560–64 jumped to over 190 edition-sheets – which (if we assume that several editions of the Grammar have been lost) probably means two presses. So if I am right in suggesting that Whitchurch brought his ornaments and at least one press into Wolfe's house to work on the prayer book, then at least two presses and perhaps three were available for quires A–F.

Whether or not the second section was put in hand at the same time as the first, John Cawood was one of the few printers whose average Marian output (about 215 edition-sheets) suggests that he had two presses. Perhaps, then, the original plan was to have him print twenty-five sheets (quires G–M) while Wolfe and Whitchurch printed their twenty-four. But if so, he must soon have been ordered to concentrate instead on three proclamations of April and May (STC 7892–4) and the first three editions of the statute of Elizabeth's first parliament (9458.7–9.5). The rest of the second section (quires H–M) was therefore handed off to Owen Rogers and Thomas Marshe, neither of whom is likely to have had more than one press. Marshe's average for his first four years (1555–58) was just over 150 edition-sheets. Rogers, by contrast, must either have printed only part-time or specialized in small jobbing items (or both), because the books he is known to have printed in the same period amount to only forty-eight edition-sheets in total (twelve a year).[B] But we do not have to assume that work on the second section slowed to half speed when Cawood left. Given that there was virtually nothing in that part of the text that needed to be revised, Rogers and Marshe could easily have divided the 1552 sheets between them in any way they chose, and then printed their sections simultaneously.

The first two printers who worked on the third section (quires N–P and the ordinal) were also men whose output suggests that they may have used two presses. Payne's average in 1556–59 was approximately 170 sheets, but his printing house had belonged to Henry VIII's royal printer, and had

---

[A] STC lists three pirate editions dated 1557, but 15611.7 was really printed in or after 1561 to imitate 15612 (see 'Two Tales of Piracy'). A lost pirate edition dated 1558 is mentioned in two depositions of June 1559 (TNA: PRO, C 24/50 part 2, Hilary, 2 Eliz., *Wolfe v. Veale*).

[B] If the twenty-two sheets he contributed to the prayer books are included, the annual average for the last three years of his printing career (1559–61) was just over thirty edition-sheets.

certainly been capable of exceeding that figure before Berthelet died. And John Kingston's annual average of between 180 and 190 sheets is second only to Cawood's among the Marian printers considered so far.

What prevents a comparatively neat and tidy reconstruction is the advent of Richard Jugge near the end of the story. If we imagine three separate teams, each starting simultaneously and working with two presses at a time, before section three the only 'irregularity' is that after Cawood stepped out of the picture the two presses working on quires H–M (Rogers and Marshe) were doing so in different printing houses. Section three began with Payne printing most of quire N, but with Jugge contributing sheet N3:6 and mistakenly including the Black Rubric on N3^v. At some point in this sequence the ordinal was printed, although it is difficult to explain the way it was divided among Kingston (AA1–2,4:5,7–8 and BB5:6), Payne (BB1–3:8–10), and Jugge (AA3:6).[A] It is even less apparent why William Copland was brought in to print sheet BB4:7. Meanwhile (or perhaps thereafter) Payne and Kingston each printed part of quire O while Jugge produced quire P by himself and then cancelled A1, C2:7, and N3.

If all three sections, A–F, G–M, and N–P plus the ordinal had been started at the same time, Jugge could in theory have begun printing some time before Wolfe and Whitchurch had finished quires A–F. But Jugge's contributions use nineteen initials formerly belonging to Whitchurch (and one to Wolfe) that had already been used in quires A–F (three of them in quire E and two in quire F itself). Apparently, then, Jugge could not have begun work (on either the ordinal or quire P) before quire F had been finished and he had taken over at least part of the Whitchurch ornament stock.

But despite the eventual irregularities it seems distinctly possible that the original plan was to have three two-press printers – (1) the partnership of Whitchurch and Wolfe, (2) John Cawood, and (3) either Richard Payne (who had once briefly been Whitchurch's next-door neighbour in Fleet Street) or John Kingston – working simultaneously in the interests of haste. But Cawood's other commitments led him to delegate to the two single presses of Rogers and Marshe, and the third group had not made much progress before Whitchurch and Wolfe finished their share and Jugge acquired much of Whitchurch's former equipment. Altogether, the job must have taken at least a few weeks longer than expected.

[A] The only explicable part of the division is that Queen's Printer Jugge printed AA3:6, which has an extract from the Act of Supremacy on AA6^v.

Meanwhile Grafton was busy printing most of the other first edition on his own. His Edwardian productivity had been slightly lower than Whitchurch's at a little less than 530 edition-sheets a year, but he too must have been using either three or four presses during his heyday. When Robert Caly took over the business under Mary he never used anything like the full capacity of the house, averaging less than 140 edition-sheets a year, so it is impossible to know how many presses were still present and in working order when Grafton evicted him. But it seems likely that Grafton began setting his preliminary quire at about the same time as the Jugge team started on theirs, so it is certainly possible that he may sometimes have been able to have more than two presses working simultaneously. In any event he seems to have been able to work at more or less the same overall pace as the printers of the Jugge edition.

Exactly when the first two editions were finished and put on sale is unrecorded. If we assume that Grafton originally printed every sheet of his edition except the calendar, including the ordinal and the two sheets that Kingston would later cancel, with two presses each producing a perfected sheet each day those seventy-nine sheets would have been finished on the fortieth day. So if he had been able to start in the afternoon of the day the queen assented to the Act of Uniformity and dissolved Parliament (8 May), working seven days a week he could have 'finished' at the end of the day on 16 June – leaving exactly a week before the use of the revised book became compulsory. And since Kingston would not yet have cancelled sheet $^\pi$A4:9 or the title sheet there would have been barely enough time left for even the incumbents of all *London* churches to acquire copies and familiarize themselves with the contents. Moreover, neither the Grafton nor the Jugge-and-Cawood title-page could have been printed before Kingston had cancelled the list of contents. So even if Grafton had been able to put a third press to work for at least part of the time, neither of the first editions could have been on sale more than two or three weeks before the official deadline.

But whether or not they were yet on sale in large numbers, copies apparently were available by or soon after that deadline. An undated entry in the wardens' account of the Stationers' Company for the financial year that ended on 10 July reads as follows: 'William Ionys ys fyned for that he solde a Comunion boke of kynge Edward*es* for one of the newe – – xxd'.[A] It is just possible that the offending volume could have been a copy of the Grafton edition containing rather too many recycled sheets from

---

[A] Arber, I, 94.

1552. (Not only sheet A2:5 as in the Bodleian and Corpus Christi copies, but perhaps also B3:4 with Edward specifically named on B4^v.) In that event, though, the fault would have been Grafton's, whereas the fact that Jones was fined suggests that he had acted knowingly. The incident does, however, at least show that copies of 'the newe' book must have been finished and on sale either in or before early July.

CHAPTER 6

The Preliminaries: Collaboration and Cancels

For reasons that will become obvious, the preliminaries of the two first editions can best be discussed together. Each edition begins with a twelve-leaf quire signed A, which (because the main text also begins with a quire signed A) is therefore called πA^{12}. That is followed in each edition by a six-leaf calendar which in Grafton's edition is signed b (as in all editions of 1549–52) and therefore called b^6. In the Jugge-and-Cawood edition, however, it is not given a signature letter at all, and the second and third leaves are signed only 'ii.' and 'iij'. The revised STC and most derivative sources call this quire π^6, which is acceptable under the Bowers rules. But since the quire follows one signed A it makes better sense to infer (and therefore italicize) the letter B and call it πB^6 instead.[A]

The Lectionary Errors of 1552

In addition to the changes to the table of proper lessons that were required by the Act (and which will be discussed later in this chapter), the editions of 1559 each made a few necessary corrections in the lectionary columns of the calendar – and since comparatively few modern readers will be exactly *familiar* with those columns it may be useful to begin by explaining a few basics.

For the purpose of the liturgical year, the Bible was divided into three parts: the New Testament, the Book of Psalms, and the rest of the Old Testament (which before 1640 was considered to include the Apocrypha). Each day of the year had readings from each of those parts assigned to it. The 150 psalms were divided into thirty groups (of five, or more or fewer depending on length), and one group was assigned to each day of the month. The first and last of February's thirty groups were given to 31

[A] See the second example on p. 216 of Bowers, *Principles of Bibliographical Description*.

January and 1 March respectively;[A] after April any 31st day repeated the selection for the 30th. In a full year, therefore, each psalm would be read at least twelve times (and those assigned to the 30th day, seventeen times).

From the rest of the Bible, each day had two 'lessons' assigned to Morning Prayer and two to Evening Prayer. Each lesson was usually a whole chapter, and the first lesson in each pair was from the Old Testament. The second morning lesson was from the Gospels (including Acts);[B] the second evening lesson from the Epistles. The comparative brevity of the New Testament meant that each second lesson was read three times a year. But with more than 900 chapters available in the Old Testament and Apocrypha, even a whole year's 730 first lessons could not include everything. So as the principle was stated in the preliminaries:

> The old Testament ... shalbee redde through euery yere once, except certain bookes and Chapiters, whiche bee least edifying, and might best be spared, and therefore are left unred.[C]

Left out completely were 1 and 2 Chronicles, the Song of Solomon, and (almost) all the Apocrypha after Baruch. But while the apocryphal books that were included had very few chapters omitted, substantial portions of several canonical books were rejected as insufficiently edifying (Exodus, Leviticus, Numbers, and Ezekiel).

Apart from one or two misprinted numbers, only one 1549 New Testament reading was changed in 1552,[D] and no further changes were made in 1559 – but the Old Testament is another story. In 1549 everything seems regular. Six days in the year have special readings assigned to them outside the basic sequence: Circumcision (1 January), Epiphany (6 January), John the Baptist (24 June), All Saints (1 November), Christmas (25 December), and Innocents' Day (28 December). Otherwise the Old Testament chapters begin on 2 January with Genesis 1 and end on 27 November with Baruch 6. There are only two departures from the Biblical order. The chapters for 3 September are identified as Daniel 13–14, and accordingly placed after Daniel 12. They are indeed so described and placed

---

[A] So in a standard year, February was assigned the psalms for days 2–29 of a standard month, while March's 31 days were assigned those for days 30 and 1–30. In a leap year the selection for 25 February was repeated on the 26th.

[B] Only two days in the year had readings from the Apocalypse (Revelation): All Saints' Day (evening only) and the feast of St John the Evangelist (morning and evening).

[C] STC 16268, πA2ᵛ.

[D] On Christmas morning, Matthew 1 was replaced by Luke 2 ('2' correct in the Table, but misprinted '22' in the calendar until corrected by Christopher Barker in his second edition of 1577: STC 16306.9, ¶7ᵛ).

in the Vulgate – but in all English translations (including the Great Bible, which was still the version authorized for church use) they are placed in the Apocrypha as the books of Susanna and of Bel and the Dragon. The other deviation is that Isaiah, much of which is particularly appropriate during Advent and Christmas, follows Baruch as the last book of the year, beginning on 28 November.

A comparison between the first Whitchurch edition of 1552 and any of its 1549 predecessors reveals several differences, all in the first half of the year. The first is that the morning lesson of 21 January is shown as Genesis 39 instead of Genesis 38. Given that the preceding and following lessons are chapters 37 and 39 respectively, this seems to be nothing more than an obvious misprint – but for the moment what matters is to record it.

For 16–24 March, the eighteen consecutive lessons in 1549 are Joshua 3–20, in order. But in 1552 the chapters for those days are recorded in the order 3, 3, 4, 4, 5, 5, 6, 6, 7, 7, 8, 8, 9, 9, 10, 11, 12, and 20. Nowhere in 1549 is a single chapter assigned to both the morning and the evening of the same day, and the most likely cause of this sequence seems to be that someone (either Whitchurch's compositor or more probably the scribe who penned the copy he followed) set or copied the lectionary not line by line but column by column. Finding himself lost after copying seven entries from the wrong column, he improvised his way from 10 to 20 instead of going back and correcting from the start of the problem.

Whoever it was managed to get through April without incident, but went astray again in May and June. Here, however, it is necessary to explain the mid-Tudor names of the books, which do not accord with modern usage. In English bibles before the Geneva version the book of Ruth was followed (as in the Vulgate) by 1–4 Kings,[A] 1–2 Chronicles, and 1–2 Esdras, while after twenty-three intervening books, the Apocrypha began with 3–4 Esdras. The modern naming was used in the Geneva Bible of 1560, but it was not until 1576 that a Geneva version was printed in England, and not until 1611 that an English version using the modern names was authorized for use in churches. When discussing the lectionary in this book I shall adopt its mid-Tudor usage, as follows:

[A] The Coverdale Bible of 1535 followed the Vulgate in naming 'The fyrst boke of the kynges, otherwyse called the first boke of Samuel' (STC 2063, cc1^v), but made no mention of Samuel when heading the second book (gg4^r). The 'Matthew' Bible of 1537 followed the Hebrew in naming the first two books for Samuel first and the kings second (STC 2066, n8^r, p4^v), using 'Samuel' in verso headlines and 'Kinges' in rectos – but nevertheless gave priority to the Vulgate numbering of books 3 and 4. The Great Bible followed 'Matthew', but the lectionary columns of the prayer books understandably opt for 1–4 Kings rather than complicate the numbering with Samuel.

Mid-Tudor	Modern	Mid-Tudor	Modern
1 Kings	1 Samuel	1 Esdras	Ezra
2 Kings	2 Samuel	2 Esdras	Nehemiah
3 Kings	1 Kings	3 Esdras	1 Esdras
4 Kings	2 Kings	4 Esdras	2 Esdras

The first scrambled sequence in May is a short one, where in days 6–10 the first nine lessons from 1 Kings are recorded as chapters 1, 1, 2, 2, 3, 4, 5, 9, and 9 (followed by 10–22 as in 1549). The next thirty-eight lessons reprint the 1549 text without alteration – but things go awry again on the evening of 29 May, when the morning's 4 Kings 25 is repeated instead of 1 Esdras 1. What should then follow is 1 Esdras 2–10 and 2 Esdras 1–12; what actually follows is 1 Esdras 1–4, 4–6, 6, 7, 7, 8, 8, 9, 10, and then 2 Esdras 1, 3–6, and 8–9. Order is restored on the evening of 9 June with the correct 2 Esdras 13, and the rest of the year follows 1549 without incident.

What makes it seem likely that these were errors in what Archbishop Cranmer called 'the copy which m^r Spilman deliuered to the printers to printe by' (see p. 40, n.A) is that they are followed with only one exception by every 1552 edition, whether by Whitchurch or Grafton. They were not noticed or corrected by Cranmer himself, or by whoever in either printing house actually compiled the few perfunctory errata lists that were printed. The only variation is that in Whit.4 and Whit.5 the first evening lesson for 30 May is misprinted as 1 Esdras 3. In 1549 that would have been correct; in the 1552 context it makes the first four chapters 1, 3, 3, and 4.

The Grafton/Kingston Calendar of 1559

It seems likely that by 1559 Grafton no longer had either a compositor skilled in setting tabular material or a pressman with experience in printing in red and black. He therefore decided to subcontract the calendar quire to his former apprentice John Kingston, who had already printed four sheets of ordinal and two of prayer book for the Jugge team, and had printed several two-colour liturgies during Mary's reign. It is impossible to be certain whether it was Grafton or Kingston who suggested revising the layout, but Kingston would print at least two more calendars in substantially the same style before the end of 1559. In each of them he omitted the first column (of the Golden numbers, which had not been included in 1549) and replaced it with the column of psalm references (in this edition using arabic numerals) that had formerly adjoined the lectionary columns in roman numerals.[A] In setting it for Grafton, however, he neglected to move the 'Psalmes' heading with the numbers, and left it misplaced above the Morning Prayer columns (see Plate 4).

In the columns for Old Testament lessons in January, March, and early May he unfortunately failed to correct any of the 1552 blunders – but before he reached the end of May something seems to have alerted him to the Esdras fiasco, and he was able to correct the errors from 29 May to 9 June (presumably by consulting an edition of 1549). That the Jugge team first noticed the need for correction at exactly the same point in the calendar suggests that the cooperation evident in quire $^{\pi}A^{12}$ may have already begun. But whoever marked the corrections in the copy being used by Jugge failed to consult a 1549 calendar, and wrongly assumed that the errors began on the morning of 30 May rather than the previous evening.[B] I therefore suspect that 'cooperation' had not yet matured into actual collaboration.

The Jugge-and-Cawood Calendar and Sheets $^{\pi}$A5–8: Reyner Wolfe

That Kingston did not correct the errors in January (b1^r) and March (b2^r) suggests that those months had already been printed before he began on May (b3^r), and therefore that he began working on the calendar with the outermost forme (January:December) and worked inwards. Whoever printed the calendar for Jugge and Cawood evidently declined to consult a 1549 edition when miscorrecting those errors, so we cannot trust the same logic to determine *his* printing order – but his design of the headings, rules, and braces above the lectionary columns evolved as the setting progressed, and shows with little doubt that he too worked from the outermost forme to the innermost.

That quire of the Jugge-and-Cawood edition is in some ways the most difficult to assign to a particular printer, because no head-ornaments or display initials are used on any page. The most distinctive decoration is a woodcut approximately an inch tall of the letters KL

[A] To be precise, they are references to the table of Psalms only through March. In and after May, the last day of each long month is numbered '31' instead of repeating '30' – so from the beginning of April they are *day*-numbers.

[B] He therefore began with 1 Esdras 1 on the morning of the 30th (misprinting the correct 'iii' in the evening instead of the incorrect 'ii') and had to omit 2 Esdras 12. He did, however, correct the morning lesson for 21 January that Kingston had overlooked. It may be no coincidence that in the revised calendar of 1561 (see Chapter 10), which was evidently based on Wolfe rather than Kingston, 1 Esdras 2 and 2 Esdras 12 were among the chapters ousted.

(for *Kalends*), printed in red on each page as a quasi-heading for the column in which the Kalends, Nones, and Ides of the Roman calendar are recorded (see Plate 5).[A] There are only two such woodcuts, each used once in each forme – so there can be no doubt that the quire is the work of a single printer throughout. Most liturgical calendars printed for use in England, whether Catholic or Protestant, use a pair of considerably smaller lombardic capitals when they 'decorate' that column at all. I have never seen a printed equivalent of these two KL cuts at any date, before or since, but they closely resemble (and were doubtless copied from) medieval manuscript examples. They presumably rule out all the English printers known to have printed liturgical calendars both before and after 1559 (Grafton, Whitchurch, Kingston, Jugge, and Cawood), and point to someone unusually interested in the aesthetics of the printed page (which I take, perhaps unfairly, as eliminating Owen Rogers).

The conclusion towards which that points receives additional support from 'Ianuary' in the heading of the first page. Each month's heading is set in 230 textura of a design common to most English printing houses. The sole exception is the initial I of 'Ianuary', which is considerably more ornate than the I actually belonging to that fount and used in both 'Iune' and 'Iuly'. It is neither the regular capital belonging to the 270 'Bible Fraktur' nor the titling version sometimes known as a 'Kanzlei' capital.[B] Never having seen a verifiable example of the I that belonged to the Wolfe Fraktur, I cannot be certain that this is it – but I have described Wolfe elsewhere as a printer who 'had strong ideas about what good printing should look like', and he commissioned woodcuts for several of his more important books.[C]

The likelihood that Wolfe printed the calendar quire is increased by the decorative braces, approximately 30 mm in length, used horizontally on each page to group the lectionary columns into two pairs: morning lessons and evening lessons. There are three different designs, none of which I have noticed in any other book (although there were plural copies of at least two of the designs, hard to distinguish from each other). In the calendar columns the printer uses at least three examples of the design I call A and one each of designs B and C,[D] while two examples of design C are found in

---

[A] Strictly speaking it is not really a heading, but the entry in that column for the first day of the month.
[B] Oastler, *John Day*, 11; *Stationers and Printers*, 11, 640nC.   [C] *Stationers and Printers*, 1, 493–5.
[D] Designs A and B are reproduced in Plate 5, under the headings for Morning and Evening Prayer respectively.

96   The Preliminaries: Collaboration and Cancels

the preceding quire in the 'Table for the Ordre of the Psalmes' on page $^{\pi}$A8^{v}. Above those braces the first line of the heading of that table is set in Wolfe's 230-mm Fraktur, while on the recto of that leaf appears a small Whitchurch woodcut T that Wolfe would continue to use into the 1560s. Meanwhile on the recto of the conjugate leaf $^{\pi}$A5, the Preface begins with a 70-mm initial T that was originally used by Wolfe in 1556 on the first page of Robert Recorde's *Castle of Knowledge* (STC 20796, A1^{r}) – for which book it was almost certainly commissioned.[A] From that page the preface continues in the same type to $^{\pi}$A6^{r}, on the verso of which the essay 'Of Ceremonies' begins with a Whitchurch O that would also remain with Wolfe in later years.[B] I therefore have no real doubt that both quire $^{\pi}$B^{6} and sheets $^{\pi}$A5–8 were printed by Reyner Wolfe. Whether or not Whitchurch himself was still actively involved is impossible to determine, but I have chosen to assume that his second brief career as a printer ended when Jugge acquired a substantial share of his ornament stock before printing quire P.[C]

Like John Kingston, Wolfe evidently felt no compulsion to preserve the layout of the 1552 calendars, but took a direction of his own. While his rival dropped the column of Golden numbers and introduced arabic numerals in his relocated psalms/days column, Wolfe left the column layout alone but decorated the headings with his KL woodcuts and ornate braces. And having done that, he went a step farther and added some new information to the 'miscellaneous' column in which special holy days, the dates of the legal terms, and astrological phenomena were recorded. At or near the top of each month's column he used either three or four lines to report the times of sunrise and sunset at the beginning of each month – and being Wolfe, did so in roman type instead of textura. Given the difference between the two printers' approaches to the calendar, it seems unlikely that either of them had been given any official instructions about it at all.

[A] The T is reproduced in my 'Initials Within Initials', p. 451.
[B] Wolfe used the O in 1562 in STC 2096 (printed for Richard Harrison, but ostensibly 'by' him), on II2^{v}, KK7^{r}, etc. The small T mentioned above also appears in that book, on A1^{v}, E1^{r}, etc. The choice of that particular O in 1559 is one of numerous similar clues suggesting that Wolfe was printing from a copy of Whit.4 (which, unlike Whit.5, uses the same initial).
[C] STC 11972 claims to have been printed by Whitchurch in 1560, and all the initials used in it are from his old stock. But they are all ones that had passed to Reyner Wolfe, whose 230 Fraktur also appears, so the colophon should presumably be interpreted as 'Imprinted at London by [Reyner Wolfe, for] Edwarde Whitchurche' (X8^{v}).

The New Act of Uniformity and Table of Proper Lessons: John Kingston

While Wolfe was printing leaves ᵖA5–8 from leaves a2–5 of Whit.4, for his part Grafton reprinted the same leaves from his last edition of 1552, Graf.6. That they each signed the first two rectos 'A.v.' and 'A.vi.' suggests that they had consulted each other about both the size and the contents of that quire.

But the relationship between the two editions of leaves ᵖA2–4 (the Act of Uniformity) and their conjugates ᵖA9–11 (the table of proper lessons) is quite different. In the Jugge-and-Cawood edition those three sheets are the work of John Kingston, while in the Grafton edition they were originally printed by Grafton himself. The two settings of the Act agree for the most part line for line, and in the few places where a minor discrepancy arises, agreement is always restored within a line or two. One must therefore have been printed from the other. Moreover, while the Jugge version of the first page begins with an eight-line drop capital W owned by its actual printer (John Kingston), Grafton uses a smaller W but nevertheless breaks the lines beside and below it at the same points in the text – including line 8, which therefore begins with 37 mm of space-metal below the seven-line capital. Evidently, then, the Act was first printed from manuscript copy by Kingston for the Jugge edition, and Grafton worked from Kingston's printed sheets. That was only to be expected because, as one of the Queen's Printers, Jugge would have had privileged access to the official manuscript copy that had first been used by his partner-in-office Cawood when printing the queen's first statute (STC 9458.7).

In that book Cawood used italic capitals for the opening word or phrase of each section of the statute, but that practice has left no visible trace in Kingston's setting, and where Cawood also used italic for the definition of 'open prayer' in section II, Kingston chose roman. But even though the Jugge team evidently preferred to trust Kingston with an official manuscript rather than printed copy, Cawood's edition of the statute had shown that the Act would fill at least six pages unless set in unsuitably small type. The material already printed in sheets ᵖA5–8 occupied eight pages, while the title-page, contents list, almanack, and introduction to the proper lessons would add four more to make eighteen. A preliminary quire of five sheets would contain twenty pages, leaving only two for the expanded table of proper lessons – which in 1552 had filled four pages and was now to be enlarged with 'one alteraci*o*n or addici*o*n of c*er*ten lessons to be vsed on eue*r*y Sonday in the yere'. It was therefore agreed that the quire would have to contain six sheets instead (twelve leaves, or twenty-four pages), which left six pages available for the revised table.

While most of the days with proper lessons in 1552 could fall on Sundays, only three of them *always* did so: Easter, Whitsun, and Trinity Sunday. Most years have fifty-two Sundays, while those that begin on Sunday (and leap years that begin on Saturday) have fifty-three, so the printers would probably have expected the promised revisions to add at least fifty proper lessons or psalms to those tabulated in 1552. What they would have done if they had been warned that instead of fifty, the revisions would add more than three times that number (155, for a total of 227) I cannot guess – but in the event they crammed the revised table into a mere four pages, and thus left two pages ($^{\pi}$AII^{v}–12^{r}) without anything significant to fill them.

In 1549 the proper lessons and psalms had not been tabulated at all, but were prescribed in the section of Introits, Collects, Epistles, and Gospels whenever one of the ninety holy days required one or more special readings. In 1552, when the Introits and various other things were omitted from that section, the seventy-two proper readings were listed instead in a two-column table (in the same order as in 1549), with the holy days in small type in the first column and the pertinent reading(s) in larger type to their right. (The compiler's omission of the 1549 second lesson for the day of Sts Philip and James may have been inadvertent, but would become permanent.)

The moveable feasts in the liturgical year divide into two groups: those linked to Christmas and those linked to Easter. In the 1559 table, the first group includes eleven Sundays: four of Advent, two after Christmas, and five after Epiphany. Those linked to Easter are more numerous, being forty-four in number: nine from Septuagesima to the sixth Sunday in Lent (Palm Sunday), nine more from Easter to Trinity Sunday inclusive, and twenty-six after Trinity. The total for the year is therefore fifty-five – two more than any calendar year can have. But because Easter can be as early as 22 March and as late as 25 April, Septuagesima can sometimes coincide with (and outrank) any of the Sundays after Epiphany except the first, while the first Sunday of Advent can occur as early as (and outrank) the twenty-third after Trinity. Why the revisers limited the number of Sundays to fifty-five is unclear, because two more were arguably needed, and would in future centuries be added. What the 1559 table fails to provide for is that whenever Easter falls on or before 26 March, as it did in 1559 itself,[A] there is

---

[A] Also in 1565, 1576, 1603, etc. After the Gospel for the twenty-fifth Sunday, a rubric notes that 'Yf there be any moe Sundayes before Aduent Sundaye, to supplye the same shall bee taken the seruyce of

The New Act of Uniformity and Table of Proper Lessons 99

	Mattens.	Euesong.		Mattens.	Euesong.
Sainct Jhon.			Goodfryday.	Gene. xxii.	Esaie. liii.
i. Lesson.	Eccle. v.	Eccle. vi.	Easter euē.	Zach. ix.	Exod. xiii.
ii. Lesson.	Apoc. i.	Apoc. xxii.	Mōdaye in easter weke.		
Innocētes.	Jere. xxxi vnto moreouer I hearde Ephraim.	Wisdō. i.	i. Lesson.	Exod. xvi.	xvii.
Circumcision daye.			ii. Lesson.	Mathew. xxviii.	Act. iii.
i. Lesson.	Gen. xvii.	Deut. x. & nowe Israel, &c. Coloss. ii.	Twesdaye in easter.		
ii. Lesson.	Rom. ii.		i. Lesson.	Exod. xx.	Exo. xxxii.
Epiphanie daye.			ii. Lesson.	Luk. xxiiii. vnto. And beholde. ii. of them.	i. Corinth. xv.
i. Lesson.	Esa. lx.	Esa. xlix.	S. Marke.	Eccle. iiii.	Eccle. v.
ii. Lesson.	Luke. iii. and it foztuned, &c.	Jhon. ii. after this he wēt to Capernaū	Philippe and Jacob.	vii.	ix.
Couersion of s. Paule.			Ascension daye.	Deut. x.	Deut. xi.
i. Lesson.	Wisdō. v.	Wisdō. vi.	Mondaye in whitson weake.		
ii. Lesson.	Act. xxii. vnto, they heard him	Act. ii.		xxx.	xxxi.
Purification of ý virgin Mary.	Wisdō. ix.	Wised. xii.	Twesdaye in whitson. weake.	xxxii.	xxxiiii.
Sainct Matthie.	Wisd. xix.	Eccle. i.	Sainct Barnabe.		
Annunciation of our Ladye.	Eccle. ii.	iii.	i. Lesson.	Eccle. x.	Eccle. xii.
			ii. Lesson.	Act. xiiii.	Ac. 15. vnto After certein daies.
Wensday afoze Easter.	Osee. xiii.	Ose. xiiii.	S. Jhon Baptiste.		
			i. Lesson.	Mala. iii.	Mala. iiii.
Thursdaye befoze Easter.	Dan. ix.	Jere. xxxi.	ii. Lesson.	Math. iii.	Mathew. xiiii. vnto, when Jesus heard.

Figure 10 Third page of the table of proper lessons.
(© The British Library Board, C.25.m.7, ᵖA10ᵛ.)

some of those Sundayes that were omitted betwene Epiphanye and Septuagesima' (STC 16292, K5ᵛ). But while the table lists lessons for a twenty-sixth Sunday on ᵖA10ʳ, none are provided for a twenty-seventh.

a Sunday lacking either a name or a proper lesson between the twenty-sixth after Trinity and the first of Advent. Similarly, when Easter falls on or after 22 April (or on 21 April in a leap year), there is a similarly unprovided Sunday between the fifth after Epiphany and Septuagesima.[A] For some reason, though, it was not until the book was revised in 1662 that the sixth Sunday after Epiphany was assigned lessons of its own, while the twenty-seventh Sunday after Trinity was not formally recognized in the table until the nineteenth century.

As can be seen in Figure 10, the 1559 table consists of three columns: one to identify the day – and, where relevant, whether the prescribed reading is a first (Old Testament) or second (New Testament) lesson – and a column each for Morning and Evening Prayer (headed 'Mattens' and 'Euẽsong', even though those names had been deliberately dropped in 1552). That triple-column list, moreover, is arranged in two 'master-columns' that would have been better separated with a double rule to make the layout clearer. But note that the heading 'Circumcision daye' in the first column is confusingly aligned with the third and fourth lines of the definition of the morning lesson for Innocents' Day, while neither the heading nor the morning reference for the second lesson is aligned with the evening reference. Elsewhere on that page the headings for the Conversion of Paul and for the Purification start before the previous entries have finished, as does that for St John the Baptist near the foot of the fourth column. In almost any other context such misalignments would suggest that the compositor was trying to squeeze rather too much text into not enough space – but in these pages the real problem was much too much space and not nearly enough text. If the manuscript copy had been arranged as a simple and clear three-column list, however long, the compositor could have cast it off by dividing it into as many as eleven 'master-columns' to precede the final half-column of proper psalms. That it is printed as only seven master-columns, some of them severely cramped, suggests that the copy itself was so arranged. The clerics who decided which days needed one or more proper lessons, and who chose appropriate chapters for the purpose, would probably not have given much thought to the eventual arrangement on the printed page. But whoever was given the task of providing a compositor with the needed information – perhaps a minor cleric told by the compilers to reduce it to a form intelligible to artisans; perhaps a scribe asked by

---

[A] As in 1570, 1573, 1581, 1592, 1600, etc. After the Gospel for the fifth Sunday, a brief rubric notes that 'The .vi. Sunday (if there be so many) shal haue the same Collect, Epistle and Gospell, that was vpon the fyfth Sundaye' (STC 16292, D1ᵛ), but no lessons are provided in the table.

Kingston to translate a poorly prepared manuscript into usable printer's copy – may well have tried too hard to be helpful by mistakenly arranging it in only four pages (as in 1552).

Apart from its bottom right corner, the best-designed of the four pages is the first, $^{\pi}$A9^v – but, as it happens, that page is probably a cancel printed to correct some problem whose nature can now only be guessed. One of the most unexpected features of the 1559 preliminaries is that there is only one extant setting of sheet $^{\pi}$A4:9, which is found both in the Jugge edition *and also in Grafton's*. The most plausible explanation is that Kingston's first setting of the sheet must have contained some serious error in at least one page, and the problem escaped notice until after Grafton had used it as copy for his own edition.[A] Given that the book was both almost finished and eagerly awaited, and that the fault was probably Kingston's, having him print enough cancels to equip both editions was not only the quickest and most efficient solution, but also the fairest. Leaf $^{\pi}$A4 contains the last two pages of the Act, in which any really serious misprint ought to have been caught at an earlier stage. The recto of $^{\pi}$A9 was reprinted line for line from a6^r of the 1552 edition (Graf.6) with only one substantive revision: in the fourth paragraph the phrase 'proper Psalmes or Lessōs appoynted for any feast' is expanded to 'proper Psalmes or Lessons appointed for the Sondayes or for any feaste', and it is difficult to imagine that even omitting the four added words would have warranted cancelling both editions of the sheet. I therefore suspect that whatever the problem was, it was in the first page of the table.

One possible objection could be raised against the conclusion that Grafton must have used Kingston's printed sheets as copy for the Act (and therefore also the table on the conjugate leaves). On page $^{\pi}$A11^v of the Jugge edition, Kingston has printed 'A briefe declaration when euery Terme beginneth and endeth', filling the space above and below it with the head and foot of one of his four-piece title-page borders.[B] But in Grafton's edition that page is left blank – and since the facing page $^{\pi}$A12^r is blank in both editions, Grafton's empty opening is a conspicuous eyesore.

It is, however, easy to believe that the sheet given to Grafton as copy did not contain that 'declaration', which is an irrelevance that was probably

---

[A] Another possibility is that Grafton was the only one to err (in $^{\pi}$A4, $^{\pi}$A9, or both), and that while Kingston's sheet is a cancel in Grafton's edition, in the Jugge edition it is the uncancelled original. But that would require Grafton to have printed his Act of Uniformity before Kingston's (rather than *from* it as the evidence suggests).

[B] The border is McK & F 38, which unquestionably belonged to Kingston, and was apparently not among the ornamental material he lent to Jugge for the second half of 1559.

foisted in rather late for no other purpose than to avoid an empty opening in the Jugge edition. While the starting dates of two of the legal terms (Easter and Trinity) were determined by the date of Easter, nothing in the liturgy itself depends on the legal calendar. Those dates had, in fact, already been included in the 1552 calendars in the pertinent months, in the column used for other miscellaneous non-liturgical facts (such as the date the sun entered each sign of the zodiac) – and although Kingston's calendar quire for the Grafton edition had dispensed with the term dates, Wolfe's had already recorded them before Kingston printed his part of the Jugge preliminaries. It is possible that the redundant 'declaration' was added as a stop-press alteration (hardly a 'correction'), and that Grafton was given one of the early copies that lacked it. Perhaps Kingston was subsequently asked to add it as an afterthought by putting Jugge's copies of sheet $^{\pi}$A2:11 through the press a second time. Or perhaps Grafton simply (and rightly) declined to consider the legal terms to be liturgically relevant.

Title-page, Contents, and Almanack: Jugge and Kingston

Sheet $^{\pi}$A4:9 is not the only part of the preliminaries that is identical in both editions, although the other example is not a sheet but only a single page: the contents list on the verso of both Jugge's title-page and Grafton's.

Identifying the printer of that page was not easy: it contains many short lines that reduce the amount of visible type to work with. There are no damaged types so distinctive that they could provide probative evidence, and there were other printers in London using founts of essentially the same great primer textura with a mixture of the same two designs of w. The nearest approach to 'ornamentation' is a cast Aldine leaf preceding the heading. The only printer in this group who uses that particular design of leaf in either of the prayer books themselves is Richard Payne (on O2^r), but the mixed w's rule him out. John Kingston, however, owned at least one such leaf, and used it on the title-page of Fabyan's *Chronicle* at about the same time in the same year (STC 10663–4, dated 26 April: see Figure 11). Moreover, I can find no tell-tale differences between Kingston's type and that of the list. Given that the only other pages in the whole project that are found in both editions are also in the preliminaries and printed by Kingston, I feel reasonably confident in attributing the list to him as well.

Because $^{\pi}$A12^r is blank, Kingston's list of contents is the only printed matter in the inner forme of either edition of sheet $^{\pi}$A1:12, while in each the outer forme contains both the 30-year almanack and the title-page. It is difficult to imagine circumstances that would have led both teams to produce their two-colour outer formes first and then to decide that only Kingston was qualified to perfect them with a simple thirty-three-line list of contents. The most plausible scenario seems to be that each team had printed and perfected its own version of sheet $^{\pi}$A1:12, but that something in at least one page of each was belatedly found unacceptable. With luck, the type for one or more of the outer-forme pages in at least one edition may still have been more or less intact, but printing the outer forme in both red and black was still a more complicated procedure than resetting and reprinting the single-page inner forme. So whatever had necessitated cancellation, it would make sense for Kingston's press to have printed the contents list first while each outer forme was made ready by its respective printer.

When a page of type was printed the types dug into the damp paper, leaving a landscape of visible grooves and dents on the printed side and slightly less prominent ridges and peaks on the reverse. If a page was then printed on the verso, its own grooves and dents were pressed into those ridges and peaks, tending overall to flatten them and distort the grooves on the recto. If the paper is preserved in good condition, therefore, it is usually fairly easy to see (even without magnification) which side was printed last. Title-pages usually get more than their fair share of handling, but the Benton copy of the Jugge-and-Cawood title-page is in unusually good condition. Although I have not seen it in person, it seems clear from high-definition photographs (perhaps especially in the italic types of the imprint) that the contents list was printed first and the title-page second. And while the British Library title leaf is substantially more worn, it tends to confirm that rather than contradict it.

There can be little doubt that the title-page and almanack were printed by Jugge himself, rather than by any other member of his team. He had evidently acquired the woodcut border as part of the Whitchurch ornament stock, and it had been altered accordingly: Whitchurch's initials had been removed from the bottom corners and the arms of Queen Catherine Parr removed from the small shield between them.[A] Those alterations may possibly have been made by one of Kingston's employees, because it was Kingston who had first actually *used* the modified border when he printed the title-page of the ordinal that will be discussed in the next chapter. But it was undoubtedly Jugge who now owned the block, which would be used on all subsequent folio editions until he died. So after Kingston had

---

[A] The block had also acquired some parasites while in storage, as witness several wormholes not found in Edwardian impressions.

printed the contents list on the inner forme of cancel sheet ᵗᵗA1:12 for *both* 1559 first editions, Jugge perfected his copies with his own title-page and almanack.

In layout, line-division, and orthography, the 1552 list of contents most closely followed by Kingston is that of Whit.4: the edition that served as copy for those parts of the 1552 preliminaries that were reprinted by the Jugge team. There are, however, two important differences. The first is that, unlike any Whitchurch edition (but like Grafton's settings in Graf.5 and Graf.6), Kingston's text and numbering begin with 'An act for the vniformitye of Common prayer'. For the last few months of Edward's reign, the items hitherto numbered i–xxi (and still so numbered by Whitchurch) were numbered ii–xxii in the newest Grafton editions. It is unlikely that anyone was ever seriously inconvenienced by this discrepancy. But if the first setting of the 1559 Jugge list had followed Whit.4 in every respect, the difference between that and a Grafton list that included the Act might well have been considered grounds for cancellation.

In such a case, however, the extant Kingston setting would presumably have originated in the Grafton preliminaries, and only Jugge would have had to cancel his title sheet. But that hypothesis would fail to explain why Kingston followed Whitchurch for everything *except* the first item – and there is an even more important difference between the lists of 1552 and 1559. The final item in all the Edwardian lists was what is now called an ordinal, but no Elizabethan edition in any format would ever either list or include one.[A]

In 1552, the twenty-five lines of Edward's second Act of Uniformity that actually concerned the new prayer book twice specified that it was to be accompanied by an ordinal, and one was duly appended to each of the folio editions and listed as the final item in the contents. Elizabeth's much longer and more detailed Act included no such requirement, and neither mentioned the ordinal nor prescribed any revisions to it. As we shall see in the next chapter, each team of printers nevertheless printed an ordinal in the apparent belief that one was required. It could perhaps be suggested that they did so mistakenly, without authority, and only because the 1559 Act said nothing about removing it – but both extant ordinals include revisions that can only have come from the same source as the changes made (some with explicit parliamentary sanction and some without it) in

---

[A] The unique copy of the third edition and the Fisher copy of the fourth each has a copy of the 1559 'Jugge' ordinal bound after it. But the prescribed price for each of those prayer books is printed on its final page, so there are no valid grounds for contradicting the contents list and treating the ordinal as *part* of it.

the prayer book itself. Evidently, then, someone in authority instructed the printers to revise the ordinal – but as we shall see in the next chapter, there is also unequivocal evidence that the Privy Council did not want it treated as an integral and necessary part of public worship. It needed to exist, and needed to be revised, but it was not to be part of the book of *common* prayer.

The decision to detach the ordinal may have been made belatedly, although the failure of the Act to mention revising it could perhaps suggest otherwise. But both teams of printers seem to have assumed when they printed it that it was still essentially an appendix rather than a separate publication. And that was undoubtedly why their original contents lists had to be cancelled in order to remove it.

The 'Grafton' Title-page and Almanack

There are four features of the outer forme of sheet $^{\pi}$A1:12 in the Grafton edition that merit discussion: the 230-mm textura used for the first line each of the title ($^{\pi}$A1^r: see Plate 2) and the almanack ($^{\pi}$A12^v), the capitula that begin those two lines, Grafton's title-page border, and lines 7–13 of the title-page text.

The 230 textura, first used in England by Robert Wyer in 1531 (STC 1914), rapidly became as popular there as in Europe. By the late 1540s there were few London printing houses of any size that did not have at least a small supply, and it remained widely used for more than a century.[A] Grafton used it fairly frequently during the 1540s, but in 1550 he acquired a supply of the 270-mm fount I have called 'Bible Fraktur' (Figure 5*d–e*). He seems to have become very fond of it, not only as a large fount for the opening lines of titles and headings, but also as a source of three-line or four-line drop capitals to use with much smaller founts in quartos and octavos. In his books of 1551 that I have seen, I have found only a single capital I of 230 textura, on page L6^r of STC 13646. In his quartos and octavos of 1552 there are no more than scattered occurrences,[B] and the only examples in folio are in the ordinals appended to his earliest editions of the new *Book of Common Prayer*. On Aa2^r in each of his first four editions the large textura is used for the heading 'The Preface', while there are three

---

[A] Described as measuring 220 mm by Isaac (*1501–35*, [173], figure 69a, etc.; *1535–58*, [18], figure 26, etc.) and Vervliet (*Printing Types*, 88–90), but more realistically as 230 mm by Dreyfus (*Type Specimen Facsimiles II*, 8, no. 6) and *Stationers and Printers* (1, 370, n.A).

[B] One in STC 14992.5 (E2^v), two in 25810 (P3^v, P4^v), five in 16057 (two on the title-page; one each in c8^r, e3^r, e4^r, e4^v), and seven in 2380a.5 (four appearances of an O, two of a T, and a single G).

drop capitals in Graf.1 (Cc5^r and Cc6^v) and two in the next three editions (Cc2^r). Otherwise, all the large type in those books is Bible Fraktur. In 1553 there are fewer examples still, and the drop capitals in the psalter appended to Grafton's quarto prayer book (16290) include only three textura O's (AA4^v, GG5^r, OO3^r).[A] I have been unable to determine the precise shares of Grafton and Nicholas Hill in their quarto bible (2092), so some or all of the four textura drop capitals and the first line of the 'Richarde Grafton' colophon may be Hill's. During Mary's reign Robert Caly printed no known folios with the Grafton materials, and the only 230 textura in any book attributed to him by STC is a T found four times in 7605.5 (B5^r, B8^r, C3^v, O6^v).[B] It is therefore hardly surprising to find that in the sheets of the 1559 *Book of Common Prayer* and the ordinal that Grafton printed before the preliminaries, the 230 textura is limited to a single G, used as a drop capital on K1^v, K6^v, L5^v, and L6^r.

Turning now to capitula: as discussed in Chapter 1 (p. 15, n.A) the modern paragraph mark (¶) resembles a mirror-reversed capital P, but with the bowl filled in and the stem represented by a pair of parallel lines. Pilcrows of that design certainly existed in the sixteenth century, but there were also older and larger versions resembling only the top of that symbol: a filled-in capital C for *Capitulum* or Chapter (see Plates 2–6 and Figures 3, 5b–c, 11, 15–16, 18, and 19). In the sheets that Grafton printed before the preliminaries there appear to be only five capitula used with the Bible Fraktur, each of them individually recognizable.[C] None of them precisely matches the design usually found with the 230 textura, but the one I have numbered 2 is apparently cast on a body slightly smaller than the Fraktur, because when followed by a T it does not always align with the same part of that letter. On D2^r and N3^r it sits at least a millimetre lower than it does on ^{π}A5^r and the second setting of X1^r, so it could well be on a 230 body. At least no. 1 and probably also no. 5 are woodcuts, but even if either or both of nos. 3 and 4 are castings, it seems unlikely that either is original to the Fraktur fount itself.

The capitula on the title-page and in the heading of the almanack, however, are cast types of the design usually found with the 230 textura.

[A] Or perhaps more realistically, three appearances of a single O.
[B] But the STC attribution of that book is very far from certain, and anyway acknowledges that 'the 82 mm. roman used for the . . . Latin was app. borrowed or otherwise acquired from J. Kingston and H. Sutton' (I, 343).
[C] In order of appearance in the main text, ordinal, and preliminary sheets ^{π}A2–11: no. 1 appears on A1^r, E5^r, I6^v, M6^r, Aa3^r; no.2 on D2^r, F3^r, K4^r, N3^r, T3^v, V6^r, X1^r (2nd setting), Bb2^r, ^{π}A5^r; no. 3 on G1^r, I3^v, P2^r, Q2^r, T1^v; no. 4 on H3^v, I1^r, I1^v, T1^r, V2^v, X4^v, Aa1^r, Aa2^v, ^{π}A6^v; no. 5 on M6^v, X1^r (1st setting), X3^v, Aa2^r, Aa6^v.

In both, if we mentally erase the black fill and the vertical line, the circumference and serifs together form a capital letter which (because the tip of the lower serif bends rather abruptly upwards) more resembles a G than a C.

On a rather larger scale, the title-page border (McK & F 67) was cut for Grafton in 1548 for use on Hall's Chronicle (*The Vnion of ... Lancastre & Yorke*, STC 12721), and he used it quite frequently until 1553 when the Marian regime imposed Robert Caly on the business as manager. Caly printed no known books in folio, and during his tenure the border was lent to at least three other printers. Richard Tottell, who would marry Grafton's daughter Joan in January 1558, used it in 1555 (STC 9922) and 1556 (9582), and on a book whose date is extremely uncertain and may be several years later than STC's hesitant '[1557?]' (9424). Once in late 1553 and again in 1557 it was used in books associated with Grafton's former apprentice John Kingston. The 1557 example was Guevara's *Diall of Princes* (12427), with a title-page claiming it as '*Imprinted at London by Iohn Waylande*' who by then no longer had access to Edward Whitchurch's presses or types. As STC notes, it was actually printed for Wayland by Thomas Marshe – but three of the initials used in it were borrowed by Marshe from Kingston.[A] The opportunity to borrow the border possibly arose when Marshe shared the printing of Kingston's Latin missal (16219), as discussed in Chapter 5 (p. 78).

A few years earlier, the same border was used on James Peele's accountancy manual, *How to Kepe a Perfecte Reconyng* (STC 19547), which claims to have been '*Imprinted at London, by Richard Grafton, printer to the kinges Maiestie*' and is dated '1553'. In 1932 McKerrow and Ferguson suggested that 'only the title and verso were printed by Grafton, the remainder by J. Kingston and H. Sutton' (McK & F, p. 71), and STC accepted that guess. But the types used throughout the book match those of the same sizes on both sides of the title leaf, the italic of the imprint is certainly not Grafton's, and both the title and the list of contents begin in 230 textura rather than Bible Fraktur. The book is explicitly identified as a New-Year's gift to the dedicatee. If the occasion was 1 January 1553 (when Grafton was still King's Printer),[B] then it must have been printed for him by Nicholas Hill. But the title-page border is in a state later than that of Grafton's last

---

[A] Specifically, the T used on A1^r, L6^v, and O3^r; the O on e3^r, and the W on v2^v and C6^v.
[B] Given the widespread fallacies, I should note (a) that 'New Style' calculation of leap years was still thirty years in the future, but (b) that while legal-year dating (as distinct from calendar-year dating) considered the 'Year of Grace' to begin on 25 March, no day except 1 January was ever called or celebrated as 'New Year's Day'.

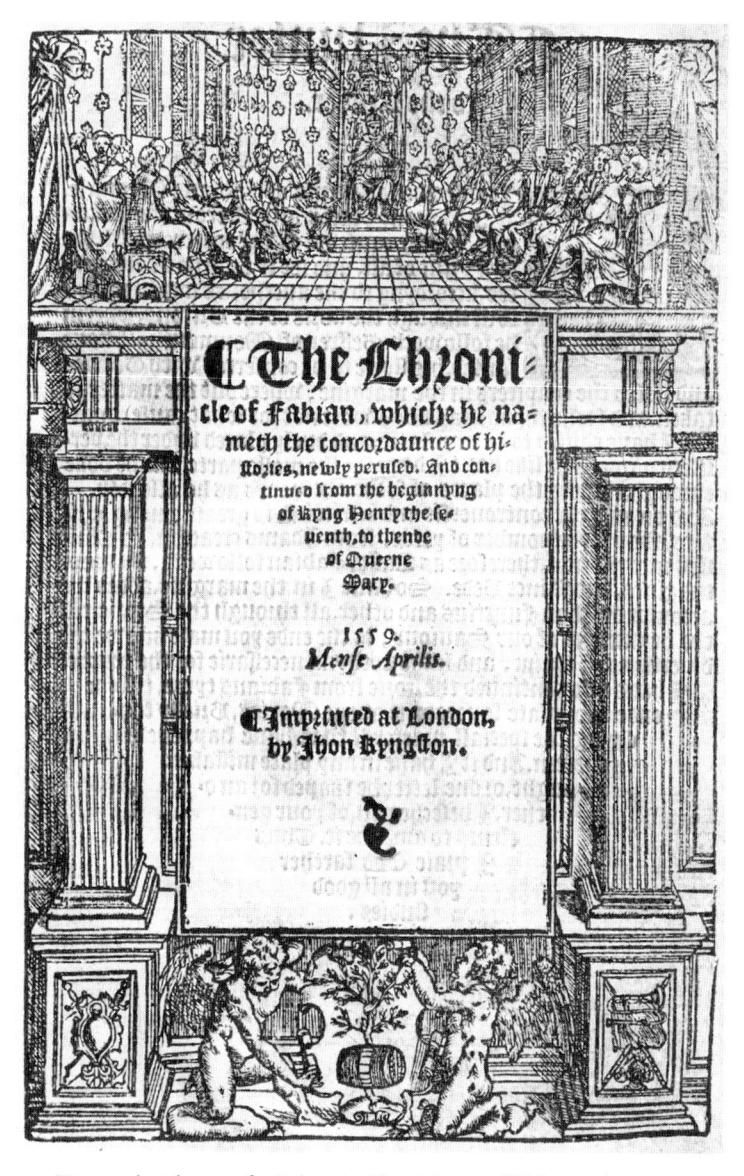

Figure 11 Kingston's title-page for Fabyan's *Chronicle*, 1559 (STC 10663).
(Lambeth Palace Library, [ZZ] 1559.2, A1ʳ.)

'1552' prayer book (Graf.6), which was almost certainly printed in early 1553. So the New Year must have been 1554 (when Hill's materials had passed to Kingston and Sutton), and the imprint is deliberately misleading.

Neither the 1559 Act of Uniformity in the prayer-book preliminaries nor the Oath of Sovereignty in the ordinal could have been printed before the royal assent was given to the pertinent acts on 8 May. A few days earlier, John Kingston finished printing the first issue of his 1559 edition of *The Chronicle of Fabian* (STC 10663), which is dated April 1559 in both the colophon and the title-page (Figure 11). Not only does the title use Grafton's border, but the first line is set in 230 textura and begins with what appears to be the same dented capitulum that precedes the 230 textura headings of Kingston's calendar pages for January, February, May, July (see Plate 4), September, and October.

It therefore seems to be the case that in addition to the calendar quire and the presumed cancel sheet ᵀA4:9, John Kingston also printed both sides of the 'Grafton' title sheet itself. Setting aside ᵀA4:9, what the other four Kingston sheets have in common is that they all contain fairly complex tables – and are also the only sheets in the book printed in both red and black. I think it safe to conclude that during five years of substantially lowered production under the anti-Protestant management of Robert Caly, Grafton's printing house had probably lost many of its most skilled employees. Meanwhile Kingston (initially in partnership with Henry Sutton) had printed more than a few Catholic liturgies in two colours, and was evidently willing to lend a hand to his former master.[A]

The text of the title-page itself also calls for comment. Throughout their 1552 editions, both Grafton and Whitchurch began the book's title in essentially the same way. In each case the first line began with an ornament printed in black: a capitulum for Grafton but a pair of Aldine leaves for Whitchurch (Figures 3 and 4). The first line of text was in Bible Fraktur printed in red; the next five in great primer textura, with alternating lines in black and red, and the text divided as follows: 'The Boke of | common praier, and ad= | ministration of the | Sacramentes, | and other | rites'. Apart from the ornaments, the only differences were that Whitchurch spelled 'prayer' with a 'y' and that Grafton capitalized 'Rites' in his last edition

---

[A] In his title-page for the Jugge-and-Cawood ordinal Kingston was apparently the first printer after 1556 to use Whitchurch's woodcut border with the initials removed, so it could reasonably be suspected that it was also Kingston who printed the Jugge-and-Cawood title-page on the other side of his contents list. But while the almanack in the same forme as Kingston's 'Grafton' title-page is clearly modelled on Jugge's (albeit rather narrower, and with the widths of columns 2 and 3 more precisely fitting their contents), they are not the work of the same printer.

(Graf.6). In 1559 both Kingston and Jugge divided those lines at the same points, both printing 'praier' and 'rites', and both using a capitulum and 230 textura in the first line. The only material difference was that Jugge, whose border had a wider compartment for the text, spelled 'Booke' with two o's (Plates 2 and 3). The remainder of the title, however, was divided differently in 1552, with Grafton using five lines ('and Cere= | monies in the | Churche | of | Englande.') but Whitchurch only three ('and Ceremonies in | the Churche of | Englande.'). In 1559 both Jugge and Kingston followed the Whitchurch layout – and since it seems likely that Kingston became a member of Jugge's team before also assisting Grafton, he may well have used the Jugge title-page as copy for much of the one he provided for Grafton. That impression is reinforced by the imprints and privilege statements. Both 1559 imprints begin with '*Londini, in officina*' in black, and continue in red. Jugge prints '*Richardi | Iugge, & Iohannis | Cawode.*' in red except for the black ampersand, while Kingston has only the single name '*Ri= | chardi Grafton*' to print in red. And on both title-pages the privilege statement is rendered in black roman as 'Cum priuilegio Regie | Maiestatis.' – a formula introduced in 1554 by the Queen's Printer John Cawood (STC 7862), and hitherto used only by him and the Queen's Typographer in Latin, Greek, and Hebrew, Reyner Wolfe.

On the prayer books of 1552 each printer had identified himself in two lines, dividing his Christian name: '*Londini, in officina Ri- | chardi Graftoni:*' and '¶ *Londini, in officina Edo= | vardi Whytchurche.*' (with later variations '*Ed= | vvardi Whytchurche*', '*Edo= | vardi Whitchurche*', and '*Edo= | vard Wihitchurche*'). Grafton, however, was able to add a third line unavailable to Whitchurch, identifying himself as '*Regij Impressoris.*' All three of Grafton's lines were in black; Whitchurch printed his capitulum and the second line in red. For what little the evidence may be worth, in this respect too, Kingston's 1559 'Grafton' imprint seems more in the Whitchurch tradition. But the use of only black for the privilege claim and date is admittedly more reminiscent of Grafton in 1552 than Whitchurch, who used to start with a red capitulum, capitalize both 'ImPri=' (corrected to 'Impri=' in Whit.5) and 'Solum', and use red for the second line.

If I am right in assuming that both 1559 title sheets are cancels, reprinted in order to remove the ordinal from the contents list, it is possible that the pre-cancellation Grafton version had been printed in his house by his own workmen. As we shall see in the next chapter, the compositor who set the ordinal's colophon in 1559 followed the wording of 1552 and changed only the date, thus inaccurately describing Grafton as if he were still the royal printer with an exclusive privilege. Had a similar mistake been made on the title-page it could have provided an additional motive for cancellation.

Summary

My need to explain each of the many separate deductions above has probably made it difficult to see the overall picture, so it will be useful to attempt a short summary of the printing of the preliminaries. What almost certainly happened first was that Kingston and Wolfe each began printing a calendar quire at approximately the same time and presumably also finished at about the same time.

Once the size of the main preliminary quire had been decided, Wolfe proceeded to reprint the Preface and 'On Ceremonies' on the two innermost sheets ($^{\pi}$A5–8) for the Jugge team while Grafton did the same for his own edition, each reprinting what had been $^{\pi}$A3–6 of the 1552 edition he was using as copy (Whit.4 and Graf.6 respectively). Meanwhile Kingston started work on the Act of Uniformity and the tables of proper lessons and psalms ($^{\pi}$A2^{r}–4^{v} and 9^{r}–11^{v}) for the Jugge team. When Grafton finished the innermost sheets of his quire he reprinted each of Kingston's sheets as it became available. The precise order of the last few events is impossible to determine, but it almost certainly included the setting and printing of each title sheet, one by Jugge for his own edition and one for Grafton's by either himself or John Kingston.

At this point a copy of one or other of the preliminary quires was shown to someone in authority, who objected to the presence of the ordinal in the list of contents. Something problematic was also found at about this time in at least one page of sheet $^{\pi}$A4:9 (most probably $^{\pi}$A9^{v}, the first page of the table of proper lessons), though whether or not it was found on the same reading or by the same person is beyond guessing. Kingston was therefore asked to reprint enough copies of both that sheet and the contents list to serve both editions. Jugge then took his share of the new contents sheets and reprinted his two-colour title forme on the clean side while Kingston (perhaps influenced by the wording of Jugge's first setting) either reimposed or reset and reprinted the Grafton version.

The most important consequence of this series of events is that neither edition could have been put on sale in its present form before its title-page had been printed on the other side of Kingston's contents list. Neither edition can realistically be called the 'second': they are simultaneous firsts.

A rather less significant conclusion is that if sheets $^{\pi}$A1:12 and $^{\pi}$A4:9 in each of the first two editions are cancels, their first quires do not collate

$^{\pi}A^{12}$ but $^{\pi}A^{12}(\pm{}^{\pi}A1,4:9,12)$. In the absence of evidence that any of Grafton's own 1559 sheets are cancels, neither the 1552 leftovers in specific copies nor the two settings of R3:4 and X1:8 need to be reflected in the formula for the main text, so the complete formula for that edition reads:

2°: $^{\pi}A^{12}(\pm{}^{\pi}A1,4:9,12)$ b^6, A–V^6 X^8.

That of the Jugge-and-Cawood edition, however, becomes:

2°: $^{\pi}A^{12}(\pm{}^{\pi}A1,4:9,12)$ $^{\pi}B^6$, A^8($\pm$A1) B^8 C^8($\pm$C2:7) D–K^8 L^{10} M^8 N^8($\pm$N3) O–P^{10}.

CHAPTER 7

The Orphaned Ordinal

History and Name

In sixteenth-century England, the book to be discussed in this chapter was never called an *ordinal*, either formally or casually. The only book so called in and before Tudor times was a collection of the (Latin) rubrics from the Catholic breviary, briefly indicating the proper mass and office for each day of the liturgical year. Ordinals were therefore included by name among the Catholic service books that in 1552 were 'clerelye and utterlye abollished extinguished and forbidden for ever to be used or kepte in this Realme', and were therefore 'to be openlye brent or otherwayes defaced and destroyed'.[A]

What the word means today in English-speaking churches (and elsewhere in this study) is a handbook setting out the forms of service used when deacons, priests, bishops, and archbishops are ordained. And here we encounter another lexical difficulty, because although the verb *to ordain* and the noun *ordination* were known and sometimes used in their present ecclesiastical senses both in and after the fifteenth century, neither word appears anywhere in the Edwardian ordinal of 1550. That book and its immediate descendants instead use only *to order* and *ordering*. The first recorded reference to this handbook as an ordinal dates from 1658,[B] and that is what it has since been called for more than three and a half centuries. To insist today on using only its original title (in modern spelling, *The Form and Manner of Making and Consecrating of Archbishops, Bishops, Priests, and Deacons*) would be beyond perverse.

[A] 3 & 4 Edw. VI, c. 10 (*Statutes*, IV, i, 110–11).
[B] *OED*, ordinal, *n.*¹, 1b. The recently added quotation from '>1395', translated from Latin *ordinalia siue rubrice*, is evidently misplaced, and clearly refers to ordinals of the pre-Reformation kind (sense 1a rather than 1b).

After the 1549 prayer book was published, several months passed before the need for a non-Catholic ordination ritual seems to have registered. It was not until 8 January 1550, more than two-thirds of the way through Edward's third Parliament, that a bill 'touching the Form and Ordering of Ecclesiastical Ministers of the Church' was introduced in the Lords and read for the first time. What became of that version is unrecorded, but it must have been either extensively revised or completely replaced by the 23rd, when a new bill 'for the ordering of Ecclesiastical Ministers' was first read. After a second reading on the 24th and a third on the morning of the 25th the bill was passed, but with five of the fourteen bishops present dissenting.[A] Later that day it was received by the Commons and read twice, followed on the 28th by a third reading and on the 29th by a highly unusual fourth – but still without being passed. On the 30th, presumably after even more changes, the process started again with both a first and a second reading, and after yet a third reading later that day it was finally passed and sent back up to the Lords. On the morning of the 31st the Lords read it once; in the afternoon they read it a second and third time and finally passed it – though with the same five bishops still dissenting.[B] Exactly why this short act, which occupies only nine and a half lines in the original manuscript,[C] took so much longer to pass than had the 1549 Act of Uniformity itself can only be conjectured. But one of the sticking points may well have been the explicitly anti-papal oath of supremacy required of all those ordained. Bishop Heath's subsequent refusal to swear that oath would cost him his bishopric in 1551.[D]

The act received the royal assent on 1 February, and required the new form of ordination to be devised 'by six Prelates and six other men of this Realme learned in godes lawe by the Kinges Maiestie to be appointed and assigned ... and sett forthe vnder the greate Seale' by 1 April.[E]

[A] PArch, HL/PO/JO/1/2, pp. 173, 186–8 (*LJ*, 1, 376–7, 383–4). Those dissenting were Cuthbert Tunstall (Durham), Nicholas Heath (Worcester), Robert Aldrich (Carlisle), George Day (Chichester), and Thomas Thirlby (Westminster).
[B] PArch, HC/CL/JO/1/1, fols. 30ᵛ–31ᵛ; HL/PO/JO/1/2, pp. 193–4 (*CJ*, 1, 15–16; *LJ*, 1, 386–7).
[C] PArch, HL/PO/PU/1/1549/3&4E6n12.
[D] Henry VIII and Elizabeth, in their respective Acts of Supremacy, each included an oath of allegiance that had to be sworn by anyone appointed to either public or ecclesiastical office. No comparable act was passed by any of Edward's parliaments, so it is not always realized that in his reign, too, a similar oath was required of all those ordained in his Church. (It does not, however, seem to have been required for any secular office.)
[E] PArch, HL/PO/PU/1/1549/3&4E6n12, lines 7–8 (*Statutes*, IV, i, 112). The seeming hurry may be connected with plans to transfer Bishops Thomas Thirlby from Westminster to Norwich and Nicholas Ridley from Rochester to London in April, and to nominate John Ponet for Rochester and John Hooper for Gloucester in June and July.

On Sunday, 2 February, the Privy Council recorded that 'The Busshop and learned whose names be vnder written' were appointed accordingly – but no names were ever actually under written.[A] Whenever it was that Grafton printed the new book in quarto, he dated its colophon March 1549, and it is usually assumed that this is a legal-year date meaning early March 1550. But it should be remembered that all Grafton's '1549' editions of the prayer book also display that same date on their title-pages, so it is possible that the intention was simply to associate the ordinal with the rest of the liturgy.

In 1552, however, the new Act of Uniformity explicitly and repeatedly announced that the King and Parliament, having perused, explained, and perfected the prayer book itself, have added to it

> a fourme and manner of making and consecrating Archebisshoppes Busshoppes preistes and Deacons to be of Lyke force aucthoritie and vallewe as the same Lyke foresaide booke . . . and to be accepted received used and estemed in Lyke sorte and manner.[B]

Accordingly, every folio edition of the 1552 *Book of Common Prayer* was therefore printed with an appended ordinal.

When the Privy Council eventually decided on the maximum retail prices that could be charged for the prayer book, they seemed to hold out the possibility of paying less for a copy with no ordinal. First they set the limits for a complete unbound copy at 2*s*. 6*d*. (30 pence), for a softbound copy 'in parchement or forell' at 3*s*. 4*d*. (40 pence), and for a hardbound copy (whether covered in leather or paper, with or without clasps) at 4*s*. (48 pence). Having established that, the note continues: 'And at the next impression, the imprinter leauyng out the [ordinal], shal sel thesaid booke' unbound at 2*s*. (24 pence), softbound at 2*s*. 8*d*. (32 pence), or hardbound at 3*s*. 4*d*. (40 pence).[C] But whether or not deliberately, the printers themselves turned this into a catch-22 by printing it on the final leaf of the ordinal itself. The only place where a prospective buyer could find that information was in a copy *with* an ordinal, where it clearly states that the offer applies only to 'the nexte impression' as distinct from the one

---

[A] TNA: PRO, PC 2/3, 72 (*APC*, ii, 379).
[B] PArch, HL/PO/PU/1/1551/5&6E6n1, lines 35–8 (*Statutes*, iv, i, 130).
[C] Quoted from the verso of what STC calls 'Errata 4' (ii, 92), which is perhaps an integral part of STC 16285.5 (Graf.2b). Neither printer's first edition includes the price note, and I have been unable to confirm that it first appeared at the end of the second edition of either ordinal.

in hand. I cannot believe that many copies were ever actually sold without the ordinal.[A]

One of the many differences between the Catholic church and the reformed churches of the sixteenth century concerned the distance between the clergy and the laity: whether or not the priesthood was, or should be considered, uniquely qualified to understand the scriptures and the mysteries of theology, or whether all members of the congregation could or should have access to God's word and laws in their own language. To apply the modern political sense of words such as *democracy* or *transparency* to the ideals and motives of the Edwardian Reformation is hopelessly anachronistic, but not entirely irrelevant. One difference between the reigns of Henry VIII and of his son is neatly illustrated by their injunctions concerning religion. Henry's first injunctions of 1536–37 are described as 'gyven by thauctoritie of the kynges highnes to the clergie of this his realme', while those of 1538 are more simply headed 'for the clerge', and address them in the second person: 'Fyrst that ye shall truely obserue ...', 'Item that ye shall prouyde ...', etc. And perhaps because the clergy amounted to only a fraction of the literate population, each set of injunctions is known from only two surviving editions.[B] In 1547, however, the Edwardian injunctions were explicitly described as 'geuen by the Kynges Maiestie, aswell to the Clergie *as to the Laitie* of this Realme' (my italics), and went through at least eight editions.[C]

It therefore seems perfectly in character for the Edwardian authorities to make the rituals of ordination, at all levels from deacon to archbishop, as widely accessible to any interested reader as the liturgy itself. In little more than a year at least twelve folio editions of the prayer book were printed and sold with the ordinal appended, which probably means between twelve and eighteen thousand copies. Under Elizabeth, however, the ordinal printed by Grafton as if part of his 1559 prayer book may perhaps have been officially suppressed, and the one printed by the Jugge team as if part of their edition was apparently sold only as a separate item. The next known editions were in 1576 (though with the title-page date of 1559 misleadingly reprinted), 1596, 1607, 1618, and 1627 – let us say the equivalent of six post-Edwardian editions in sixty-nine years. In 1552–53 the supply must have

---

[A] The only extant copy of John Oswen's STC 16287 (if the 22 leaves in a made-up Whit.2 at the Bodleian are disqualified as 'a copy'), which lacks at least quire N[8], has no ordinal. It does, however, have an unsigned leaf bound after S6 with Oswen's colophon, two errata, and the full text of 'The prices of this boke'. That does not quite prove that he printed the whole ordinal – but it is strongly suggestive, and the copy of Whit.2 from which he worked must have included one.
[B] STC 10084.7–85 (1536–7); 10086–7 (1538).   [C] STC 10087.5–93.7.

hugely exceeded the demand, but the Edwardian authorities evidently wanted the congregation to have the opportunity to become familiar with the process of ordination. The more conservative Elizabethan church, however, either declined to encourage a curiosity that had anyway proved to be limited, or perhaps deliberately discouraged it.

Because only five copies of the first Jugge-and-Cawood edition of the prayer book are known to have survived, the simple fact that none has an ordinal bound with it is not quite enough to prove that the two were not issued together. But while the original binding of the British Library copy has been rebacked in modern times, the boards and their paste-downs are original. And since both the title-page and the front paste-down were signed by the original owner – Sir Nicholas Bacon (see Plate 3), Keeper of the Great Seal and leader of the Privy Council – it seems safe to take the absence of an ordinal (both from that copy and from all 1559 contents lists) as reflecting the official view.

The Corpus Christi Copy

The only extant copy of Grafton's 1559 ordinal is bound as if part of the uniquely important copy of his prayer book in the library of Corpus Christi College, Oxford (shelfmark Phi.F.3.7). As explained in Chapter 2, that copy was almost certainly one of the first to be collated and assembled (above, p. 61), and it was delivered to the Privy Council to help them with a material deliberation. When their decision had been made and recorded on a convenient blank page (signature R6^v), the councillors endorsed it by subscribing their signatures in descending order of Council precedence, as can be seen in Figure 12. The signatures are those of Sir Nicholas Bacon C[ustos] S[igillarum], Francis Russell (earl of Bedford), William Herbert (earl of Pembroke), Edward Fiennes de Clinton (Lord Admiral), William Howard (Lord Howard of Effingham, Lord Chamberlain), Sir Thomas Parry, Sir Francis Knollys, Sir William Cecil, and Sir Ambrose Cave.

In her 2016 article, Cyndia Clegg uses this page to support her belief that the Grafton edition was the first of the 1559 folios to be printed, suggesting that it was inspected by the Council before Parliament assembled on 23 January (115–21). After it had been approved, one reason why the passage through Parliament of the Acts of Supremacy and Uniformity was so lengthy and complex was that both houses had somehow to be forced to accept the already-printed revisions exactly as they stood. This is simply not credible.

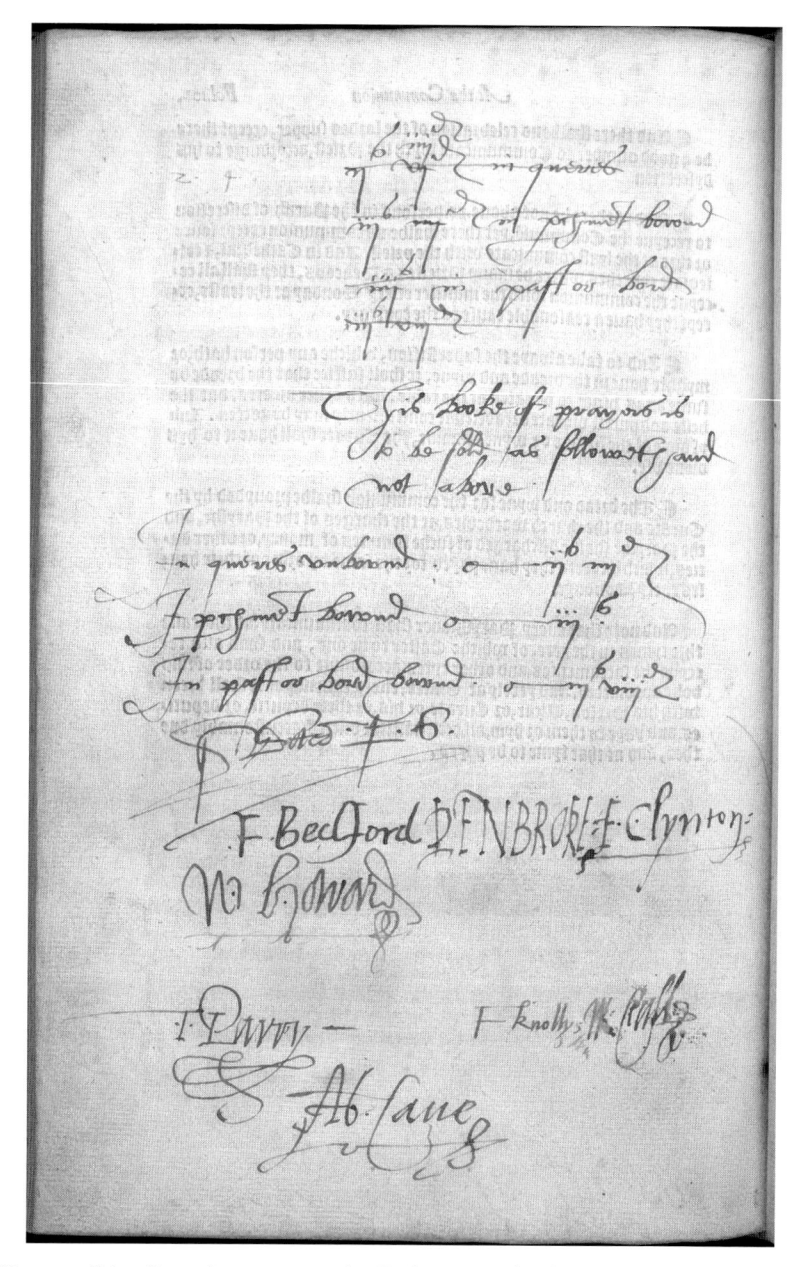

Figure 12 Privy Council signatures in the Grafton prayer book.
(Corpus Christi College, Oxford, Phi.F.3.7, R6^v.)

Because a mission to France caused Lord Chamberlain Howard to be absent from 21 January to 14 April inclusive, Clegg seeks a date before his absence when the attendance records match the signatures – but no such date exists. Her own favoured compromise is 19 January, although Sir John Mason was also present (but might have declined to sign) and Knollys was absent (but might have signed outside the formal attendance period). Failing that, she is willing to accept the end of 1558 from 24 to 29 December inclusive, when all the signatories were present (although so were between one and six others who did not sign). But Clegg's reading of the evidence is shaped by her apparent belief that the signatures represent some kind of formal conciliar approval of the book's contents – and they do not.

After the Council had finished with it, the volume in question was somehow acquired by Richard Cobbe, a fellow of Corpus Christi whose bequests to the college when he died in 1597 included his books. At the time this prayer book was unbound (though presumably at least stitched, since it was described as a 'book'), so in 1604 the library spent twenty pence 'for binding an olde comūnion book geven by Mr Cobbe'.[A] The final leaf of the ordinal, Cc6, is missing, and the staining and annotations on Cc5^v make it obvious that Cc6 was lost some considerable time before the volume was bound. What is now the last page contains the colophon, which is notable because the compositor has reproduced it almost literatim from the last 1552 edition, apart from omitting 'Mense Augusti.' from the date and changing the final figure of the year from 2 to 9. The result reads as follows: '*RICHARDVS GRAF-* | *tonus, Typographus Regius* | *excudebat.* | *Anno Domini*, 1559. | Cum Priuilegio ad Imprimen- | dum solum.' (Figure 13).

It is clear that Grafton printed the booklet with the permission and approval of at least the Privy Council, or he would not have been given access to the revisions. Elizabeth herself may perhaps have added her own agreement, although I see no obvious reason why she would not have left such details to her advisers. But by no stretch of the imagination could Grafton have been given permission to call himself 'Typographus Regius'. Despite what Clegg thinks that 'Cum Priuilegio' might imply,[B] a printing privilege at this date was a commercial monopoly, and Grafton could not possibly have been given a monopoly of a book that belonged to the office

---

[A] Corpus Christi College Archives, C/1/1/7, 61^r.
[B] It is untrue that 'all books printed by the royal printer were printed with privilege', or even that all 'statutes and statute books, acts of parliament, [and] proclamations ... bore some form of the imprint *cum privilegio*' (Clegg, 'The 1559 Books of Common Prayer', 118).

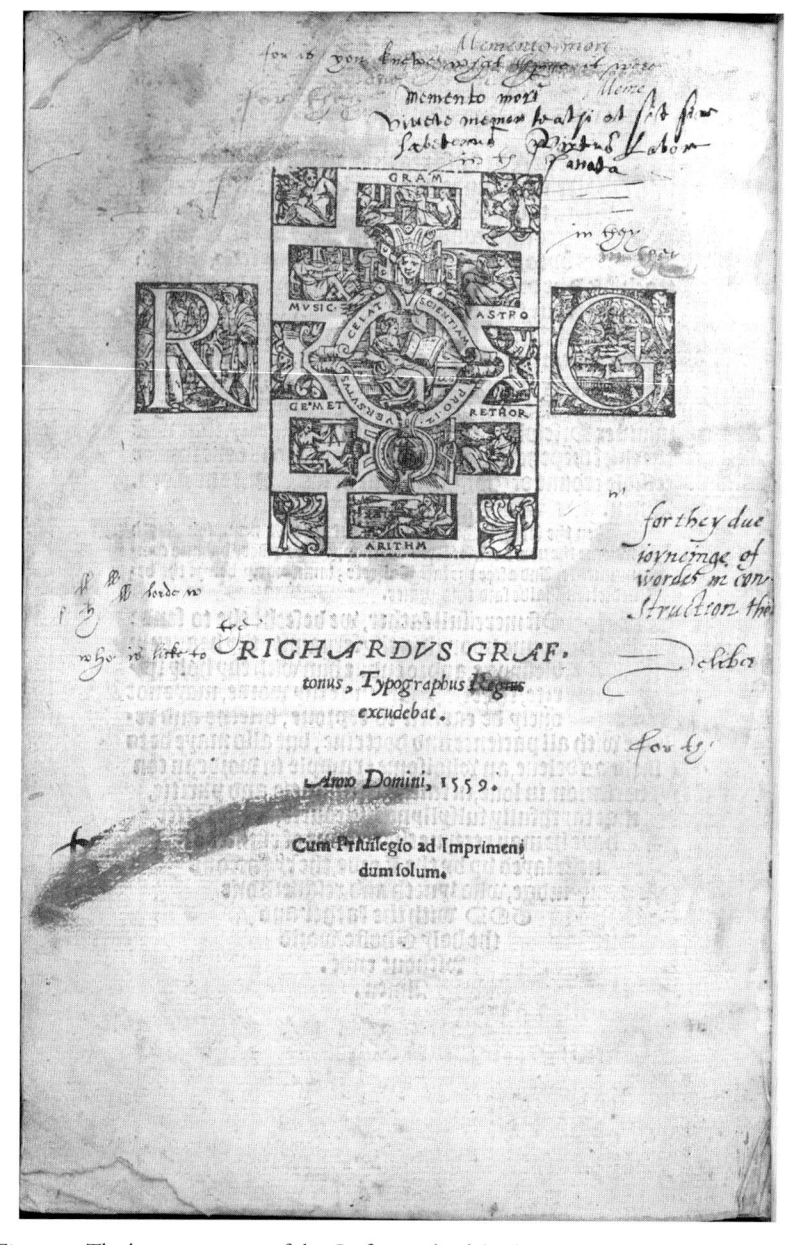

Figure 13 The last extant page of the Grafton ordinal (with colophon).
(Corpus Christi College, Oxford, Phi.F.3.7, Cc5[v].)

of the real Typographi Regii. Katharine F. Pantzer suggested that the Grafton edition 'represents an unsuccessful attempt ... to gain a share in the Queen's Printing Office',[A] but I find it difficult to see that colophon as Grafton's own gesture of pointless bravado. To my mind it is more likely to be an example of a compositor following copy a little too slavishly and without full attention.

But whichever explanation is closer to the truth, it is reasonable to guess that whoever set the recto of the now-missing final leaf would likewise have reprinted what stood on Cc6^r of the 1552 edition he was using as copy: a statement that the book was truly and diligently imprinted, followed by the paragraph on prices that I have already discussed. In 1559, what was first written on blank page R6^v of the Corpus Christi copy was what had been printed on page Cc6^r of the compositor's copy: the maximum permitted retail prices for complete copies of the Edwardian book (those including the ordinal): 'ij^s vj^d in queres | iiij^s iiij^d in p*a*rchme*n*t bownd | iiij^s in past or bord'. What the penman of 1559 did next – presumably after some discussion by those present – was to strike out 'vj^d' in line 1 and write 'iiij^d' above it,[B] to delete 'iiij^d' in line 2 without replacing it, and to delete 'iiij^s' in line 3 and write 'iij^s viij^d' below it. Probably after another interval while the wording was discussed, the writer then copied out the revised prices more formally with an introductory explanation, crossed out the working notes, and handed the book to the councillors so they could authorize it with their signatures.

This booke of prayers is
to be sold as followeth and
not above

In queres vnbovnd ———— ij^s iiij^d
I p*a*rchme*n*t bownd ———— iij^s
In past or bord bownd ———— iij^s viij^d

The Corpus Christi volume itself could hardly have been used as copy by John Kingston when he printed those words and prices above Jugge's device on the final page of the third edition (Figure 14), so the statement

---

[A] See the note to entry 16291 (STC, II, 93). It seems obvious, however, that the suggestion was inspired by the hypothesis put forward by John R. Hetherington that Pantzer goes on to outline. While a false claim to be the Queen's Printer is an offence that could have been punished by making Grafton print paste-on cancel colophons (or even reprint the whole sheet Cc2:5), the real Queen's Printers could have suppressed it themselves by declining to market it once Grafton had abandoned the book trade (for which see below, pp. 145–6).

[B] Whether he wrote the faint '2. 4.' to the left of that line before or after altering it is indeterminable.

This boke of prayers is to be solde as foloweth, and not aboue.

In Queers vnbounde. ii.s.iiii.d.
In Parchement bounde. iii.s.
In Paste, or Borde bounde. iii.s.viii.d.

Figure 14 Prices as printed in the second Jugge-and-Cawood edition.
(York Minster Library, XI.F.19(1), P10ᵛ.)

must then have been written out at least one more time (with the second 'In' given its missing 'n') to serve as printer's copy. It was far too late to add it to either of the first two editions, which were already complete.

There are two reasons why that page is of historical importance. For the first we need to consider the implications of the actual sums. In 1549, when the first edition of the first Edwardian prayer book contained ninety-three sheets, the price set for unbound copies was 2*s*. (24 pence), or three and seven-eighths sheets for a penny. When the size of the next editions rose to ninety-five sheets, the price went up to 2*s. 2d.* (26 pence), or approximately three and two-thirds sheets for a penny. In 1552, when the first editions that included the ordinal contained either ninety (Grafton) or ninety-two sheets (Whitchurch), the price unbound was 2*s*. 6*d*. (30 pence), or only 2*s*. if a copy without an ordinal could be found. Thanks to the continued Edwardian inflation, a penny would now buy only three sheets (or without the ordinal, three and one-third).

The Marian regime had failed to halt inflation, so if the Elizabethan book had included an ordinal the prices should have risen rather than falling. The new price of 2*s*. 4*d*., then, must presumably have been for a copy *without* an ordinal (as the contents list implies). At twenty-eight pence for Grafton's seventy-three sheets or Jugge's seventy-two, the number of sheets a penny would buy in 1559 had dropped to approximately two and three-fifths – while the few who wanted an ordinal would have to pay whatever the booksellers chose to ask for it. So what we can deduce from the Council's annotations is that the ordinal's absence from the list of contents was no accident, but official policy.

The second significant fact is that what Grafton sent or took to the Council was a book – probably not actually bound, but certainly collated and at least stitched. The presence in it of Kingston's title-page with the revised list of contents on the verso shows that the decision to omit the ordinal had already been taken, so perhaps Grafton included his ordinal in the expectation or hope that it too might be given an official price, albeit a separate one.[A] But the whole book was evidently finished, and that fact eliminates all question of a date before either the Act of Uniformity (reprinted in the preliminaries from Kingston's 'Jugge-and-Cawood' setting) or the Act of Supremacy (from which the oath on page Aa6^v of the ordinal is quoted verbatim). Both Acts had been passed by Parliament at the end of April and had received the royal assent on 8 May 1559. It is beyond possibility that the

---

[A] Or perhaps simply because it served as evidence of the Edwardian prices.

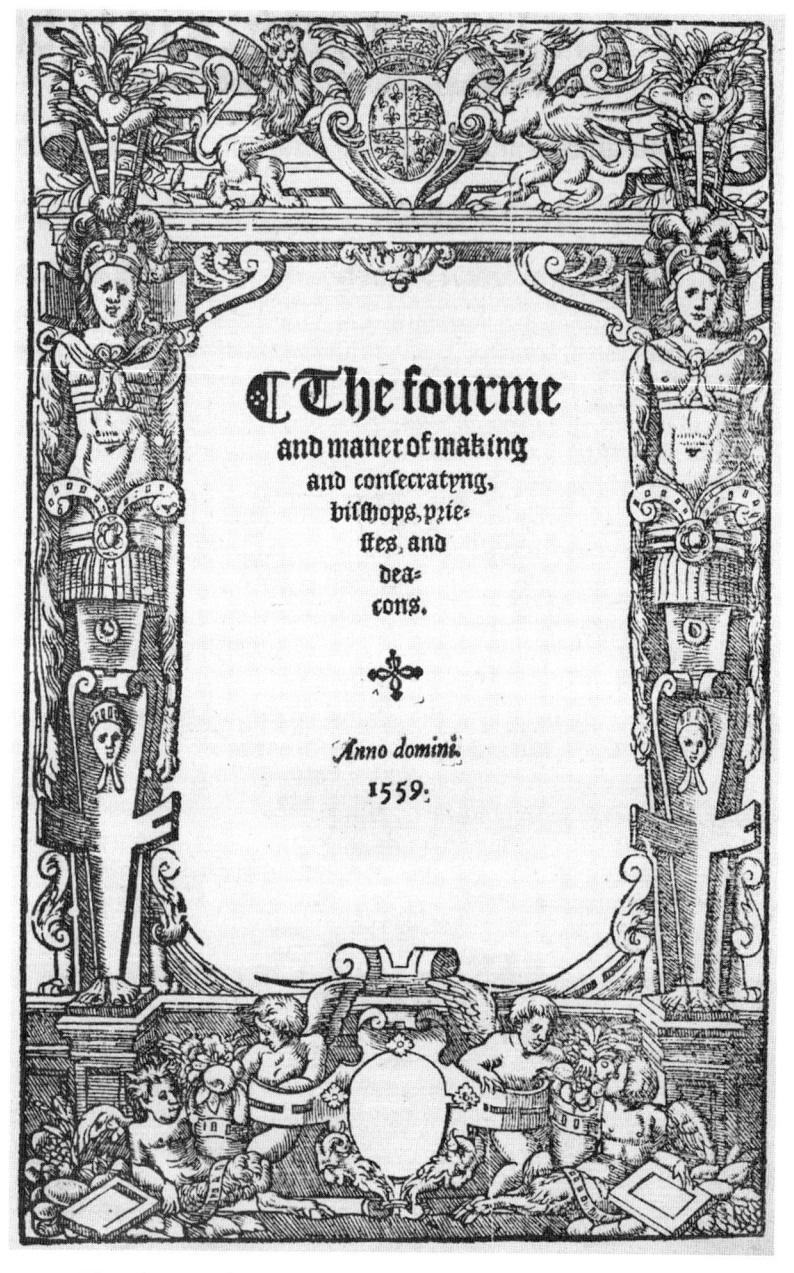

¶ The fourme
and maner of making
and consecratyng,
bisshops, prie-
stes, and
dea-
cons.

Anno domini
1559.

Figure 15 The title-page of the Jugge ordinal.
(Thomas Fisher Rare Book Library, stc 01220, AA1ʳ.)

precise wording of either could have been predicted in December 1558 or January 1559. The reason why Clegg could find no day on which the Council attendance precisely matched the signatures is that there is a gap in the Privy Council Registers between 12 May 1559 (four days after those Acts received the assent) and 28 May 1562. The Grafton prayer book, which could not possibly have been completed before late May, could not have been inspected by the Council before that three-year gap began.

The Printers of the Jugge Ordinal

The ordinal printed by the team responsible for the first Jugge-and-Cawood prayer book must have been produced towards the end of the project, because none of the printers who worked on it printed any part of the main text before quire N. It consists of only nine sheets – two quires, collating AA^8 BB^{10} – which one might imagine would have been given to only one or at most two printers.

In the first quire, Richard Jugge himself printed only the single sheet AA3:6 – perhaps because page AA6^v contained only the revised 'Othe of the Quenes Soueraintee', which as part of the Act of Supremacy 'belonged' to the Queen's Printer. John Kingston contributed the three other sheets of that quire, including the title leaf on which Whitchurch's old woodcut border (now host to some woodworm that moved in while it was in storage) made its first appearance since Jugge had acquired it and removed Whitchurch's initials (Figure 15).

In the second quire the three outer sheets were printed by Richard Payne, including page BB10^v which contained the larger of the two devices that had been cut for Jugge in 1552 before he became a printer. So although the ordinal displays what were now Jugge's two principal trademarks, one at each end, neither of them was actually printed there by Jugge himself. The innermost sheet (BB5:6) was printed by Kingston, and its later history will be discussed below. Meanwhile sheet BB4:7 was, for reasons both unknown and unguessable, printed by a newcomer to the increasingly crowded prayer-book field, William Copland.[A]

Two quires, four printing houses.

[A] Probably the son of the author, translator, and printer Robert Copland (*fl.* 1505–47), to whose printing materials he succeeded, Copland specialized in popular literature and (like Grafton's associate Robert Wyer) usually printed only in formats smaller than folio.

The Revisions

Like *The Book of Common Prayer* itself, the ordinal was revised in 1559, but the revisions were apparently neither considered nor authorized by Parliament. Superficially, it would seem that they probably should have been: like the 1549 prayer book, the 1550 ordinal was printed at Parliament's insistence, and in 1552 the two books had been formally joined together by comparable authority. But even the 1552 Act treats the ordinal as something distinct from and appended to the prayer book rather than actually part of it. So when the 1559 Act identifies the book that is to be revived and revised by quoting the full title of the 1552 *Book of Common Prayer*, it cannot be taken for granted that the ordinal is implicitly included.

The first changes are in fact the same ones made in the prayer book's Litany, which is recited in a slightly modified form near the beginning of the service for ordaining deacons. Both the Grafton and Jugge editions duly decline to mention the bishop of Rome's detestable enormities; both also replace Edward's name with Elizabeth's in the first state prayer and make the necessary changes to the pronouns in the next two petitions. Jugge, however (who printed the relevant page, AA3^v), slips up once by asking that 'she maye alwayes haue affiaunce in thee' as in Edwardian editions, whereas in both the 1559 octavo *Letanye* and all subsequent editions of the prayer book itself the third word is 'euermore'.

After the three petitions concerning the queen herself, the Litany usually goes on to ask for the bishops to be illuminated, the lords of the Council to be endued with grace, wisdom, and understanding, the magistrates to be given grace to execute justice, and the people to be blessed and kept. In the Edwardian ordinal, however, a special petition for the ordinands themselves was inserted between those for the bishops and the Council, as follows:

> That it maie please thee to blesse these menne, and sende thy grace vpon them, that thei maie duely execute the office, now to be committed vnto theim, to the edifying of the Churche, and to thy honor, praise, and glory.[A]

Exactly why this was omitted in 1559 is unclear. Perhaps it was considered that although in ecclesiastical matters the bishops might well take precedence over the Privy Council, those who were not yet even deacons should not. But if precedence had been the problem, the ordinands could simply

---

[A] STC 16462, B2^r.

have been moved to a position either before or after the magistrates, so perhaps there was another reason.

Once again, Grafton made the change correctly – but the Jugge team's ordinal was being shared among printers. Sheet AA4:5 was printed by Kingston, and in the copy from which his compositor was setting, AA4^r began with the petition for the lords of the Council, so he duly followed copy and set it as the first few lines of the page. But sheet AA3:6 was printed by Jugge, and in *his* compositor's copy AA3^v must have ended with the crossed-out petition for the ordinands. Not unnaturally, the compositor looked at AA4^r in his copy to see what should follow the omission, and duly set the lines about the lords of the Council at the foot of his page instead. And that is why the Council petition appears twice in the Jugge edition.

What is probably the most important change is that the original 'Othe of the Kynges supremacie' in the service for deacons is replaced by the new and shorter 'Othe of the Quenes Souerainte' (Grafton's spelling: Jugge has 'Soueraintee'). The text itself is preceded by a rubric explaining that the bishop is to administer the oath, which in the Edwardian version was described as 'against the vsurped power and aucthoritie, of the Bishop of Rome'. In 1559 this was softened to 'against the power and authoritie of all foreyn potētates'.[A] In Grafton's editions that rubric appears on the same page as the oath itself, and so it is no surprise that where the Edwardian editions call it the oath of the 'Kynges supremacie', in 1559 that was appropriately changed to the 'Quenes soueraintie'.

While similar rubrics appear in the services for priests and bishops, the oath itself is not repeated. In the third of those rubrics, on Cc3^r, Grafton likewise replaced 1552's 'Kynges Supremacie' with 'Quenes Soueraintie' – and probably did the same on Bb5^v. But in the only surviving copy, sheet Bb2:5 is a leftover from 1552 in which the rubric consequently reads 'Kynges Supremacie'.

In the Jugge edition from which all subsequent editions descended, the oath itself with its 'Quenes Soueraintee' heading is on page AA6^v in the inner forme, but the rubric is on the recto in the outer forme. I cannot tell whether the two pages were set either on the same day or by the same Jugge compositor, but while whoever set the rubric correctly changed 'Kynges' to 'Quenes', whether or not his copy had been emended he nevertheless set 'supremacye'. The second rubric, on BB3^r, is in one of Richard Payne's sheets, while the third on BB7^r was printed by William Copland. In both

---

[A] Ibid., C3^r; Grafton's 1559 edition, Aa6^v.

cases the queen correctly replaces the king, but the oath remains one of supremacy rather than the 'Soueraintee' on which its heading on AA6^v insists. And despite the fact that in almost all subsequent editions the first rubric appears immediately above the oath, for more than three centuries the rubrics always claimed supremacy while the heading insisted on sovereignty. On occasion, a compositorial slip can cast a long shadow.

Whatever Happened to Sheet BB5:6?

I have been able to verify the existence of seven copies of the Jugge ordinal of 1559. The two in best condition are the one at Keble College, Oxford (shelfmark Brooke 214), and the copy acquired in 2017 by the Thomas Fisher Rare Book Library at the University of Toronto (shelfmark stc 01220).[A] Both are complete, and the Keble copy is individually bound. The Fisher copy is bound after a copy of the fourth edition of the prayer book (STC 16292a); the present binding is no earlier than the eighteenth century, but the condition of both items suggests that they have been together since the beginning. In both the Keble and Fisher copies, and in the imperfect copy in the Oxford University Press Archives, sheet BB5:6 (the innermost sheet of quire BB^{10}) is the work of John Kingston (Figure 16), who also printed most of quire AA.

The copy at York Minster is also bound after a prayer book: the unique copy of the third edition, shelfmark XI.F.19(1). The two had evidently been bound together for some considerable time, and all the text pages had been carefully ruled in red, before that volume was rebound with a Jacobean prayer book of 1620 appended (STC 16353). Before that happened, 'Mrs Anne Forster her Booke' was written below the Jugge device on BB10^v, followed on the same line in another hand (but in what appears to be the same ink) by the word 'Witness', and in a second line below, the signature 'Edward Emery 1671'. That was almost certainly written before the book was put in its present binding, because 'Witness' is uncomfortably close to the gutter and there was plenty of space to the left of the signature.

The only serious physical defect in the ordinal is the absence of sheet BB5:6, which has been replaced (after the present volume was bound) by Cc1 and Cc2 from a somewhat narrower copy of one of the 1552 Grafton editions (Graf.4). It is impossible to know when or how that sheet was lost,

---

[A] I am grateful to Ben Higgins for examining the Keble copy for me in 2018 before I was able to see it myself.

or whether it was ever present, but the evidence of the remaining copies raises the distinct possibility that it was never there.

None of the other copies is bound with a prayer book. The complete copy at Jesus College, Oxford, is the third item in a collected volume (R.9.12.Gall.), where it is followed by Robert Barker's edition of 1607 (STC 16467). The Huntington Library copy (438000:581) is separately bound and textually complete, but wants the final leaf (blank except for Jugge's device on the verso). Neither copy, however, has the original Kingston sheet BB5:6 of 1559. What they have instead is a substitute printed by Thomas Dawson – a former apprentice of Jugge's, freed in 1568 and a master printer from 1577 (Figure 17). It is fortunately possible to date that sheet quite precisely, because of minor damage sustained by the outer frame of the 38-mm initial T used on BB6^v. The impression on that page shows a break in the top line 11 mm from the left, which happened during the printing of STC 18006 in 1580. (In that book, on the recto of leaf I1 the frame is undamaged, but on the verso the break appears for the first time.) Moreover, in the ordinal the bottom line of the outer frame is intact, whereas in all its appearances in and after 1581 that I have seen it has a small break in the exact centre.[A] The text contains a few readings that differ from the Whitchurch tradition followed by Kingston in 1559, and show that Dawson copied the missing pages from one of Grafton's 1552 editions.

The British Library copy (shelfmark 468.b.9) is also separately bound and textually complete, but in that copy sheet BB5:6 was printed by Thomas Purfoot the elder, who began his printing career during the 1560s (Figure 18). Progressive damage to the frames of the A on BB5^v and the I on BB6^v is difficult to date precisely because its appearance varies with inking.[B] But the date can be narrowed down to the early 1580s, and I have not found the M on BB5^r in Purfoot's work before 1581. Unlike Dawson, Purfoot took the text from either a Whitchurch edition of 1552 or Kingston's 1559 setting itself. Whether or not the Dawson and Purfoot sheets should be considered as defining 'issues' of the 1559 ordinal is a tricky question, but even though the sophistication was performed only a generation after the original printing, in my opinion the three copies in question are more realistically described as made-up copies.

Neither Dawson nor Purfoot would have gone to the trouble of reprinting the whole sheet if he had only a handful of defective ordinals – so

---

[A] See, for example, STC 4437 A1^r, 11421 A1^v, and 17771 P1^r, all three of 1581.
[B] The extent of the damage to the top right corner of the I (or bottom left on its frequent appearances upside down) is particularly difficult to ascertain. In 1581, for example, see STC 4401 A2^r, A3^r; in 1582, 5116 H1^r; in 1583, 1212 A2^r and 6275 K3^r and L2^v.

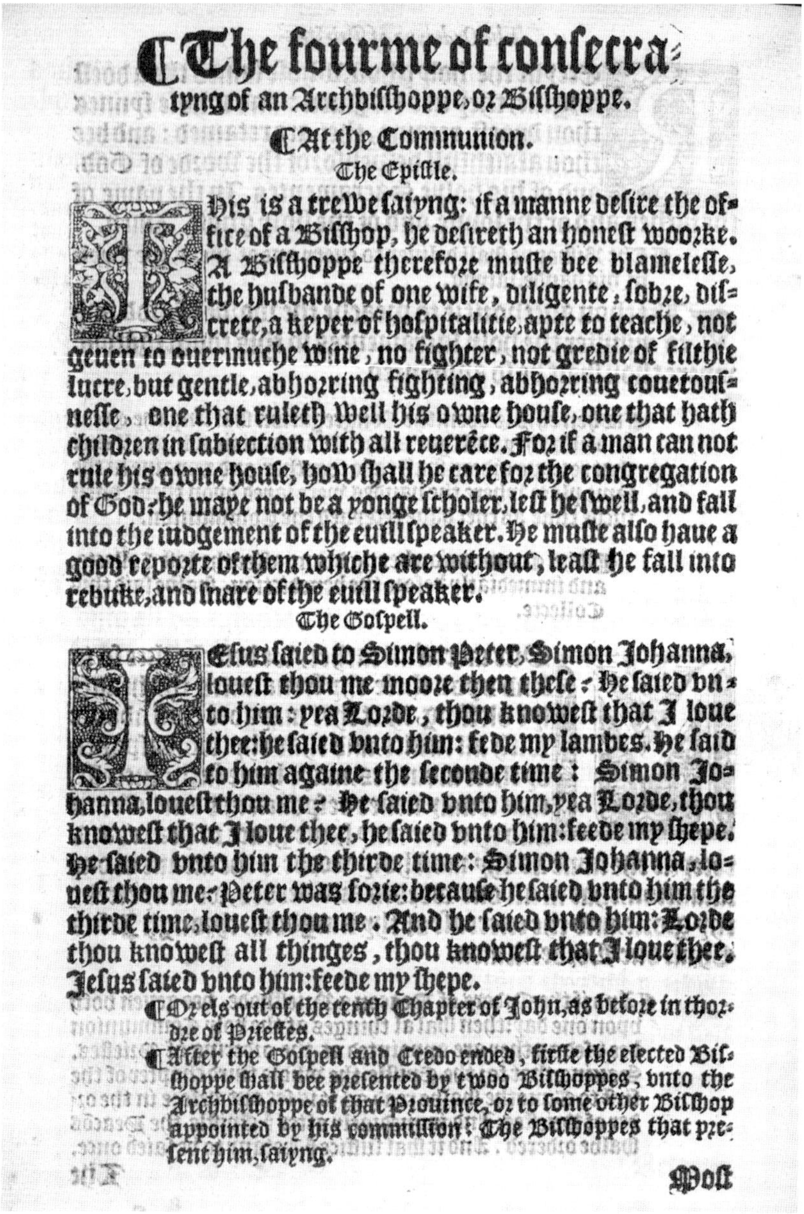

¶ The fourme of consecra-
tyng of an Archbisshoppe, or Bisshoppe.

¶ At the Communion.

The Epistle.

This is a trewe saiyng: if a manne desire the office of a Bisshop, he desireth an honest woorke. A Bisshoppe therefore muste bee blamelesse, the husbande of one wife, diligente, sobre, discrete, a keper of hospitalitie, apte to teache, not geuen to ouermuche wine, no fighter, not gredie of filthie lucre, but gentle, abhorring fighting, abhorring couetousnesse, one that ruleth well his owne house, one that hath children in subiection with all reuerence. For if a man can not rule his owne house, how shall he care for the congregation of God? he maye not be a yonge scholer, lest he swell, and fall into the iudgement of the euill speaker. He muste also haue a good reporte of them whiche are without, least he fall into rebuke, and snare of the euill speaker.

The Gospell.

Iesus saied to Simon Peter, Simon Iohanna, louest thou me moore then these? He saied vnto him: yea Lorde, thou knowest that I loue thee: he saied vnto him: fede my lambes. He said to him againe the seconde time: Simon Iohanna, louest thou me? He saied vnto him, yea Lorde, thou knowest that I loue thee, he saied vnto him: feede my shepe. He saied vnto him the thirde time: Simon Iohanna, louest thou me? Peter was sorie: because he saied vnto him the thirde time, louest thou me. And he saied vnto him: Lorde thou knowest all thinges, thou knowest that I loue thee. Iesus saied vnto him: feede my shepe.

¶ Or els out of the tenth Chapter of Iohn, as before in thordre of Priestes.

¶ After the Gospell and Credo ended, firste the elected Bisshoppe shall bee presented by twoo Bisshoppes, vnto the Archbisshoppe of that Prouince, or to some other Bisshop appointed by his commission. The Bisshoppes that present him, saiyng.

Most

Figure 16 John Kingston's original sheet BB5:6, 1559.
(Thomas Fisher Rare Book Library, stc 01220, BB6^v.)

THE FORME

of consecrating of an Archbishop,
or Bishop.

The Epistle at the Communion.

1.Tim 3.

THis is a true saying, if a man desire the office of a Bishop, hee desireth an honest worke. A Bishop therfore must be blamelesse, the husbande of one wife, diligent, sober, discrete, a keeper of hospitalite, apte to teach, not giuen to ouermuch wine, no fighter, not greedie of filthie lucre, but gentle, abhorring fighting, abhorring to couetousnesse, one that ruleth well his own house, one that hath children in subiection with all reuerence. For if a man cannot rule his owne house, how shall hee care for the congregation of God? He may not be a young scholler, least he swell, and fall into the iudgement of the euill speaker. He must also haue a good report of them which are without, least he fall into rebuke and snare of the euill speaker.

The Gospell.

Iohn.10.

IEsus said to Simon Peter, Simon Iohanna louest thou me more then these? he said vnto him, yea, Lord thou knowest that I loue thee: he said vnto him, feede my lambes. He saide to him againe the second time: Simon Iohanna, louest thou mee? Hee saide vnto him, yea, Lord thou knowest that I loue thee: he saide vnto him, feede my sheepe. He saide vnto him the thirde time, Simon Iohanna, louest thou mee? Peter was sory, because he saide vnto him the thirde time, louest thou mee, and hee said vnto him: Lord thou knowest al things, thou knowest that I loue thee. Iesus saide vnto him, feede my sheepe.

Or els out of the x. Chapter of Iohn, as before in the order of Priestes.

After the Gospell and Creede ended, first the elected Bishop shalbe presented by two Bishops, vnto the Archbishop of the Prouince, or to some other Bishop appointed by his Commission: The Bishops that present him, saying:

Most

Figure 17 Thomas Dawson's replacement sheet BB5:6, 1580.
(Jesus College, Oxford, R.9.12(4) Gall., BB6^v.)

¶ The fourme of consecrating of an Archbishoppe, or Bisshoppe.

◦ At the Communion,
The Epistle.

This is a true saying: if a man desire ye office of a Bisshop he desireth an honest worke. A Bisshop therfore must be blamles, ye husband of one wife, diligent, sobre, discreete, a keper of hospitalitie, apt to teache, not giuen to ouer much wine, no fighter, not greedy of filthy lucre: but gentle, abhorring fighting, abhorring couetousnes, one yt ruleth well his owne house, one yt hath children in subiection, wt all reuerence, for if a man cannot rule his owne house, how shall he care for ye congregation of God. He may not be a yong scholer, least he swel, and fall into ye iudgement of ye euill speaker, he must also haue a good report of them which are with out, least he fall into rebuke, and snare of the euill speaker.

The Gospell.

Iesus said to Simon Peter, Simon Johanna, louest thou me more then these? He saide vnto him, yea Lord, thou knowest that I loue thee he said vnto him, feede my lambes. He said to him again the second time, Simon Johanna, louest thou me? He said vnto him, yea Lord, thou knowest that I loue the. He said vnto him, feede my sheepe. He said vnto him the third time, Simon Johanna, louest thou me? Peter was sorie because hee said vnto him the third time, louest thou me? And he said vnto him, Lord thou knowest all things, thou knowest that I loue thee, Jesus said vnto him, feede my sheepe.

¶ Or else out of the tenth Chapter of John, as before in thorder of Priestes.

¶ After the Gospell and Creede ended, first the elected Bisshop shalbe presented by two Bisshops, vnto the Archbisshoppe of that prouince, or to some other Bisshope appointed by his commission: The Bisshops that present him saying.

Most

Figure 18 Thomas Purfoot's replacement sheet BB5:6, *c.* 1581.

(© The British Library Board, 486.b.9, BB6[v].)

somehow, a few years after Jugge died, each presumably acquired a sizeable batch of copies lacking only BB5:6. How and where they found them is impossible to guess. The ordinal was certainly completed before Jugge bound Dawson as his apprentice in August 1559,[A] so Dawson cannot have worked on the original book, and no connection is known between Purfoot and either Jugge or Kingston. Had the defective copies been misplaced in some corner of Cawood's premises, after his death in 1572 they would have passed to Jugge, who added most or all of the late Cawood's printing equipment to his own. But if Jugge had those copies in the early 1570s he could have reprinted the missing sheet himself, because the date 1559 would evidently not have rendered them unsaleable. Instead, in 1576 he reprinted the whole ordinal (dispensing with large display initials and thus compressing it from nine sheets to seven) but dated it '1559' – which suggests that he was unaware that the leftover stock still existed.

[A] Arber, I, 120.

CHAPTER 8

The Third and Fourth Editions

Disentangling Some Facts

The book listed by the revised *Short-Title Catalogue* as the third folio edition of 1559 (STC 16292a, whose title-page is reproduced as Figure 19) is the one that has been most substantially misrepresented by the revisers. The main entry gives the location of only four copies, each of which was believed (in one case wrongly) to be imperfect, sophisticated, or both. Seemingly uncertain which parts of the preliminaries in those copies could be considered 'original', the revisers briefly described each of them in turn (only once accurately), and then defined the edition as 'series 2/22' in the table of collations on page 88 of that volume – referring the reader back to those four descriptions as if each copy somehow defined a legitimate variety sanctioned by Jugge and Cawood. Moreover, because two of those copies have had parts of their original preliminaries replaced by cancel quires printed in 1561, both the STC entry and the table of collations misleadingly suggest that 1561 might really be the date of the edition itself, which is certainly not the case. It was printed in the second half of 1559 by five of the printers who had worked on the first Jugge-and-Cawood edition, and its collation differs from that of series 2/21 only in that there are no cancels and the calendar quire is signed B instead of being left unsigned.

What really happened in 1559 was that five of the printers in the Jugge-and-Cawood team quickly proceeded to print two more folio editions – their haste perhaps prompted by their belated discovery of the Litany blunder in quire B (see Chapter 5, pp. 66–7). Those two are the third and fourth editions of the revised *Book of Common Prayer* as a whole, which creates a minor terminological problem. In STC, the first of the three Jugge-and-Cawood editions is listed as if the second edition, following (as distinct from simultaneous with) the Grafton edition. The second

Jugge-and-Cawood edition (the third edition overall) was not known to the revisers and is therefore not listed at all in STC, while STC 16292a (listed as if the third edition) is really the fourth. To avoid having to pretend that STC 16292 is the 'second' edition, in order to discuss the three Jugge-and-Cawood editions as parts of a coherent sequence of bibliographical events I shall temporarily call them JC1 (16292), JC2 (not in STC) and JC3 (16292a). The unique copy of JC2 in York Minster Library unfortunately lacks both preliminary quires, which have been replaced by a ten-leaf cancel printed in 1561 and resembling (but distinct from) that found in Keble copy 2 of JC3. The main text of JC2, however, is complete and in good condition.

When Jugge and Cawood had finished assembling complete copies of JC1 from the heaps of sheets contributed by the various printers, there would necessarily have been at least a few copies of at least a few sheets left over, some of which found their way into copies of the next two editions. As I shall suggest below, there is probably a special reason why five of the nine extant leftovers are sheets from quire P of JC1 found in copies of JC3. Two of the other examples are sheets from JC1 found in the unique JC2 (Rogers's H2:7 and Payne's N2:7); the other two are Marshe's sheet L3:8 from JC1 and Kingston's P1:10 from JC2, both found in British Library copy 1 of JC3 (shelfmark 6.d.9).

With only one exception, each of the fifteen quires of the main text exists in what I shall call three distinct *versions*. In most cases that means that each forme of each sheet is found in three different editions, or distinct settings of type. There are, however, a few occasions on which a page or a forme was either reimposed (put back in the chase, often with some or all of the incidentals reset – the running title, catchword, shoulder notes, and occasionally one or more small-type headings within the type-page) or simply put back on the press with no visible alteration. The exception is quire F, reprinted by John Cawood from the Wolfe-and-Whitchurch setting of JC1, which appears to be identical in JC2 and all copies of JC3.

In all fourteen of the other quires, collation of the text leaves no reasonable doubt about which of the two reprinted versions is the second and which the third. In two cases, however, the York copy of JC2 has the third setting, while what is clearly the second is found only in a copy of JC3: Cawood's quire G in the Fisher copy and Rogers's quire I in Keble copy 2. It would seem, therefore, that the editions followed each other with little or no interval, and that some of the gathered quires for JC3 were delivered to the publishers before the heaps of JC2 quires had all been assembled into copies. In at least a few cases, some or all of the newer quires were placed in

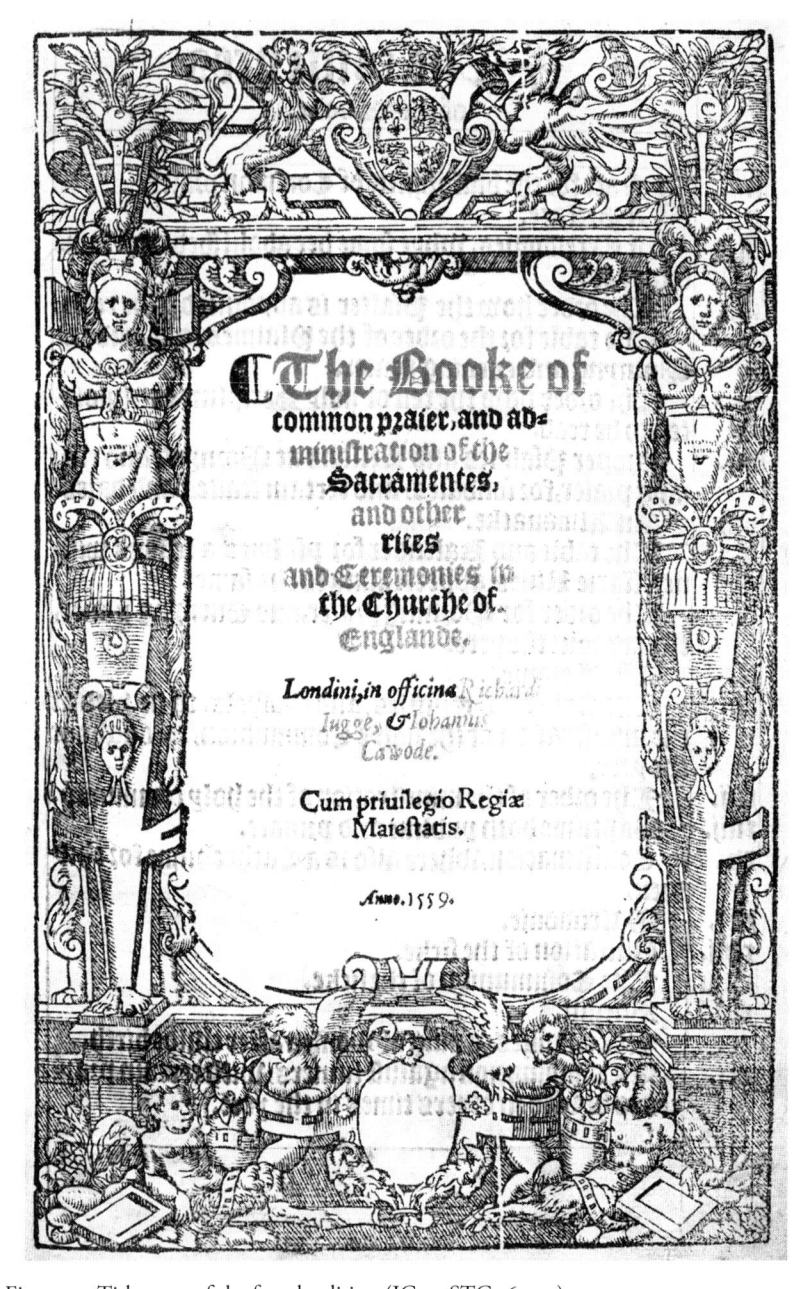

Figure 19 Title-page of the fourth edition (JC3 = STC 16292a).
(Thomas Fisher Rare Book Library, STC 01220, ᵖA1ʳ.)

front of (or on top of) the existing heaps instead of behind (or under) them. Given that one of the 'misplaced' JC2 quires is Cawood's quire G, it is quite possible that a Cawood setting of quire F 'proper' to JC2 once existed.

Although JC2 and JC3 are the work of the same five printers, the division of labour among them is not the same throughout. Quires A–I and L in each edition are the work of the same men, but in quires K and M–P only four sheets (O2–9) were produced by the same printer in both editions. Despite that divergence, however, the two editions are so closely interconnected that it makes sense to discuss them in tandem rather than separately.

Quires A–E: Richard Jugge

Bibliographically speaking, perhaps the most interesting feature of Jugge's work in JC2 and JC3 concerns his choices between his two great primer founts. Given that in JC1 he used the w^{2+} fount only in the cancels, it is natural to think of it being 'later' than the w^{5c} fount that it would eventually displace, especially if the latter really was a fount that had been formerly owned and used by Whitchurch. That assumption seems to be corroborated by JC2, in which the w^{5c} type is used for all but one sheet of quires A–B, the exception being sheet B4:5 (the corrected reprint of JC1's unrevised Litany sheet). Thereafter in JC2 Jugge uses the 'older' w^{5c} fount for only one sheet of quire D (D2:7) and five formes of quire L (sheets 1:10, 3:8, and forme 2^r:9^v). In general JC3 seems to reinforce the idea, because after quire B in that edition Jugge uses only the w^{2+} fount. But for no very obvious reason, in quires A–B the pattern is exactly the same as in JC2, with only B4:5 in w^{2+} and all the rest in w^{5c}.

The only other significant irregularity in the first five quires is that for some reason two copies of JC3 (British Library copy 1 and the Lambeth Palace copy) have the complete quire D in the JC2 setting. But since both those copies contain a few other sheets from earlier editions,[A] they were presumably gathered at a time when sheets and quires from the previous editions were showing up in several of the dwindling heaps.

[A] British Library copy 1 also has P1:10 from JC2 and both L3:8 and P4:7 from JC1; the Lambeth Palace copy has P1:10 and P3–4:7–8 from JC1. STC's claim that quire D in British Library copy 1 is also from JC1 is mistaken.

Quires F–G: John Cawood

As already noted, all extant copies of JC2–3 have the same Cawood setting of quire F. In JC1 Cawood's only contribution had been quire G, and his setting of that quire in the single extant copy of JC2 is the same as that found in five of the six known copies of JC3. But the Fisher copy of JC3 has a very different version, in which three of the formes are reimposed from the JC1 setting. In the case of G2^v:7^r the whole forme differs only in a very few small type-shifts and the loss of 's' from 'Iames' in the shoulder note on G7^r. Forme G4^r:5^v is almost as little changed, except that the running title on G5^v has shifted a few millimetres to the left. But in G4^v:5^r the running titles and catchwords are new, the formerly textura shoulder notes have been reset in italic, and on G5^r the lines of small type containing the headings 'The Collect.' (now 'Collecte') and 'The Epistle.' have also been reset.

With six of its sixteen pages almost entirely in the same setting of type as in JC1, there can be no doubt at all that this is the setting intended for JC2, and the absence of any similar links with the later setting suggests a greater interval between them. And the fact that the only extant copy of JC2 has the setting clearly intended for JC3 raises the distinct possibility that an earlier version of quire F once existed, perhaps also printed by Cawood.

The Return of Owen Rogers

Quires H–K of JC2 were all printed by Owen Rogers, half reprinted from his own previous settings (quire H and sheets I1:8 and I2:7) and half from pages set by Thomas Marshe (who was not involved in JC2–3). Having learned to expect irregularity from Rogers, I am not unduly surprised to find that there appear to be only two settings of sheets H4:5 (the second found in both JC2 and JC3) and H2:7 (the second found only in JC3, while JC2 has the JC1 setting). Like sheet H4:5, forme H3^v:6^r has only two known settings: JC1 and a setting common to JC2 and JC3. But the JC2 setting of the perfecting forme H3^r:6^v differs from all copies of JC3, so there are certainly three versions of sheet H3:6 (and three uncomplicated editions of H1:8).

Quire I is comparatively straightforward, with three versions of each forme in each sheet, except that both formes of the JC2 version of I2:7 are reimposed from JC1 (although with reset running titles and shoulder notes). The catch, however, is that once again the only extant copy of the intermediate version is found in a copy of JC3 (Keble copy 1) rather

Figure 20 Owen Rogers initials in JC2–3.
(a, c: Keble College, Oxford, Brooke 217, I1^v),
(d, e: Thomas Fisher Rare Book Library, STC 01220, I8^v, I2^v),
(b, f, i: Lambeth Palace Library, [**] H5415.A4R5 1559, I8^r, I2^v, I8^r),
(g: STC 16246, d1^v, used by permission of the Folger Shakespeare Library),
(h: © The British Library Board, 6.d.9, I8^r).

than in the only copy of JC2 itself. The most noticeable difference between JC3 and its predecessors in this quire is that for some reason Rogers decided to set it in great primer instead of large english. Quire K – printed by Marshe in JC1, by Rogers (in large english) in JC2, and by Cawood in all copies of JC3 – presents no serious difficulties. While Rogers continued to improvise when short of display initials, in JC2 he did so with a modicum of restraint. On four occasions he used his 18-mm T with its crossbar packed to serve as an I, and its companion V was inverted three times as a substitute for A.[A] His only 'new' trick appeared on I1^v, where he used both

---

[A] Packed T on H8^r, I1^r, I3^r, and K1^v; inverted V on I3^v, I7^v, and K7^r.

of his T's with their crossbars packed but upside down (Figure 20*a*, *c*). The relevant grooves in the smaller letter were, however, evidently too narrow and shallow to hold the packing convincingly.[A]

It was in JC3 that Rogers outdid himself in ingenuity. There was little new that he could do with his 18-mm T, which he used with its crossbar packed either upright as before (I4^v) or inverted (H8^r, I1^v: Figure 20*c*). Having had little success in obscuring the crossbar of his smaller T (Figure 20*a*), he simply used it upside down three times (I1^r, I6^r, I8^r) with no attempt to hide the crossbar (Figure 20*b*). At some point he wisely decided to add to his supply of initials, and acquired a new W to match (at least in height) his 15-mm alphabet (Figure 20*d*). London printers had access to several skilled manufacturers of printing ornaments and initials (either of wood or metal), both overseas and in London itself. But Rogers seemingly considered quality too expensive, and either commissioned an amateur or found a suitable piece of wood and did it himself. The W was certainly a sensible addition – and one would think that whoever carved it could easily have produced one or more comparable I's. But no: Rogers evidently preferred to improvise.

What he needed to find in his 15-mm alphabet, therefore, were letters with wide stems of full height but not too close to either side of the enclosing frame. For page I8^v he chose his B, inverted it, and packed the bowls and the surrounding decoration as best he could to hide its identity (Figure 20*e–f*). For page I8^r he chose his E instead, and used it in much the same way (Figure 20*g–h*). But because the grooves and other low areas in these letters were evidently shallow (as he had found with the 15-mm T), the packing failed to behave as desired, and both shifted and came away during the printing. In the Lambeth Palace copy the letter is almost completely exposed (Figure 20*i*).

Quires L–P

The history of the next two quires is relatively straightforward. In JC1 quire L was printed by Thomas Marshe and quire M by Rogers. In JC2 quire L was reprinted by Richard Jugge and quire M by John Kingston;[B] in JC3

[A] This being the forme that needed four I's, it is interesting that in the other page (I8^r) what he used in addition to his 15-mm I was simply a capital I from his 230 textura. Since he made frequent use of such capitals elsewhere for initials A, B, G, K, L, O, P, and W it is hard to understand why, in all the sheets he printed for the prayer book, he only ever used such an I once.

[B] On page M1^r, Kingston's compositor omitted the fourth line of the first (4½-line) paragraph, but the omission was noticed and corrected at press. State 1 is in British Library copy C.25.l.6; state 2 in copy 6.d.9.

Jugge printed both quire L and the two outer sheets of quire M while the two sheets M3–6 were contributed by John Cawood. Apart from the single leftover Marshe sheet L3:8 from JC1 found (as already mentioned) in British Library copy 1 of JC3, each extant copy of each edition contains the appropriate sheets. Jugge's contribution to these two quires is of special interest because of information it provides about Richard Grafton – but that will be separately discussed below.

In JC1, most of quire N was printed by Richard Payne, but with Jugge first contributing sheet N3:6 and then cancelling leaf N3. In JC2 the whole quire is Payne's, but there is a complication. Sheets N4:5, N3:6, and the outer forme of sheet N1:8 behave as expected, with the JC2 settings being simple reprints of those of JC1. In the inner forme of N1:8, however, page N1^v is reimposed from the type of JC1. And while that in itself creates no uncertainty, it proves that at least part of Payne's JC1 setting still existed when he began on JC2. So when we find that sheet N2:7 appears to be in exactly the same setting in both JC1 and JC2, it is impossible to be certain whether that sheet is just a lone leftover (in which case there was presumably a second setting of that sheet 'proper' to JC2 but now lost) or whether Payne still had both formes intact when he was asked to participate in a second edition. Edition JC3 provides no additional evidence, its quire N having been printed by John Cawood.

In Chapter 5 (p. 81) I remarked that there seems to be no obvious reason why Payne did not print all the sheets in quire O of JC1, and why Kingston printed the innermost and outermost sheets (O5:6 and O1:10 respectively). I am equally unable to explain why Cawood (last seen in quire G) contributed the single sheet O1:10 to the JC2 version of the quire otherwise printed by Payne. But at least in JC3 Payne finally printed the whole quire, which is otherwise unremarkable.

As I mentioned earlier in this chapter, three of the five sheets of quire P of JC1 are also found in the Lambeth Palace copy of JC3, while one of them is also found in two other copies.[A] These leftovers, however, seem unlikely to indicate any significant irregularity in the printing – nor does the presence in British Library copy 1 of a single copy of P1:10 from JC2. The original quire P was the first complete quire that Jugge is known to have printed, so he may have overestimated how many 'extra' copies he needed to produce to allow for accidents. And because that quire was

---

[A] Sheets P1:10, P3:8, and P4:7 in the Lambeth Palace copy; copies of P4:7 also in British Library copy 1 and the Fisher copy.

printed by Kingston in JC2, when Jugge was the one who reprinted it for JC3 he would have had his own leftovers handy.

That it was Kingston who printed the final quire of JC2 raises an interesting issue, because in all three editions page P10^v contains Jugge's trademark device (McKerrow 125). An elaborate panel with his monogram in a compartment at the foot, this is one of three trademarks that were cut for him in 1552,[A] and used by Steven Mierdman in the books he printed for Jugge in that and the following year. Used on Jugge's behalf by Richard Payne in the colophon of the 1559 ordinal, it was next used by Jugge himself in JC1, then by Kingston in JC2, and again by Jugge in JC3. Meanwhile the woodcut border obtained by Jugge from Edward Whitchurch (McK & F 68, from which Whitchurch's initials were consequently removed) was used first by Payne on the title-page of the ordinal, then by Jugge himself on that of JC1, and lastly by Kingston on that of JC3 (of which he printed both preliminary quires). Since the preliminaries of JC2 are lost one can only conjecture – but if Kingston printed the calendar of JC2 he may well also have printed quire $^\pi$A (including the title-page). It should moreover be remembered that the only two appearances in 1559 of Grafton's trademark border (on Fabyan's *Chronicle* and the Grafton prayer book) were on pages likewise printed by Kingston. While a device may usually indicate that the title-page or colophon displaying it was printed *for* its owner, it is not always safe to assume that it was printed *by* him.

A Brief Summary

Having worked through the quires in order of appearance, I have reported and described so many irregularities (both major and minor) that some readers may be wondering whether the York copy really does qualify as a distinct edition. So let me summarize the overall pattern of the evidence in a different way. With the exception of quire F and two sheets of quire H, every extant sheet exists in three distinct versions that are easy to place in chronological order. Moreover, in each quire except F and H the only 'irregularities' are a few odd sheets in the first setting found in one or more copies of either JC2 (N2:7) or JC3 (L3:8, P1:10, P3:8, P4:7), or in one case a sheet from JC2 found in a copy of JC3 (P1:10). That covers quires A–C, E, K–P, and part of H: ten quires and a half out of fifteen. Two copies of JC3

[A] The others were McKerrow 123 (a smaller version of the same design) and a compartment of four separate pieces (one bearing Jugge's initials in a circle with the motto 'Omnia desuper') overlooked by McK & F but reproduced here in Plate 8. One or more of these were used in 1552 and 1553 in STC 2867–70 and 2090.

have the second setting of quire D instead of the third; in quires G and I the second of three settings is found not in the York copy but only in a single copy of JC3; quire F and part of H are known in only two settings (perhaps because settings proper to JC2 have failed to survive).

The Preliminaries

Both the preliminary quires of JC3 were printed by John Kingston. There is little in quire πA^{12} that calls for comment, but the calendar quire is of interest because it follows the pattern of the one Kingston printed for the Grafton edition. The only notable changes of layout are that the '¶Psalmes' heading is now correctly placed at the extreme left above the column of psalm selections, and that while those numbers are now in roman rather than arabic numerals, the numbers in the 'Kalends' column are in arabic rather than roman. In the lectionary columns, moreover, the few 1552 blunders that Kingston had overlooked when correcting the calendar in the Grafton edition are now brought back into conformity with 1549. The JC2 calendar is lost, but had it been reprinted from Wolfe's JC1 setting I doubt that Jugge would have allowed Kingston a completely free hand in JC3, so I consider it likely that Kingston had also printed the lost calendar of JC2.

The calendar in JC3 (and presumably JC2) is a special exception to what I said at the beginning of Chapter 4 about the Jugge-and-Cawood edition being the direct ancestor of all subsequent editions (p. 52). From mid-1559 to late 1560, the calendars followed the one that Kingston had contributed to the Grafton edition. Neither of the two 1559 quartos still has its calendar, but the complete octavo edition follows the layout of JC3, as does the only extant edition of 1560 whose calendar survives (STC 16294, in which it is printed by Jugge).[A] But as I shall explain in Chapter 10, in 1561 the calendar was extensively revised, and what Jugge used as the model for the revised version was the Wolfe setting in JC1. So what little influence the Grafton edition had on its successors was confined to the calendar and lasted no more than two years.

Richard Grafton Gives Up Printing

The motley assortment of initials that Jugge used during his first few months as a printer, some permanently acquired and others merely

---

[A] Large sections of that calendar are in fact reimposed from one that Jugge contributed to a bible otherwise printed by Cawood (STC 2094), as discussed (and illustrated) in Appendix C below.

Figure 21 Some initials of Grafton, Jugge, and Payne.
(*a*) Grafton's uncial M... (*b*) used as T by Jugge.
(*c*) Jugge's ex-Mychell A... (*d*) sometimes used as V.
(*e*) Q mutilated for use as O (Payne). (*f*) F mutilated for use as E (Jugge).
   (*a*, *c*, *d*: © The British Library Board, C.25.l.9, N2^r; C112.c.10(1), D3^v, K1^v.)
   (*b*, *f*: York Minster Library, XI.F.19(1), L8^v, L4^v)
   (*e*: Thomas Fisher Rare Book Library, STC 01220, O8^r.)

borrowed, has caused a number of his early productions to be misattributed to other printers. Amid that confusion, however, one small cluster of initials provides an important piece of information. Those he used in his two editions of quire L (JC2–3) and two sheets of quire M (JC3 only) include nine that had not been seen before in either JC1 or quires A–E of JC2. Seven of them, however, can be found in *Grafton's* edition, and both the others had been used in one or more Grafton editions in 1552.[A] The most plausible explanation for their appearance as a cluster is that Jugge had only just acquired them, and since the book in which Grafton last used most of them is the only book he is known to have printed during Elizabeth's reign, it presumably follows that soon after finishing the prayer book he began to discard his printing materials.

One of those initials is a very old-fashioned uncial M, more typical of the 1520s and '30s than the late '50s. Grafton himself was perfectly capable of recognizing it, but one of Jugge's compositors evidently mistook it for a T and so used it upside down (Figure 21*a*–*b*) – not only in JC2 but on page D3^v in all four editions of Elizabeth's *Injunctions* of the same year (STC 10099.5–10100.5). Whether or not the same Jugge compositor was responsible I cannot say, but a rather splendid A that Jugge somehow acquired from the estate of the late John Mychell is found in each of the quarto editions to be discussed in the next chapter, both on D3^v as an A and upside-down on K1^v as a V (Figure 21*c*–*d*). Improvising with initials was in fact rather more widespread than has usually been realized, and among the more common forms of the practice was mutilating an O to serve as a Q or vice versa. What appears to be an O on Richard Payne's page O8^r in all three Jugge-and-Cawood folios (and also on O10^r in JC3) began life as a Q but was discreetly deprived of its tail at some time in its past (Figure 21*e*). But mutilation was not always as unobtrusive, and I hope that Jugge himself was not responsible for turning John Mychell's favourite F into the extremely clumsy E found on L4^v of JC2 (Figure 21*f*).[B] I draw no important conclusion from such practices, except perhaps that while Owen Rogers can be considered noteworthy, he was far from unique.

At the end of Chapter 2 (p. 61) I suggested that the Cambridge University Library copy was probably the last of the five known copies of Grafton's edition to be gathered and made ready for sale. Whether or not that is true, there is evidence strongly suggesting that it was not sold wholesale to any retail bookseller until after Grafton gave up the book trade (an event that did not necessarily coincide with his giving up printing). In addition to its two second-setting sheets and a recycled 1552 sheet found in no other 1559 copy, the special features of that copy include a small cancel slip that until

---

[A] Specifically: **A**$_1$ was used by Grafton in STC 16291 on D3^v, I2^v, M1^r, M5^v, R2^r, R3^v and by Jugge in JC2 (L1^v, L8^r) and JC3 (L1^v, M7^r); **A**$_2$ by Grafton on D2^r, G4^r, H3^v, I4^v, O1^r, O3^v and Jugge in JC2 and JC3 (L3^r, L7^v); **I**$_1$ by Grafton on L5^r, O2^v and Jugge in JC2 and JC3 (L2^r); **I**$_2$ by Grafton on L4^v, L5^r, O2^v, X1^r (both settings) and Jugge in JC2 and JC3 (L2^r); **M**$_1$ by Grafton on N2^r and Jugge in JC2 (L3^v, L8^v); **V**$_1$ by Grafton on K1^v and Jugge in JC2 and JC3 (L2^r); **W**$_1$ by Grafton on D6^r, E3^r, E5^r, K5^r and Jugge in JC2 (L8^v) and JC3 (L1^r, L5^v). **B**$_1$ was used in Graf.5 on C6^r, D6^r and by Jugge in JC3 (L6^v); **B**$_2$ in Graf.6 on N5^r, O6^r, Aa2^v and by Jugge in JC2 (L4^r) and JC3 (L4^r, M8^r).

[B] It also appears on I4^r of the first of the quarto editions (STC 16293.3).

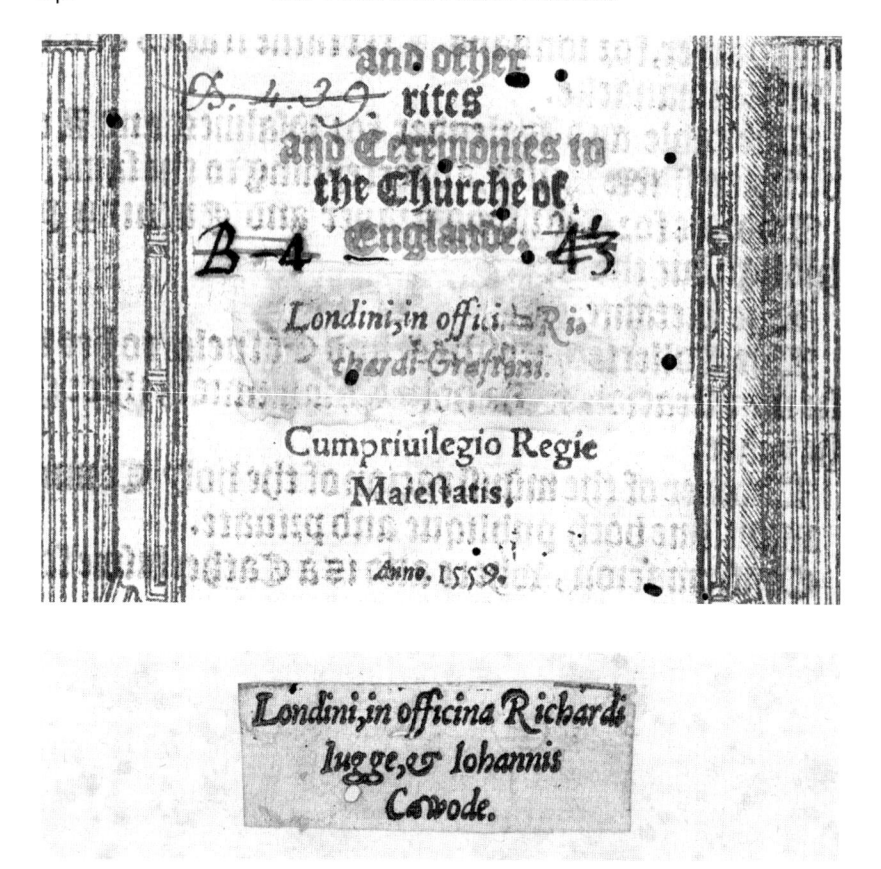

Figure 22 The cancel slip formerly pasted over Grafton's imprint.
(Cambridge University Library, Sel.3.221, title-page and facing flyleaf.)

comparatively modern times was pasted to the title-page to cover Grafton's imprint. Measuring approximately 52 × 19 mm, it replaced the two lines '*Londini,in officina Ri-* | *chardi Graftoni.*' (in black and red) with the three lines '*Londini,in officina Richardi* | *Iugge,& Iohannis* | *Cawode.*' (all black). That slip has since been removed, and transferred to the facing verso of the modern flyleaf. But its former position is easily seen because it has left a clear mark on the title-page (see Figure 22). Also in Cambridge, the St John's College copy wants the first four leaves ($^\pi$A1–4), so it is impossible to know whether it was ever modified in the same way. The British Library copy has what may be traces of the former presence of a similar slip, but neither of the copies in Oxford shows any sign of having been treated likewise.

Richard Grafton Gives Up Printing

What has been accepted (at least since 1976) as the probable explanation for the use of that cancel is spelled out in the notes to the entry for STC 16291.

> As no other book with Grafton's imprint after 1553 is known, this ed. possibly represents an unsuccessful attempt by him to gain a share in the Queen's Printing Office. Mr. Hetherington suggests that this ed. was pr. by Grafton as agent for Jugge and Cawood and that he improperly put his name in the imprint, since his licence as Queen's Printer was revoked by Queen Mary in 1553 and never restored. (STC, 2:93)

Had either Hetherington or the STC revisers known of the existence of the ordinal in the Corpus Christi copy, its implicit claim in the colophon on Cc5^v that Grafton was still somehow '*Typographus Regius*' might have seemed to support the first of those sentences – but the title-page imprint over which the cancel was pasted made no such claim.[A] Moreover, while a sample of only four title-pages may be far from adequate for statistical purposes, some copies were apparently sold without the cancel.

It should be remembered that while an imprint or colophon could certainly include a proud printer's boast that he was the one who manufactured a book, its principal function was to inform retail booksellers where (or from whom) they could buy copies at wholesale prices. Neither the original imprint nor the cancel claims credit for the actual printing, but each identifies what was presumably the best source of stock: Grafton's house for copies marketed before he gave up the book trade, and the houses and shops of the Queen's Printers thereafter. For an earlier parallel, at the turn of 1545–46 the lawbook publisher Henry Smith produced *Intrationum liber omnibus legum Anglie* (STC 14117) with a colophon dated 1 November 1545 and a title-page imprint dated 1546, each giving his address at the sign of the Trinity in the parish of St Clement Danes. A few months later he left the book trade, and the equipment used by his usual printer Jean Le Roux also changed hands. By May his unsold copies had been acquired by a former rival, William Middleton at the sign of St George in the parish of St Dunstan in the West – so Middleton printed cancels with his own address for both the imprint (still dated 1546) and

---

[A] Immediately below the imprint, Grafton claims to have printed the book 'Cum priuilegio Regie Maiestatis', which is certainly untrue unless *priuilegio* was being used (without precedent) merely to indicate that he had printed it at the request (or at least with the permission) of the Queen's officers. That phrase did not need to be covered up by the cancel, because the substitution of the Queen's Printers in the imprint rendered it truthful.

the colophon (now dated 1 May 1546).[A] Given that Grafton's printing materials were being dispersed even before the third edition of the prayer book was finished, the acquisition by Jugge and Cawood of some of the late-gathered Grafton copies need cause little surprise. As I have noted elsewhere, the purpose of the cancel was probably 'not to write Grafton out of history, but to prevent booksellers from wasting their time seeking copies from someone who no longer stocked them'.[B]

Which Edition is the 'Best'?

Some of those who have examined the folio editions of 1559 in the past (whether or not very closely) have done so in an attempt to determine which edition, or which copy of it, ought to be considered the definitive version of the 1559 text. But no extant copy of any of the four comes close to that impossible ideal. In 'practical' terms (albeit for a wholly impractical quest) one might isolate all readings known or suspected to be 'official' revisions to the 1552 text, whether mandated by the Act of Uniformity (such as the conflated words of administration in the Communion service), less explicitly allowed by it (the so-called 'ornaments rubric'), or evidently commanded but without parliamentary sanction (omitting the Black Rubric and detaching the ordinal). Those revisions could then be made to an ostensibly 'ideal' version of the 1552 text.

But although all editions of 1552 have a common ancestor in the edition I have elsewhere called Whit.1 (Whitchurch's first edition of that year, STC 16279), that edition itself derives from manuscript copy that manifestly mangled its own sources in at least the calendar section. And those lost sources in turn depended in uninvestigated ways on an ancestry that included 'Whitchurch' and 'Grafton' branches diverging from the lost printers' copy of 1549.

If the comparison is limited to the two first editions of 1559 – Grafton's and 'JC1' – the litany blunder of Wolfe and Whitchurch clearly indicates that Grafton's STC 16291 is the better. But no modern edition has yet been based wholly on what Grafton and Kingston printed in 1559, because each of the extant copies contains between one and twenty-nine sheets actually printed in 1552 (and because two sheets exist in distinct 1559 settings). In one particular quire there can be only one practical answer, and that is the

---

[A] Cambridge University Library has one copy with neither cancel (Syn.7.54.7), one with only that for the colophon (SSS.1.3), and one with both (Syn.7.54.8).
[B] *Stationers and Printers*, II, 765 nA.

calendar quire. As already discussed, both Kingston (in Grafton's edition) and Wolfe (in JC1) corrected some of the 1552 errors in the lectionary. But the first known editions in which all those errors have been corrected is JC3 (itself perhaps following the lost preliminaries of JC2), which is otherwise far from being an ideal copytext.

To determine the chronological order of each extant quire of JC2 and JC3 I had to collate the texts in sufficient detail to ascertain whether each page of each forme appeared to share the same status. Had I intended to edit the text I would have needed to work far more slowly and meticulously – but I can certify that apart from the calendar quire and lines B4^{v}21–5^{v}27, the only rational choice of copytext for the 1559 ancestor of all subsequent editions of *The Book of Common Prayer* would be JC1 (STC 16292). Both JC2 and JC3 are replete with the kinds of compositorial error to be found in virtually all early modern reprints of any text. Terminal letters are added or omitted, sometimes inadvertently and sometimes perhaps misguidedly, thus changing number (disciples/disciple, destroyer/destroyers) and creating either 'indifferent' variants or nonsense (shal/shalt, and/an, hath/hat). Prepositions, articles, and other short words are occasionally added but more often omitted (all, also, as, but, in, one, out, some, the, to, were), and obvious typos are far from rare (afrer, fillek, lenger, pleople).

When recording variants I worked on the assumption that unless the reverse was obvious, the JC1 readings were usually correct and departures from them were errors (which more often than not proved to be the case). In the following discussion, therefore, reference by signature and line is to the JC1 reading, and may not always quite match that of the reprints.[A] Apart from obvious typographical errors, JC2's departures from JC1 are usually followed by JC3. In one of the more notable examples, JC2 turns 'O God make spede to saue vs' into 'O God make haste to spede vs' (A2˙13). A few pages later, in 'he sitteth on the right hande of the father ... from whence he shal come' (B1^{v}4–5), JC2 substitutes '&' for the first 'he' and 'thence' for 'whence'. Not quite without precedent, at P2^{v}7 Kingston's compositor in JC2 alters 'there is no other name' to 'there is none other name', and as with the previous two examples, JC3 follows suit.[B] Another error is not merely repeated by JC3 but made worse. At I8^{v}30–31, JC1 reads 'Thou shalt loue the Lord

---

[A] I adopt this rule mainly because while JC1 is readily available online (in EEBO, search STC 16292), JC2 at York Minster is not easy for most readers to access.
[B] Curiously, 'none' revives a reading otherwise unique to Grafton's first edition of 1552 (STC 16286.5, sig. &1^{v}32), which is hardly a source one would expect to find influencing JC2.

thy God', and after JC2 had rendered the last four words as 'the Lord the God', JC3 compressed them to 'thy lord god'.

Those and other errors make it reasonably clear that most of the printers of JC3 used JC2 as copy. Cawood, however, may have been an exception, because his sheets are less prone to follow JC2 errors. At G3^{v}35, where JC2 transformed 'downe from the tre' to 'downe from the the', the error was perhaps obvious enough for Cawood's compositor to have corrected without assistance, but that is rather less likely at K4^{v}11, where JC1's 'bādes of all those synnes' is not self-evidently more correct than JC2's 'handes of all those sinnes' (JC3 has 'bandes').

When I began checking the earlier history of some of these readings, however, it became clear that a significant number of the variants in both JC2 and JC3 were the results of two distinct attempts to correct earlier errors that either originated in JC1 or were perpetuated by it. One blunder of JC1's own is the omission of 'come to' from 'We do not presume to come to this thy Table' at M8^{v}11, which might not have been beyond the ability of Kingston's compositor to correct in JC2 without help. But the erroneous 'for to forgeue vs' at L5^{r}9, also found in all 1552 editions but not in JC2–3, is a rather less obvious misquotation of 'for to geue vs' in *Benedictus* (where it is correct in all editions of 1549, 1552, and 1559).

Two other errors that were first committed in Edward's reign, repeated by JC1, but corrected in JC2–3, are the omission of the bishop's '¶Let vs pray' after O4^{v}18 and the substitution of 'hath pleased the Lorde' for 'pleaseth the Lorde' in the burial service at P3^{v}24. Both errors originated in Whitchurch's second edition of 1552 (STC 16281). But the bewildering variety over the years on the various occasions when the versicle '{Lord/O Lord} hear {our/my} {prayer/prayers}' is answered by 'And let {our/my} cry come {to/unto} thee' defies easy definition of what, in any given case, is an error and what a correction.[A]

If, however, an effort was indeed made to correct the text in preparation for JC2, it was less effective than a second reading undertaken before JC3 was printed. One of the textual errors introduced by JC1 and repeated in JC2 was in the litany, when the congregation asked to be delivered 'In al our time of tribulation' instead of the correct 'In al time of our tribulation', which JC3 duly corrected. More surprisingly, the obsolete reference in JC1 to 'the king and his ministers' was unthinkingly repeated in JC2, and left for JC3 to correct to 'the Quene & hir ministers' (O3^{v}15). Requiring rather more alertness was an error found in all 1552 editions and JC1–2. On I1^v the

---

[A] In JC1, see O4^r, O7^v, O9^v, P6^v, and P9^v.

number of those fed by seven loaves ought to have been 'about' four thousand as in the Great Bible (Mark 8:9), all 1549 editions, and again in JC3 – not 'aboue' four thousand as in all intervening editions.

But even though JC3 corrects some significant errors in its immediate predecessors, it cannot claim to be the 'best' of the 1559 folios. The inevitable accumulation of careless misprints by the compositors of both JC2 and JC3 can be only partly offset by the occasional corrections. For every misplaced long 's' such as that in 'Our sather which art in heauen' (JC1, N6^v), JC3 can supply a misplaced 'f' as in 'O ye spirites and foules of the righteous' (A4^{v}17). Likewise, it can turn the 'felowshippe of the mistery' into that of the 'ministerye' (C5^{v}1), ask for the congregation to be 'offended' instead of 'defēded' (D2^{r}30), and transform the 'natural' into the 'carnall' (P5^{r}1). For all the many shortcomings of the first Jugge-and-Cawood edition (STC 16292), if we set aside sheet B4:5 and the calendar quire it remains unquestionably the most authoritative extant version of the 1559 text as prescribed by Parliament, Elizabeth, and her Privy Council.

CHAPTER 9

The Quarto and Octavo Editions

When the new English liturgy was intoduced in 1549, the immediate and urgent demand was for books to be used by the clergy. In an age lacking the technical ability to make the customized correction of vision easy, affordable, or widespread, what were needed first were editions set in type large enough to be sight-read by clergy whose eyes were no longer young. Accordingly, during the limited period in which '1549' editions were being printed, all but one of the known editions were printed in folio. The lone exception is a quarto printed in Worcester by John Oswen and dated 24 May – thus unexpectedly preceding his folio edition dated 30 July.[A]

Despite the '1549' date on all editions of the first Edwardian prayer book printed in England, some of them were probably printed in 1550, while the only known Dublin edition is dated 1551.[B] It is likewise possible – indeed, likely – that the latest of the '1552' editions were printed in early 1553. But they all necessarily antedate Mary's accession in July of that year, so they were being produced for only half as long as their '1549' predecessors. Unsurprisingly, folio editions greatly outnumber those in smaller formats. But two quarto editions printed by Whitchurch have survived, and he and Grafton each printed at least one edition in octavo.

In 1559, however, only four editions in folio are known to have been printed before the printers turned their attention to smaller formats. The factors that influence survival will be discussed in more detail in Chapter 10, but for the present I shall simply observe that when all else is equal (as it rarely is), large books have a better chance of surviving than do small ones. So while there are five known copies of each of the first two folio editions and six of the fourth, like JC2 each of the quarto editions is known only from a single imperfect copy.

[A] STC 16271 (quarto) and 16276 (folio). [B] STC 16277.

The Two Quartos

The revised STC lists the quarto editions in the wrong order, so I shall begin with STC 16293.3 (Plate 8). If we ignore for a moment the appended psalter, at first sight it would appear that the prayer book itself is complete. It is a quarto in eights, collating a–b^8, A–T^8 V^{10}. Each quire except the last has eight leaves, made up of two sheets of which each is folded into four leaves. The sheets were folded first and then quired: leaves 1–2 and 7–8 are the outer sheet and leaves 3–6 the inner sheet. The only exception is the final quire V^{10}, which has an additional halfsheet in the middle forming leaves 5–6. The first fourteen quires (a–b and A–M) were printed by Richard Jugge; the last eight (N–V) by John Cawood – and the most interesting peculiarity of this edition is that on page R1^r Cawood includes the Black Rubric. Moreover, it is material to note that in order to do so he had to make the page two lines longer than any other, and even then had to run the Black Rubric on without a break from the previous rubric.[A] There is only one explanation that makes sense of Cawood's mistake: the copy from which he was printing included the Black Rubric, but he (or his compositor) had not been told that it should be omitted.

The printers were evidently setting from one of the two Whitchurch quartos of 1552–53, having decided for reasons of their own to take the main text with which Whitchurch had filled thirty sheets (A–P^8) and spread it over forty and a half (A–T^8 V^{10}). On average, then, each of the Elizabethan pages ought to contain only three-quarters as much text as its Edwardian source. But comparatively few pages consist of nothing but text, and there are numerous large-type headings, indented rubrics and responses in small type, frequent white lines (consisting only of space), and display capitals of a wide variety of sizes. If we limit our consideration to text-only pages, Whitchurch's norm was thirty-seven lines measuring approximately 108 mm (total 3.996 metres); Jugge's is thirty-three lines of approximately 96 mm (3.168 metres) and Cawood's thirty-two lines of 93 mm (2.976 metres).

Cawood begins his quire Q exactly halfway down Whitchurch's M2^r, and first expands four and a half Whitchurch pages into six of his own (Q1^r–3^v). His next page (Q4^r) begins at the same point as Whitchurch's M4^v, and he stretches the next seven Whitchurch pages (M4^v–7^v) into ten of his own (Q4^r–8^v), ending at exactly the same point in mid-sentence in

---

[A] The STC entry claims that the rubric was 'apparently erroneously added in this ed[ition] as the page is 2 lines longer than the others', but if 16293.3 had been a reprint of 16293 that would hardly have been possible.

the fourth of the Communion rubrics ('And yf anye of | the bread or wine remaine'). So when he began work on quire R he assumed that he could fit the text from Whitchurch's M8^r into his own page R1^r. In Whitchurch's edition, that text – thirty-five lines of 73-mm type, set to a measure of 105 mm – occupied only three-quarters of a page. But twenty-two of those lines were the Black Rubric.

In whatever order the pages of quire R were set, when Cawood's compositor came to R1^r he ran into trouble. He was using an 82-mm fount where Whitchurch had used one of 73 mm, and found that even setting in a measure 7 mm wider than he had used for the rubrics on Q8^v was not enough to solve his apparent space problem. Instead of Whitchurch's three-quarters of a page, Cawood's compositor needed forty lines of text in a page whose 'usual' length was only thirty-seven. The second of those lines would have contained only the last three-letter word of the fourth rubric, so he was able to save a line by making the Black Rubric run on from it instead of starting a new line. But he found no other ways of taking up any slack, and so had to settle for an unusually long page of thirty-nine lines. Evidently, then, whoever marked up the Whitchurch copy for setting had failed to delete the Black Rubric (without which page R1^r would have contained only fourteen lines).

But despite first appearances, the extant copy is not quite complete. Although the way in which the psalms and other scriptures are distributed throughout the year is explained on preliminary b3^r–4^r, and while the tables of proper lessons and psalms follow on b4^v–8^r and the dates of the legal terms on b8^v, there is no calendar. The collation shown in STC's chart of editions as 'Heth. 3' (11: 88) includes a hypothetical quire c^6, presumably conjectured by John R. Hetherington, whose work on quarto editions was an important source. But in the STC entries for the two quartos, the notes on imperfections make no mention of the absent calendar, so the revisers may perhaps not have realized that the preliminaries themselves are incomplete. Hetherington's c^6 would be a plausible guess if all that was missing was a calendar with a month on each page. But the contents list on A1^v calls for the calendar to be preceded by an almanack, so even if both sides of leaf c8 were left blank, a complete quire c^8 is more likely.

The second quarto edition, STC 16293, is more seriously incomplete. All that survives was printed by Richard Jugge without Cawood's assistance, but the only parts that unquestionably 'belong' to this edition are quires D–L^8 and N–T^8. Quire V^{10} is lost, while quire M and everything present before D1^r (namely quires a–b^8, A^8, and leaf B1) are in the same setting as the previous edition. When two editions are produced in quick succession it is quite possible for an occasional sheet or quire proper to one of them to be found in the other (as witness the appearance of quires D, G, and I of JC2 in copies of JC3). But while I am quite prepared to accept that explanation for quire M, the fact that everything before quire D is either missing or 'proper' to the previous edition is suspicious. Books usually suffer the most extreme damage at either the front or the back (or both), and I find it easy to imagine a book that had lost its first six quires being supplied with three quires and a leaf from an even more defective copy of another edition. The alternative – an accident that destroyed fifteen leaves between B1 and D1 but left everything before and after in good condition – seems less likely. What might seem even more difficult to explain is that in each case the presumed quire c^8 is missing, but without having left any traces on either $b8^v$ or $A1^r$ to suggest how or why it was lost. As we shall see in the next chapter, however, there is a special reason why, in or after 1561, the calendars in 1559 prayer books might have been deliberately removed – as indeed they were from one extant copy of Grafton's folio edition, the only known copy of JC2, and two extant copies of JC3.

It is, of course, possible that Jugge, having printed only enough copies of quires C–L and N–V for one edition, then decided to print twice as many copies of quires a–b, A–B, and M in order to make a start on a second edition. But I cannot consider it likely.

The Psalter

While each folio prayer book of 1552 was printed with an appended ordinal, the quarto and octavo editions had a psalter appended instead:[A] the complete 'Psalter or Psalmes of Dauid' in the Great Bible translation, divided into the thirty 'days' defined by the liturgical calendar and followed by two dozen 'Godly Prayers'. What accompanied at least the first of the 1559 quartos was a psalter of exactly that kind, except that the last two prayers were omitted. But although this psalter was manifestly intended to accompany a prayer book, and although their royal patent gave Jugge and Cawood a monopoly of all 'books which we, for the service of God in the

---

[A] In *The Book of Common Prayer*, 783, the third sentence of Cummings's notes on the Psalter is a little misleading. In 1549 Oswen printed a psalter compatible with his quarto prayer book; Grafton and Whitchurch each printed quarto psalters, but no extant prayer books to match. In 1552–62 psalters were printed to accompany editions in quarto and octavo, and from 1564 a psalter was included in every edition.

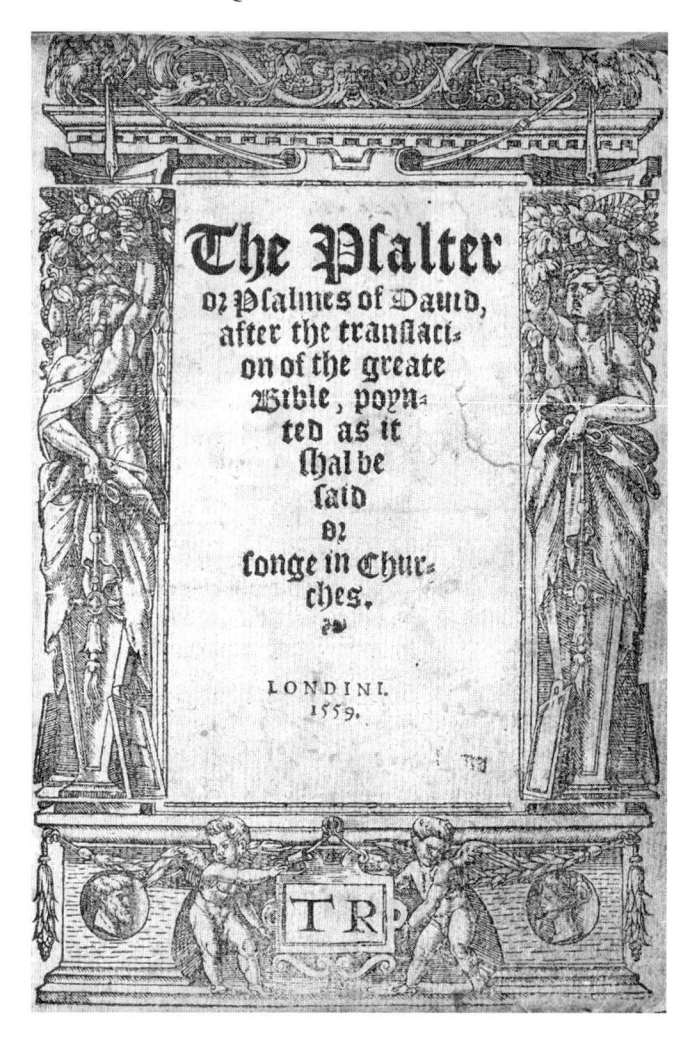

> The Psalter
> or Psalmes of Dauid,
> after the translati-
> on of the greate
> Bible, poyn-
> ted as it
> shal be
> said
> or
> songe in Chur-
> ches.
>
> LONDINI.
> 1559.

> ¶ Imprinted at London by Wyllyam
> Seres dwellinge at the weste
> ende of Poules, at the signe
> of the Hedghoge.

Figure 23 Title-page and colophon of the Seres psalter.
(© The British Library Board, C.194.a.207, A1ʳ, M8ᵛ.)

churches of this our Realm of England, will have commanded hereafter to be used',[A] it was printed neither by nor even *for* the Queen's Printers.

Two copies of this psalter survive, both at the British Library. One is bound with the first of the quarto editions (STC 16293.3), but lacks the final quire M⁸. The other is complete, but bound alone as if an independent book. The treatment of this copy by the STC revisers is mystifying. Suggesting without any justification that the final quire 'may not belong' (which it unquestionably does), they treat the psalter as self-evidently belonging to what they failed to recognize as the second of the quarto editions (16293, about whose own psalter we have no evidence at all) instead of the edition to which the other extant copy is actually appended.[B] It is, of course, conceivable that enough copies of that same psalter could have been printed to serve for both quarto editions of the prayer book – but the only edition with which we can confidently associate it is the first.

The colophon of that psalter claims that it was 'Imprinted at London by Wyllyam Seres dwelling at the weste ende of Poules, at the signe of the Hedghoge' (M8ᵛ: Figure 23). That is not literally true, because Seres was never an actual printer, but as a publisher he almost invariably had his publications described as printed 'by' rather than 'for' him. A former household servant and continued protégé of Sir William Cecil's,[C] while Cecil was Edward's principal secretary Seres had been granted a six-year patent of monopoly for 'all man*er* of book*es* of private prayers called . . . prymers bothe in grete volumes and small . . . sett furthe agreagle [*sic*] and acco*u*rding to the booke of com*m*en prayers'.[D] But a year and a half later Mary cancelled that patent, and when she called in all books 'concerning' the Edwardian liturgy Seres not only lost a substantial stock of primers but reportedly also spent some time in prison.

In early July 1559, with Cecil now principal secretary to a second monarch, Seres received a new patent by the accelerated process known as an 'immediate warrant'.[E] This new grant was for life rather than a

---

[A] In the original warrant of 20 March 1559, 'libro*rum* quos nos p*ro* dei seruicio in templis huius Regni n*ost*ri Anglie imposte*rum* vti mandaue*r*imus' (TNA: PRO, C/82/1062/24).

[B] As a consequence, ESTC misleadingly credits the British Library with two copies of the unique STC 16293: the actual defective copy lacking a psalter, and the separate psalter treated as a defective volume lacking that specific edition of the prayer book. Meanwhile, the Library catalogues the first quarto edition and its appended psalter as if they were separate and unrelated items, (1) and (2), sharing a single binding (C.112.c.10).

[C] Blayney, 'William Cecil and the Stationers', 26–9.

[D] TNA: PRO, C 82/962/31, lines 15–17 of main text.

[E] For a description of the procedures by which patents were granted, see *Stationers and Printers*, Appendix D (II, 952–9).

specified number of years, and to compensate for his Marian losses it was expanded to include

> psalters both in great volumes and in small in Latine or englishe, whiche now be, or at anie tyme herafter shalbe setfurthe and permitted by vs our heires and Successours or by anie other persons therto authorised by vs ... Anie other priuiledge or anie other order hertofore graunted or taken to the contrarie notw*it*hstanding.[A]

What the authorities may have intended this to cover was a special form of separate psalter without the added prayers but prefaced by a short selection from the prayer book (the list of proper lessons and psalms, Morning and Evening Prayer, and the Litany). But taken literally, the wording as granted appears to override the Queen's Printers' right to include psalms in either prayer books or even bibles – and that is apparently how Seres himself intended it and tried to enforce it. So the psalter appended to the first quarto prayer book of 1559 was printed neither for nor by Jugge and/or Cawood. The first eight quires (A–H^8) were printed for Seres by Kingston's former partner, the Stationer Henry Sutton,[B] and the last four (I–M^8) by William Copland.

In the surviving Whitchurch quartos of 1552 (STC 16288–8a), the psalter fills twenty-one sheets (A–I^8 K^4 aa^8), and a typical page contains thirty-seven lines of text. The Seres version, however, fills twenty-four sheets of thirty-two-line pages. In Sutton's section, whoever marked up the 1552 copy apparently placed at least one of his marks ambiguously, next to the first line of the last verse of Psalm 79. The compositor setting page G8^v evidently thought that the mark was placed after that line, which he therefore set as the final line of his page. But whoever set page H1^r thought the mark came before the line, and set it again as the first line of *his* page. In the section allotted to Copland, the 1552 editions of the Godly Prayers had filled thirteen pages, beginning on the third page of the last quire and ending on the final recto (aa2^r–8^r). Copland also found himself beginning those prayers on the third page of what would be his last quire, but in his shorter pages the twenty-second prayer ended more than halfway down the final verso (M8^v). He would have needed at least another half-sheet (four pages) to include the

---

[A] TNA: PRO, C 82/1066/[32], lines 10–14 of main text. Unusually even for an immediate warrant, below the text Cecil has written and signed the note, 'This may passe to ye Gr: seale immediatly | W. Cecill'.

[B] The title-page border (McK & F 37) was originally initialled T P for Thomas Petyt, but when it passed to his ex-apprentice Thomas Raynald the younger, a 'leg' (perhaps a piece of wire bent into a square-cornered staple) was added to turn the P into an R. By 1559 the border had passed to John King (who simply ignored the initials), from whom Sutton evidently borrowed it.

last two prayers – and I suspect that they were omitted only because either Copland or Seres was reluctant to use up any more paper.

But Elizabeth can surely not have intended Seres to have a complete monopoly of psalms in all possible contexts. It was less than four months since she had granted her royal printers a patent for all books used for church services (which necessarily included psalms in the Great Bible translation), and Reyner Wolfe had a pre-existing royal right to print any Latin books of interest to the Crown. When she signed the immediate warrant for Seres it is highly unlikely that Elizabeth first read through the whole document. She probably read only a brief docket that would have described the scope of the grant as merely 'primers and psalters'. It is more difficult to excuse Cecil, who was evidently trying to compensate a loyal retainer for whatever difficulties Mary's cancellation of his former patent had created. But during the first few months of Elizabeth's reign even her indefatigable secretary may not have foreseen all the possible implications of a comparatively minor book-trade grant.

Seres himself, however, evidently knew exactly what he was trying to achieve, and he is the one who would have drafted the document (albeit probably with professional assistance) to further his own ambitions. The preamble may or may not be free of exaggeration when it recounts how Seres

> had by the graunt of our late deare brother of worthie memorie king Edward the sixte licence to printe all maner of Primers . . ., And in the tyme of our late dere Syster Quene Mary was not only defeated therof to his great losse, but was also imprisoned long tyme and depriued of great multitude of the said prymers, and also of other great nombres of book*es* whiche tended to his vtter vndoing.[A]

But there can be little doubt that his move was carefully planned. Jugge and Cawood either temporarily agreed (pending arbitration) not to print a psalter for their first quarto, or were simply unable to prevent some or all copies being sold with the Seres psalter appended. Some kind of compromise would have had to be negotiated in short order, and given that Jugge, Cawood, Wolfe, and Seres were all Stationers, the most likely venue would have been the Court of Assistants at Stationers' Hall (of whose proceedings in 1559 no records survive). A deal must evidently have been arranged substantially before the end of the year, because in and after the octavo edition of 1559 the psalter was always printed either by or for the Queen's Printers without mention of Seres. His own subsequent Elizabethan

---

[A] TNA: PRO, C 82/1066/[32], lines 2–6 of main text.

psalters were separately published, each prefaced by a very short selection from the prayer book.[A]

With only one copy of the first quarto extant, we cannot know whether or not some copies included a now-lost psalter printed by Jugge and/or Cawood and intended to be part of it. Were that the case, some copies of the Seres psalter may have had to be sold separately – and as it happens the only extant perfect copy survives as a singleton. Depending on how quickly the arbitration succeeded, the second quarto (STC 16293) may well have had its own psalter printed by one or other of the Queen's Printers (perhaps Cawood, who otherwise printed none of it). Since nothing after quire T survives there is no way to know – but the present assumption that the Seres psalter 'belongs' to that edition has no foundation.

The Extant Octavo

The only small-format edition of 1559 that has survived intact is an octavo (STC 16293.5) of which the only copy is in the Morgan Library & Museum, New York. The prayer book itself fills twenty-nine sheets of paper, and the imprint credits it to Jugge and Cawood (Figure 24). The psalter has its own title set in the same woodcut border, but has only the date 'Anno.1559.' and no imprint. The colophon on page ²R3ᵛ, however, likewise attributes it to both Queen's Printers, so the problem of the conflicting monopolies had evidently been solved. Moreover, this is the first 1559 edition to have been printed from start to finish by a single printer – but at this stage in the narrative it should come as no great surprise that he was neither Jugge nor Cawood but John Kingston.

The Newcastle Fragment

After the entry for the Kingston octavo in the revised STC is added a brief note:

> NEK has a frag. of an unrecorded 8° ed., w. heading on A8ʳ: 'A briefe declaration ...'; this appears on ♒ 8ᵛ of the present ed.[B]

[A] All parties may have been equally content with the compromise. In May 1560 the High Commision required the Master and Wardens of the Stationers to co-opt the Queen's Printers in their efforts to 'stay' the presses that were apparently infringing the Seres patent (Arber, II, 62, from Stationers' Hall, Liber A, 2ᵛ–3ʳ). For the Seres psalter of 1562–3 (the earliest extant edition, STC 2384.5) Richard Jugge lent one of his monogrammed title-page borders (McK & F III) to the printer of the Psalms themselves (Leonard Askell, a Seres dependant who contributed sheets ²A–R⁸) for use on the part-title.

[B] The zigzag symbol is not a letter but part of a set of zodiac signs that I have not seen elsewhere. Its name is Aquarius.

The Booke of Common Prayer,

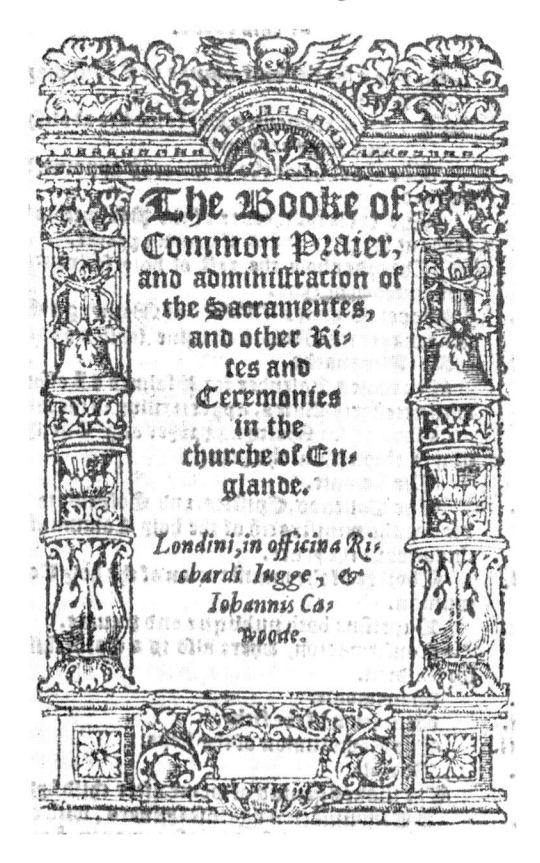

and administration of the Sacramentes, and other Rites and Ceremonies in the churche of Englande.

Londini, in officina Richardi Iugge, & Iohannis Cawoode.

¶ Imprinted at London by Richard Iugge, and John Cawoode, printers to the Quenes Maiestie.

M.D.LIX.

Cum Priuilegio.

Figure 24 Title-page and colophon of the complete octavo edition (STC 16293.5). (The Morgan Library & Museum, New York, PML 5421, πA1^r, R3^v.)

This information was reported to the revisers before 1976 (perhaps not long before), but the reporter apparently failed to leave a permanent record of the fragment's precise location in Newcastle University Library, and its whereabouts are no longer known. A lot can nevertheless be deduced from that note, despite its terseness. To begin with, the fragment was evidently never catalogued as a separate printed item, which probably means that it was (and with any luck, still is) a piece of printing-house waste used as one or more endpapers in an early modern binding – presumably a London binding, although not necessarily on an English book.

Had the date been uncertain, that fact would probably have been mentioned in the note. I therefore assume that appending it to the entry for Kingston's 1559 octavo strongly implies that the date was not in doubt – which suggests that part or all of the title leaf was present and legible.

The most important clue is the reporter's apparent certainty that the page headed 'A briefe declaration' (of the dates of the four law terms) was page $A8^r$ – or, as we shall see, more probably $^{\pi}A8^r$. The only way of knowing that the quire was signed 'A' (rather than ¶ or *, or another of the indeducible symbols common in preliminaries) would have been if at least one surviving page actually had a signature.

Now if an uncut, unbound sheet of common octavo is placed with the long side horizontal and the title-page in the bottom right corner, the page immediately to the left of the title is signature 8^v – but neither the title leaf nor its neighbour would have displayed a signature on either side. Above those two pages, printed upside down, would once have been pages 5^r (left) and 4^v (right). So if we assume that this right-hand half of the original octavo sheet survived in generally sound condition, there would probably have been a signature at the foot of page 4^r. And had the whole sheet survived, at the extreme left leaves 2 (upright) and 3 (inverted) would probably also have been signed on their rectos. If, therefore, an extant signature identified the sheet as quire A^8 (or $^{\pi}A^8$), it would seem that the fragment included at least a substantial part of the right-hand half of a sheet signed A. Moreover we can, I believe, go a step or two beyond that.

The presence of the 'briefe declaration' on $A8^r$ is of particular interest. I know of only two Elizabethan editions in any format in which that declaration appears on signature 8^r of a quire signed A. Neither is an octavo, but each is a quarto in 8's with the preliminaries printed by Richard Jugge himself, one in 1560 (STC 16294) and the other in 1562

(16295).^A Those are the only known early editions in which the 'declaration' immediately precedes (and is backed by the first page of) the Act of Uniformity – although despite the rearrangement of the preliminaries, both editions reprint the folio contents list without change. If the Newcastle fragment does likewise, the Act probably begins on A8^v with an ornamental W that will allow the printer to be identified. The prime suspect being Jugge, it will probably be the only small W he is known to have owned at this date (and which is reproduced twice in Figure 6).

In both those quarto editions, what fills the space between the contents list ($^\pi$A1^v) and the declaration ($^\pi$A8^r) is the twelve-page calendar. And if the fragment is ever rediscovered, a comparison between what survives of its calendar and the one in Jugge's 1560 quarto could be of considerable interest, as will be seen in the next chapter. So despite the brevity of the revised STC's note, it allows several plausible deductions to be made, including that the most likely printer of quire A^8 (or more probably $^\pi$A^8) was Richard Jugge himself.

[A] Both were shared with John Cawood, who printed almost everything after quire P, including the whole psalter. The one difference is that for unknown reasons in 1560 (STC 16294), Jugge printed the middle halfsheet V5:6 in what was otherwise Cawood's quire V^{10}.

CHAPTER 10

The 1561 Revision of the Calendar

The Lectionary from 1549 to 1560

As noted in Chapter 6 (pp. 91–2), with the single exception of a lesson on Christmas morning, all the differences in the lectionary between the calendars of 1549 and 1552 were either simple misprints in one or other edition or blunders made in 1552 by whoever prepared the manuscript copy on which both printers depended. And while the 1552 table of proper lessons was extensively revised in 1559, in the actual calendars of the first two 1559 editions the only changes are corrections (and in Wolfe's case also miscorrections) of some but not all of the blunders of 1552. No copy of the third edition's calendar survives, but in the fourth edition the only departure from the lectionary of 1549 is the Christmas morning lesson already mentioned. Both the extant quarto editions are missing their calendars, but the extant octavo agrees in all lectionary essentials with the fourth of the folios, as does the sole surviving quarto of 1560 (STC 16294).

All would therefore seem to have been settled, except for one significant oversight. Most of the readings newly assigned in the preliminary table of proper lessons in 1559 were for moveable feasts, to be read instead of the lessons assigned by the calendar for the days on which those feasts happened to fall in any given year. The revised table also assigned new proper lessons to nineteen fixed feasts, each of which fell on the same date in every year – but the calendar itself continued to assign the 'traditional' lessons to those days instead.[A]

[A] 25 January, 2 and 24 February, 25 March, 25 April, 1 May, 11 and 29 June, 25 July, 24 August, 21 and 29 September, 18 and 28 October, 30 November, and 21 and 26–28 December. On the last of those dates only the first evening lesson was affected; on the other days the first lessons for both morning and evening were changed.

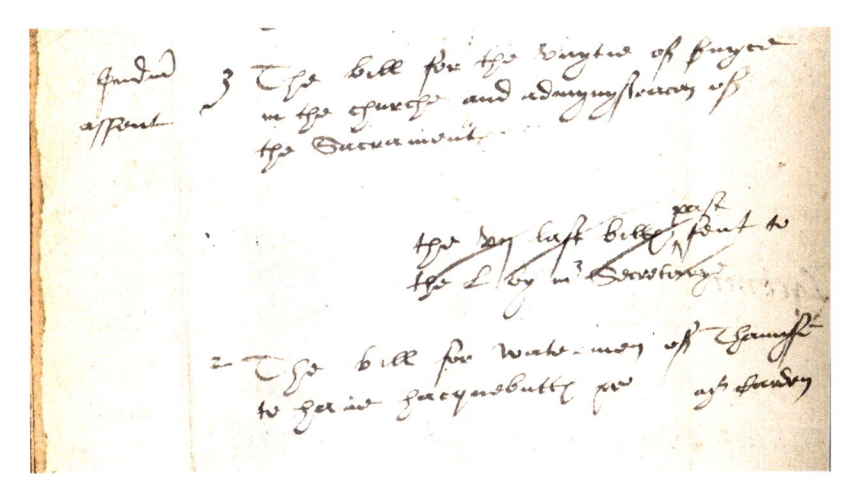

Plate 1a 20 April 1559. The Act of Uniformity is passed by the Commons, but their attempt to deliver it to the Lords is unsuccessful.

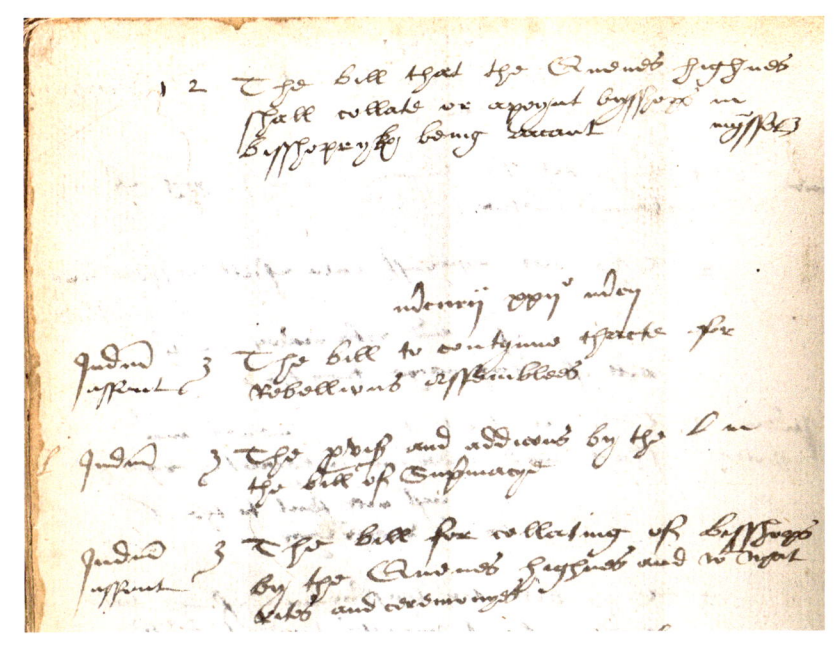

Plate 1b 21–22 March 1559. The (lost) Act for Collating Bishops is read, engrossed, and passed, and the royal assent is recorded in the margin.
(Parliamentary Archives, HC/CL/JO/1/1, pages (a) 210^v and (b) 204^v.)

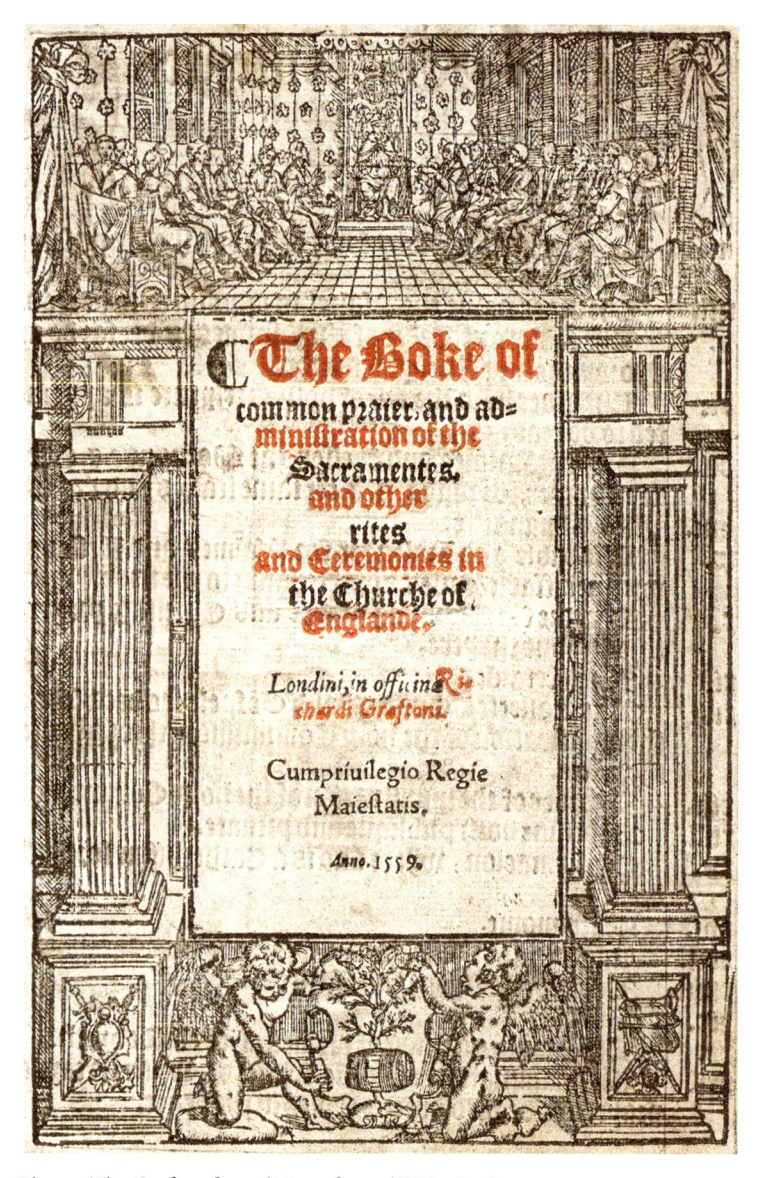

Plate 2 The Grafton first edition of 1559 (STC 16291).
(Corpus Christi College, Oxford, Phi.F.3.7, $^{\pi}$A1^{r}.)

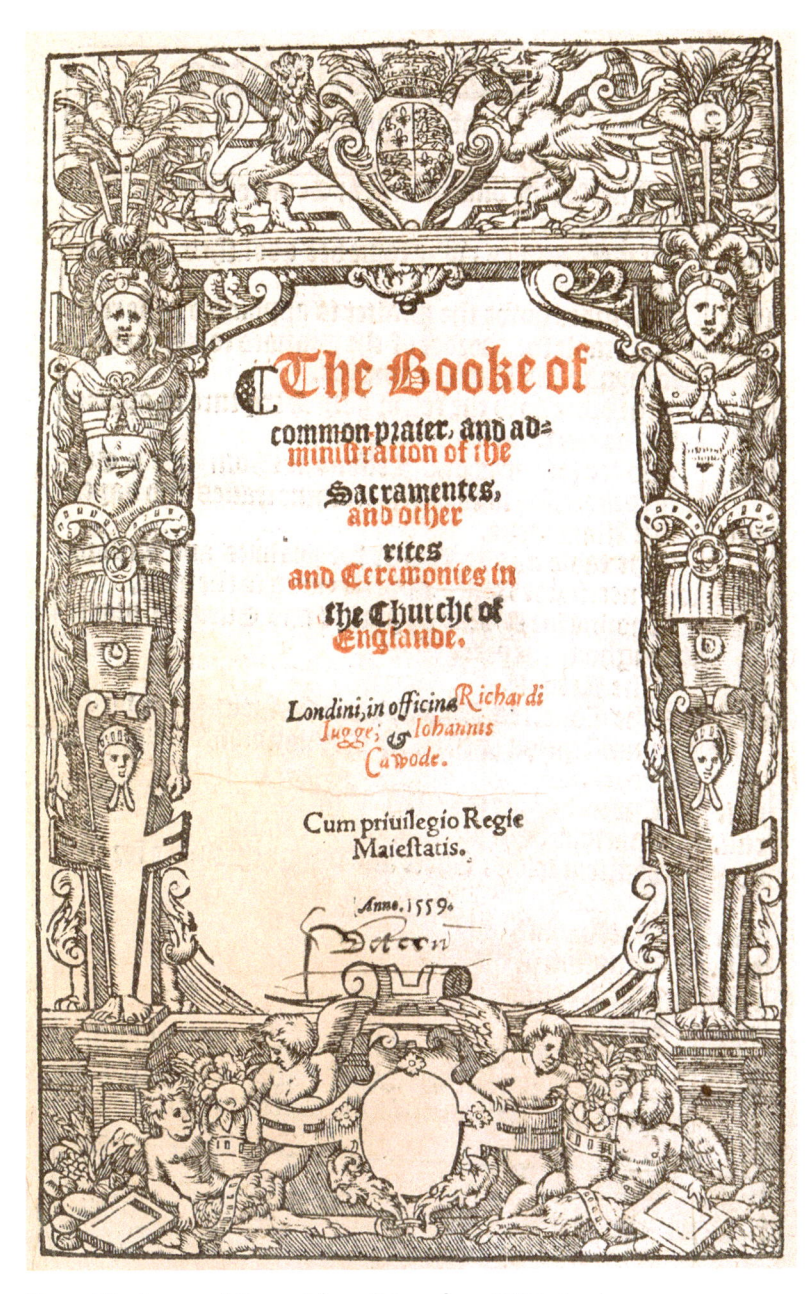

Plate 3 The Jugge-and-Cawood first edition of 1559 (STC 16292).
(© The British Library Board, C.25.m.7, $^{\pi}$A1^{r}, signed by Sir Nicholas Bacon.)

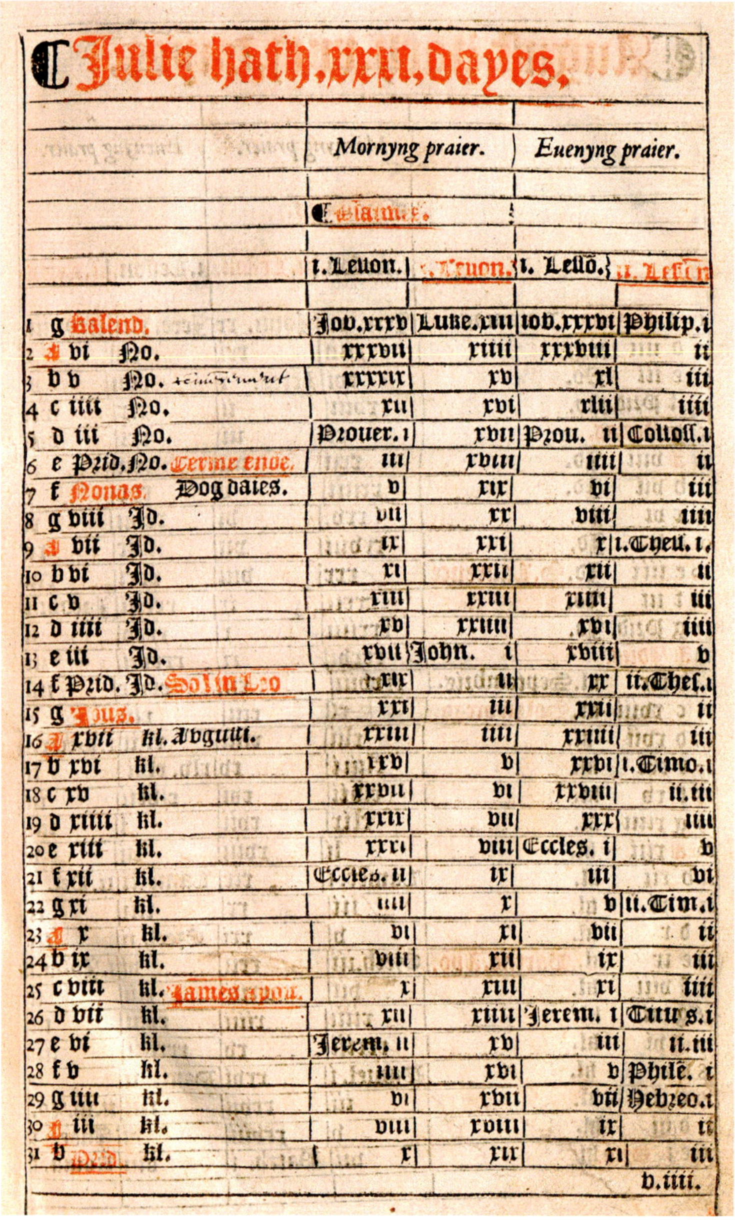

❡ Julie hath .xxxi. dayes.

			Mornyng praier.		Euenyng praier.	
			❡ Biamus.			
			i. Lesson.	ii. Lesson	i. Leśő.	ii. Leſſő
1	g	Kalend.	Iob.xxxv	Luke.xiii	Iob.xxxvi	Philip.i
2	A	vi No.	xxxvii	xiiii	xxxviii	ii
3	b	v No.	xxxix	xv	xl	iii
4	c	iiii No.	xli	xvi	xlii	iiii
5	d	iii No.	Prouer.i	xvii	Prou. ii	Colloſſ.i
6	e	Prid.No. Terme ende.	iii	xviii	iiii	ii
7	f	Nonas Dog daies.	v	xix	vi	iii
8	g	viii Id.	vii	xx	viii	iiii
9	A	vii Id.	ix	xxi	x	i.Theſſ.i
10	b	vi Id.	xi	xxii	xii	ii
11	c	v Id.	xiii	xxiii	xiiii	iii
12	d	iiii Id.	xv	xxiiii	xvi	iiii
13	e	iii Id.	xvii	John. i	xviii	v
14	f	Prid. Id. Sol in Leo	xix	ii	xx	ii.Theſſ.i
15	g	Idus.	xxi	iii	xxii	ii
16	A	xvii kl. August.	xxiii	iiii	xxiiii	iii
17	b	xvi kl.	xxv	v	xxvi	i.Timo.i
18	c	xv kl.	xxvii	vi	xxviii	ii.iii
19	d	xiiii kl.	xxix	vii	xxx	iiii
20	e	xiii kl.	xxxi	viii	Eccles. i	v
21	f	xii kl.	Eccles. ii	ix	iii	vi
22	g	xi kl.	iiii	x	v	ii.Tim.i
23	A	x kl.	vi	xi	vii	ii
24	b	ix kl.	viii	xii	ix	iii
25	c	viii kl. Iames apoſ.	x	xiii	xi	iiii
26	d	vii kl.	xii	xiiii	Ierem. i	Titus.i
27	e	vi kl.	Ierem. ii	xv	iii	ii.iii
28	f	v kl.	iiii	xvi	v	Philē. i
29	g	iiii kl.	vi	xvii	vii	Hebreo.i
30	A	iii kl.	viii	xviii	ix	ii
31	b	Prid. kl.	x	xix	xi	iii
						b. iiii.

Plate 4 Kingston's calendar for the Grafton edition (STC 16291).
(St John's College, Cambridge, A.4.13, b4ʳ.)

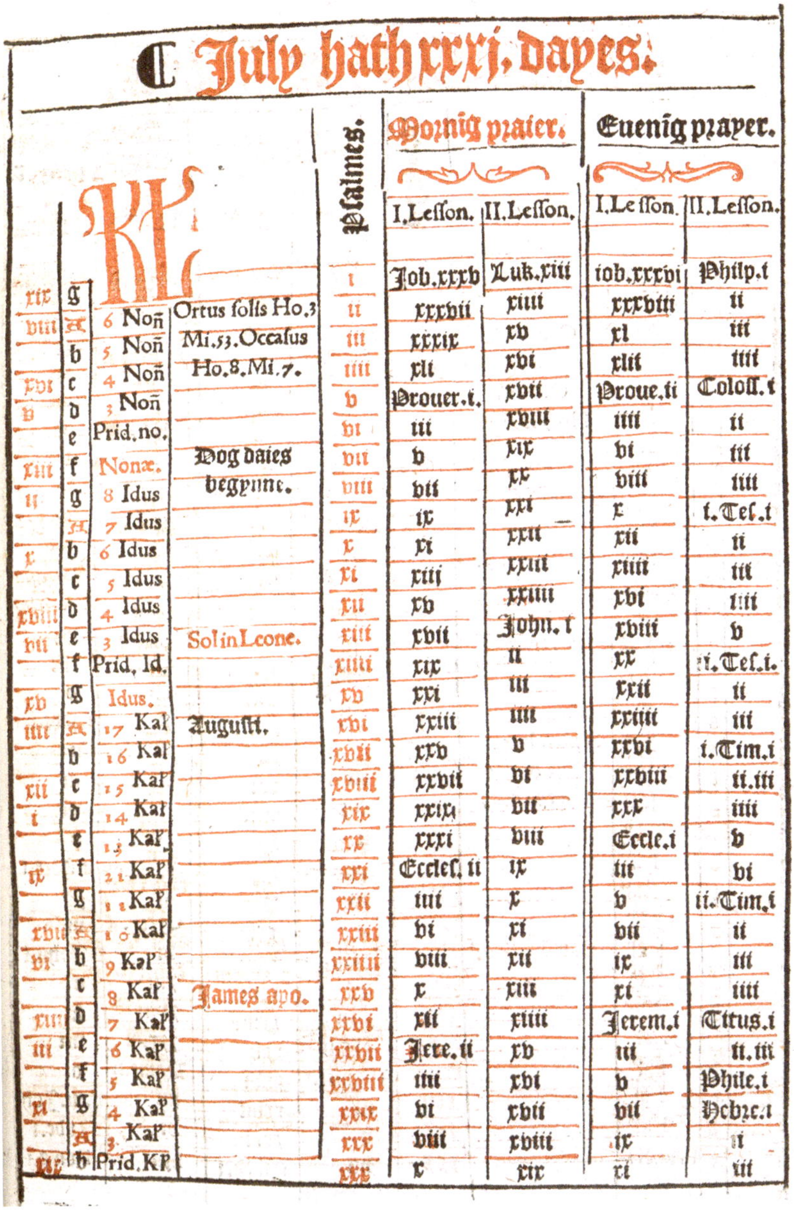

☾ July hath xxxi. dayes.

				Psalmes.	Mornig prater.		Euenig prayer.	
					I. Lesson.	II. Lesson.	I. Lesson.	II. Lesson.
xix	g	KL		i	Job.xxxv	Luk.xiii	iob.xxxvi	Philp.i
viii	A	6 Non	Ortus solis Ho.3	ii	xxxvii	xiiii	xxxviii	ii
	b	5 Non	Mi.53. Occasus	iii	xxxix	xv	xl	iii
xvi	c	4 Non	Ho.8. Mi.7.	iiii	xli	xvi	xlii	iiii
v	d	3 Non		v	Proue.i	xvii	Proue.ii	Coloss.i
	e	Prid. no.		vi	iii	xviii	iiii	ii
xiii	f	Nonæ.	Dog daies	vii	v	xix	vi	iii
ii	g	8 Idus	begynne.	viii	vii	xx	viii	iiii
	A	7 Idus		ix	ix	xxi	x	i.Tes.i
x	b	6 Idus		x	xi	xxii	xii	ii
	c	5 Idus		xi	xiii	xxiii	xiiii	iii
xviii	d	4 Idus		xii	xv	xxiiii	xvi	iiii
vii	e	3 Idus	Sol in Leone.	xiii	xvii	John.i	xviii	v
	f	Prid. Id.		xiiii	xix	ii	xx	vi.Tes.i
xv	g	Idus.		xv	xxi	iii	xxii	ii
iiii	A	17 Kal	August.	xvi	xxiii	iiii	xxiiii	iii
	b	16 Kal		xvii	xxv	v	xxvi	i.Tim.i
xii	c	15 Kal		xviii	xxvii	vi	xxviii	ii.iii
i	d	14 Kal		xix	xxix	vii	xxx	iiii
	e	13 Kal		xx	xxxi	viii	Eccle.i	v
ix	f	12 Kal		xxi	Eccles.ii	ix	iii	vi
	g	11 Kal		xxii	iiii	x	v	ii.Tim.i
xvii	A	10 Kal		xxiii	vi	xi	vii	ii
vi	b	9 Kal		xxiiii	viii	xii	ix	iii
	c	8 Kal	James apo.	xxv	x	xiii	xi	iiii
xiiii	d	7 Kal		xxvi	xii	xiiii	Jerem.i	Titus.i
iii	e	6 Kal		xxvii	Jere.ii	xv	iii	ii.iii
	f	5 Kal		xxviii	iiii	xvi	v	Phile.i
xi	g	4 Kal		xxix	vi	xvii	vii	Hebre.i
	A	3 Kal		xxx	viii	xviii	ix	ii
xix	b	Prid. Kl		xxxi	x	xix	xi	iii

Plate 5 Wolfe's calendar for Jugge and Cawood (STC 16292).
(© The British Library Board, C.25.m.7, $^{\pi}B4^{r}$.)

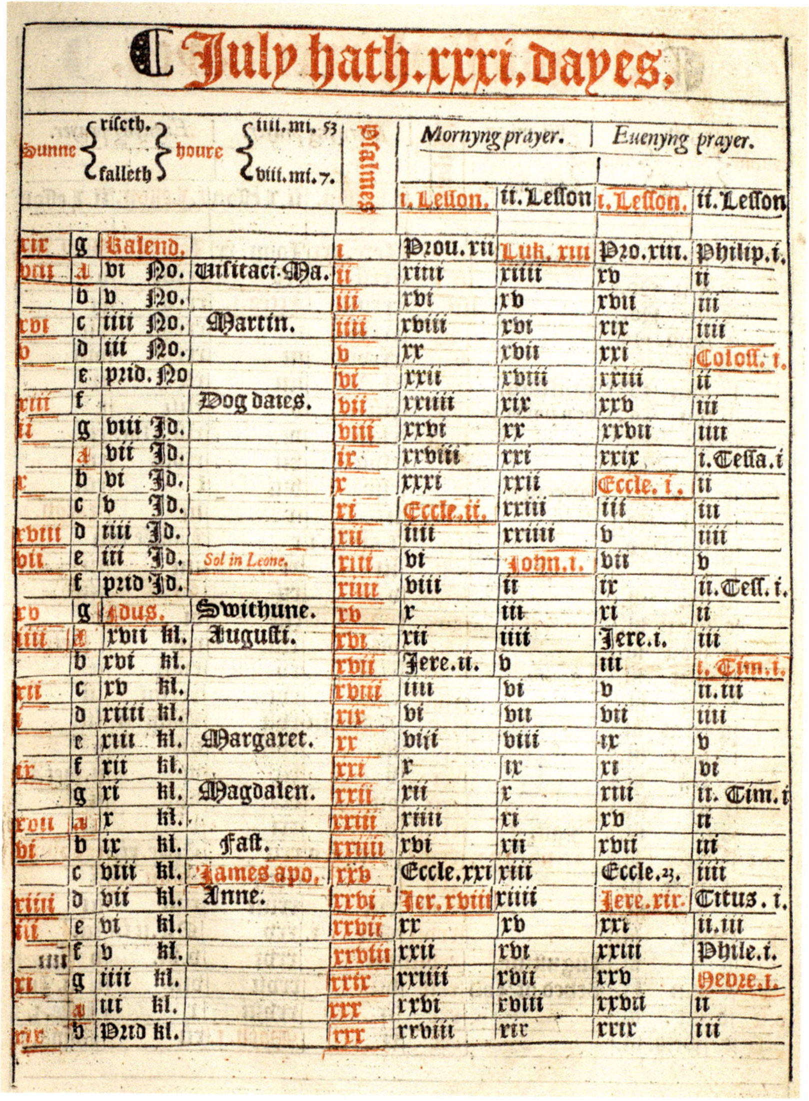

Plate 6 The first edition of Jugge's cancel calendar, 1561.
(York Minster Library, XI.F.19(1), ¹B6ʳ.)

July hath .xxx. dayes.

Sunne			riseth / falleth		houre	vi.mi. 18. / v.mi. 42.	Psalmes	Mornyng prayer.		Evenyng prayer.	
								i. Lesson	ii. Lesson	i. Lesson	ii. Lesson
xix		g	Kalend.	Visitaci. Ma.			i	Prou. xii	Luk. xiii	Pro. xiii	Philip.
viii		A	vi No.				ii	xiiii	xiiii	xv	ii
		b	v No.	Martin.			iii	xvi	xv	xvii	iii
xvi		c	iiii No.				iiii	xviii	xvi	xix	iiii
v		d	iii No.				v	xx	xvii	xxi	Colloss. i.
		e	prid. No	Dog dayes.			vi	xxii	xviii	xxiii	ii
xiii		f	Nonas.				vii	xxiiii	xix	xxv	iii
ii		g	viii Id.				viii	xxvi	xx	xxvii	iiii
		A	vii Id.				ix	xxviii	xxi	xxix	i. Thes. i.
x		b	vi Id.				x	xxxi	xxii	Eccle. i.	ii
		c	v Id.				xi	Eccle. ii.	xxiii	iii	iii
xviii		d	iiii Id.	Sol in Leone.			xii	iiii	xxiiii	v	iiii
vii		e	iii Id.				xiii	vi	John. i.	vii	v
		f	prid. Id.				xiiii	viii	ii	ix	ii. Thes. i
xv		g	Idus.	Swithune.			xv	x	iii	xi	ii
iiii		A	xvii kl.	Augusti.			xvi	xii	iiii	Jere. i.	iii
		b	xvi kl.				xvii	Jere. ii.	v	iii	i. Tim. i
xii		c	xv kl.				xviii	iiii	vi	v	ii iii
i		d	xiiii kl.				xix	vi	vii	v	iiii
		e	xiii kl.	Margaret.			xx	viii	viii	ix	v
ix		f	xii kl.				xxi	x	ix	xi	vi
		g	xi kl.	Magdalen.			xxii	xii	x	xiii	ii. Tim. i
xvii		A	x kl.				xxiii	xiiii	xi	xv	ii
vi		b	ix kl.	Fast.			xxiiii	xvi	xii	xvii	iii
		c	viii kl.	James Apo.			xxv	Eccle. xxi	xiii	Ecl. xxiiii	iiii
xiiii		d	vii kl.	Anne.			xxvi	Jer. xviii	xiiii	Jer. xix	Titus. i.
iii		e	vi kl.				xxvii	xx	xv	xxi	ii iii
		f	v kl.				xxviii	xxii	xvi	xxiii	Phile. i.
xi		g	iiii kl.				xxix	xxiiii	xvii	xxv	Hebre. i.
		A	iii kl.				xxx	xxvi	xviii	xxvii	ii
xix		b	prid. kl.				xxx	xxviii	xix	xxix	iii

Plate 7 The third edition of Jugge's cancel calendar, 1562.
(Lambeth Palace Library, [**] H5145.A4W4 1552, ¹A8ʳ.)

The booke of

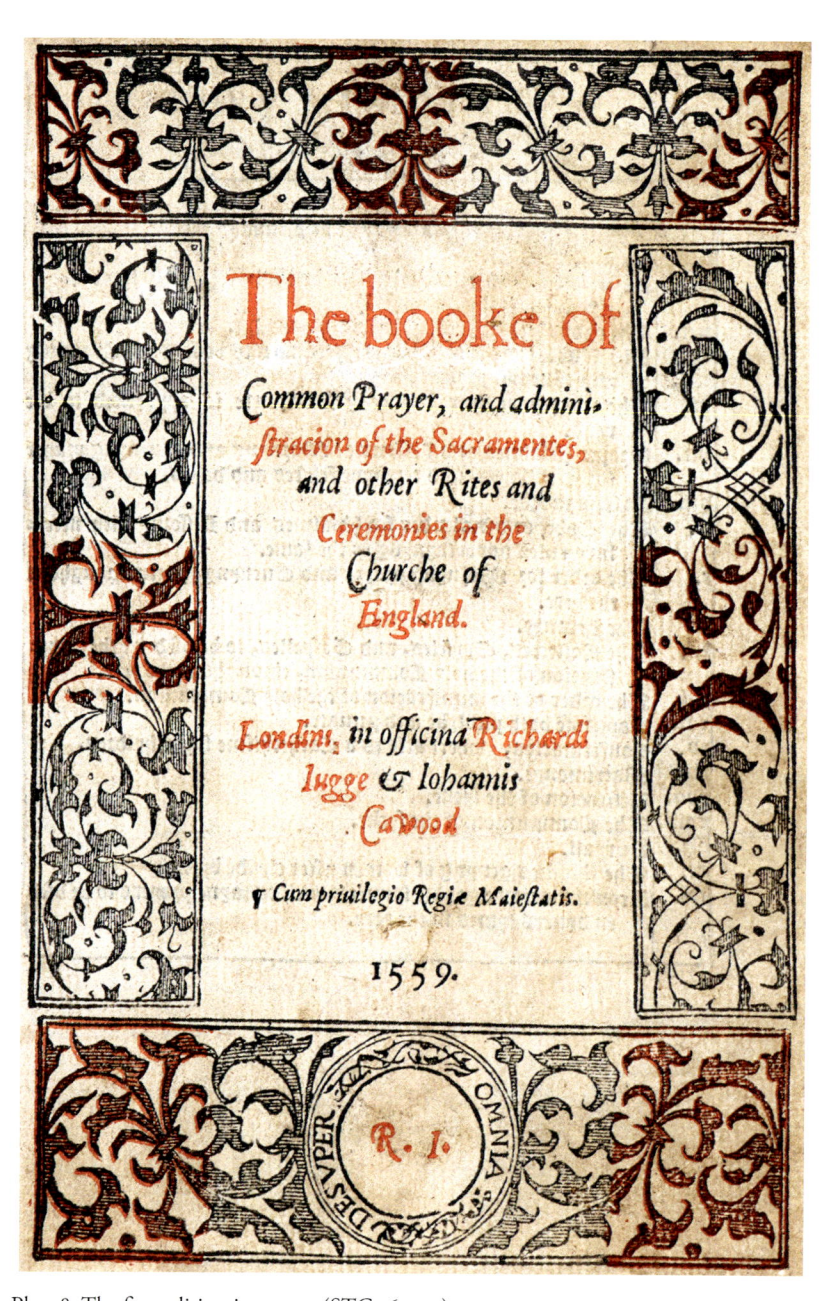

Common Prayer, and admini-
stracion of the Sacramentes,
and other Rites and
Ceremonies in the
Churche of
England.

Londini, in officina Richardi
Iugge & Iohannis
Cawood

¶ Cum priuilegio Regiæ Maiestatis.

1559.

Plate 8 The first edition in quarto (STC 16293.3).
(© The British Library Board, C.53.c.61, a1ʳ.)

Elizabeth Intervenes

On 22 January 1561, Elizabeth wrote an important letter to Archbishop Parker of Canterbury, Bishop Grindal of London, and the Court of High Commission, expressing concern about two matters that needed reformation.[A] The second of these, which she discussed at greatest length, was that the interiors (and especially the chancels) of many churches and chapels were disgracefully unfit for their reverent purposes. She writes of 'open decaies and ruines of coveringes walles and wyndowes', and of

> vnmeete and vnseemely Tables wth fowle clothes for the Communion of the sacramentes, and generallye leavinge the place of prayres desolate of all cleanelynes and of meete ornamentes for such a place whereby it might be knowne a place provided for diuine service. (14–17)

One of her suggested improvements would have interested printers:

> that the Tables of the Commaundementes maye bee comelye sett or hunge vpp in the Est end of the Chauncell to bee not only red for edification but aloe to geve some comelye ornament and demonstrac*i*on that the same is a place of Religion and prayre. (26–9)

But no such printed tables have survived from the reigns of either Elizabeth or her first two Stuart successors.[B]

The other matter concerned the prayer book itself, and the calendar and lectionary in particular.

> Wee ... vnderstandinge that there bee in the saide booke certaine Chapiters for lessons and other thinges appoynted to bee read which might bee supplied wth other Chapiters or parcells of scripture tendinge in the hearinge of the vnlearned or laye people more to there edification ... have thought good to require you our cōmissioners ... auctorized by our greate Seale for causes eccl*es*iasticall or fowre of you ... to pervse the order of the sayde lessons throwgh out the whole yere, and to cause some newe Callenders to bee imprinted whereby such Chapters or p*ar*cells of lesse edification maye bee removed, and other more profitable maye supplie there roomes. (6–8, 18–23)

Because the prayer book itself owed both its existence and its contents to the successive Acts of Uniformity, Elizabeth evidently felt it necessary to explain

---

[A] Lambeth Palace Library, Reg. Parker 1, 215^r (line numbers here given parenthetically).
[B] The only known example printed before 1700 is either Henrician or Edwardian: STC 23877.3 (ESTC S124487).

what gave her the authority to make changes. So after the formal addresses to each of the recipients with which the letter began, she had set out her interpretation of the relevant provisos in the most recent of those Acts.

> Lettinge you to vnderstande, that where it is provided by acte of Parliament holden in the firste yere of our Raigne, that whensoeu*er* wee shall see cause to take further order in any rite or ceremonie appointed in the booke of cōmon prayre, and our pleasure knowne therein either to our Cōmissioners for causes eccl*es*iasticall or to the Metropolitane, that then eftsoones consideraci*o*n should bee had therein. (3–6)

In other words, whenever Elizabeth chooses to make changes to any rite or ceremony, and so informs either the Commissioners or the Archbishop, her wishes should be carried out without delay.

But the Act does not exactly say that. What it says about the potentially contentious subject of 'ornaments' (which included not only church furnishings but also vestments) is as follows:

> Prouided alwaies & be it enacted that suche ornament*es* of the churche & of the ministers thereof shalbe reteyned and be in vse as was in this churche of Englond by auctoritie of p*ar*liame*nt* in the seconde yere of the reign of king Edwarde the vjth vntill other order shalbe therein taken by thauctoritie of the quenes ma*ies*tie w*ith* the advise of her comyssione*rs* appointed and auctorized vnder the grete zeale of Englond for causes ecclesiasticall/ or of the metropollytan of this realme.[A]

That certainly supports the queen's right to make new rules about 'ornament*es* of the churche' with the advice (or in this case, the subsequent 'consideraci*o*n') of the Commissioners. But what it says about what Elizabeth calls 'any rite or ceremonie appointed in the booke of cōmon prayre' is distinctly different.

> And also that if there shall happen any contempt or irreverence to be vsed in the ceremonies or Rites of the churche by the misvsing of the orders appointed in this boke, The quenes ma*ies*tie may by the like advise of the said cōmissioners or metropollytan ordeyn & publish suche farder ceremonies or Rites as may be most for the advauncement of gods glorie the edifiyng of his churche and the due reue*re*nce of christ*es* holie mysteries and sacram*entes*/[B]

Yet in her letter Elizabeth makes no attempt to claim that the existing lectionary has led to the 'misvsing of the orders appointed in this boke' or

---

[A] PArch., HL/PO/PU/1/1558/1Eliz1n2, lines 144–9. [B] Ibid., lines 149–53.

has caused 'any contempt or irreuerence to be vsed in the ceremonies or Rites'.[A]

The question of whether or not she really had the authority to revise the calendar depends on the constitutional paradox inherent in the first two acts of her first Parliament. Only the queen could summon Parliament; only Parliament could pass an act that declared her to be (in the words of the Oath of Supremacy) 'thonly supreme gouernour of this Realme ... aswell in all spirituall or ecclesiasticall thinges or causes as temporall';[B] and that Act of Supremacy could become law only if she assented to it. But once her governorship of the Church of England had been acknowledged as supreme, how could Parliament have the authority to impose conditions or limits on it?

According to the letter, revision was needed because some of the lessons in the 1559 lectionary were 'parcells of lesse edification' that could usefully be replaced by 'other more profitable'. But while that may perhaps have been Elizabeth's intention, that was not what was actually done. The revisions of 1561 did remove thirty-five chapters from the corpus, but the only addition was Leviticus 26.

If we start in 1549, in Cranmer's 'original' calendar each day was assigned four chapters or passages as 'lessons'. As I outlined in Chapter 4 (p. 91), Matins had two lessons, the first from the Old Testament and the second from one of the Gospels or from the Acts of the Apostles; at Evensong the first was again from the Old Testament but the second from one of the Epistles. Given the brevity of the New Testament the series of second lessons was read three times a year, and remained almost completely unchanged after 1549. With the exception of the Apocalypse (Revelation, of which three chapters each made a single appearance each year),[C] no chapter or part of any New Testament book was ever considered less than edifying before 1561.

The Old Testament, however, was different. If we exclude the psalms which have their own monthly and annual cycle, and include the

---

[A] As divided here, the proviso's discussion of rites and ceremonies begins at 'And also', and permits changes only as a response to 'contempt or irreverence' – which the wording (and the punctuation of Kingston's ᵖA4ᵛ29 in STC 16291–92) suggests is the intention. But the original act (line 149) has no punctuation between 'realme' and the capitalized 'And'. In the first four printed editions (STC 9458.7–59.7) there is a period and space after 'boke' (in my second quotation), and 'The quenes' appears to begin an unindented paragraph. If so interpreted, that 'paragraph' gives Elizabeth permission to change rites or ceremonies without cause.

[B] PArch., HL/PO/PU/1/1558/1Eliz1n1, lines 123–4. Note that 'or ecclesiasticall' is interlined above a caret, although it is impossible to know whether this was the simple correction of a scribal omission or (perhaps more likely) one of the many amendments this bill endured.

[C] Chapter 19 on the evening of 1 November; chapters 1 and 22 on the morning and evening of 27 December.

Apocrypha,[A] the canonical Old Testament and the Apocrypha together have 950 chapters from which to select 730 second lessons. On ten days of the year a lesson consisted of two chapters, which raised the total to 740. For the most part the chosen chapters were assigned to the morning and evening of each day in Biblical order, except that Isaiah was placed out of sequence at the end of the year, beginning on 28 November. But on each of six special holy days, the continuity was interrupted for a particularly relevant chapter that also appeared in its proper place in the main sequence. On Innocents' Day (28 December) only the morning's first lesson was a specially prescribed one, but on the other five days both Old Testament lessons were 'propers', so the final number of Old Testament chapters included was 729.

That figure, however, applied only to what could be recorded in the lectionary columns of the calendar itself, and the number of those chapters actually read in a given year was always smaller than 729. The prayer books of 1549 and 1552 also assigned particular Old Testament lessons to six moveable feasts on which those lessons were read instead of the ones shown in the calendar: in the morning only on the Wednesday and Saturday before Easter and on Trinity Sunday, and in both morning and evening on the Thursday before Easter, Good Friday, and Easter Day itself. But although no individual year saw all 729 chapters actually read, that was how many were available in the corpus. Given Elizabeth's stated goal, therefore, we should expect to find a significant number of those chapters rejected as lacking merit and replaced by a similar number of 'new' and more edifying substitutes. That, however, is not at all what happened.

In all the 1552 calendars, the errors in March, May, and June that I discussed in Chapter 4 inadvertently removed a dozen chapters from the full corpus of 729, but the only intentional changes were limited to the moveable feasts of the Wednesday, Thursday, and Saturday before Easter. In 1549 there was no special reading for the Wednesday morning, but the first lesson in the evening was Lamentations 1. On Thursday the first lessons were chapters 2 and 3 respectively, and the morning of Easter Eve was one of the few occasions when the first lesson included two chapters, namely Lamentations 4–5. In 1552 the Wednesday before Easter had an evening lesson of two chapters: Hosea 13–14. The morning lesson on Thursday was Daniel 9 while the evening had Jeremiah 31 (a chapter regularly heard on 10 August and also specially assigned to the morning

---

[A] Counting the Prayer of Manasses (or Manasseh) as a single-chapter 'book', but considering the Song of the Three Children as part of Daniel 3.

Elizabeth Intervenes

of Innocents' Day, December 28). And on the morning of Easter Eve, Zechariah 9 replaced the two chapters of Lamentations.

The Act of Uniformity ordered that the 1559 prayer book should come into use on 24 June, and from then to the end of the year the actual calendar readings were the same whether one was using the first Jugge-and-Cawood edition (whose miscorrections of the 1552 errors were all in earlier months), the Grafton edition with Kingston's actual 1559 calendar, or a Grafton copy with the recycled calendar quire from 1552. Clergymen who read all the new preliminaries with care would eventually notice, however, that not only had proper lessons been newly introduced for both morning and evening on twenty-seven moveable Sundays,[A] but that twelve fixed holy days now had new proper lessons that were not indicated in the calendar itself.[B]

To illustrate just how extensive the changes really were, let us imagine a street with a church at each end in calendar year 1560 (beginning on 1 January). In one church the 1559 Kingston calendar (whose lectionary columns agree with those of 1549) is being used by an older incumbent who once memorized the list of proper lessons for the six moveable feasts so commemorated in Edward's reign and has not yet read the new table. He will end the year having read 720 of the 729 chapters in the full 1549 corpus – twenty of them twice and one (Jeremiah 31) three times. In the other church, the younger minister has carefully read the new table of proper lessons, and has noticed all the revised readings for both the moveable feasts and the fixed holy days. He will end the year having read only 602 of the 729 chapters, 131 of them twice and five of them three times.[C]

What was actually done to the lectionary by the revisers of 1561 suggests that an attempt to lessen this effective shrinking of the corpus was given a higher priority than replacing less edifying chapters with better ones. Wherever a fixed holy day had been given new proper readings, the revised Old Testament sequence skipped over that day instead of losing two chapters as in 1560. But such events were rather more numerous than the targeted omission of unprofitable chapters, so the two sequences spent the first half of the year growing steadily farther apart.

The first two holy days of January are Circumcision on the 1st and Epiphany on the 6th. In the revised calendar each day kept the same proper readings it had been given in 1549.[D] On the 2nd the sequential journey

---

[A] The fourth to the twenty-sixth after Trinity and the first four of Advent.
[B] Morning and evening on the feasts of Sts Peter, James, Bartholomew, Matthew, Michael, Luke, Simon & Jude, Andrew, Thomas, Stephen, and John the Evangelist; evening only on Innocents' Day.
[C] Those who check the numbers carefully will notice that 1560 was a leap year.
[D] Gen. 17 and Deut. 10 on the 1st; Isa. 60 and 49 on the 6th.

through Genesis begins, and on the four days before Epiphany the first eight chapters of Genesis are assigned to the same services as before. But after Genesis 9 on the morning of the 7th, in the evening where 1549 had Genesis 11 (chapter 10, which lists the descendants of Noah, having already been omitted as of limited spiritual benefit), the revisers dropped that chapter too (the tower of Babel and the genealogy of Abraham) and substituted chapter 12. From the 8th to the 19th of January the readings continued in sequence but half a day ahead of 1549, until on the 20th the revisers dropped chapter 36 (the descendants of Esau) and thus increased the gap to a full day. As a consequence, after they had inserted the two proper lessons for the 25th (the Conversion of St Paul: Wisdom 5 and 6 from the Apocrypha), the Genesis sequence returned to its 1549 pattern, followed by the beginning of Exodus. But on the morning of the 30th, the omission of Exodus 6 put the revised calendar half a day ahead again.

In February the two diverged even farther. On the two fixed holy days in that month (the Purification on the 2nd and St Matthias on the 24th) the new proper lessons from Wisdom and Ecclesiasticus in the Apocrypha, together with the addition of the hitherto-unused Leviticus 26, could have put the revisers four lessons out of step in the other direction, except that before the month ended two more chapters of Exodus and nine of Numbers had been removed from the 1549 corpus – which left them *seven* lessons behind. By early June, thanks to the deliberate omission of twelve chapters of Joshua (seven of which had been accidentally lost in 1552 but briefly recovered in 1559) that gap had widened to twenty-three lessons. The first chapter of Esther, assigned to the morning of 10 June in 1549, had been read on the evening of 29 May in the revised calendar.

After June, however, the revisers omitted only one more chapter from the 1549 corpus (Proverbs 30), and so each time a new pair of proper lessons was inserted the gap shrank, until by Christmas the two calendars were only five lessons apart. When five new proper lessons were inserted in December, therefore (on the 26th, 27th, and the evening of the 28th), the last three days of the year were back in step. Other than five and a half holy days when the calendars shared the same proper lessons,[A] only eleven days in the year had the same lessons assigned in both 1549 and 1561.[B]

One might think that since the fixed proper lessons now merely interrupted the sequence of chapters (rather than permanently replacing those previously assigned to the same holy days), the total number of chapters

---

[A] Circumcision, Epiphany, John the Baptist, All Saints, Christmas, and the morning of Innocents' Day.
[B] 2–5 January, 26–29 January, and 29–31 December.

read during the years after 1561 would have risen significantly from the 602 of 1560. But the revisers of 1559 had also increased the number of moveable feasts with proper lessons from the six Edwardian examples to sixty-five. So in any given year after 1558 each of those feasts replaced two of the lessons listed in the lectionary columns – and in 1562 the total number of chapters read was only 610 (out of a possible 705), of which 123 were read twice and four others three times.

That is what the revisions achieved – but it is worth remembering that what the revisers had been instructed to do was to prepare (and have printed) new calendars 'whereby such Chapters or *pa*rcells of lesse edification maye bee removed, and other more profitable maye supplie there roomes'. They succeeded in removing a total of thirty-five chapters,[A] a number of which probably were considered somewhat lacking in the power to edify. It is, however, both interesting and perhaps significant that nine of those thirty-five (Joshua 13–19; 2 Esdras 7 and 11) had been among the fifteen accidentally omitted in 1552 when the printer's copy for the lectionary columns of March and June was scrambled. Meanwhile only a single chapter was added to the corpus – and unless Elizabeth considered that Leviticus 26 alone could out-edify all thirty-five of those omitted, it is difficult to argue that her wishes had been carried out.

The Folio Miscellaneous Column before 1561

In the Edwardian prayer book of 1549, each month of the year had its own page in the calendar, and each folio page was divided into nine columns. The last five constituted the lectionary: column 5 indicated the numbered selection of psalms allocated to each day, which in most days of most months was the same as the number of the day itself; columns 6–9 identified the assigned lessons: two for Matins and two for Evensong.

In column 1 were listed the so-called Dominical letters: the letters A and b–g repeated over and over through the year, beginning on 1 January with 'A'. In each year the letter belonging to the first Sunday was called the Dominical letter, and knowing it enabled the reader to identify all the Sundays (and consequently all the other weekdays) in any month. Column 2 gave the dates as in the Roman calendar, while column 3 numbered the days of the month itself.

[A] To be really precise, thirty-six from the calendar itself – but while Deuteronomy 12 no longer appears in the lectionary columns it survives as the proper lesson for the evening of the Sunday after Ascension.

Column 4 was the widest (albeit only slightly wider than column 2 in Grafton's editions), although in 1549 its 365 lines contained only twenty-five entries: one each in March, April, May, and August, two each in February, July, and September to November, three in January and June, and five in December. These were the twenty-five fixed holy days of the Edwardian church, including Circumcision, Epiphany, the Conversion of Paul, the Purification of Mary, the Annunciation, All Saints' Day, Christmas, and Innocents' Day. The remaining seventeen were the feast days of the twelve Apostles and four Evangelists (a total of twelve days),[A] and of St Barnabas, John the Baptist, Mary Magdalene, St Michael, and St Stephen.

In 1552 changes were made to the folio layout (including the replacement of 'Matins' and 'Evensong' with 'Mornyng prayer' and 'Euenyng prayer'), although the five lectionary columns remained arranged as before. The first four columns, however, were no longer separated from each other by vertical rules, and often strayed into each other's space. The days of the month were no longer listed, leaving the psalm selections in column 5 as the only clues. This was an inconvenience in February (numbered 2–29) and March (in which 30 preceded 1–30), and occasionally led to a holy day being marked one day too early (February) or too late (March). A new column 1 presented an intermittent sequence of so-called Golden numbers, whose nature and purpose would have been understood by only a tiny percentage of readers. Column 2 presented the Dominical letters and column 3 the Roman calendar, while column 4 was substantially widened and contained more than twice as many entries as before. Now the only month with fewer than four miscellaneous entries was May (which gained its own fourth in a few editions), while January, June, and November each had six and December seven.

All but one of the twenty-five entries of 1549 remained in place, although Mary Magdalene was ejected. Each month an additional entry recorded that the sun had moved into a new sign of the zodiac; each month another entry noted, after the Roman Ides, the name of the next month towards whose Kalends the countdown then began. Several additions concerned the dates of the four law terms. All the folio editions marked the beginning of Hilary term and both the beginning and end of Trinity and Michaelmas terms. The dates of Easter term varied with the date of Easter itself, and (as

---

[A] Matthew and John were both Apostles and Evangelists; Matthias replaced Judas Iscariot (who has no feast), and two days are each shared by a pair of Apostles (Philip & James the Less and Simon & Jude).

defined by the 'briefe declaration' added to the Jugge-and-Cawood editions of 1559) the term could begin as early as 8 April or end as late as 7 June. In three of Grafton's folios (Graf.1 and Graf.3–4) the end of a term was rather arbitrarily marked on 30 May, but no other edition followed suit, and none offered a date for its beginning. Meanwhile those three editions and Graf.5–6 (but not Graf.2 or any Whitchurch edition) noted the end of Hilary term on 12 February. Four of the remaining additions were equally unconnected with the liturgy: the vernal equinox on 11 March (but not its autumnal counterpart in September), Lammas on 1 August, and the beginning and end of the 'dog days' (7 July and 5 September). The only three additions with any real claim to be considered holy days were the feasts of England's patron St George and the rather less significant Sts Laurence and Clement.

As I explained in Chapter 6 (p. 94), while the only differences between the lectionary columns of the first two folios of 1559 were confined to a few 1552 errors corrected by John Kingston in the Grafton edition (but miscorrected by Wolfe in that of Jugge-and-Cawood), the layout of their pages differs quite strikingly. Kingston (Plate 4) follows the 1552 pattern in doing without vertical rules between the first few columns, and when he does divide columns, does so with short line-high verticals set between the page-wide horizontal rules.[A] He dispenses with the Golden numbers and puts the days of the month (or in January–March, the allotted selection of psalms) in the first column in arabic numerals. In the headings, however, he forgets either to omit the 'Psalmes' heading or to move it to the left. The only changes he makes in the miscellaneous column are to omit any mention of the beginning or end of either Hilary or Easter term (although he does follow 1552 in marking each end of both Trinity and Michaelmas terms).

Wolfe, by contrast, substantially redesigns the layout (Plate 5), choosing to have it set by a more difficult (but visually superior) method in which the vertical rules are of full height and the red horizontals a series of short lines.[B] His headings are more elaboratively decorative than Kingston's and

---

[A] The compositor, in other words, set each line of the table in his composing stick in much the usual way, lining the types up on a setting rule on which a series of scratches marked the divisions between columns, and setting a short vertical rule on each mark. When each line was finished he placed a line-length rule on top of it, retrieved the marked setting rule from underneath, and began a new line.

[B] This requires each column to be set separately in a composing stick adjusted to the appropriate short measure, with the lines separated by short, column-wide rules. When the first column has been completed and is leaning against one side of the tilted page-galley, a rule is placed against it and the next column constructed alongside that rule, etc. In the January and December pages (only) he took advantage of the fact that red and black were printed separately, and printed the red horizontals *across*

he retains the previous edition's Golden numbers as column 1. He does not hesitate to insert three or four lines of text into the miscellaneous column at the beginning of each month to record the times of sunrise and sunset on the first day, to divide an entry into two lines rather than abbreviating it (thus creating uncertainty about which day it applies to), or to take several lines to explain how to calculate a term date – and he is perfectly happy to misplace a zodiac entry when something else is in the way. In January he follows 1552 in marking the beginning of Hilary term but in February omits its end. He inserts his own descriptions in March of when Easter term begins, in May of when it ends, and in June of when Trinity term begins and how long it lasts. While following copy for when the dog days begin (July) and end (September), he also erroneously marks them as ending in August, and in September he adds the autumnal equinox to balance the vernal one in March.

All told, the year's miscellaneous column has 365 lines available for text. In a typical 1552 folio edition, only sixty-two of those lines are used at all, and more than 300 remain empty. In the folio calendar Kingston printed for Grafton in 1559, omitting the four entries concerning the first two law terms left him using only fifty-eight lines. Wolfe's willingness to use empty space, on the other hand, gave him an overall total for the year of 129 lines – more than twice as many as Kingston. Evidently, then, while each printer both expected and attempted to follow copy as precisely as possible in the lectionary columns, each also considered that he could impose his own ideas on the overall design of each page and to some extent on even the content of the columns in the left-hand half of the page. For saints' days and other matters concerning rites and ceremonies, however, both men followed their 1552 copy without either adding or subtracting anything. That, of course, seems only to be expected – but as we shall find later in the chapter, any such expectation is a consequence of tunnel vision.

Printing the Cancel Calendars (1)

Once the calendar had been revised, in all subsequent editions beginning with the quarto of 1562 (STC 16295) the revised version replaced the old. Meanwhile, however, several thousand people had bought copies of one or other of the nine known editions of 1559–60. I know of no evidence that any thought was given to the purchasers of the small-format editions whose

---

some of the black verticals (grouping them as if there were only three columns: actual columns 1–4, 5–7, and 8–9). He chose not to repeat that complication in the other ten pages.

calendars were now obsolete, but something needed to be done about those owning folio copies, who in many cases (and probably most) were clergymen who needed to know which chapters should be read on which days. It was possible (as was proved by the owner of British Library copy 6.d.9 of the fourth edition) to take a pen and laboriously annotate the whole year's columns of Old Testament lessons – but trying to fit everything in legibly must have taken many hours.

When Elizabeth had instructed her High Commissioners 'to cause some newe Callenders to bee imprinted', she is unlikely to have meant only in subsequent editions. Her instructions for all matters covered by her letter of 22 January had, moreover, included the directive 'that the alteration of anythinge hereby ensuinge bee quietlie donne *with*out shewe of anye Innouation in the Church'.[A] While one can hardly call changes to the national liturgy 'surreptitious', that clearly ruled out title-pages proudly boasting that they had been 'Newly revised and augmented according to order'. Richard Jugge therefore began by printing cancel quires to replace the obsolete calendars in existing folio copies, so that the owners could pull out or cut out the unrevised calendar quires (and, as it turned out, also the four leaves preceding them) and insert the cancels in their place.

Each of the two earliest known printings consists of two quires (both printed by Jugge): a single bifolium A^2 to replace leaves $^\pi A9$–10 of any of the four 1559 folios, followed by a four-sheet quire B^8 to replace leaves $^\pi A11$–12 and the whole calendar quire (b^6, $^\pi B^6$, or $^\pi B^6$, depending on edition). In both editions A^2 is in the same setting, and since the third edition more sensibly combines the pages into a single quire A^{10}, it seems likely that the original plan was limited to the single quire B^8 (signed B because it was to follow $^\pi A1$–10). But having revised the calendar itself, the authorities decided to make a few additional changes to the instructions for 'The order howe the rest of holye Scripture . . . is appoynted to be read' (originally $^\pi A9^r$) and the table of proper lessons ($^\pi A9^v$–10^v). A new bifolium (signed A) was therefore prefixed to B^8, and because a second edition of that quire was either planned or already in progress, A^2 was apparently printed in sufficient numbers to supply both editions.

If we begin as Jugge did with quire B^8, the first page is a simple reprint of page $^\pi A11^r$ in one of the Jugge-and-Cawood folios of 1559 (hereafter simply 'the Jugge folios', STC 16292 and 16292a). This page (which in both Jugge folios was printed by John Kingston) contains the final column of the table of proper lessons and the short table of proper psalms, and includes no

---

[A] Lambeth Palace Library, Reg. Parker 1, 215^r, lines 44–5.

significant changes. There is, however, one reading that differs interestingly from the other editions of 1559, and that is the number of the psalm assigned to Morning Prayer on Whitsunday. In all editions of both Edwardian prayer books it was Psalm 48 (xlviii), and in 1559 that number was preserved unchanged by Grafton in his folio, by Jugge in at least the first of his surviving quartos, and by Kingston in his surviving octavo.[A] In both the Jugge folios whose preliminaries survive, however, the reading assigned is Psalm 45 (xlv) – which seems likely to be the result of the simple and accidental omission of 'iii' from the first of those editions – in both of which the page in question was set by Kingston. As I explained in Chapter 4, the text of the Act of Uniformity shows that Grafton's forme $^\pi$A2^v:11^r was printed from Kingston's setting, so his 'xlviii' is a correction of Kingston's error. But there is abundant evidence that what Jugge used as copy for the 1561 tables and calendar relied on the preliminaries of the first Jugge-and-Cawood folio: Wolfe's calendar, and Kingston's tables with the misprint.

Grafton seems to have been the only person involved in 1559 who realized that the Whitsunday psalm should have been the forty-eighth and not the forty-fifth. So with the lone exception of Jugge's 1560 quarto (STC 16294), all subsequent editions of the prayer book before it ceased to be printed in the early 1640s followed the misprinted 'xlv'. So did most of the editions of 1660 when the ban was overturned. But at least two of them finally restored the correct number as arabic '48' (Wing B3618A and B3618aA), and were followed by at least most of the editions of 1661–62 that appeared before the 1662 revision made it official. It had taken just over a century for Kingston's misprint to be noticed and corrected. During those decades there must have been at least a few parish clergy who privately wondered what there was about Psalm 45 that made it especially appropriate for Pentecost, but none of them spoke up when the book was being revised again in 1604.

In all the folio editions of 1559, the last page of quire $^\pi$A^{12} contains the thirty-year almanack for 1559–88.[B] In Grafton's edition both pages between the table of proper psalms and the almanack are blank; in the Jugge editions the first of them ($^\pi$A11^v) contains the dubiously relevant 'declaration' of the dates of the law terms. In the cancel calendar the extensively

---

[A] ⁌STC 16291, $^\pi$A11^r; 16293.3, b8^r; 16293.5, w/1^v.
[B] One difference between them is that in the 'Epact' column for year 1576 the Grafton edition (set by Kingston) uses an arabic 0 to record a 'null epact'. The Jugge editions record it as 'xxix' – but in the first of them the initial 'x' is slightly damaged and almost exactly resembles a 'c'. The epact therefore appears to be an impossible 119.

revised almanack (now covering 1561–90) was moved to B1ᵛ while Jugge used the next two pages for completely new material. The 1559 almanack had consisted of six columns with all the figures in roman numerals: the year, Golden number, Epact, Solar cycle, Dominical letter, and (essentially rendering columns 2–5 redundant for anyone not a compiler of almanacks) the date of Easter. The revised version used arabic numerals for all numbers except the Golden ones, and could thus increase the number of columns to ten. The first three were the year, Golden number, and Dominical letter; the others usefully provided seven precalculated dates for each year: Septuagesima, Lent, Easter, the beginning of Rogation week, Ascension, Whitsunday, and Advent Sunday. On the facing page was the first of the new additions: a table 'To fynde Easter for euer'.

The final page before the calendar itself (B2ᵛ) contained three things. The first was a simple list of seven special Sundays, noting how many weeks either before or after Easter they occurred; the third was the familiar declaration of the term dates. Between them was a new and more important list, officially declaring which days in the year were to be considered holy: 'These to be obserued for holy dayes, and none other'. Listed first were 'all Sundayes in the yere', after which were enumerated twenty-seven days that were to be observed as holy regardless of the day of the week. Twenty-two of them had been among the twenty-five special dates named in the miscellaneous column of the 1549 calendars, discussed above (p. 172). The three omitted were the Conversion of Paul and the feasts of St Barnabas and Mary Magdalene; the five newly added were Ascension Day, the Monday and Tuesday of Easter week, and the Monday and Tuesday of Whitsun week.

Perhaps no less important than the holy days themselves was the heading's insistence that 'none other' days should be treated as holy. As we shall see, the miscellaneous columns of Jugge's revised calendars were very much fuller than their immediate predecessors, with notes of the days associated with a substantial number of lesser saints, and of several other festivals treated as particularly notable in Catholic liturgies. For the most part these names and notes were printed in black to distinguish them from the red-lettered holy days. But the demarcation was not always absolute – zodiac notes too were almost always printed in red – and inadvertently printing one colour where the other was needed was an ever-present possibility.

The reason why that would matter is that in addition to the holy days listed on B2ᵛ, the miscellaneous columns in the revised calendar on pages B3ʳ–8ᵛ record the beginning of Elizabeth's reign, the first of the Advent antiphons ('O sapientia'), the Conception, Nativity, and Visitation of Mary, the Exaltation and the 'Invention' of the Holy Cross, the Transfiguration and the Name of Jesus, the Beheading of John the Baptist, thirteen fasts (each on the eve of a red-letter holy day), and no fewer than fifty-one additional saints' days.[A] In at least the three known Jugge cancel calendars, the only entries printed in red are the twenty-two fixed holy days, the twelve zodiac entries, the single word 'Æquinoctium' (but not the following 'Autumnale') in September in the first edition only, and 'Init.reg.Elizabet.' commemorating the first complete day of her reign on 18 November (rather than her actual accession, because St Hugh was occupying the 17th).[B] But the erratic use of red in other columns of the cancels shows that it was at least *possible* for a lesser saint to be misprinted as a major one – and it was always likely that at least a few readers would assume that every entry in the miscellaneous column was equally important.[C]

That the calendar was re-revised in 1561, so soon after the revision of both the liturgy itself and the table of proper lessons, is probably not very widely known. The comparative few who know that Elizabeth herself commissioned the revision are (I suspect) also likely to have assumed that all the changes, including those in the miscellaneous column, were made at her instigation. The more radical reformers during her reign probably saw the sudden multiplication of saints, and the increased prominence of Mary and the Cross, as a revival of Catholic traditions – and some modern historians may have similar suspicions.

[A] Agatha, Agnes, Alphege, Ambrose, Anne, Augustine of Canterbury, Augustine of Hippo, Benedict, Blaise, Boniface, Brice, Catherine of Alexandria, Cecilia, Chad, Crispin, Cyprian, David, Denys, Dunstan, King Edmund, Edward the Confessor, Edward the Martyr (feast and translation), Etheldreda, Fabian, Faith, Giles, Gregory, Hilary, Hugh, Jerome, John ante portam Latinam, Lambert, Leonard, Lucian, Lucy, Machutus, Margaret, Martin of Tours (feast and translation), Mary Magdalene, Nicholas, Nicomedes, Perpetua, Prisca, Remigius, Richard, Swithun, Sylvester, Valentine, and Vincent.

[B] In 1580 Christopher Barker would add the Nativity of Queen Elizabeth in red on 7 September (STC 16307, ¶9ʳ). This being the day before the Nativity of Mary (in black), the Catholic Edward Rishton considered it a gesture of contempt for Mary: see his continuation of Nicholas Sander's *De origine ac progressu schismatis Anglicani* (Cologne, 1585, Y3ᵛ). The entry was dropped in 1603 after Elizabeth died (STC 16325, ᵠB6ʳ), and replaced in black in the 1604 revision by 'Enurcus bish.' (St Evurtius: 16326, ᵠB6ʳ). For the suggestion that 'The discreet placing of a black-letter day with the initial letter "E" may have been a ... way of keeping her flame alive, unnoticed by a jealous successor' see Cummings, *The Book of Common Prayer*, 755.

[C] In the undated quires (*c*. 1566) that replace the 1552 prelims of one Huntington copy of Graf.6 (call no. 438000:387), and in an undated prayer book *c*. 1573 (Huntington 438000:783), for no obvious reason the (black) name of St Valentine (14 February) is preceded by a right-pointing red manicule. In the former but not the latter, a similar red manicule precedes St Martin (11 November).

But it is clear from the differences between the Kingston and Wolfe calendars of 1559 that each printer felt entitled to modify the layout as he saw fit, and to make his own decisions about what was useful to include in the miscellaneous column. To suggest that the unquestionably Protestant Richard Jugge might have taken it upon himself to add saint after saint and fast after fast to that column without being ordered to do so by the very highest authority may at first sight seem very far-fetched. But there is a substantial amount of neglected evidence that even such champions of the Reformation as Richard Grafton and Edward Whitchurch were willing and able to do precisely that during Edward's reign. The calendar revisers of 1561 were insistent that (Sundays aside) only the twenty-seven specially prescribed days were to be observed as holy – so most of the new blackletter saints' days, feasts, and fasts seem to be intended as mere calendrical trivia: miscellaneous memorabilia from the history of Christendom, with no more liturgical significance than the beginning of the dog days or the arrival of the sun in Aquarius. More modern attention might have been paid to them had their Edwardian antecedents not been rendered largely invisible by two simple facts: that some books are far less likely to survive than others, and that some which survive are less likely to be studied than others. At first sight the following section may seem to be a mere digression of little general interest – but the facts discussed in it have had consequences.

The Survival of the Biggest

On the increasingly few occasions when copies of the first Edwardian prayer book come up for sale, the 1549 version is usually described as 'extremely rare'. This seems only reasonable, given that it was in production for no more than a couple of years before being officially rejected and replaced, and that most extant copies are now institutionally owned and unavailable to collectors. The same, however, is no less true of its successor of 1552, which was revived under Elizabeth with comparatively few changes. Being very nearly the same as the liturgy that would define the Church of England for several centuries, the 1552 book perhaps seems rather less antiquated and more accessible. But both Edwardian versions were banned by Mary in 1555, and were supposed to be handed in to the clergy within fifteen days of the proclamation and either burned or otherwise disposed of. So perhaps they are both extremely rare.

If we assume that the online English Short-Title Catalogue (ESTC) is reasonably accurate in the number of known copies it lists of each edition (an assumption I see no obvious reason to question here), there are still more than 140 copies of the 1549 prayer book in existence (including three copies of the belated Dublin reprint of 1551). Some of those 'copies' are far from complete, and a few can fairly be described as mere fragments, but most of them presumably survived Mary's attempted destruction as substantially complete books before time took its usual toll. When we add more than 110 recorded copies of the 1552 replacement (including a few printed and dated in early 1553), the number of Edwardian prayer books still in existence may seem surprisingly large for a pair of extremely rare books – not to mention being an eloquent comment on the obedience of Mary's subjects and the effectiveness of her ban.

What is less surprising is the preponderance of folio editions among the 250-odd survivors. As I have already observed, the initial need in both 1549 and 1552 was for copies to be used by the clergy during services, which in practical terms meant copies in fairly large type. Only eight of the extant copies are from the lone quarto edition printed by John Oswen in 1549. Two undated Whitchurch quartos of the second Edwardian version survive, one in eleven copies and the other in seven, accompanied by an octavo each from Whitchurch (one copy) and Grafton (three copies, of which one lacks the psalter and one is a psalter lacking the prayer book). All told, about 88 per cent of the surviving Edwardian prayer books are folios.

Before I turn to the calendars themselves, some Elizabethan statistics merit comparison. Of the four folio editions of 1559 only seventeen copies are known, accompanied by two quarto editions (two copies and a psalter) and two octavos (a unique copy and an untraced fragment). Then follows a drought: from 1560 a quarto (five copies) and an octavo (unique); from 1561 nothing; from 1562 a quarto (four copies); from 1563 nothing; and from 1564 an octavo (two copies) and the first known folio edition since 1559 (four copies). The total from 1560–64 is four copies in folio, nine in quarto, and three in octavo. If we add those to 1559 we have a six-year total of thirty-eight surviving copies to compare with the Edwardian total of about 250. To match the total from four and a half years of Edward's reign with recorded copies from Elizabeth's reign we have to include her first *forty* years (approximately 250 extant copies from 1559–98, fewer than 30 per cent of them folios).[A]

[A] While these figures include the abbreviated editions ('the Bible version') printed from 1586 as booklets to be bound into bibles (and which omit the prescribed Epistles, Gospels, and Psalms that can be found in the bibles themselves), they do not include similar editions printed as part of the

Among the reasons for that extreme discrepancy, perhaps the most significant is that one of the leading causes of the destruction of books is use. Had the 1549 books remained in common use for several decades, many of the clergy's original folio copies would have needed to be replaced. But once that version of the liturgy was retired and superseded in 1552, all surviving copies became essentially useless, and unless discarded could remain in good condition indefinitely. Much the same was true of the 1552 folios under Mary, although in 1555 preserving copies of either version became a crime (often, perhaps, committed in the hope that one day they could be openly used again). The comparative liturgical stability of Elizabeth's reign allowed the re-revised editions printed in and after 1559 to age, wear out, and perish of natural causes – although it is also apparent that the demand for folio editions seems to have declined as more and more quartos were printed.

The reason why these statistics matter is that they have tended to restrict research to a few of the most easily acquired sources. After the Restoration, serious liturgical scholars interested in the ancestry of the revived and newly revised prayer book of the 1660s would naturally have tried to locate the earliest available editions of each of the previous versions. Whether or not they knew which of the Edwardian folios of each year were the earliest, folios would anyway have been easiest to acquire (and probably preferred). In the nineteenth century the focus on a few landmark folio editions was narrowed even more when William Pickering published his 1844 reprints of the early Whitchurch editions of 1549 and 1552, Grafton's of 1559, and the key editions of 1604 and 1662. The tradition of foliocentric scholarship has, however, overlooked some rather interesting facts.

The Edwardian Quartos and Octavos

The first English prayer book printed in quarto was produced by neither Grafton nor Whitchurch but by John Oswen in Worcester. He had been given a royal patent to print, specifically and only for sale in Wales and the Marches, the service books otherwise covered by the Grafton and Whitchurch patent. It would have been very unwise of him to depart in any material way from the text of the authorized London editions, and within the rather elastic standards of Edwardian printing his quarto can count as a faithful reprint, calendar included. It is not very likely that either

preliminaries of some quarto and folio bibles between 1560 (STC 2094: see Appendix C) and 1585 (2144).

Grafton or Whitchurch printed a small-format edition of the whole book in 1549, but if they did no copies have survived. What they each did, however, was to print a very abbreviated version of the prayer book in the preliminaries to a quarto edition of the psalter, and in each case the calendar's miscellaneous column was restricted to the same twenty-five holy days as in the 1549 prayer book.[A]

Sometime in 1552, however, Edward Whitchurch printed two undated quarto editions of the complete prayer book, and the miscellaneous columns in their calendars differ materially from both the folios and each other. In the earlier of the two Whitchurch omitted the Annunciation from March (presumably by accident) and also the note that somewhat randomly marked the end of the (moveable) Easter term as 30 May. But his additions included twenty-three of the saints' days that would be added in Jugge's cancel calendar of 1561,[B] and four additional feasts (the Invention of the Cross and the Conception, Nativity, and Visitation of Mary) that would also resurface in the cancel. He also inserted several entries that would not reappear in 1561: a two-line indication of 'the place of the lepe yere' (to which I shall return), the Assumption of Mary, six saints' days,[C] and a commemoration of the so-called 'Seven Sleepers' (July 27). A few were inserted on the wrong days. St Valentine and Edward the Martyr were each entered beside what would have been the correct number had it been the day of the month, but because it was really the number of the psalm selection instead they were erroneously placed on 13 February and 19 March. It was probably a misreading of a manuscript roman numeral that gave St Margaret the 15th rather than the 20th of July.

Exactly when in 1552 that quarto was printed is uncertain, but it was probably before the end of the year. In 1553 the immigrant French printer Thomas Gaultier, who in 1550–53 frequently worked in close collaboration with Whitchurch,[D] printed a French translation of the 1552 prayer book. This must have been published before Edward died in July, but the translator probably began work in 1552 rather than 1553. His calendar follows the first Whitchurch quarto in all respects, including the omitted Annunciation and the misdated Valentine, Edward, and Margaret.[E]

[A] STC 2376.5, ¶3ʳ–8ᵛ (Whitchurch); 2377, ✠3ʳ–8ᵛ (Grafton). In the Latin translation of the prayer book printed in Leipzig in 1551 the 1549 miscellanea are translated with no additions or subtractions (STC 16423, D2ʳ–E3ᵛ).
[B] Agatha, Agnes, Ambrose, Augustine of Hippo, Blaise, Catherine of Alexandria, Chad, Crispin, David, Edward the Confessor, Edward the Martyr (feast *and* translation), Faith, Hilary, Jerome, Leonard, Lucy, Margaret, Martin of Tours (feast only), Mary Magdalene, Nicholas, and Valentine.
[C] Anthony, Bernard, Edmund of Abingdon (translation), Helen, John of Beverley, and Mildred.
[D] *Stationers and Printers*, 11, 624–8.   [E] STC 16430, d1ʳ–e2ᵛ.

The second of Whitchurch's two undated quartos antedates his 1553 octavo but was probably finished early that year. Either he or his employees continued to tinker with the contents of the miscellaneous column, albeit on a smaller scale. The omitted Annunciation was restored, and the five remaining notes about the law terms were removed. Only four new days commemorating five new saints were added,[A] but St Clement (23 November) was erroneously repeated on 23 December.[B] There was also one significant innovation: the insertion of a 'Fast' immediately before each of ten special days: the restored Annunciation, Christmas, and the feasts of (in calendar order) John the Baptist, Peter, James, Bartholomew, Matthew, Simon & Jude, Andrew, and Thomas.

What was almost certainly Whitchurch's last prayer book was an octavo dated 1553, which made yet more changes. They were not all additions: his omissions of Sts Adrian, Edmund of Abingdon, Laurence, and Leonard may have been deliberate, although the loss of Pisces from the zodiac notes and the fast from 27 October seem more likely to have been accidents. He also made several corrections, deleting the erroneous December appearance of St Clement, and moving Valentine, Nicholas, and the sign of Libra to their correct dates. But when moving King Edward the Martyr from the 21st to the 20th of June he accidentally left him at the 21st as well. Among his completely new entries is an ambiguous one: 'Trãs.Iesus.' on 6 August. In all subsequent calendars in which 'Transfiguration' is marked on the 6th it is immediately followed by 'The name of Ie[sus]' on the 7th, and in Grafton's octavo of 1552–53 the two are flagged simply as 'Transfiguration' and 'Iesus' respectively. So did Whitchurch perhaps combine what should have been two separate entries into one? Meanwhile he added eight more of the saints who would appear in 1561,[C] accompanied by six who would not.[D]

Two changes are of particular interest: the substitution of 'Fish' where the second quarto had called for a 'Fast', and of 'Sun' for 'Sol' in the zodiac entries. Grafton too flagged the fast days as fish days in his octavo, although he retained 'Sol' for the zodiac. I suspect that Whitchurch assumed a lower level of education in the typical purchaser of the smaller and cheaper

---

[A] Adrian, Dorothy, Fabian & Sebastian, and Vincent. Fabian (but not Sebastian) and Vincent would be included in the 1561 roster; Adrian and Dorothy would not.
[B] Part of the line of type was apparently transferred from the November page to December, although exactly how and why that could have happened is unclear.
[C] Anne, Augustine of Canterbury, Boniface, Dunstan, Giles, John ante portam Latinam, Nicomedes, and Remigius.
[D] Aldhelm (misprinted 'Adeline'), Cuthburga (misnamed as 'Cuthbert', but on 31 August), Osmund, Pancras of Rome, Petronilla, and Theodore.

octavos, and felt it useful both to translate 'Sol' and to explain that none of the suggested fasts had to mean complete abstention from food.

In Grafton's octavo the prayer book itself is dated 1552 but the psalter 1553, so the calendar is probably a little earlier than that of the Whitchurch octavo. How many of its miscellaneous entries had appeared in (lost) earlier quartos can only be guessed, and there is little point in repeating the names of 'extra' saints that we already know to have been listed by Whitchurch. Four days that would receive special attention in 1561 were first so marked by Grafton,[A] who also annotated eight other days not thus distinguished in any later edition.[B] He was also the first to move St Faith to her correct date of 6 October (from the 4th) and St Margaret to 20 July (from the 15th).

What makes all these minutiae important is simply this. We cannot be certain whether Grafton and Whitchurch were still printing editions in folio while the smaller books were produced. But even if the last folio calendars of 1552 had been finished before work began on any of the smaller editions, it cannot reasonably be imagined that each small-format calendar was the result of a careful rethinking by the authorities, or that each was separately submitted for approval before being typeset. In each printing house it must have been considered that the 'official' contents of the miscellaneous column (as prescribed by the printer's copy used by Whitchurch for his first folio edition of 1552) should be faithfully reproduced in each edition intended primarily for use by the clergy. But so long as all those items were *also* present in the smaller editions, the precise selection of added calendrical 'trivia' to be printed for wider circulation was apparently something that could be left to whoever oversaw the printing of each such edition. It was not the authorities who inserted them but the printers.

To scholars who know the calendars only from folio editions of 1549, 1552, and 1559, what seems to be a sudden and dramatic increase in the number of saints, fasts, and other celebrations in the calendars of 1561 may suggest that their appearance is somehow a consequence of the queen's decision to have the lectionary revised. It may seem, in other words, that the added miscellanea constitute another of the ways in which the Elizabethan church chose to distinguish itself from its Edwardian counterpart. But more than three-quarters of the 'added' entries of 1561 (fifty-eight

---

[A] The Beheading of John the Baptist, and the feasts of Benedict, King Edmund, and Martin of Tours (translation).

[B] Alban, the Chair of Peter, Cuthbert (20 March, as distinct from Cuthburga as 'Cuthbert' on 31 August), Edmund of Abingdon (feast), Erasmus, Felix, Linus, and Magnus.

of the seventy-five) had already appeared in Edwardian editions, and still more may have been included in lost quartos or octavos. The persons responsible for adding them were apparently not the rulers of either the church or the state. They were Edward Whitchurch and Richard Grafton: the unimpeachably Protestant suppliers of liturgies to a church even less tolerant of its Catholic ancestry than was Elizabeth's.

Other Pre-Elizabethan Calendars

Until now I have focused exclusively on calendars included in Edwardian prayer books and their Elizabethan descendants. There are, however, other pre-Elizabethan calendars that provide useful information, namely those that appear in several editions of the Bible and the New Testament.

The translation of the Bible appointed by Henry VIII to be used in every parish in the land – the Great Bible of 1539 and its seven reprints of 1540–42 – included a calendar that essentially reproduced that in the 'Matthew' Bible of 1537. It consisted of only four columns: Golden numbers, Dominical letters, miscellanea, and the days of the month. The miscellanea consisted almost exclusively of saints' days and other holy days, and include most of the saints and other miscellanea included in the small-format prayer books of 1552–53. Moreover, they include all but five of the black-letter saints and other feasts added to the miscellaneous column of Jugge's 1561 cancel calendars. So even though the Henrician Great Bible was not a product of the Edwardian Reformation it would hardly be reasonable to describe any influence it may have had on the calendar revision as 'Catholic'.

When bible printing resumed under Edward, the 'Matthew' edition of Raynald and Hill reprinted the calendar from its copy (STC 2078), Whitchurch declined to include a calendar at all in his Great Bible version (2079), and Edmund Becke's revision of 'Matthew' removed more than two-thirds of the Great Bible miscellanea and left only eighty-nine entries (2077).[A] Meanwhile Nicholas Hill, who printed a 'Matthew' edition for Robert Toy in 1551 and a Great Bible edition for Abraham Veale in 1552, in each case limited the miscellanea to the twenty-five items listed in the 1549 prayer book. And when Steven Mierdman printed a Coverdale edition for Richard Jugge in 1553 (2090), the thirty-one miscellanea he added to those 'authorized' twenty-five were restricted to the zodiac, the countdown

---

[A] Becke's second version in 1551, revised from Taverner's edition instead of from 'Matthew', reduced the miscellanea still more to 78 entries (STC 2088).

to each month's Roman kalends, term dates, dog days, equinoxes, and Lammas.

The printers of New Testaments made different choices. The little-known William Tylley printed one edition in 1548 and another in 1549. The calendar in the second of these (a Tyndale quarto, STC 2855) lists even more saints than does the Great Bible, including three of the five not yet accounted for in the 1561 cancels (Alphege, Denys, and Etheldreda). In the only extant copy of Tylley's 1548 Coverdale octavo (2839) only a few narrow fragments of the inner margins of the calendar leaves remain, but seem consistent with his 1549 calendar.[A]

Of particular interest are the otherwise unparalleled calendars printed by Reyner Wolfe in his Coverdale New Testaments of 1549 and 1550 (STC 2858–59). As is often true in biblical calendars Wolfe's columns are neither headed nor explained, which in this case is particularly inconvenient because they differ radically from the 'norm'. Rather less than half the width of the page is given to four columns on the left, with no separating rules either vertical or horizontal. Each of the first two columns presents an intermittent series of arabic numbers: the first column in red ranging from one to nineteen (presumably Golden numbers); the second in black ranging from zero to twenty-three. Neither column has an explanatory heading, although together they presumably help to calculate the date of Easter. The third column gives the days of the month in black; the fourth the Dominical letters in black lower case except (as usual) for red capital A.

To the right of those columns, rather more than half the page is available for miscellanea in red and some in black: holy days, saints' days, dog days, signs of the zodiac, solstices and equinoxes. These are mostly justified left a few millimetres from the fourth column, although a few multi-line entries are indented. All these figures and lines are set in type of which twenty lines measure approximately 54 mm. What is really unusual about this right-hand part of the page is that in each month there are also between one and four numerical entries in red justified against the *right* margin, set in arabic numerals cast on the same body as the larger textura used for each month's heading: either 82 mm or 86 mm (Wolfe owned both sizes). Given that the 54-mm miscellanea frequently extend past the beginnings of these larger red lines, the compositors must either have had to use a lot of non-matching spacing material (large 'quotation quads' and thin pieces of

---

[A] For the identification of Tylley as the printer of that edition, see *Stationers and Printers*, II, 631.

scabbord or reglet) or to print the large numerals in a separate red press-run before or after the black was printed.

The purpose of those numerical entries is not obvious, and is nowhere explained. The first, more or less aligned with 4 January and widely spaced, reads '8 :8 :4'. The second, roughly halfway between the 15th and 16th of the month, reads '8½ 7¾ 4¼'. In each new example the first number adds a half to the previous one, the second subtracts a quarter, and the third adds a quarter. All becomes clear in March, when the red figures aligned right halfway between the 10th and the 11th are '12 :6 :6', and the 54-mm text aligned left beside the 11th and 12th reads 'The day & | night equall'. The first red figure gives the number of hours of daylight on the day in question, the second is the time of sunrise, and the third the time of sunset. Reyner Wolfe was evidently particularly interested in those facts, which is presumably why in 1559 he began each month in his calendar for the first Jugge-and-Cawood folio by giving the precise times of sunrise and sunset on the first day.

But while no other printer followed his example in detail, two of them included part of that information in their New Testament calendars. The first was John Oswen in Worcester, in whose 1550 quarto the hours of daylight are omitted, and the times of sunrise and sunset given only in half-hours rather than quarters (STC 2862). For 3 January, therefore, his (unexplained) entry is simply 'At.viii.and.iiii.', while beside the 23rd and 24th he has 'At.vii.and halfe | and.iiii.and half'. The only subsequent editions to follow Oswen were those printed by Steven Mierdman for Richard Jugge (2867–70), whose miscellanea in most other respects fall somewhere between the 1549 and 1552 prayer books.

The Last Calendars before the Revision

Before 1561 only three printers had printed calendars for editions of the Elizabethan *Book of Common Prayer*: Reyner Wolfe (for the Queen's Printers), John Kingston (for both Grafton and the Queen's Printers), and Richard Jugge himself. But although Wolfe felt entitled to include his sunrises, sunsets, and term dates, he inserted no saints' days, fasts, or anything similar. The following year, however, he printed a Latin translation in quarto that had been made under the supervision of Walter Haddon: one of the four principals to whom Elizabeth would soon give the task of revising the calendar. That translation was authorized by her royal patent of 6 April 1560 to be used at Eton, Winchester, and both universities, and much of it is apparently based on a translation by

Alexander Alesius of the *first* Edwardian prayer book, published in Leipzig in 1551 (STC 16423). In the earlier translation, however, the calendar had listed only the twenty-five miscellanea found in English editions: in that of 1560 the miscellaneous column is almost full of saints' days, and of the 365 available spaces only forty-four are empty.[A]

There is no way of knowing who was responsible for those miscellanea, but for want of a shorter label I shall use Haddon's name. Many of the saints included in Jugge's 1561 cancels are among those listed, but more than a dozen are not, and even though Haddon includes thirty-six entries not even found in the Great Bible, his blank spaces include days that in 1561 would be assigned to the Exaltation of the Cross, the Invention of the Cross, King Edward the Martyr (both feast and translation), St Lucy, St Martin of Tours, and O Sapientia. Haddon does, however, include the only two saints added in 1561 for which I have found no other likely source: Brice and Machutus (13 and 15 November respectively).[B] Exactly how the Haddon calendar could be considered a 'translation' of the one in the 1559 prayer book is far from obvious – but in this case the initiative could hardly have been Reyner Wolfe's.

John Kingston printed his 1559 version of the calendar at least twice in folio (and quite probably also did so for the third edition) and then again in octavo – but unlike his 1552 predecessors he declined to add any miscellanea to his octavo edition, and had no fasts to turn into fish days. Once Richard Jugge had settled into his new premises and become an actual printer he no longer seems to have needed to collaborate with anyone but Cawood, and I have seen no sign of Kingston's work in any prayer book later than 1559.

Jugge himself, however, was almost as cavalier in 1560 as Whitchurch had been in 1552–53. In his quarto prayer book of 1560 he followed Kingston's calendars in layout, and there were two months in which he followed them in content (January and March), but in most months there was at least one unauthorized omission or addition. The omissions may well have been merely accidental, and it may be a pure coincidence that Whitchurch's 1553 octavo had also neglected to mark the sun's February arrival in Pisces. But if so it is curious that later in the same month Jugge followed the Whitchurch quartos and octavo in marking 'The place of | the

---

[A] STC 16424, π1^v–2^r (patent), c1^r–d2^v (calendar).
[B] St Brice does appear as 'briccius bys.' in the calendar included in the cancel preliminaries printed for Andrew Hester by Mierdman in 1550 to replace the Zurich preliminaries of Christoph Froschauer's quarto Coverdale Bible (STC 2080). But that calendar (which also serves as an index to the Epistles and Gospels, and includes short quotations among the miscellanea) is unlikely to have influenced any subsequent ones.

leap yere' beside the 22nd and 23rd. In May his omission of the holy day of the apostles Philip and James the Less may have been an accident,[A] but during the remainder of the year he called for either one or two fasts in each month, for a total of nine.[B] He also followed Whitchurch and anticipated the 1561 revisions in marking both the Nativity of Mary and the Exaltation of the Cross in September and St Lucy's day in December. His most unusual insertions, though (and a distinctly unusual error), were made in February, May, September, and December.

In the six lines for 15–20 February (psalm selections 16–21), Jugge informs (or reminds) his readers that 'Wensday | Fryday and | Saterday, | the first weke | in Lent is | Imber.' Ember days (to use the modern spelling) are the Wednesday, Friday, and Saturday of a particular week that are devoted to fasting and prayer, and occur four times a year: the first week in Lent, Whitsun week, and the weeks after Holy Cross (14 September, but misplaced by Jugge at the 11th) and St Lucy's day (13 December). In May Jugge breaks his note into five lines: 'Wensday,fri | day and sater | day in Whit= | son weke is | Imber.', and in December he manages with only four: 'Wensday,fry= | day & saterday | after.S.Lucie | is Imber'. December is printed on page $^{\pi}$A7^{v} in a quarto quire in eights: part of the inner forme of the outer sheet. That forme must have been set, printed, and partly distributed before the inner forme of the inner sheet – because the latter forme contains page $^{\pi}$A6^{r}, in which the four-line 'Imber' note beside September 13–16 was printed from exactly the same four lines of type found beside December 14–17 (which must have been where they were first set because there is no St Lucy's day in September).[C]

By far the most unexpected feature of this particular calendar, however, is that it also appears – with four of its pages and parts of three others in essentially the same settings of type – in the preliminaries of a quarto bible printed in the name of John Cawood, with a title-page dated 1560 and a colophon dated 1561. But that is a matter best reserved for discussion in Appendix C.

[A] This may, however, be connected with the 1552 omission of the second lesson for the feast of Sts Philip and James on 1 May, noted on p. 98 above.

[B] Of the thirteen that would be called for in the cancels, he failed to mark the first three (1 and 23 February and 24 March). The one that the cancel calendars mark on Halloween, however, was not anticipated by Whitchurch, Grafton, *or* Jugge's quarto.

[C] Had he removed line 3 the note would have served perfectly well – but that is not the only problem in mid-September. Holy Cross is misplaced at the 11th instead of the 14th; the correct Imber note should properly have begun at the 15th; what follows the incorrect one at the 17th is 'Sol in Libra.' which is usually placed at the 13th. Moreover, the evening first lesson on the 16th, which should be Jonah 1, is mistakenly printed 'Abdi. ii.' – which is doubly incorrect because 'Abdi' (Obadiah) has only a single chapter.

Printing the Cancel Calendars (2)

In at least the fourth of the folio editions of 1559 (and probably also the third), Jugge had John Kingston print the calendar in the same layout he had used for Grafton's edition, and Jugge himself followed the Kingston layout in his own quarto calendar of 1560. In the 1561 cancels, however, Jugge's model was the calendar that Wolfe had provided for the first Jugge-and-Cawood folio, STC 16292. He did not follow Wolfe in setting it as columns rather than lines, and his headings were not as elaborately decorative (see Plates 5 and 6), but Wolfe's influence is clear in such details as the restoration of the Golden numbers in the first column, the use of rules (or their equivalent) to separate the left-hand columns, and setting the 'Psalmes' heading vertically. Perhaps the most obvious influence on the content is shown by the inclusion of the times of sunrise and sunset for the beginning of each month, although Jugge more sensibly confines them to the heading area. But there are also frequent traces of Wolfe in the miscellaneous column, especially when Jugge follows his 'non-standard' placement of Cancer, Leo, and Libra, and when he aligns Aquarius, Pisces, and Sagittarius with the first rather than the second lines of Wolfe's two-line notes.[A]

Yet although some features of the 1561 calendar clearly show that its design was a matter decided by the printer rather than the High Commissioners, the responsibility for the contents of the miscellaneous column cannot be easily determined. The presence of Walter Haddon among the appointed revisers necessarily makes the calendar of 'his' 1560 translation a factor to consider, even though it is impossible to know how active a role he is likely to have played in either that translation or the revision of the lectionary. On balance, however, it seems to me that both the overall character of the added miscellanea and their (comparatively) modest numbers are more reminiscent of what Whitchurch and Grafton added to the same column in their quartos and octavos of 1552–53 than of the Haddon calendar, and so Jugge remains my prime suspect.

When Jugge decided that a second edition of quire B^8 was needed, the first was reprinted quite carefully and with very few changes that can be confidently classified as either corrections or misprints. There are, however, some puzzling differences in the use of red ink in the almanack, the guide to finding Easter forever, and the lectionary columns of the calendar itself. I can find no obviously logical or consistent system in either edition.

[A] Jugge's 'late' placement of Aries, however, is a consequence of including St Gregory on 12 March.

Printing the Cancel Calendars (2) 191

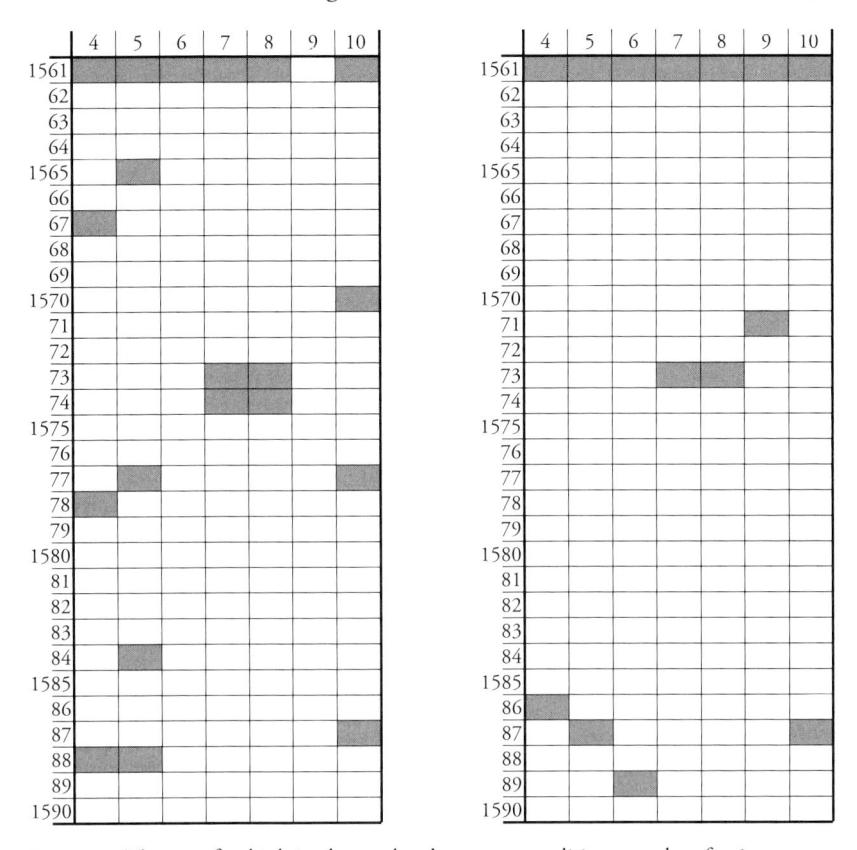

Figure 25 The use of red ink in almanack columns 4–10, editions 1 and 2 of 1561.

As already noted, columns 4–10 in the almanack give the dates of seven significant Sundays in each year. Figure 25 illustrates the seemingly random nature of the use of red in the first two editions. After the line for 1561 itself, the only 'cells' using red in both editions are columns 7 and 8 in 1573 and column 10 in 1587. In the calendar itself the variation seems equally unpredictable – but the use of red in edition 3 essentially follows edition 2, so some of the differences between editions 1 and 2–3 can be seen by comparing Plates 6 and 7.

Whoever chose what to put into the 1561 miscellaneous column, the decision that changes also needed to be made in the two leaves preceding cancel quire B^8 was unquestionably made by the revisers. Whether this was decided before or after work began on the second edition of B^8 can only be guessed, but unless the unique copy of edition 2 is a hybrid it would seem that enough copies of A² were printed to accompany both editions of B⁸.

In the table of proper lessons on pp. A1ᵛ–2ᵛ there are three changes *back* to 1552 readings, and these are almost certainly deliberate corrections of 1559 misprints. On A2ʳ, for example, the evening lesson for the 11th Sunday after Trinity was changed back from 4 Kings '19' to 1552's chapter 9, while on the verso the second evening lesson for 25 January (the Conversion of Paul) was changed back from Acts '2' to chapter 26 and the second morning lesson on 24 June (John the Baptist) from Matthew '3' to chapter 13. But when the first morning lesson on Ascension Day was changed from Deuteronomy 11 to 4 Kings 2; when the two first lessons for Whit Monday were changed from Deuteronomy 30–31 to Genesis 11:1–9 and Numbers 11:16–30; when Whit Monday also acquired 1 Corinthians 12 as a second evening lesson and Whit Tuesday's first lessons were changed from Deuteronomy 32 and 34 to 1 Kings 19:18–24 and Deuteronomy 30: in all those cases it seems safe to attribute the changes to the ecclesiastical authorities.

The revisions in sheet A², however, are not limited to the table of proper lessons, and two important changes made in 'The order howe the rest of holye Scripture (besyde the Psalter) is appoynted to be read' (A1ʳ) are interesting in very different ways. The first is the replacement of a paragraph that had remained essentially unchanged from the very first edition of 1549 through Jugge's quarto of 1560.

> This is also to bee noted, concernyng the leape yeres, that the .xxv. daie of February, whiche in leape yeres is coumpted for twoo daies, shall in those two dayes, alter neither Psalme nor Lesson: but thesame Psalmes and Lessons, whiche be saied the first daie, shall serue also for the second daie.[A]

There is no ambiguity here: in a leap year February's extra day is accommodated by treating the 26th as an exact repetition of the 25th.

But in nearly all the calendars in bibles from 1539 and New Testaments from 1548, when the leap year (or 'bissextile') is mentioned at all it is marked on the 23rd of February rather than the 25th. The only exceptions are Wolfe's New Testaments of 1549 and 1550, where beside the Dominical 'A' of the 26th begins a three-line note: 'In the leape yeare this | letter A. must be twyse | rekened' (STC 2858, π2ᵛ), and Oswen's Worcester edition of 1550 where 'The place of the | lepe yeare' is printed beside the 25th and 26th (2862, *3ᵛ) – and it is quite likely that all three of those editions were

---

[A] STC 16268 (1549), A2ᵛ.

printed after, and influenced by, the instruction in the first Edwardian prayer book. Once again Whitchurch's small-format editions prove of unexpected interest, because while all three print the paragraph quoted above about the 25th and 26th, in the February calendar page itself they follow the bibles and New Testaments in printing 'The place of | the lepe yere' beside the 22nd and 23rd.[A]

The cancels of 1561 replace the paragraph quoted above with the following on A1^r:

> When the yeres of our Lorde may be deuyded into foure euen partes, which is euery fourth yere: then the Sunday letter leapeth, and that yere the Psalmes and Lessons which serue for the .xxiii. day of February, shalbe read againe the day folowyng, excepte it be Sunday, which hath proper Lessons of the olde Testament appoynted in the Table, seruyng to that purpose.

It is difficult not to read this as a tacit acknowledgement that in 1552 and 1560 (the only two Februaries in which it would have applied) the Church of England had repeated the wrong day's lessons.

A few lines later the 1561 cancel ends A1^r with a completely new paragraph that would ultimately prove more significant.

> Item so oft as the first Chapter of Saint Mathie is read eyther for Lesson or Gospel: ye shall begin the same at. The byrth of Iesus Christ was on this wyse, &c. And the thyrde Chapter of Saint Lukes Gospell shalbe read vnto. So that he was supposed to be the sonne of Ioseph.

What this means is that Matthew 1:1–17 and Luke 3:24–38 were not to be included in any day's lessons – a ban that would become one of the targets of the Puritan campaign against *The Book of Common Prayer* in the 1630s and '40s.[B] The Puritans called the suppressed sections 'the Genealogie of Christ', although it would be more accurate to describe them as the genealogy of Mary's husband Joseph. And it is not difficult to understand why the authorities preferred not to have attention drawn to them three times a year. According to Matthew, Joseph's father was Jacob, a twenty-fourth generation descendant of King David's son Solomon, while according to Luke he was Heli, a thirty-ninth generation descendant of David's son Nathan – and discrepancies of that order rather complicate the notion of 'Gospel truth'.

[A] STC 16288, ¶1^v. Grafton's octavo, however, does not mention the leap year at either point in the miscellaneous column (16290, b2^v).

[B] For example, Hughes, *Certaine Greevances*, 1640, D3^r (STC 13917.5); *The Protestation of the Two and Twenty Divines*, 1643, A3^r (Wing P 3871).

Only two copies of Jugge's first cancel calendar have been reported: one is simply inserted after leaf $^\pi$A11 in the Cambridge University Library copy of the Grafton prayer book; the other replaces all the preliminaries in the unique York Minster copy of the third edition. The second edition of the cancel is known only from Keble copy 2 of the fourth folio prayer book (STC 16292a), in which it replaces leaf $^\pi$A12 and quire $^\pi$B^6. There is no way of knowing how many copies were printed (or how they were advertised and sold), but the owner of at least one copy of the fourth folio preferred to correct his copy by pen.[A]

When those editions sold out a continued demand led Jugge (perhaps in 1562) to print a third cancel more sensibly arranged as a single quire A^{10}. In new folio editions of the prayer book from 1564 until 1592 that quire was then simply reprinted as ¶^{10}, following a four-sheet quire signed either ∴ or *. Unfortunately A^{10} was less carefully printed than its predecessors, and some of its errors were repeated for years by subsequent editions. In June, for example, St Nicomedes was misplaced two days late on the 3rd, and in July the Visitation of Mary, the translation of St Martin, the beginning of the dog days and the Sun in Leo (which should have been on the 2nd, 4th, 7th, and 13th respectively) were all misplaced one day early.[B] All five errors were still being repeated in London editions in 1640 (STC 16421), and although the Cambridge editions of 1629 and 1638 corrected the three holy days (though not the dog days or Leo: 16375, 16410), their successor of 1640 evidently assumed that London printers sometimes knew what they were doing and wrongly moved Nicomedes back to the 3rd (16420).

Only one copy of the third edition of the cancel has been found in a 1559 prayer book, where it replaces only the calendar quire $^\pi$B^6 in British Library copy C.25.l.6 of the fourth edition. It is difficult to guess how many cancel calendars were printed overall, because the prayer books into which they were most likely to be inserted were those in most regular use, and therefore among those least likely to survive. Of the seventeen extant folio copies of 1559 only four include cancel calendars, although they are probably not a representative sample.[C]

But it should be remembered that the Elizabethan *Book of Common Prayer* differed comparatively little from the second Edwardian version of

---

[A] British Library copy 6.d.9 of STC 16292a.
[B] See Plate 7, where the July heading also credits the month with only 30 days while the times of sunrise and sunset are actually those for March.
[C] The Bodleian copy of Grafton's folio has no calendar at all, and so may once have had a cancel loosely inserted to replace it.

1552. To those who were prepared to spend a little time with a pen, crossing out the few omissions and copying the few additions into the margin, 1552 books were perfectly usable if a copy of the new table of proper lessons was somehow acquired – at least until the calendar itself was radically changed in 1561. The two other known copies of the third cancel calendar are found in copies of Whit.5 'doctored' for Elizabethan use (STC 16282.7). In the Lambeth Palace copy it replaces quires b^6 and ^{2}a^2, and the loss of the first quire of text (A^8) is presumably unconnected with the cancellation. In the Houghton Library copy at Harvard it likewise replaces b^6 and ^{2}a^2, and the loss of the preceding leaf a6 is also probably a separate matter. Whether one counts them as two out of six of the known cancels (33 per cent) or two out of three of the last known separate edition (67 per cent), it seems likely that more than a few cancel calendars were thus (mis)used to update Edwardian editions.

Whoever was really responsible for augmenting the miscellaneous column in 1561, once the calendar had been revised it remained essentially unchanged in all formats for the rest of Jugge's printing career. When Christopher Barker succeeded him as Queen's Printer in 1577 he seems to have considered the contents of the calendar as no less established than the rest of the book, and (unless the 1580 addition of Elizabeth's nativity on 7 September was his own idea) shows no sign of wanting to improvise. So although the process certainly began in 1559, the revision of the Edwardian prayer book into its 'settled' Elizabethan form cannot be said to have been completed until 1561. And the first edition into which the revisions were incorporated (as distinct from inserted as a cancel) was the quarto edition of 1562, STC 16295.

CHAPTER 11

Concluding Summary

If research projects are not carefully watched and controlled, they can spread faster than weeds. The printed book with whose archaeology this project began was STC 16292: the first 'Jugge and Cawood' folio edition of the 1559 *Book of Common Prayer*. Because that book was shared by so many different printers, identifying who printed which parts of it was far from easy, especially because the types and many of the display initials used by Richard Jugge towards the end of the book had belonged to others at the beginning. Given that STC 16292a was clearly the work of at least some of the same printers, what I then believed to be the third edition also had to be investigated – and because sheet ᵖA4:9 and the list of contents are identical in both the first Jugge-and-Cawood folio and Richard Grafton's edition of the same year, the Grafton edition was also found to have been shared (though with only one other printer). Extending the study to the quarto editions of the same year uncovered yet more sharing, and while the only complete octavo edition was printed by one man throughout, he was neither of the two named in the imprint and colophon. Meanwhile another problem had revealed itself in the shape of cancel calendars implicitly dated 1561 that have been inserted into the preliminaries of some of the folios, so they too had to be scrutinized. At which point I drew a line in the sand and refused to step into 1562.

It was, however, also necessary to look backwards, because each of the first editions of 1559 was essentially a revised reprint of a particular edition of the second Edwardian prayer book (1552), and many of the ways in which they differed from each other were consequences of how those Edwardian editions differed. But the editions of 1552 seemed to have been less directly shaped by the differences between their own predecessors of 1549, so when I first considered this book to be 'finished', most of the present Chapter 1 did not exist and parts of the present Chapter 2 were scattered among later chapters. At that point, however, Brian Cummings suggested that if I expanded the Edwardian material, all three of the early

Concluding Summary

English prayer books could at last be subjected to the same kind of bibliographical (or archaeological) scrutiny. Having already recorded most of the shared printing in the Edwardian editions elsewhere,[A] I therefore decided to investigate why Richard Grafton chose to place his dated colophon four-fifths of the way through his first prayer book rather than at the end. And (perhaps because a prayer book is an appropriate context for an epiphany) I finally realized that shared printing was the answer to that as well. Grafton had printed part 1 while Whitchurch had printed part 2. Each printed his dated colophon at the end of his share (Whitchurch on 7 March, Grafton a day later), and the first few hundred copies of the book were issued in that form. The rest, however, were held back while each man reprinted the other's share, and then issued the remaining copies as books printed entirely by himself.

Close examination shows clearly that the text was still a work in progress when the printing began. Grafton knew approximately how much space the orders of Matins and Evensong would occupy, but began work with the Introits section in quire B. The copy for the texts prescribed for Easter Monday had either been misplaced or was not yet written when Grafton printed quire K^6, and so he later had to replace it with an eight-leaf quire to include them. When the copy for Matins and Evensong arrived, four essential canticles were included only by name but without their texts, which Grafton belatedly supplied as a bifolium appended to some (but not all) copies of the first edition. And the complete omission of the Litany was noticed and rectified only later, when Grafton reissued the first edition with his own part 2 replacing Whitchurch's.

During the two years that followed, each of the printers went his own way, sometimes compacting the text into fewer pages to reduce his costs, and often subcontracting part of the work to another printer (Whitchurch to Nicholas Hill, Grafton to Robert Wyer). But among those who opposed the book on religious grounds, radicals who considered that the reforms had not gone far enough were in the ascendant, and so in 1552 that first prayer book was replaced by a substantially revised version. This time both printers were able to print their first few editions without assistance,[B] and only later resorted to sharing: Whitchurch with Steven Mierdman for his fourth and fifth editions, and Grafton with both Nicholas Hill and John Day for his sixth.

[A] *Stationers and Printers*, II, 1050–51.
[B] Once again, however, one text had been included only by title (Psalm 98, see p. 35), and its full text was not included until each printer's second and later editions.

The accession of Mary, however, brought the production of Protestant liturgies to a halt for more than five years. Nearly two years would pass before the Edwardian editions were specifically and prominently included in a proclamation that called for heretical books to be surrendered within fifteen days and then burnt.[A] But very soon after Mary was proclaimed queen the new regime had begun to purge the book trade, whose most prominent members had been champions of the Edwardian Reformation. The authorities seem to have tried to preserve the printing houses of Grafton and Whitchurch as valuable assets by putting each one under the management of a trustworthy Catholic. But Robert Caly seriously compromised the productivity of Grafton's establishment, and by 1556 Edward Whitchurch had quarreled with John Wayland, given up his lease of the printing house, and stored his equipment somewhere to prevent Wayland from using it. By the time Mary died there were no printing houses in London capable of production on the scale seen in 1549–53. Grafton's establishment still existed, and (given time) could probably be brought back to something like its former capacity. Whitchurch's types and ornaments could still be accessed, though whether or not any of his presses were still usable is uncertain. But both the immigrants who had done so much to help him produce his Edwardian prayer books (Hill and Mierdman) had hastily returned abroad on Mary's accession, and there was now a distinct shortage of printers capable of production at Edwardian levels.

As a consequence, the most important of the Elizabethan prayer books of 1559 are the products of collaboration among a completely unprecedented number of printers. If that were not complexity enough, the revisions required by Parliament were not all clearly explained, and during the printing the authorities apparently continued to devise new instructions and to change their minds. The Elizabethan part of the story has many layers, sometimes necessitating a guess at the intentions of the authorities, sometimes a close focus on a particular printer, a specific edition, an individual quire, leaf, or page, or even a single display capital or type. The variety of different kinds of evidence that have had to be considered has prevented me from reconstructing the story in a single, straightforward sequence. It may therefore be useful to try to summarize the overall history of the Elizabethan *Book of Common Prayer* as a more direct narrative.

[A] STC 7865, 1^r–2^r (TRP 422, p. 59).

At the beginning of 1559, Elizabeth started the ball rolling by having the recently appointed 'Printer vnto the Quenes Maiestie', Richard Jugge, publish the revised English Litany that she was using in her own chapel. Not yet being an actual printer, Jugge paid John Day to print it in his name. Seeing a potential problem, either the queen or one of her advisers decided that a printer who both owned and knew how to run a printing house would be a useful addition, and persuaded Mary Tudor's printer, John Cawood, to become printer to a second queen as Jugge's partner-in-office.

Under Mary, the Church of England had been reunited with Rome, so until Parliament could repeal Mary's statutes the Pope would remain the supreme authority in matters of religion. Elizabeth's first requirement, therefore, was a new statute appointing her the supreme governor of the English Church – but since all England's archbishops, bishops, and abbots had been appointed by either Mary or Henry VIII and were members of the House of Lords, that would be no easy task. Secondly, something would have to replace one or other of the two Edwardian prayer books, both of which had been condemned by Mary.

Elizabeth's first Parliament met on 23 January 1559, and on 9 February what would become the Act of Supremacy began its long and complicated evolution with the first of what would eventually be nine readings in the Commons – although it would not finally pass until after its sixth reading in the Lords on 29 April. What was probably the ancestor of the eventual Act of Uniformity was first read by the Commons on 15 February, but disappeared after a second reading the following day. The version of that bill that would eventually be passed by the Lords (with a majority of only three) first appeared in the Commons on 18 April, and the Lords finally passed it on the 28th. It would probably have been obvious in February that the book to be defined by the eventual Act of Uniformity would closely follow the Edwardian prayer book of 1552. It is, however, highly unlikely that any realistic start could have been made on the printing before that bill was first read in April.

But who would print it? In 1557 Mary had granted the Stationers' Company of London a nationwide monopoly of printing. Even if Grafton and Whitchurch had been in a position to repeat their Edwardian roles, Grafton was a freeman of the Grocers' Company and Whitchurch of the Haberdashers, so neither had the legal right to print anything at all in 1559 (unless Elizabeth granted him a royal patent, which she never did). Meanwhile, Richard Jugge was still trying to set up a suitable printing house, to staff it, and to learn how to run it. That left the queen's other printer, John Cawood, as the fourth most obvious choice. But his output during Mary's reign had never come near that of either Grafton or Whitchurch under Edward – and until Jugge became a printer in reality, Cawood was needed to print the various official publications for which the office of Queen's Printer existed.

What the authorities evidently did was to involve all four of those men. One team, probably led by Jugge, was to reprint one of Whitchurch's last editions of 1552, essentially page for page but incorporating the comparatively few revisions required by the Act. Whitchurch himself (who was now married to Cranmer's widow) apparently brought at least some of his equipment out of storage, and began working in a temporary partnership with Reyner Wolfe (who was still the royal Printer in Latin, Greek, and Hebrew, as he had been under both Edward and Mary). Work on that edition may even have been started before the Act of Uniformity had been passed or given the royal assent. Somehow or other, the middle sheet of quire B was simply reprinted from the 1552 Whitchurch sheet, without the most important of the revisions in the Litany (even though the revised Litany had been published by Jugge in or before January). That could have been an isolated blunder – but the very first page of the order for Morning Prayer contains two rubrics whose revision was required by the Act, and the leaf on which they appear is a cancel: a pasted-in replacement printed by Jugge after he had set up his own house and bought the Whitchurch ornament stock. Moreover, later in the volume leaf N3, printed by Jugge himself, was likewise cancelled by him – this time almost certainly to remove the so-called Black Rubric of 1552 which was omitted (although without parliamentary sanction) from Elizabethan editions.

It was probably a little later that Grafton, who had evicted his Marian supervisor but had not yet started printing again, was separately commissioned to reprint *his* last edition of 1552 with the same revisions. He was able to incorporate all the Litany revisions without undue difficulty, and I have found no evidence suggesting cancellation in his opening rubrics or the page from which the Black Rubric has gone. What most distinguishes the main text of his edition is the presence in all extant copies of sheets printed in 1552. He had evidently ignored Mary's proclamation of 1555 that ordered all Edwardian prayer books to be burnt, and had concealed a substantial number of as-yet-unbound sheets from his last edition of 1552. So if his new edition were to consist of (say) 1,500 copies, and he had a hundred copies of a given 1552 sheet that required no significant textual revision, he needed to print only 1,400 new copies because he could recycle the old ones. Five copies of his 1559 edition survive: two contain only one recycled sheet each, one contains eight, another twenty-three, and the last twenty-nine. (Because parts of his 1552 edition had been contributed by other printers, in two of the extant copies the recycled sheets include one or more printed by John Day, and in three copies one or more of the 1552 leftovers were printed by Nicholas Hill.)

Returning to the other edition: Wolfe and Whitchurch printed the first six quires of the main text (a total of twenty-four sheets of paper: forty-eight leaves, or ninety-six pages). The next quire (quire G) was the only part of the book printed by John Cawood: sixteen pages containing no revisions. Perhaps he had been intended to print more, but the need to print the statutes from Elizabeth's first parliament took priority. So either Cawood himself or Jugge farmed the next five quires out to two young and comparatively inexperienced printers. The younger of the two (Owen Rogers) contributed quires H and M; the slightly more experienced Thomas Marshe printed quires K–L, and they each printed two sheets of quire I. Marshe's sheets are notable because this is one of only two known books in which he marked most of his contribution by setting his initial M below the text in one page (seemingly chosen at random) of eight of the eleven sheets he printed – thus pioneering (or anticipating by almost seventy years) the use of what are now known as 'press figures'. Rogers, meanwhile, distinguished himself in this and the next two editions by his ingenuity in improvising substitutes for a display initial I (of which he owned only one, but sometimes needed as many as four).

The next two quires are the work of three more printers: Richard Payne (married to the widow of the second of Henry VIII's royal printers, but not himself a Stationer and therefore not legally entitled to print); John Kingston (an ex-apprentice of Richard Grafton's, and therefore a Grocer not legally entitled to print); and Richard Jugge – who had by now acquired much of Whitchurch's printing material and had at last become an actual printer. The final quire of the text (quire P) is the first to be printed by Jugge from start to finish.

Whichever of the two editions of the main text was finished first, work on the two sets of preliminaries evidently started at about the same time. Grafton set the middle two sheets of the first preliminary quire from the relevant pages of his own 1552 edition; for the other team those sheets were set from Whitchurch's penultimate edition by Reyner Wolfe (apparently now working without Whitchurch). Wolfe also set the calendar quire for that edition – but setting tabular pages and printing them in both black and red required especially skilled workmen, and the best of those who had worked for Grafton in 1552 would not have been needed by his less productive Marian manager. So although Grafton's ex-apprentice John Kingston was more closely associated with the Jugge team, it was Kingston who printed the 'Grafton' calendar.

Four sheets were still needed for each edition. One – the outermost sheet of the quire – would contain the title-page and the thirty-year almanack for 1559–88 on one side, while the only printing on the other side would be the list of contents backing the title-page. Of the remaining three sheets, the first three leaves would contain the six pages of the full text of the Act of Uniformity; the last three the greatly expanded tables of proper lessons and psalms. As it happened, those tables themselves would be arranged to fill only four pages, although spreading them over five or six could have made them clearer. Those three sheets were printed for Jugge by John Kingston, with the Act apparently set from the manuscript supplied to the Queen's Printers and used by Cawood for his edition of the statute (rather than from Cawood's printed text itself). And what Grafton used as printer's copy for the Act was evidently Kingston's printed sheets. At this point we encounter the first of three significant anomalies – because the sheet containing the last two pages of the Act and the first two of the table (sheet $^{\pi}$A4:9) is exactly the same Kingston setting in both editions.

The only explanation that makes sense seems to be that Kingston had made a significant mistake on at least one of the four pages (more probably in the table than the Act), and that because Grafton had then reprinted the erroneous material from Kingston's setting it seemed both efficient and fair for Kingston to print enough corrected sheets to serve both editions.

The second anomaly is that the list of contents that backs each title-page is also a single setting by Kingston found in both editions. The layout, line-division, and spelling of that list show clearly that it was based on the Whitchurch setting in the edition used as copy by the Jugge team, from which, however, it differs in two important respects. It begins by correctly listing the Act of Uniformity as the first item: a feature found only in the lists in Grafton's last three editions of 1552–53 (two folios and an octavo), none of which actually *placed* the 1552 Act there. And perhaps more importantly, in 1559 the list does not include an ordinal as the final item. That ordinal will be discussed below, but I believe that the original settings of the list were cancelled for the specific purpose of omitting it. The printers of each edition had certainly assumed that an ordinal was to be included as in 1552, and each team had actually printed one, duly updated for Elizabeth's reign and with an oath prescribed by her Act of Supremacy. But the authorities evidently (and belatedly) decided that it should be sold only as a separate publication, and ordered that the list of contents should be reprinted accordingly. That made it necessary for the title-page of each edition (and the almanack in the same forme) to be reprinted on the other side of the sheets containing Kingston's reprinted $^{\pi}$A1^{v}.

The third anomaly is that while the Grafton title-page is set in the same woodcut border he had used on all his folio prayer books in Edward's reign, both that title-page and the tabular almanack printed on the same side of the sheet (each in both black and red) contain types that did not belong to Grafton, and (like the two-colour tabular pages of the calendar) were also printed by Kingston (who had borrowed the title-page border for a book of his own in April), despite the presence of Grafton's name in the imprint.

Each of the 1559 ordinals contained nine sheets of paper, and the Grafton edition really was printed by him. The one intended for the Jugge-and-Cawood edition is mostly the work of the printers of the last three quires (N–P) of the prayer book proper: four sheets by Kingston, three by Payne, one by Jugge himself, and one by the unexpected newcomer William Copland. Seven copies of that edition survive (none bound with the first Jugge-and-Cawood prayer book), but only one copy of Grafton's. That copy, however, is a crucially important one, joined to a copy of his prayer book that was assembled and stitched (although apparently not actually bound) for submission to the Privy Council so that the maximum permitted price could be determined. The prayer book itself is complete, and has the cancel contents list, so I imagine that Grafton must have included the ordinal in the hope that the Council would at least set a price for it as a separate item – but their signed memorandum on an otherwise blank page sets prices only for the prayer book itself. Moreover, the compositor who set the ordinal's colophon slavishly followed his 1552 copy except for altering the date to 1559. And since in that year Grafton was no longer 'Typographus Regius' and had no 'Priuilegio ad Imprimendum solum', the failure of any other copy to survive may indicate that his ordinal was suppressed (either by the authorities or unofficially by the Queen's Printers themselves).

The year 1559 saw two more editions of the prayer book in folio, the earlier of which was recognized as a distinct edition only during the research for this book. Each is the work of five of the printers of the first Jugge-and-Cawood edition: both Queen's Printers, Owen Rogers, Richard Payne, and John Kingston. But while some quires were printed by the same printer in each edition, others were not. The only extant copy of the earlier of those editions (the third edition overall) lacks the preliminaries; seven copies of the fourth are known, some of which contain a sheet or two (or in two cases a whole quire) proper to the third. Collation of the texts shows that while each edition made an occasional attempt to correct a few of its predecessor's errors, most of the changes are typical of the textual degeneration commonly found in reprints.

After finishing those folio editions the Queen's Printers turned to smaller formats, and produced two known editions in quarto. One copy of the first (mistakenly listed as the second by the revised STC) has survived almost complete, while the substantially defective copy of the second has been partly made up with sheets from a defective copy of the first. Neither edition has either its almanack or calendar, probably as a consequence of the 1561 revision to be discussed below.

While all known folio editions of 1552 included an ordinal, editions in smaller formats (intended more for the congregation than the clergy) had a psalter and a few added prayers appended instead. The extant copy of the first 1559 quarto includes all but the last quire of a psalter of which a complete copy has also survived as a separate book – but it is not the work of the Queen's Printers, and was printed for the publisher William Seres (partly by Henry Sutton and partly by William Copland). In July 1559 Seres was granted a new version of a patent for primers that had originally been granted by Edward VI but cancelled by Mary I. As a former servant of Elizabeth's principal secretary (Sir William Cecil), Seres had managed to have the patent revised so that it included not only primers but also (to compensate for his Marian losses) psalters. It is unlikely that Elizabeth read more than a brief docket before granting the requested patent, but as worded it gave Seres the exclusive right to print psalters of all kinds, notwithstanding any former grant to anyone else. Interpreted literally, this deprived the Queen's Printers of the right to include psalms in either prayer books or bibles – so an arbitration must soon have been made (probably by the Court of Assistants of the Stationers' Company, whose earliest extant records date from 1565). This evidently gave Seres the exclusive right to publish psalters separately (prefaced by a few essentials from the prayer book), but left Jugge and Cawood their monopoly of psalters both in bibles and in prayer books for use in church.

Before the year ended at least two editions of the prayer book had also been printed in octavo, although one of these survives only as a fragment whose precise location is at present unknown. The other is complete, and both the prayer book and the psalter are explicitly attributed to Jugge and Cawood. Perhaps inevitably, it was printed for them from start to finish by John Kingston.

The Elizabethan revision, however, was not yet quite finished. Whoever had compiled the greatly extended table of proper lessons in 1559 had assigned Old Testament readings to both the morning and evening of sixty-four moveable feasts, only six of which had been so treated before. Those readings necessarily replaced the lessons assigned by Cranmer to the days in question in the 'basic' calendar of 1549. The new table also assigned new lessons to nineteen fixed feasts, whose former lessons were therefore no longer relevant – but remained unrevised in the calendar itself.

How Elizabeth either noticed or was informed that the lectionary now had problems is unknown, but in January 1561 she wrote to Archbishop Parker, Bishop Grindal, and the rest of the High Commission, instructing them 'to cause some newe Callenders to bee imprinted whereby ... Chapters or p*ar*cells of lesse edification maye bee removed, and other more profitable maye supplie there roomes' – but that the changes 'bee quietlie donne w*i*thout shewe of anye Innouation in the Church'. Once the required changes had been made it was easy enough to incorporate them in all new editions without drawing attention to the fact that they had been newly revised and augmented by royal command. But several thousand copies of the 1559 book had already been sold, a substantial percentage of them to clergymen who now needed to be informed of the extensive new changes. Richard Jugge therefore printed an eight-leaf cancel to replace the almanack and calendar of the folio editions, signed 'B' because it was to follow leaf $^\pi$A10 in the preliminaries. But at some point before it was circulated, the Commissioners made a few corrections and some more significant changes in the table of proper lessons itself, so a bifolium signed 'A' was printed to cancel old $^\pi$A9–10 and thus precede the new quire B^8. By then it seems to have become obvious that many more copies of B^8 would be needed, so enough copies of A^2 were printed to serve both editions.

A close comparison of the lectionary columns in the old and new calendars reveals hundreds of alterations – but outside the clergy few readers would appreciate how extensive the changes really were. What would stand out, however, was that in the 'miscellaneous' column of the calendar, where comparatively few special holy days printed in red were interspersed with notes on the zodiac and the dates of non-liturgical occasions (Lammas, the dog days, the law terms, etc.), a substantial number of additions included the feasts of several dozen 'minor' saints, events in the life of Mary, celebrations of the Exaltation and 'Invention' of the Holy Cross, and a number of fasts preceding major saints' days. To some reformers then (and to some historians today), those additions may have suggested a resurgence of Catholic traditions – a conclusion to which I confess that I likewise jumped when I first began comparing the revised calendar with its Edwardian ancestors.

But the overwhelming majority of the surviving Edwardian prayer books are folio editions printed primarily for the use of the clergy during church services. In those of 1549 the entries in the miscellaneous column are limited to twenty-five holy days; in those of 1552 nearly all the thirty-eight additions are astrological and secular, except for Sts George, Laurence, and Clement. Liturgiologists naturally tend to focus on the key folio editions: the presumed first editions of 1549, 1552, 1559, 1604, and 1662. But in 1552–53 Edward Whitchurch printed two known editions in quarto and one in octavo. Each has its own selection of miscellanea: the first adds twenty-nine saints and six other feasts to those mentioned in Whitchurch's folio editions, the second has a slightly different selection of thirty-two added saints, the same six feasts, and ten fasts before major holy days; the octavo has forty-five added saints, seven other feasts, and nine fasts (but identified as 'Fish' days) . Meanwhile in his sole surviving octavo of 1552–53, Richard Grafton has fifty added saints, five other feasts, and eleven fish days.

We can hardly assume that each of those four editions had its added miscellanea individually approved by the Edwardian authorities, and that leaves only one plausible answer to the question of who selected and inserted them: the printers themselves. It would be absurd to suspect either Whitchurch or Grafton of attempting to revive Catholic traditions – and not only are the number and nature of the added miscellanea of 1561 very similar to those of 1552–53, but many of them are precisely the same. They seem to have been added simply as calendrical trivia, of little more liturgical importance than the term dates and the sun's progress through the zodiac. I therefore consider their most likely source to have been the printer Richard Jugge himself.

Looking back at how this project began (with simple curiosity about whether the first Jugge-and-Cawood folio edition really was printed by both of them) I find it hard to recapture the naivety with which I first framed the question. Once I realized that the volume was the product of a completely unprecedented level of shared printing I began to wonder why, and whether any of the other 1559 editions were similar. That led me to the Grafton edition (with its recycled sheets, its Kingston title-page and calendar, and its unique ordinal) and what I now know to be the fourth folio edition (some copies of which contain Jugge's 1561 cancel calendars). And so the excavation grew to include the Journals of both Houses of Parliament and several Original Acts, William Seres's predatory patent of 1559, and the calendars in several dozen prayer books, bibles, and New Testaments from 1537 to the 1660s and beyond. Much of what I uncovered appears to have been both unknown and unsuspected – but archaeology can often reveal new details about history.

It has long been known that the progress of the Acts of Supremacy and Uniformity through Parliament was far from smooth, and that what emerged from numerous rounds of hard-fought compromise nevertheless barely scraped together a tiny, last-minute majority in the Lords. What a close study of the books themselves shows clearly is that the passage of the Act of Uniformity was by no means the end of the story. The requirement that

> suche ornament*es* of the churche & of the ministers thereof shalbe reteyned and be in vse as was in this churche of Englond by auctoritie of p*ar*liam*en*t in the seconde yere of the reign of king Edwarde the vjth vntill other order shalbe therein taken

fails to explain how the book's opening rubrics should express that – and in the first Jugge-and-Cawood folio, the extant leaf containing the revised rubrics is a cancel printed much later than the rest of the quire. The Act says nothing about removing the Black Rubric of 1552 – but removed it was, and the pertinent leaf in that same edition is also a cancel. The Act required 'one alterac*i*on or addic*i*on of c*er*ten lessons to be vsed on eue*ry* Sonday in the yere', but the printers evidently found the copy for the revised table of proper lessons difficult to divide among the available preliminary pages, and the leaf containing the first of those pages is a cancel in both first editions. The Act says nothing about the ordinal, although both extant editions of it show that revisions had been made, communicated, and printed. But it is also clear that at the last minute the authorities decided that it should be issued only as a separate booklet, and the contents list that omits it is a cancel in both first editions of the prayer book. Moreover, when it was realized that the revision of the proper lessons had seriously reduced the number of Old Testament chapters read during the year, a substantial revision of the calendar in 1561 (which nevertheless failed to implement the queen's express wishes) required the belated cancellation of the calendars and some adjacent leaves in at least four existing folio editions.

It seems appropriate to give the penultimate word to Katharine F. Pantzer, in the sentence I quoted in the Preface: 'Most bibliographers are hesitant to deal with liturgies from the period before, during, and after the Reformation.' Not all liturgies, of course, are likely to reward the unhesitant with quite as many 'archaeological' problems to solve as have those of 1549–61, although unless they are studied carefully we shall never know for certain. One of the reasons why such extraordinary events occurred was that during a period when religion and politics demanded extraordinary efforts from the producers of books, printers who had formerly been partners had to begin to think and act more like rivals (Grafton and Whitchurch in 1549–52), and former rivals found themselves pressed into partnerships (the printers of 'Jugge-and-Cawood' editions in 1559). There were probably few such periods in the history of English liturgical printing,[A] but similar circumstances could arise whenever politics rather than religion led to hyperactivity in the book trade.[B] And as field archaeology can sometimes enhance or alter the findings of even the most diligent of archival historians, analytical bibliography can sometimes reveal evidence of events completely unrecorded in the archives.

[A] The period between the revival of *The Book of Common Prayer* in 1660 and its official revision in 1662, however, might repay investigation.
[B] The analysis by Stanley Rypins of 'The Printing of *Basilikòn Dôron*, 1603' (*PBSA*, 64 (1970), 393–417) barely scratches the surface of another extraordinary outbreak of shared (and competitive) printing.

APPENDIX A

The Etymology of 'Black Rubric'

As I explained in Chapter 2 (p. 32), the 252-word passage now usually known as the Black Rubric was written in October 1552, probably by Cranmer himself, between the 7th (when he politely informed his fellow Privy Councillors that they had acted precipitately) and the 22nd (when the king both approved and signed what is described in the official record as 'an article . . . declaring the right meaning of kneling').[A] A rubric, on the other hand, is 'A direction in a liturgical book as to how a church service should be conducted, traditionally written or printed in red ink'.[B] One of the real rubrics in the 1552 Communion service requires the elements to be delivered 'to the people in theyr handes kneling', and Cranmer's 'article' defends that kneeling against John Knox's accusation of idolatry.

Less than a year after the passage was first printed, Mary's accession made the Edwardian prayer books obsolete, although it was not until 13 June 1555 that they were explicitly banned by proclamation.[C] While Elizabeth's Act of Uniformity neither required nor even permitted the declaration to be suppressed, it was omitted from almost all the editions of the revised book in 1559. In the first of the 'Jugge and Cawood' folios Richard Jugge apparently printed it on page N3ʳ and had to cancel leaf N3 to remove it, and in the only extant copy of the first of the 1559 quartos John Cawood mistakenly printed it on R1ʳ – but apart from those two oversights it was not printed again for more than a century.

In 1660, after *The Book of Common Prayer* had gone for seventeen years without a legally printed edition, the resumption of printing at the Restoration prompted debate about additional revisions. But none of those whose views were published and discussed – such as Cornelius Burges, who misdescribed Cranmer's declaration as a *'Rubrick'* when

---

[A] TNA: PRO, SP 10/15, 34ʳ–5ʳ (Cranmer's letter); BL, MS Royal 18.C.xxiv, 262ᵛ (record of the sign manual).
[B] *OED*, rubric *n*. A.1.a. In that definition, 'traditionally' seems excessively sweeping in an English dictionary, given that Anglican rubrics were printed only in black ink for at least two and a half centuries.
[C] STC 7865, 1ʳ–2ʳ (TRP 422, p. 59).

Figure 26 The Black Rubric, 1663.
(Reproduced by kind permission of Bridwell Library Special Collections, Southern Methodist University, AEU4343/A, I11^r.)

reprinting and commending it in at least two pamphlets – is reported as having called it 'Black'.[A]

[A] Wing B5686 (collating A⁴), reprinted in B5679 on C2^r–D1^v (the '*Rubrick*' appearing on A2^r and C3^r respectively).

Appendix A

When the prayer book was duly revised in 1662, a shortened version of the declaration (reduced from 252 words to 190) was reinstated. Not being a rubric, it was usually distinguished from the real rubrics by being set in a different typeface – as were two new and shorter non-rubrics inserted at the end of the service for public baptism. When the services were in textura and the rubrics in roman, the three non-rubrics were set in italic (as in Wing B3622); when the services were in roman and the rubrics in italic, the non-rubrics were in roman (B3623). The first edition known to have the declaration set in textura is ESTC R236138: a duodecimo of 1663 collating A–R^{12} S^6, with the declaration on I11^r (Figure 26).[A] This was followed in 1664 by an octavo (Wing B3628, declaration on K7^r), and in 1680 by a quarto (Wing B3659, declaration on C2^v).[B] Each of those editions was closely reprinted in subsequent years, the two smaller formats most frequently, so by the time Abraham Woodhead called the declaration 'the *Black Rubrick*' in 1688 at least fifteen editions had been printed in the most popular formats with the declaration printed in textura – which then as now was commonly known as '**black** letter'.

I have rejected the notion that the nickname could have meant 'black-ink-as-distinct-from-red' on the grounds that all Edwardian rubrics were printed in black. It may therefore seem inconsistent to suggest that it meant 'blackletter-as-distinct-from-other-typefaces' when textura was the default face for virtually every part of every Edwardian (and Elizabethan) liturgy. But the nickname is not recorded before the Restoration, and by the 1660s textura was very far from the usual face in editions smaller than the folios and large quartos used by the clergy during services (and even in those volumes the rubrics themselves were seldom in textura). While the revised version of Cranmer's declaration was unquestionably not a rubric, the most immediately obvious feature

---

[A] This is one of two 12° editions included in Wing entry B3626A: the other (ESTC R211843) collates A–F^{12} G^6 and has the declaration in roman type.

[B] Griffiths (*Bibliography*, p. 115) reports an edition of 1662 (no. 1662/4), allegedly collating a–b^{12} A–P^{12} Q^6 with the declaration in blackletter on G11^r, which he identifies as Wing B3624 and locates at both Lambeth Palace and the Huntington Library. I have been unable to trace any such edition in either Wing or ESTC at any date, and no copy matching that description is found in either library. The real B3624 (which collates A–F^{12} G^6) is recorded by Griffiths without a Wing number as no. 1662/5, and there wrongly identified as ESTC R4629. *That* number really belongs to the Cambridge octavo (Wing B3625) correctly listed by Griffiths as no. 1662/6. To assume that the *Bibliography* (2002) must be more up-to-date and trustworthy than either STC vol. 2 (1975) or Wing vol. 1 (1994) would be a mistake.

that distinguished it from its neighbouring rubrics was neither its content nor its function but its typeface.

It would be pointless to suggest that we should start calling it the Blackletter Rubric instead (especially since it is still not an actual rubric), but an explanation that fits both the facts and the chronology may make a welcome change.

APPENDIX B

The Missing Act of 1559

As I reported in Chapter 7 (p. 115), the 1552 Act of Uniformity twice specified that the ordinal devised in 1550 should be appended to each edition of the second Edwardian *Book of Common Prayer*. Whitchurch and Grafton apparently considered that the instruction need not apply to editions in quarto or smaller formats, but every known folio edition of 1552 did indeed have an ordinal printed to accompany it. Although the 1559 Act of Uniformity made no mention of the ordinal, someone in a position of authority apparently prescribed several revisions to it. But although both Grafton and his rivals printed a revised version accordingly, evidently believing that to be the official intention, it was subsequently separated from the service book – presumably by someone with authority equal to or higher than that of the reviser.

But as I also reported, the word *ordinal* was not applied to the publication in question until a century later. The name given to it by the title-page of the first edition (and by which it is identified in the 1552 Act of Uniformity) was *The Forme and Maner of Makyng and Consecratyng of Archebishoppes Bishoppes, Priestes and Deacons*. It is therefore of more than passing interest that although only twenty public acts are known to have received Elizabeth's assent in 1559, and that only those twenty are printed in the nine Elizabethan editions of her first statute, the 'Table' in the first two editions (STC 9458.7–59) lists twenty-one. And the fifth of those – which does not actually appear in any edition – is identified as 'An acte for the admitting and consecrating of Archbysshoppes and Byshoppes' (A1^v).

In the printed statute itself, the act described as 'The fourth Chapter' on B5^v is followed on C6^v by 'The .vi. Chapter', and the remaining numbers follow accordingly – not only in those two editions, but also in the next three (STC 9459.3–9.7), although in those the phantom Chapter 5 is at least removed from the Table. Not until the sixth edition (9460) are Chapters vii–xxi renumbered (in both Table and text) as vi–xx (although in both that and the last three Elizabethan editions the text of the 'real'

Chapter 5 remains numbered 'vi', so there are two consecutive acts identified as Chapter 6). Given the similarity between the titles of the ordinal and the missing act, it seems useful to record what little is known about the latter, since its failure to survive has led to an understandable neglect.

To begin with an essentially unrelated red herring, on 15 February 1559 the Commons Journal records the first reading of 'The bill for order of Servyce and mynysters in the churche', and on the following day what is listed as the first reading of 'The boke for com*m*on pr*a*yer and mynystra-*cion* of sacrament*es*'.[A] As I have already noted in Chapter 3 (p. 47, n.C), in *Faith by Statute* Norman Jones suggested that the first of these might have been connected with the ordinal (91–2) – perhaps because the ordinal had been established by 'An Acte for the orderinge of Ecclesiasticall Ministers' (3 & 4 Edw. VI, c. 12). But it seems more likely that both entries refer to the same bill, and that while the second should have been numbered '2' for a second reading, the word 'mynysters' in the first is an error for some contracted form of 'mynystracion'.

A more obvious candidate for the missing act began its parliamentary journey in the Commons on 21 March with the first and second reading of 'The bill that the Quenes highnes shall collate or apoynt bysshops in bishopryk*es* being vacant', which was then sent to be engrossed. On the following day it was passed after a third reading, and later sent up to the Lords – this time under a description whose last six words raise at least the possibility of a link with the ordinal: 'The bill for collating of bisshops by the Quenes highnes and w*ith* what rites and ceremonyes' (see the first and last entries shown in Plate 1*b*).[B] What is of particular interest here is the word 'assent' subsequently added in the left margin and which will be discussed below.

Later that day (Wednesday, 22 March) the bill 'For the admitting and consecrating of Archebisshopp*es* and Busshopp*es*' was the fourth of five bills received in the Lords from the Commons, and was read there for the first time in what was apparently the morning.[C] That is the last mention of this bill in the extant Journal, but Sir Simonds D'Ewes had a better source, and also records several events of an afternoon session, including the second reading of 'The Bill for Admitting and Consecrating of Archbishops'. And while the extant Lords' Journal records nothing at all for Thursday the 23rd, D'Ewes records that 'The Bill for Admitting and Consecrating of Archbishops and Bishops' was read for the third time and

---

[A] PArch, HC/CL/JO/1/1, fols. 189ᵛ–90ʳ (*CJ*, 1: 54).   [B] Ibid., fol. 204ᵛ (*CJ*, 1:58).
[C] PArch, HL/PO/JO/1/4, 42 (*LJ*, 568).

passed.[A] The only extant manuscript source for the 23rd neither lists those present nor identifies any who opposed the bill. It is, however, safe to assume that all the lords spiritual who had voted against the Act of Supremacy on the 19th, and who were present at the adjournment on the morning of the 24th (with the possible exception of James Turberville of Exeter, not listed as present on the 22nd), not only heard the third reading but also voted against it.

At the time the bill was passed, Elizabeth still seems to have intended to end the session on the 24th (Good Friday), and apparently said as much to Count Feria that evening.[B] As emended by the Lords on the 19th and reluctantly passed by the Commons on the 22nd, the intended Act of Supremacy had been seriously maimed by a committee which (as Jones summarized it in *Faith by Statute*) 'was persuaded to destroy those portions of the bill which would have altered the church service, leaving only the royal supremacy' (100). In addition to rejecting any revival of the Edwardian prayer book,

> the committee members had refused to grant Elizabeth clear recognition of her claim to be supreme head of the Church of England . . . declaring, in effect, that they would abide by her decision but would not sanction it. (101)

While a very long way from ideal, if this were supplemented by an act that explicitly allowed the queen to appoint bishops to the sees currently vacant (most importantly the archdiocese of Canterbury), the balance of power in the Lords could be altered in preparation for a renewed campaign in some future parliament. There was, however, a danger in allowing the Latin liturgy to remain the norm for however many months or years were required. So Elizabeth decided instead to keep Parliament in session, perhaps hoping (or intending) that the planned disputation at Westminster between eight Catholics and eight Protestants would help weaken the opposition. Beginning on Friday, 31 March, it ended in useful disarray on the second day (Monday, 3 April), after two of the bishops had shown sufficient disobedience to land them in the Tower while the others had been fined for contempt and ordered to appear daily before the Privy Council.

When Parliament resumed, the absence of two of the fiercest critics of the desired reforms significantly shifted the balance in the Lords. The

---

[A] D'Ewes, *Journals*, 26; see also Sainty, 'Further Materials', 29, nos. 93, 98. In *Faith by Statute* (115) Jones cites Sainty for the third reading and passage, but apparently overlooked the second reading.
[B] Jones, *Faith by Statute*, 114.

supremacy debate was accordingly reopened in the Commons on 10 April with a revised bill, and was followed on the 18th by a new bill for uniformity of church service. Both were eventually passed, albeit with only tiny majorities.

Once the Act of Supremacy reached its final form on 29 April and was passed by the Lords, the queen no longer needed a special act to allow her to appoint bishops. Not only was she now officially the Supreme Governor of the Church of England, but among the acts repealed by Mary and now revived by Elizabeth in section 2 was 25 Hen. VIII, c. 20, which prescribed how Henry and (crucially) his heirs and successors should set about appointing them. But it seems distinctly possible that on 7 May, when the clerks of the two houses were told which of the acts were to receive the Queen's assent during the following morning's ceremony (and annotated them accordingly),[A] that the Act for Admitting and Consecrating of Archbishops and Bishops was among the favoured ones. John Seymour (the clerk of the Commons) evidently thought so, and when copies of the public acts were delivered to John Cawood to be printed, the numbered list of their titles that accompanied them included that act as the fifth item. Had it actually been present it would presumably have been printed – but even after coping with its absence in the first edition (STC 9458.7), Cawood reprinted the list without omitting it when contributing sheets A1:6 and B1:6 to the second edition (9459, mostly printed by Jugge).

What interests me most about this lost act is not only that its title is so reminiscent of that of the ordinal, but that its contents must presumably have either mentioned the ordinal or quoted at least part of its text. On its second appearance in the Commons Journal it was, after all, described as 'The bill for collating of bisshops ... *and with what rites and ceremonyes*' (my italics). If it included any excerpts from (or discussion of) the ordinal, it may also have spelled out the few revisions required by that book – or may even have formally required it to be detached from the prayer book.

Perhaps Elizabeth really did initially give the act her assent. And perhaps she changed her mind before the copies reached the printer, either because the act was redundant or because it set a bad precedent by implying that Parliament had the authority to direct exactly how the Supreme Governor should govern her Church. Or perhaps she rejected it without hesitation, but Seymour somehow inexplicably mistook her intention. Whatever the details, the loss of its text is regrettable.

[A] The ceremony itself is briefly described by Elton, *The Parliament of England, 1559–1581*, 126–7.

Appendix B

When he wrote *The Parliament of England, 1559–1581*, Sir Geoffrey Elton was unaware that the Lords had both re-read and passed the bill. Commenting that 'In the battles of 1559 not everybody overlooked the fact that Mary's repeal of Edward VI's act for a protestant ordinal left the Church without a lawful system for making bishops', he called the act's supposed expiration 'another success for the Marian bishops'. But the act was not only passed: it apparently received the royal assent and very nearly made it into the printed statute, and the only person who could have been responsible for stopping it was Elizabeth herself. Elton's attempt at explaining its disappearance holds no water: the Edwardian act that established the ordinal was only one of nine included in Mary's act of repeal, and all nine came back into force when Elizabeth's Act of Supremacy repealed that repeal. Although detached from the prayer book at the last minute for reasons unknown, the 1559 ordinal was evidently revised by authority, and I know of no evidence suggesting that the Jugge edition was suppressed.

As Elton also reported, in 1563 a bill 'for the Collation of Bishops of the Queens's Presentment, with such Ceremonies as the Time of K. E.' was read for the first time on 8 March, read again on the 12th and sent to be engrossed,[A] and then disappeared without trace (perhaps because someone pointed out that a revised 1559 ordinal already existed). It seems, however, to have become widely rumoured among the laity that none of the bishops or archbishops appointed by Elizabeth had been legally ordained, so on 14 October 1566 the Commons read a 'Bill affirming the Consecration of Archbishops and Bishops of this Realm' for the first time. It was read again on the 17th, read a third time and passed on the 22nd, and sent up to the Lords on the 23rd.[B] There it was read (as the bill 'declaring the Manner of making and consecrating of the Archbishops and Bishops of this Realm to be good, lawful, and perfect') on the 26th and 30th, and committed to the Chief Justices and Attorney General on the 31st. On 6 November it was read again with a new proviso attached, and passed but with eleven peers dissenting. Back in the Commons the Lords' proviso was read on the 6th and 7th. But a new proviso to replace it was then read on the 23rd and 25th, and passed on the 28th. Finally, on 2 December 1566, the bill with that proviso was read three times in the Lords and passed unanimously.[C] It is difficult to avoid concluding that if the act of 1559 had not been withdrawn, none of the efforts of 1563 and 1566 would have been necessary.

One last matter may be of rather wider importance, and that is the marginal 'assent' written beside the last record of the lost act in Seymour's

---

[A] *CJ*, 68, 69.   [B] Ibid., 74–5; *LJ*, 636.   [C] *LJ*, 635–6, 638–41; *CJ*, 76, 78; *LJ*, 651.

'scribbled book' (as shown in Plate 1*b*). In the *Journals* as published, if the number indicating whether a reading is the first, second, or third is preceded by an 'L' in the manuscript (as in the penultimate entry in Plate 1*b*), that letter is printed approximately where it is written (with an editorial period after both it and the numeral). If, however, the word 'nova' appears in the left margin it is inserted in italic (again with a period), but between the number and the description of the bill instead of where Seymour placed it. If, on the other hand, the margin notes 'Iudm' with a terminal stroke curving up and back over the 'm' like a tilde to indicate that the bill was passed (Iud*iciu*m), the editors insert '—*Jud'm*' in italic, but *after* the description of the bill. Meanwhile various other marginal notes are omitted altogether: what looks like 'no°' (perhaps for *nota*?) beside non-legislative memoranda such as those that follow the records of the bills read on the 7th and 10th of February; 'Lycence' beside notes granting a member leave of absence, as on the 21st and 23rd; and '1 2 3 | quere p*ro* alia | postea' beside the last entry for the 25th.

Attention was first drawn to these discrepancies in the printed record by Elton in 1986,[A] when he rightly identified the omission of one particular group as 'Most serious', namely

> the systematic omissions ... of marginal notes made by the clerk in his manuscript at a later stage. Thus the originals show, as the print does not, that Seymour went over his sessional record at the end of the session, adding where appropriate a note of the assent having been given to his early entry in the margin recording passage of a bill in the House (*iudicium*).

Seymour's marginal 'assent' appears forty-three times during the course of that Parliament, but on one occasion was subsequently deleted. Every example is beside the record of a bill's passage, but not all bills that were passed are so annotated. The deleted example is of particular interest, because it is beside the passage of one of the early versions of the Act of Supremacy: the one passed on 25 February, which Jones erroneously claims was passed 'after a stormy debate' on the 23rd.[B]

The list of acts (both public and private) recorded in the Lords' Journal, contains forty entries,[C] every one of which is flagged with 'assent' beside the record of its passage in the Commons Journal. Of the remaining three 'assent' notes, one is the deleted example just discussed, one flags a genuine

---

[A] Elton, *The Parliament of England, 1559–1581*, 8–9.
[B] *Faith by Statute*, 93–4. It was read first ('*nova*') on the 21st, re-read and engrossed on the 22nd, read again and passed on the 25th.
[C] PArch, HL/PO/JO/1/4, 63–4 (*LJ*, 579).

act that is mistakenly omitted from the Lords' list,[A] and the other is the one I have illustrated in Plate 1*b* beside the lost act 'for collating of bisshops... and with what rites and ceremonyes'. Given that its title was included in the list sent to Cawood with the public acts to be included in the official statute book, it is possible that Elizabeth really did assent to it but subsequently changed her mind. And if that were the case, some connection with the belated detachment of the ordinal cannot be ruled out.

I have chosen folio 210^v of the Journal to illustrate another 'assent' note (Plate 1*a*), because of another important omission from the published edition. As I reported in Chapter 3 (p. 48), after passing the Act of Uniformity on 20 April the Commons immediately sent Cecil to the Lords to deliver that and the six other bills most recently passed. They then moved on to the second reading of another bill. But the Lords had already adjourned, Cecil could not complete his errand, and the note was accordingly deleted. Not until the 25th were those bills (plus two more passed meanwhile) successfully sent up to the Lords again by Sir Anthony Cooke. And the deleted record of the attempted delivery is something else neither included nor mentioned in the published *Journals*. Caveat lector.

[A] 1 Eliz. I, c. 17: An Acte for the preservacōn of Spawne and Frye of Fyshe. This was passed by the Commons on 24 April, read in the Lords the following day and 1 May, passed on 6 May but then sent back to the Commons with a proviso. The amended act was read there the same day, then re-read twice and passed during the morning of the 8th before receiving the assent in the afternoon (*CJ*, 60–1; Davis, 'An Unpublished Manuscript', 537, 539, 541).

APPENDIX C

The Recycled Calendar of 1560

In 1560–61 John Cawood printed the first of several quarto editions of the Great Bible (which was still the translation 'appoynted to be red in the Churches') that would appear during the 1560s under his name alone. The title-page on ¶1^r is dated 1560; the colophon on Nn6^r 1561.[A] After the title-page the first four quires (¶^{8} ^{π}A^4 ^{π}B^8 ^{π}C^{12}) contain an abbreviated form of the *Book of Common Prayer*: the almanack, the order of reading the psalms and the rest of scripture, the calendar (¶3^r–8^v), the table of proper lessons and psalms, the order for Morning and Evening Prayer, the Litany, and the Collects (only) for the principal holy days.

The title-page was evidently set in Cawood's house. The text is framed by two ornaments that he had acquired from Stephen Mierdman,[B] separated at head and foot by woodcut illustrations from Mierdman's 16° New Testament of 1548 (STC 2852) and supported by a third ornament (measuring approximately 19 × 99 mm) flanked by two pairs of large printers' flowers. The same three ornaments and four flowers are used again (though with the two woodcuts replaced by more apposite ones) for the New Testament title-page (AA1^r) in a quire unquestionably printed by Cawood himself, but that last cannot be said of quire ¶^{8}. All four formes of that quire are printed in red and black, and fourteen of the sixteen pages consist of tabular material. And in the same way that Grafton handed off his two-colour tables and calendar to John Kingston in 1559, Cawood evidently asked Richard Jugge (whose printing house was now both fully equipped and competently staffed) for expert help with his opening quire. With the exception of the title-page itself, every page in the quire is set in Richard Jugge's type, and the display capital T on page ¶2^v is one of two

---

[A] STC 2094 (ESTC S122372). The complete collation is 4°: ¶^{8} ^{π}A^4 ^{π}B^8 ^{π}C^{12}, A–Bb^8 Cc^6, a–z^8 &^{8} aa–bb^8 cc^{10}, AA-MM^8 NN^6.
[B] Illustrated as the sides of Border McK & F 110, they were used in the Coverdale Bible of 1535, came to England that year to the house of James Nicolson of Southwark, and had been used by several printers before being acquired by Mierdman in the late 1540s.

closely similar letters belonging to the 21-mm alphabet that Jugge began using at the end of 1559.[A]

But the identification of Jugge does not depend solely on comparison of the two printers' ornaments and types. More strikingly, four whole calendar pages of Cawood's inner sheet ¶ (January–March, and July) and parts of three of the other five (May, June, and August) are recognizably reimposed as pages $^{\pi}$A2^r–3^r and $^{\pi}$A4^r–5^v of Jugge's quarto prayer book of 1560 (STC 16294). Those pages were set as lines separated by narrow rules rather than as columns, and each vertical 'line' is made up of thirty-two line-high strokes, approximately aligned. The horizontal rules were evidently very thin and easily bent, and many of them are readily and unmistakably recognizable: in the two Januaries, the rules below days 2–4, 19, 23, and 25–6 (see Figures 28–9); in the Februaries, below psalm-selections 3–4, 12, 16, 26, and the blank line after 29; in the Marches, below psalm-groups 2, 18–19, 21, 24, and 29–30. Given the two-colour printing, it is unsurprising that there are some differences in the red text which, after being printed through a custom-cut colour frisket, would have been taken out and replaced by quads and spaces before the black text was printed in Cawood's bible. Those cells therefore needed to be reset before being printed in red for the prayer book. In February, though, the resetting in the miscellaneous column was rather more extensive, and while 'Sol in Pis.' was omitted, St Matthias was mistakenly moved from line 25 to line 22, and in the formerly blank lines 16–21 is inserted 'Wensday | Fryday and | Saterday, | the first weke | in Lent is | Imber.'

Now if the Ember-day notes were restricted to the Jugge edition alone we could perhaps attribute them to his own special interest (as in the case of Reyner Wolfe and the hours of daylight). But the other three 'Imber' notes are given correctly in the Cawood calendar – and as I noted in Chapter 10 (p. 189), when Jugge's compositor tried to to transfer lines 1–2 and 4 of the December note to the September page, he mistakenly included line 3 ('after.S.Lucie') as well. Perhaps, then, it was Cawood rather than Jugge who had a special interest in Ember days. If so, the inadvertent omission from February may have been corrected before the press-run was finished, and some copies of Cawood's bible may have included all four notes. If the Newcastle fragment is ever rediscovered (see above, p. 163), and proves to have been printed by either Jugge or Cawood, perhaps it may shed a little more light on the matter.

[A] See footnote on p. 83. This is not the initial used in the calendar cancels to introduce the list of holy days (B2^v in the first two editions, and A4^v in the third). That T can be found in Jugge's 1560 prayer book (STC 16294) on C6^v and D6^v; the one used in the Cawood bible appears on the facing pages C7^r and D7^r. The clearest distinctions are in the foliage along the top of the crossbar.

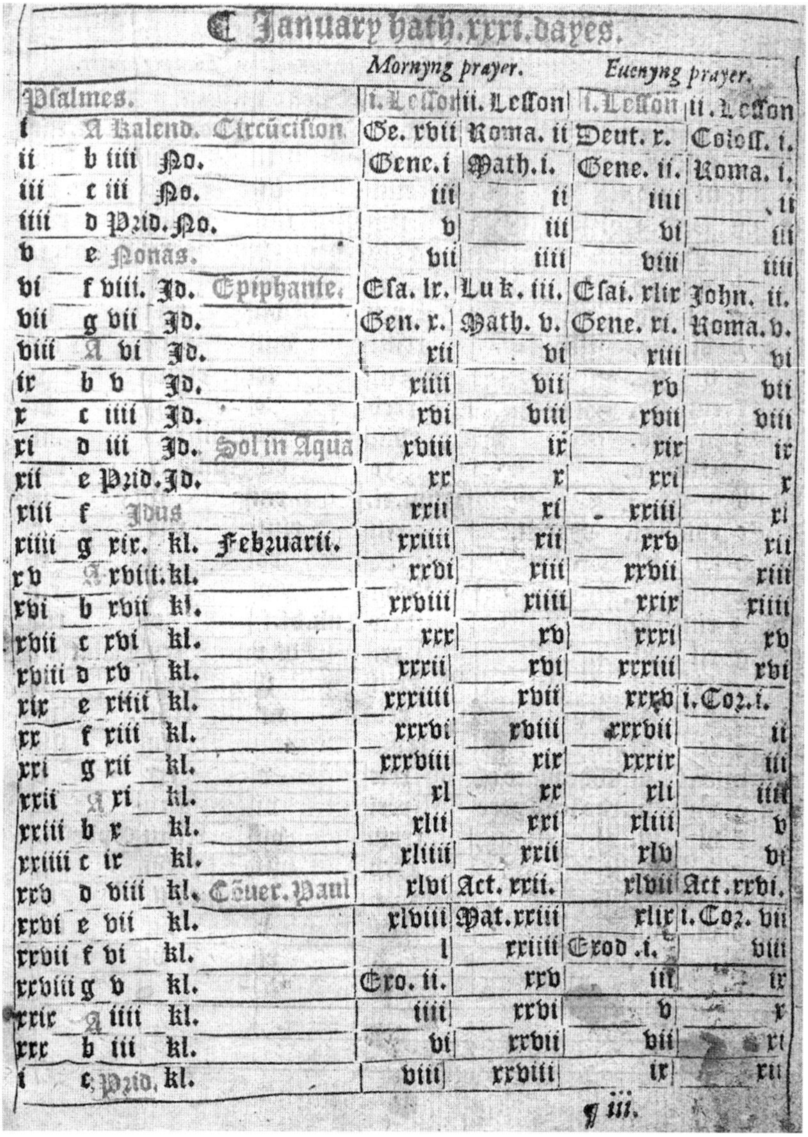

¶ January hath. xxxi. dayes.

		Mornyng prayer.		Euenyng prayer.	
Psalmes.		i. Lesson	ii. Lesson	i. Lesson	ii. Lesson
i	A Kalend. Circűcision	Ge. xvii	Roma. ii	Deut. x.	Coloss. i.
ii	b iiii No.	Gene. i	Math. i.	Gene. ii.	Roma. i.
iii	c iii No.	iii	ii	iiii	ii
iiii	d Prid. No.	v	iii	vi	iii
v	e Nonas.	vii	iiii	viii	iiii
vi	f viii. Id. Epiphanie.	Esa. lx.	Luk. iii.	Esai. xlix	John. ii.
vii	g vii Id.	Gen. x.	Math. v.	Gene. xi.	Roma. v.
viii	A vi Id.	xii	vi	xiii	vi
ix	b v Id.	xiiii	vii	xv	vii
x	c iiii Id.	xvi	viii	xvii	viii
xi	d iii Id. Sol in Aqua	xviii	ix	xix	ix
xii	e Prid. Id.	xx	x	xxi	x
xiii	f Idus	xxii	xi	xxiii	xi
xiiii	g xix. kl. Februarii.	xxiiii	xii	xxv	xii
xv	A xviii. kl.	xxvi	xiii	xxvii	xiii
xvi	b xvii kl.	xxviii	xiiii	xxix	xiiii
xvii	c xvi kl.	xxx	xv	xxxi	xv
xviii	d xv kl.	xxxii	xvi	xxxiii	xvi
xix	e xiiii kl.	xxxiiii	xvii	xxxv	i. Cor. i.
xx	f xiii kl.	xxxvi	xviii	xxxvii	ii
xxi	g xii kl.	xxxviii	xix	xxxix	iii
xxii	A xi kl.	xl	xx	xli	iiii
xxiii	b x kl.	xlii	xxi	xliii	v
xxiiii	c ix kl.	xliiii	xxii	xlv	vi
xxv	d viii kl. Cõuer. Paul	xlvi	Act. xxii.	xlvii	Act. xxvi.
xxvi	e vii kl.	xlviii	Mat. xxiii	xlix	i. Cor. vii
xxvii	f vi kl.	l	xxiiii	Exod. i.	viii
xxviii	g v kl.	Exo. ii.	xxv	iii	ix
xxix	A iiii kl.	iiii	xxvi	v	x
xxx	b iii kl.	vi	xxvii	vii	xi
i	c Prid. kl.	viii	xxviii	ix	xii

¶ iii.

Figure 27 Jugge's January in Cawood's Bible, 1560 (STC 2094).
(© The British Library Board, 465.a.3, ¶3r.)

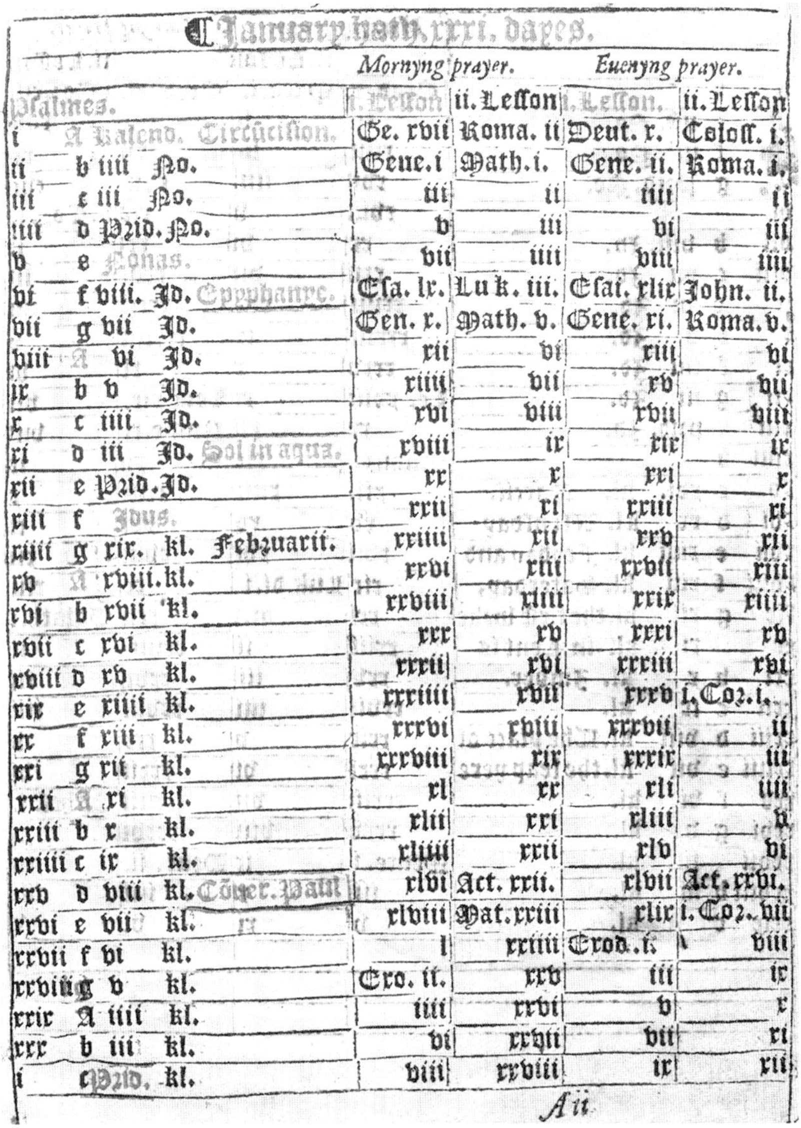

January hath xxxi. dayes.

		Mornyng prayer.		Euenyng prayer.	
Psalmes.		i. Lesson	ii. Lesson	i. Lesson	ii. Lesson
i	A Kalend. Circũcision.	Ge. xvii	Roma. ii	Deut. x.	Coloss. i.
ii	b iiii No.	Gene. i	Math. i.	Gene. ii.	Roma. i.
iii	c iii No.	iii	ii	iiii	ii
iiii	d Prid. No.	v	iii	vi	iii
v	e Nonas.	vii	iiii	viii	iiii
vi	f viii. Id. Epyphanye.	Esa. lx.	Luk. iii.	Esai. xlix	John. ii.
vii	g vii Id.	Gen. ix.	Math. v.	Gene. xi.	Roma. v.
viii	A vi Id.	xii	vi	xiii	vi
ix	b v Id.	xiiii	vii	xv	vii
x	c iiii Id.	xvi	viii	xvii	viii
xi	d iii Id. Sol in aqua.	xviii	ix	xix	ix
xii	e Prid. Id.	xx	x	xxi	x
xiii	f Idus.	xxii	xi	xxiii	xi
xiiii	g xix. kl. Februarii.	xxiiii	xii	xxv	xii
xv	A xviii. kl.	xxvi	xiii	xxvii	xiii
xvi	b xvii kl.	xxviii	xiiii	xxix	xiiii
xvii	c xvi kl.	xxx	xv	xxxi	xv
xviii	d xv kl.	xxxii	xvi	xxxiii	xvi
xix	e xiiii kl.	xxxiiii	xvii	xxxv	i. Cor. i.
xx	f xiii kl.	xxxvi	xviii	xxxvii	ii
xxi	g xii kl.	xxxviii	xix	xxxix	iii
xxii	A xi kl.	xl	xx	xli	iiii
xxiii	b x kl.	xlii	xxi	xliii	v
xxiiii	c ix kl.	xliiii	xxii	xlv	vi
xxv	d viii kl. Cõuer. Paul	xlvi	Act. xxii.	xlvii	Act. xxvi.
xxvi	e vii kl.	xlviii	Mat. xxiii	xlix	i. Cor. vii
xxvii	f vi kl.	l	xxiiii	Exod. i.	viii
xxviii	g v kl.	Exo. ii.	xxv	iii	ix
xxix	A iiii kl.	iiii	xxvi	v	x
xxx	b iii kl.	vi	xxvii	vii	xi
i	c Prid. kl.	viii	xxviii	ix	xii

A ii

Figure 28 January reimposed in Jugge's own prayer book, 1560 (STC 16294).
(© The British Library Board, C.25.h.12, A2r.)

APPENDIX D

The Editions of 1559 (and the Cancels of 1561–62)

Most of the title-pages and colophons of the books listed below are reproduced in this book. It therefore seems unnecessary to go to the trouble of transcribing them in full quasi-facsimile, using textura type, long s and ligatures, and distinguishing regular from swash italic capitals. In transcribing them, therefore, I have substituted bold roman for blackletter and have modernized the typography. I have, however, used a dotted underline to indicate red ink, since only three of the title-pages are reproduced in colour.

I have cited STC and/or ESTC for each item with an entry in one or the other (and have 'invented' STC-style numbers in quotations for two of them). I have not thought it worthwhile to cite the Griffiths *Bibliography* (whose sixteenth-century entries add nothing to their STC sources beyond additional errors) except when recording the mistakes in its entry for STC 16293.5.

STC 16291 (ESTC S93763; title-page reproduced as Plate 2)

[In black and red, within a woodcut compartment, McK & F 67]
❧ **The Boke of | common praier, and ad= | ministration of the | Sacramentes, | and other | rites | and Ceremonies in | the Churche of | Englande.** | *Londini, in officina Ri=* | *chardi Graftoni.* | Cumpriuilegio Regie | Maiestatis. | *Anno.*1559.

[No colophon. In line 10, imperfect register between black and red in the copy reproduced as Plate 2 (Corpus Christi College, Oxford) has made the black *officina* slightly overlap the red *Ri=*. In the Bodleian Library copy the two are touching but not overlapped; in the copy illustrated in Figure 23 (Cambridge University Library) there is a little space between them.]

$2°$: $\pi A^{12}(\pm \pi A1,4:9,12)\ b^6,\ A–V^6\ X^8$

Appendix D

Richard Grafton printed $^\pi$A2–3,5–8,10–11, A–V^6 X^8, original $^\pi$A4:9, and probably original $^\pi$A1:12 (70 sheets)
John Kingston printed b^6 and cancel $^\pi$A1,4:9,12 (5 sheets)

Verified copies:

British Library: C.25.l.9 (Sheets reissued from 16286.2: b^6, A2–5, F1:6, I^6, V3:4).
Cambridge University Library: Sel.3.221 (Sheets reissued from 16286.2: only Q1:6. Sheets R3:4 and X1:8 are in 1559 settings not found elsewhere. Has a copy of Jugge Cancel Calendar 1 inserted after $^\pi$A11).
St John's College, Cambridge: A.4.13 (Reissued from 16286.2: only F1:6. Wants $^\pi$A1–4, X1:8, and most of b1).
Bodleian Library, Oxford: C.P. 1559 d.1 (Reissued from 16286.2: A2–5, F1:6, G1:6, I^6, L^6, M1:6, N1:6, O^6, T^6, V1,3:4,6; from 16286.3: E2:5, H1,2:5,6. Wants calendar b^6).
Corpus Christi College, Oxford: Phi.F.3.7 (Reissued from 16286: L3:4; from 16286.2: b^6, A2–5, F1:6, G1:6, I^6, L1,2:5,6, M1:6, N1:6, O^6, T^6, V1,3:4,6; from 16286.3: E^6, H1,2:5,6, X3:6. Has the only known copy of 'STC 16464+' bound after X8: for description see below).

STC 16292 (ESTC S111841; title-page reproduced as Plate 3)

[In black and red, within a woodcut compartment, McK & F 68β]
¶ The Booke of | common praier, and ad= | ministration of the | Sacramentes, | and other | rites | and Ceremonies in | the Churche of | Englande. | *Londini, in officina Richardi* | *Iugge,* & *Iohannis* | *Cawode.* | Cum priuilegio Regie | Maiestatis. | *Anno.*1559.

[No colophon: Device McKerrow 125α on P10^v (otherwise blank)]

2°: $^\pi$A^{12}(±$^\pi$A1,4:9,12) $^\pi$B^6, A^8(±A1) B^8 C^8(±C2:7) D–K^8 L^{10} M^8 N^8(±N3) O–P^{10}

Reyner Wolfe and Edward Whitchurch printed A–F^8 (24 sheets)
John Cawood printed G^8 (4 sheets)
Owen Rogers printed H^8, I1,2:7,8, and M^8 (10 sheets)
Thomas Marshe printed I3–6, K^8, and L^{10} (11 sheets)
Richard Payne printed N1,2,4:5,7,8 and O2,3,4:7,8,9 (6 sheets)

Reyner Wolfe (probably alone) printed $^{\pi}$A5–8 and $^{\pi}B^6$ (5 sheets)
John Kingston printed sheets O5:6 and O1:10, cancel sheet $^{\pi}$A4:9, and cancel forme $^{\pi}$A1^v:12^r (3 sheets and 1 forme)
Richard Jugge printed sheet N3:6, quire P^{10}, cancels A1, C2:7, and N3, and cancel forme $^{\pi}$A1^r:12^v (6 sheets, 2 leaves, and 1 forme)

Verified copies:

British Library: C.25.m.7 (Signature of Sir Nicholas Bacon on front paste-down and title-page).
Lincoln Cathedral Library: L.402 (Wants all before B1).
Private owner. In 1976 the revisers of STC (who knew of only two Jugge-and-Cawood editions) listed a copy then owned by Sir Richard Proby. No more recent information is available.
Boston Public Library: Benton 1.95.Folio. Reproduced on EEBO from UMI film STC reel 1073, item 4.
The Huntington Library: 97019.

'STC 16292+' (not in STC or ESTC)

[Title unknown, though probably closely resembling 16292 and 16292a]

[No colophon: Device McKerrow 125α on P10^v below 5-line price note (reproduced as Figure 15)]

2°: [Unique copy lacks the preliminaries], A–K^8 L^{10} M–N^8 O–P^{10}

Richard Jugge printed A–E^8, L^{10} (25 sheets)
John Cawood printed F–G^8 and sheet O1:10 (9 sheets)
Owen Rogers printed H–K^8 (12 sheets)
John Kingston printed M^8 and P^{10} (9 sheets)
Richard Payne printed N^8 and O2–9 (8 sheets)

Verified copy:

York Minster Library: XI.F.19(1) (wants preliminaries, probably $^{\pi}$A^{12} $^{\pi}$B^6, which have been replaced by a copy of Jugge Cancel Calendar 1; has a copy of STC 16465 bound after P10: for descriptions see below).

Appendix D

STC 16292a (ESTC S93764; title-page reproduced as Figure 19)
[In black and red, within a woodcut compartment, McK & F 68β]
¶ The Booke of | common praier,and ad= | ministration of the | Sacramentes, | and other | rites | and Ceremonies in | the Churche of | Englande. | *Londini,in officina Richardi* | *Iugge,* & *Iohannis* | *Cawode.* | Cum priuilegio Regiæ | Maiestatis. | *Anno.*1559.
[No colophon: Device McKerrow 125α on P10^v below 5-line price note]

2°: πA^{12} πB^6, A–K^8 L^{10} M–N^8 O–P^{10}

John Kingston printed πA^{12} B^6 (9 sheets)
Richard Jugge printed A–E^8, L^{10}, M1,2:7,8, and P^{10} (32 sheets)
John Cawood printed F–G^8, K^8, M3–6, and N^8 (18 sheets)
Owen Rogers printed H–I^8 (8 sheets)
Richard Payne printed quire O^{10} (5 sheets)
(In all known copies, F^8 (Cawood) and H4:5 (Rogers) are in the same setting as 'STC 16292+')

Verified copies:

British Library: 6.d.9 (STC describes this copy as having the title-page from an edition of 'c. 1566' (actually from STC 16297, *c.* 1567). The absence of leaf πA10 is overlooked, and while it is true that leaves L3:8 (Marshe) and P4:7 (Jugge) are in the same setting as STC 16292, quire D and P1:10 are from 'STC 16292+'.) Reproduced on EEBO from UMI film STC reel 2312, item 1.

British Library: C.25.l.6 (STC describes this copy as having a title-page 'dated 1559, but the state of the border ... is probably later than 1559'. The four new holes made by the woodworm since 16292 can be dated only relatively, and prove only that this edition of 1559 is the later of the two. The title-page is proper to this edition, and has 'Regiæ' in the privilege statement (STC 16292 has 'Regie'). STC correctly observes that calendar quire πB^6 has been replaced by a ten-leaf quire signed A (Cancel Calendar 3) whose almanack on A3^v begins with 1561, but ends by mistakenly claiming that 'the text is the same setting as [6.d.9], except that P1, 10 are reset'. P1:10 is proper to this edition, and STC had already noted that D^8, L3:8, and P4:7 also differ between the two copies.) Reproduced on EEBO from UMI film STC reel 2312, item 2.

228   *Appendix D*

- Lambeth Palace Library: H5415.A4 1559 (Complete, but title-page re-attached after separation).
- Keble College, Oxford: Brooke 217 (The copy numbered '3' by STC, and the only perfect copy the revisers saw. Has I⁸ in the setting evidently proper to '16292+'. STC's claim that the almanack begins with 1561 is incorrect. ᵀA1:12 is original and undamaged, and the almanack begins with 1559).
- Keble College, Oxford: 'Keble copy 2'. (This is the copy numbered '4' by STC: one of two Keble books formerly numbered 'A.66' (the other is a copy of STC 16273). Since 2003 this copy has been officially known as 'Keble College Library Special Collections STC 16292', having been thus misreported to SOLO (Search Oxford Libraries Online) by an outside cataloguer – but it is not a copy of 16292. The title-page is a clumsy twentieth-century fake, misdated 1561. Leaf ᵀA12 and quire ᵀB⁶ have been replaced by the only known copy of Cancel Calendar 2, which evidently inspired the faker's date).
- Thomas Fisher Rare Book Library, Toronto: stc 01221 (Perfect. Has a copy of STC 16465 bound after P10).

STC 16293.3 (ESTC S93766; title-page reproduced as Plate 8)

[In black and red, within a border of four ornamental strips (not in McK & F), approximately 107 × 25 mm (top and left), 107 × 23 mm (right), and 106 × 34 mm (sill). All four corners and the midsections of the top and sides have red overprinted on the black. In the sill a circular band (33 mm enclosing 22 mm) includes the motto 'DESVPER OMNIA', and in its centre the initials 'R. I.' are typeset.]

The booke of | *Common Prayer, and admini=* | *stracion of the Sacramentes,* | *and other Rites and* | *Ceremonies in the* | *Churche of* | *England.* | *Londini, in officina Richardi* | *Iugge & Iohannis* | *Cawood* | ¶ *Cum priuilegio Regiæ Maiestatis.* | 1559.

First colophon on V10ᵛ (not reproduced)
❧Imprinted at Lon | don in *P*ovvles Churchyarde bi Richard | Iugge,and Iohn Cavvood, printers | *t*o the Quenes Maiestie. | Anno M.D.LIX. | Cum priuilegio Regiæ | Maiestatis.

Part-title on ²A1ʳ (reproduced in Figure 23)
[Within a woodcut compartment, McK & F 37β]

The Psalter | or Psalmes of Dauid, | after the translaci= | on of the greate | Bible, poyn= | ted as it | shal be | said | or | songe in Chur= | ches. | ❧ | LONDINI. | 1559.

Second colophon on ^{2}M8^v (reproduced in Figure 23)
⁋ Imprinted at London by Wyllyam | Seres dwelling at the weste | ende of Poules, at the signe | of the Hedghoge.

4°: a–c^8, A–T^8 V^{10}; ^{2}A–M^8

Richard Jugge printed a–c^8, A–M^8 (30 sheets)
John Cawood printed N–T^8 V^{10} (16½ sheets)
Henry Sutton printed ^{2}A–H^8 (16 sheets)
William Copland printed ^{2}I–M^8 (8 sheets)

Verified copies:

British Library: C.112.c.10 (wants ^{2}M^8). Reproduced (without imperfect psalter) on EEBO from UMI film STC reel 2295, item 1.
British Library: C.53.c.1 (a–b^8, A^8, B1, and M^8 only, bound with the imperfect copy of 16293). Reproduced on EEBO from UMI film STC 2389, item 3a, images 2–28 and 92–100.
British Library: C.194.a.207 (psalter only). Reproduced on EEBO from UMI film STC 2389, item 3b.
Neither the (almost) complete C.112.c.10 nor the fragmentary C.53.c.1 has anything between b8^v (the 'brief declaration' of the term dates) and A1^r (Morning Prayer), and both lack the calendar clearly called for in the contents list (and implied by the table of proper lessons). John R. Hetherington included a hypothetical quire c^6 in his collation (see STC, II: 88, series Heth. 3), evidently assuming that *only* the calendar was missing. But that would still have left out the almanack, so I believe that the missing quire is more likely to have been c^8 (even if it included three blank pages).

STC 16293 (ESTC S93765)

[Title, colophon, and presence or absence of an appended psalter unknown.]

4°: Unique copy consists only of D–L^8 and N–T^8 (made up with a–b^8, A^8, B1 and M^8 from a copy of STC 16293.3)

All extant leaves printed by Richard Jugge (30 sheets)

Verified copy:

> British Library: C.53.c.1. Reproduced on EEBO from UMI film STC 2389, item 3a, images 28–92 and 100–56.
>
> The prayer book almost certainly collated like the previous edition to the end (V10^v). If the patent conflict had not yet been resolved, the psalter was probably either a copy or a reprint of the known Seres edition. Otherwise an edition of unknown collation would have been printed either for or by Jugge and Cawood.

STC 16293.5 (ESTC 93767; title-page reproduced in Figure 24)

[Within a woodcut compartment, McK & F 33]
❡ **The Booke of | Common Praier, | and administracion of | the Sacramentes, | and other Ri= | tes and | Ceremonies | in the | churche of En= | glande.** | *Londini, in officina Ri= | chardi Iugge, & | Iohannis Ca= | woode.*

Part-title on ²A1^r (not reproduced)
[Within a woodcut compartment, McK & F 33]
❡ **The Psalter | or Psalmes of | Dauid, after | the tran= | slaci= | on of the greate Bi= | ble, pointed as it | shall be song | in chur= | ches.** | *Anno.1559.*

Colophon on ²R3^v (reproduced in Figure 24)
❡ **Imprinted at London by Ri= | chard Iugge, and Iohn Cawoode, | printers to the Quenes | Maiestie.** | *M.D.LIX.* | Cum P riuilegio.

8°: $^\pi$A⁸ +⁴w⁸, A–Z⁸ Aa–Cc⁸ Dd⁴, ²A–Q⁸ R⁴

> John Kingston printed the whole book (45½ sheets)

Verified copy:

> The Morgan Library & Museum, New York: PML 5421.
>
> In his entry 1559/6 (*Bibliography*, 70, col. 1) Griffiths wrongly describes this octavo as a '4°', while the note about the Black Rubric ('BR erroneously restored to R1 of part 1') is inexplicably repeated from entry 1559/5. It has nothing to do with this edition, in which the Communion begins on T8^v and does not include the Black Rubric.

'STC 16293.5+' (not in STC or ESTC)

For the fragment once reported at Newcastle University Library, see Chapter 9, pp. 160–63.

'STC 16464+' (not in STC; ESTC S498161; title-page not reproduced)

⁋ **The Forme** | **and maner of makynge, and** | **consecrating Bishoppes** | **Priestes, and Dea=** | **cons.** | (,?,) | *Anno a salutiferoVir=* | *ginis partu.* | 1559. | [34-mm rule]
[Line 1 in 'Bible Fraktur' (see Figure 5d–e), not textura.]

Colophon on Cc5ᵛ (reproduced in Figure 13)
[Device McKerrow 122, flanked by 29-mm display initials R and G]
R I C H A R D V S G R A F = | *tonus, Typographus Regius* | *excudebat.* | *Anno Domini*, 1 5 5 9. | Cum Priuilegio ad Imprimen= | dum solum.

2°: Aa–Cc⁶

Printed by Richard Grafton (9 sheets)

Verified copy

Corpus Christi College, Oxford: Ph1.F.3.7
The unique copy wants Cc6, whose recto probably reprinted the 1552 note on prices.

STC 16465 (original STC only: wrongly treated as part of 16292 by revised STC and ESTC. Title-page reproduced as Figure 16)

[Within a woodcut compartment, McK & F 68β]
⁋ **The fourme** | **and maner of making** | **and consecratyng,** | **bisshops, prie=** | **stes, and** | **dea=** | **cons.** | [Cruciform fleuron, 9 × 9.5 mm] | *Anno domini.* | 1559.

[No colophon: Device McKerrow 125α on BB10ᵛ (otherwise blank)]

2°: AA⁸ BB¹⁰

John Kingston printed AA1,2,4:5,7,8 and BB5:6 (4 sheets)
Richard Jugge printed AA3:6 (1 sheet)

232   *Appendix D*

Richard Payne printed BB1,2,3:8,9,10 (3 sheets)
William Copland printed BB4:7 (1 sheet)

Verified copies:

British Library: 486.b.9.
Jesus College, Oxford: R.9.12(4) Gall.
Keble College, Oxford: Brooke 214.
Oxford University Press Archive: NS Stack B 5/1 (title-page defective; wants BB10).
York Minster Library: XI.F.19(1).
The Huntington Library: 438000:581 (wants BB10).
Thomas Fisher Rare Book Library, Toronto: stc 01221(2).

Jugge Cancel Calendar 1 (not separately entered in STC or ESTC)

[No title-page or colophon. Heading on A1^r]
⁋ **The order howe the rest | of holye Scripture(besyde the Psalter) | is appoynted to be read.**
2°: A² B⁸

Printed by Richard Jugge (5 sheets)

Verified copies:

Cambridge University Library: Inserted after leaf $^\pi$A11 in Sel.3.221 (STC 16291).
York Minster Library: replaces preliminaries of XI.F.19(1) ('STC 16292+').

Jugge Cancel Calendar 2 (not separately entered in STC or ESTC)

[No title-page or colophon. Heading on A1^r]
⁋ **The order howe the rest | of holye Scripture(besyde the Psalter) | is appoynted to be read.**
2°: A² B⁸

Printed by Richard Jugge (5 sheets)

Verified copy:

Keble College, Oxford: cancels leaf $^\pi$A12 and quire $^\pi$B⁶ in 'Keble copy 2' of STC 16292a. In at least that copy, A² is in the same setting as Cancel Calendar 1.

Appendix D

Jugge Cancel Calendar 3 (not separately entered in STC or ESTC)

[No title-page or colophon. Heading on A1ʳ]
⁌ The order howe the rest of | holye Scripture (besyde the Psalter) is | appoynted to be read.

2° A¹⁰

Printed by Richard Jugge (5 sheets)

Verified copies:

British Library: replaces calendar quire B⁶ in C.25.l.6 (STC 16292a). Reproduced on EEBO from UMI film STC reel 2312, item 2, images 15–25.
Lambeth Palace Library: replaces b⁶ ²a² and A⁸ in H5145.A4 1552 (STC 16282.7).
The Houghton Library, Harvard: replaces a6 b⁶ ²a² in STC 16282.7.

Bibliography

Any early book whose *contents* I have cited or quoted is included below, followed by its STC or Wing number in parentheses. But if the only part quoted is the title-page or colophon, or if the book is mentioned merely as a manufactured product, it is not listed here.

Place of publication is London unless otherwise specified.

Acts of the Privy Council of England. New Series. A.D. 1542–1558, ed. John Roche Dasent. 6 vols. 1890–93.

Arber, Edward, ed. *A Transcript of the Registers of the Company of Stationers of London; 1554–1640 A.D.* 5 vols. 1875–7; Birmingham, 1894.

Blayney, Peter W. M. *The Bookshops in Paul's Cross Churchyard*. Occasional Papers of the Bibliographical Society, 5. 1990.

— 'A Dry Discourse on Wet Paper (and Ink)'. *The Library*, 7th ser., 18 (2017): 387–404.

— 'The First Issue of the First Edition of the First Edwardian Prayer Book: New College Library, Oxford, BT1.131.19'. *New College Notes* 15 (2021), no. 5, ISSN 2517–6935.

— 'Initials Within Initials'. *The Library*, 7th ser., 20 (2019): 443–61.

— 'The Numbers Game: Appraising the Revised *STC*'. *PBSA*, 88 (1994): 353–407.

— *The Stationers' Company and the Printers of London, 1501–1557*. 2 vols. Cambridge, 2013.

— *The Texts of 'King Lear' and Their Origins. Vol. 1, Nicholas Okes and the First Quarto*. Cambridge, 1982.

— 'Thomas Marshe Invents the Press Figure'. *The Library*, 7th ser., 20 (2019): 455–68.

— 'Two Tales of Piracy', forthcoming in *The Library*, 7th ser., 23 (2022).

— 'William Cecil and the Stationers'. In *The Stationers' Company and the Book Trade, 1550–1990*, ed. Robin Myers and Michael Harris, 11–34. Winchester, 1997.

The Book of Common-Prayer and Administration of the Sacraments, and Other Rites and Ceremonies of the Church, According to the Use of the Church of England. 1662. (Wing B3622)

The Book of Common Prayer and Administration of the Sacraments and Other Rites and Ceremonies of the Church According to the Use of the Church of England. Standard edition. Cambridge, 2016.

Booty, John E., ed. *The Book of Common Prayer 1559: The Elizabethan Prayer Book*. Folger Shakespeare Library, Washington, D.C., 1976

Bowers, Fredson. *Principles of Bibliographical Description*. Princeton, 1949.

Bray, Gerald, ed. *Records of Convocation, VII: Canterbury, 1509–1603*. Woodbridge, 2006.

Byrom, H. J. 'Some Exchequer Cases Involving Members of the Book Trade'. *The Library*, 4th ser., 16 (1935–36): 402–17.

Clegg, Cyndia Susan. 'The 1559 Books of Common Prayer and the Elizabethan Reformation'. *Journal of Ecclesiastical History*, 67 (2016): 94–121.

Cummings, Brian, ed. *The Book of Common Prayer: The Texts of 1549, 1559, and 1662*. Oxford, 2011.

Davis, E. Jeffries. 'An Unpublished Manuscript of the Lords' Journals for April and May 1559'. *EHR*, 28 (1913): 531–42.

D'Ewes, Sir Simonds, *The Journals of All the Parliaments During the Reign of Queen Elizabeth, Both of the House of Lords and House of Commons*. 1682. (Wing D1250).

Dickens, A. G. *The English Reformation*. Second edition, 1989.

Dreyfus, John, ed. *Type Specimen Facsimiles II. Reproductions of Christopher Plantin's 'Index sive specimen characterum' 1567 & Folio Specimen of c. 1585 ... With annotations by Hendrik D. L. Vervliet and Harry Carter*. 1972.

Elton, G. R. *The Parliament of England, 1559–1581*. Cambridge, 1986.

Gaskell, Philip. *A New Introduction to Bibliography*. Oxford, 1972.

Grant Ferguson, Meraud. 'Grafton, Richard (*c*. 1511–15730)'. In *Oxford Dictionary of National Biography*, ed. H. C. G. Matthew and Brian Harrison, 23: 166–9. Oxford, 2004.

Greg, W. W. *A Bibliography of the English Printed Drama to the Restoration*. 4 vols. 1939–59.

'A Formulary of Collation'. *The Library*, 4th ser., 14 (1933–34): 365–82.

Griffiths, David N. *The Bibliography of the Book of Common Prayer, 1549–1999*. 2002.

Herbert, William. *Typographical Antiquities: or An Historical Account of the Origin and Progress of Printing in Great Britain and Ireland .... Begun by the Late Joseph Ames .... Considerably Augmented ....* 3 vols. 1785–90.

Hinman, Charlton. *The Printing and Proof-Reading of the First Folio of Shakespeare*. 2 vols. Oxford, 1963.

Hughes, Lewis. *Certaine Greevances Well Worthy the Serious Consideration of the Right Honorable and High Court of Parliament*. [Amsterdam], 1640. (STC 13917.5).

Hughes, Paul L., and James F. Larkin, eds. *Tudor Royal Proclamations*. 3 vols. New Haven, 1964–69.

Isaac, Frank S. *English & Scottish Printing Types, 1501–35 * 1508–41*. 1930. *English & Scottish Printing Types, 1535–58 * 1552–58*. 1932.

Jones, Norman L. *Faith by Statute: Parliament and the Settlement of Religion 1559*. 1982.

Journals of the House of Commons. From November the 8th 1547 ... to March the 2d 1628. 1802.
Journals of the House of Lords, Beginning Anno Primo Henrici Octavi. Vol. 1: 1509–1577. 1846.
Loach, Jennifer. *Parliament under the Tudors.* Oxford, 1991.
MacCulloch, Diarmaid. *Thomas Cranmer: A Life.* New Haven, 1996.
McKerrow, Ronald B. *An Introduction to Bibliography for Literary Students.* Oxford, 1927, reprinted 1967.
   Printers' & Publishers' Devices in England and Scotland, 1485–1640. 1913, reprinted 1949.
   and F. S. Ferguson. *Title-Page Borders Used in England & Scotland, 1485–1640.* 1932.
Maunsell, Andrew. *The First Part of the Catalogue of English Printed Books.* 1595. (STC 17669).
Moxon, Joseph. *Mechanick Exercises on the Whole Art of Printing (1683–4)*, ed. Herbert Davis and Harry Carter, 1958.
Neale, J. E. *Elizabeth I and Her Parliaments, 1559–1581.* 1953.
Oastler, C. L. *John Day, the Elizabethan Printer.* Oxford Bibliographical Society, Occasional Publications, 10. Oxford, 1975.
The Oxford Dictionary of the Christian Church, ed. F. L. Cross and E. A. Livingstone. Third edition, revised, Oxford, 2005.
Page, William, ed. *Letters of Denization and Acts of Naturalization for Aliens in England, 1509–1603*, 1893.
The Protestation of the Two and Twenty Divines, for the Setling of the Church: And the Particulars by Them Excepted Against in the Liturgie. London, 1643. (Wing P3871).
Rypins, Stanley. 'The Printing of *Basilikòn Dôron*, 1603'. *PBSA*, 64 (1970), 393–417.
Sainty, John Christopher. 'Further Materials from an Unpublished Manuscript of the House of Lords Journal for Sessions 1559 and 1597–8'. In *A Parliamentary Miscellany: Papers on the History of the House of Lords, Published 1964–1991*, by J. C. Sainty (*Parliamentary History*, Texts and Studies 10, 2015): 25–46.
Sander, Nicholas. *De origine ac progressu schismatis Anglicani ... Editus & auctus per Edouardum Rishtonum.* Cologne, 1585.
A Short-Title Catalogue of Books Printed in England, Scotland, and Ireland, and of English Books Printed Abroad, 1475–1640. Compiled by A. W. Pollard and G. R. Redgrave. Second edition, revised by W. A. Jackson, F. S. Ferguson, and Katharine F. Pantzer. 3 vols. 1976–91.
Statutes of the Realm. Volume IV, part 1 (1547–85). 1819.
Vervliet, H. D. L. *Sixteenth-Century Printing Types of the Low Countries.* Amsterdam, 1968.
Ward, Thomas. *Englands Reformation from the Time of King Henry the VIIIth to the End of Oates's Plot.* 'Hambourgh' [Saint-Omer?], 1710.
Wing, Donald, ed. *Short-Title Catalogue of Books Printed in England, Scotland, Ireland, Wales, and British America and of English Books Printed in Other*

Countries, 1641–1700. Second edition, revised and edited by Timothy J. Crist, John J. Morrison, Carolyn W. Nelson, and Matthew Seccombe. 4 vols. New York, 1982–98.

Woodhead, Abraham. *A Compendious Discourse on the Eucharist*. Oxford, 1688. (Wing W3440A)

Index

Listings under '*Book of (the) Common Prayer, The*' are limited to general comments about the three Tudor versions. Specific printed editions are gathered under 'BCP', in a long entry that is also a glossary of the codes by which those editions are identified elsewhere in the index. Each code begins with 'BCP' and the year of publication. If the date is followed by G, W, or JC, the *title-page* (but not always the colophon) claims (but not always truthfully) that it was printed by Grafton, Whitchurch, or Jugge and Cawood. Unless otherwise specified, editions are in folio and were printed in London.

Anyone simply identified as a 'printer' was a freeman of the Stationers' Company. In May 1557 the Stationers' charter of incorporation restricted printing to (a) Stationers and (b) anyone expressly permitted by royal patent, so four of those who printed BCPs in 1559 had no formal right to do so. Printers who were not Stationers are here identified by company affiliation (Grocer, Salter, Haberdasher) or as immigrants or 'forens' (English, but not freemen of London).

In discussions of the lectionary, with one exception books of the Bible and their chapters are not indexed. Saints are indexed by their given names; signs or places named after them by 'St'. In addition to the traditional departures from alphabetical order ('Mc' and 'St' listed as if spelled 'Mac' and 'Saint'), after Cancel Calendars I have arranged 'cancels' in ascending order of size (slips, leaves, sheets, and quires). Subentries and sub-subentries are usually arranged chronologically rather than alphabetically. Page numbers in italics refer to illustrations.

Act of Supremacy (1 Eliz. I, c. 1), 47–8, 87, 199, 216
Acts of Uniformity
  1549 (2 & 3 Edw. VI, c. 1), 3–4, 24, 57
  1552 (5 & 6 Edw. VI, c. 1), 29–30, 40
    included in BCP preliminaries, 38–9
    listed in Contents of BCP1552Graf.5–6 etc., 39, 104
    probably printed first by Grafton, 39
    required an ordinal to be appended, 104, 115, 213
    to be read out loud annually, 39
  1559 (1 Eliz. I, c. 2), 48
    passed the Lords by a majority of three, 48, 199
    received the royal assent on 8 May, 48, 88, 109
    date of introduction altered, 48
    Litany updated, 55–6
    more proper lessons added, 55
    words of administration revised, 55
    Black Rubric not mentioned, 57–8, 209
    ordinal neither mentioned nor required, 104
    'ornaments rubric', 56–7
    first printed as statute by Cawood, 97
    included in BCP1559 preliminaries, 57
    printed in BCP1559JC1 by Kingston, 72, 97–8, 202
    reprinted in BCP1559G by Grafton, 72, 97
Acts of the Privy Council cited, 31, 44–5, 82, 115
Adeline, St. *See* Aldhelm, St
Adrian, St, 183
Agatha, St, 178, 182
Agnes, St, 178, 182
Alban, St, 184
Aldhelm, St, 183
Aldine leaf, 7
  on contents list of BCP1559G, 1559JC1, 102
  used by Whitchurch in 1552 title-pages, 109
Aldrich, Robert, bishop of Carlisle

opposed the ordinal, 114
Alesius, Alexander
    translated BCP1549 into Latin, 188
Alphege, St, 178, 186
Ambrose, St, 178, 182
Anne, St, 178, 183
Anthony, St, 182
Antwerp, 2
Aquarius symbol used as printed signature, 160
Arber, Edward, cited, 63, 73, 88, 133, 160
Ash Wednesday service
    in section 2b of the 1549 BCP, 14
    renamed 'A Commination' in 1552, 14
Askell, Leonard, printer, 160
'assent' noted beside bills in Commons Journal, 218–19, *Plate 1*
Augustine of Canterbury, St, 178, 183
Augustine of Hippo, St, 178, 182

Bacon, Sir Nicholas, Lord Keeper of the Great Seal
    former owner of British Library copy of BCP1559JC1, 117, *Plate 3*
    signatures, 117, *118*, 226, *Plate 3*
Bankes, Richard, printer
    18-mm T 'packed' for use as I, 74–5
Baptism services
    in section 2a of the BCP, 14
Barker, Christopher, printer, 91, 178
    succeeded Jugge as Queen's Printer, 195
BCP
    1549G1a (not in STC), 9–12, 197
        collation of the first edition, 17, 20
        Grafton colophon, *18*
        quire K, 10, 197
        Whitchurch colophon, *18*
    1549G1b (not in STC), 22
        collation of the first edition, 2nd issue, 20
        Grafton colophon, *18*
    1549G1c (STC 16268), 9, 14–16, 23, 26, 56, 197
        collation of the first edition, 3rd issue, 21
    1549G2 (STC 16269), 11, 16, 25–6, 56
    1549G3 (STC 16269.5), 11, 16, 56
    1549G3+ (not in STC), 16, 26
    1549G4 (STC 16274), 11, 23, 26–7, 56
        colophon June, 4
    1549G5 (STC 16275), 11, 23, 26–7, 56
        colophon June, 4
    1549W1 (STC 16267), 9–17, 25, 56, 197
        collation, 21
        not first but second ed., 21
    1549W2 (STC 16270), 25, 27, 56
        colophon 4 May, 4
    1549W3 (STC 16270a), 25, 27, 56
        colophon 4 May, 4
    1549W4 (STC 16272), 23, 25, 56
        colophon 16 June, 4
    1549W5 (STC 16273), 23, 25, 27, 56
        colophon 16 June, 4
    1549W5+ (not in STC), 25
    1549Worcester (STC 16276), 20, 152
        dated 30 July, 4
    1549Worcester4° (STC 16271), 20, 152
        dated 24 May, 4
    1551Dublin (STC 16277), 4, 152
    1552Graf.1 (STC 16286.5), 30, 34–5, *36*, 41, 56–7, 106, 149, 173
    1552Graf.2 (STC 16285–5.5), 43, 53, 173
    1552Graf.2b (STC 16285.5), 115
    1552Graf.3 (STC 16285.7), 34, 43, 53, 173
    1552Graf.4 (STC 16285a), 34, 43, 53, 173
    1552Graf.5 (16286), 31, 34, 39, 43, 53, 104, 173, 225
    1552Graf.6 (STC 16286.2–6.3), 34, 39, 53, 59, 61, 111, 173, 196
        used as copy for BCP1559G, 43, 97
    1552Graf.6a (STC 16286.2), 42–3, 225
    1552Graf.6b (STC 16286.3), 42–3, 225
    1552Whit.1 (STC 16279–80.5), 30, 35, 41, 53, 148
    1552Whit.2 (STC 16281), 30–1, 53, 116
    1552Whit.3 (STC 16281.5), 53, 58
    1552Whit.4 (STC 16282.3), 34, 43, 53, 77, 93, 111, 196
        used as copy for BCP1559JC1, 43, 96–7, 104
    1552Whit.5 (STC 16282.7), 34, *37*, 43, 53, 77, 93, 96, 110, 195
        used by Rogers as copy for BCP1559JC1, 76
    1552Worcester (STC 16287), 30–1, 33, 116
    1552W4° (STC 16288), 34, 152–3, 158, 193
    1553G8° (STC 16290), 34, 39, 106, 152, 193
    1553W4° (STC 16288a), 34, 152–3, 158
    1553W8° (STC 16290.5), 34, 152
    1559G (STC 16291), 52–3, 58–61, 88–9, 147–8, 176, 224–5, *Plate 2*, *Plate 4*
        no cancels in main text, 51, 200
        titlepage compared with 1559JC1, 109–10
    1559JC1 (STC 16292), 59, 62–89, 149–51, 175–6, 190, 196, 225–6, *Plate 3*, *Plate 5*
        a few sheets found in JC2, JC3, 135
        cancels in text suggest priority, 51
        titlepage compared with 1559G, 109–10
    1559JC2 (STC '16292+'), 135, 149–52, 155, 226
        a few sheets found in JC3, 135

BCP (cont.)
  1559JC3 (STC 16292a), 128, 134–5, *136*, 149–51, 155, 175–6, 196, 227–8
    a few sheets found in JC2, 135–7
  1559 4°.1 (STC 16293.3), 153–4, 157, 176, 196, 228–9, *Plate 8*
  1559 4°.2 (STC 16293), 154–7, 196, 221, 229–30
  1559 8°.1 (STC 16293.5), 160, 176, 230–1
  1559 8°.2 (STC 16293.5 note), 160–3, 196
  1560 4° (STC 16294), 143, 162–4, 176, 221, *223*
  1560 8° (STC 16294a.3), 180
  1562 4° (STC 16295), xviii, 162, 174, 195
  1564 (STC 16296), 180
  1564 8° (STC 16296.3), 180
  1566(*c*.) (not in STC), 178
  1567 (STC 16297), 227
  1573(*c*.) (not in STC), 178
  1577 4° (STC 16306.9), 91
  1580 (STC 16307), 178
  1603 (STC 16325), 178
  1604 (STC 16326), 178
  1619 (STC 16353), 128
  1629Cambridge (STC 16375), 194
  1637Edinburgh (STC 16606), 23
  1638Cambridge (STC 16410), 194
  1640Cambridge4° (STC 16420), 194
  1640 8° (STC 16421), 194
  1660 8° (Wing B3618aA), 176
  1660 12° (Wing B3618A), 83, 176
  1662 (Wing B3622), 58, 83, 211
  1662 8° (Wing B3623), 211
  1662 12° (Wing B3624), 211
  1662Cambridge8° (Wing B3625), 211
  1663a12° (ESTC R236138), *210*, 211
  1663b12° (ESTC R211843), 211
  1664 8° (Wing B3628), 211
  1680 4° (Wing B3659), 211
  2016Standard, 58
Becke, Edmund, Bible annotator
  calendar in his 'Matthew' Bible has 89 miscellanea, 185
  calendar in his Taverner Bible has 78 miscellanea, 185
Benedict, St, 178, 184
Benedictus. *See* canticles
Bernard, St, 182
Berthelet, Margery (later Payne), 80
Berthelet, Thomas, King's Printer to Henry VIII, 3, 80
Bible, the sign of the, 63
bible, versions
  Bishops'
    Elizabethan editions printed by Jugge, 72
  Coverdale, 2, 65, 92, 185, 188
  Geneva, 92
  Great Bible, 2, 13, 34, 65, 74, 92, 185
    Elizabethan editions printed by Cawood, 72
  'Matthew', 2, 92, 185
  Taverner, 185
  Vulgate, 92
bibles, printed, 14, 42
bifolium defined, 5
Black Rubric, the, 31–3, 81, 87, 209
  cancelled from BCP1559JC1, 71
  included by Cawood in BCP1559 4°.1, 153–4
  origin of the name, 32–3, 209–11
  removed without explanation in 1559, 72
Blaise, St, 178, 182
Blayney, Peter W. M.
  Stationers and Printers cited, 2, 4, 13, 30, 45–6, 62, 65–6, 80, 82, 85, 95, 105, 148, 157, 182, 197
  other publications cited, xiv, 13, 61–2, 78, 82, 85–6, 96, 157
Boleyn, Anne, Queen, 85
Boniface, St, 178, 183
Bonner, Edmund, bishop of London
  probably led the book-trade purge, 45
Book of (the) Common Prayer, The
  (For specific printed editions, see BCP)
  first Edwardian version
    written by late 1548, 3
    first edition mistaken for made-up copies, 16
    Latin translation printed in Leipzig (1551), 182, 188
    to be revised and replaced, 28, 197
  second Edwardian version, 29
    title slightly revised, 30
    section 2b revised and shortened, 40
    words of administration revised, 30, 55
  Elizabethan version
    the major revisions, 54–8
    words of administration conflated, 55
    printers' errors and corrections, 149–51
    Latin translation printed by Wolfe (1560), 187–8
    which edition is the 'best'?, 148–51
Booty, John E., 33
Bowers, Fredson, cited, xxiii, 90
Bradock, Richard, printer, Z rotated for use as N, 73
Brasenose College, Oxford, copy of BCP1549G1b
  mistaken for hybrid, 16
  really first edition, second issue, 20
  annotations on title-page, 21–3
  appended canticles now misplaced, 23
Bray, Gerald, cited, 1
Brice, St, 178, 188

Index

'briefe declaration' of law term dates
  not included in BCP1559G, 101
  added to BCP1559JC1, 52, 101–2, 173
  in fragment of BCP1559 8°.2, 162–3
British Library copy of BCP1549G1a
  mistaken for hybrid, 16
  really first edition, first issue, 20
Bucer, Martin, *Scripta Anglicana* (1577), 23
Burges, Cornelius, 209
Burial service in section 2a of the BCP, 14
Byrom, H. J., cited, 65

calendar, the
  tabular setting, 8, 93, 109, 173
  printed in two colours, 8–9, 93, 109
  1559 version, 90, 143
    missing from Bodleian copy of BCP1559G, 59, 155, 194
    missing from both extant quartos, 154, 164
    missing from British Library copy 2 of BCP1559JC3, 194, 227
    missing from Keble copy 2 of BCP1559JC3, 155, 194
    missing from York copy of BCP1559JC2, 135, 155, 164
  revised version first included in BCP1562 4°, 174
calendars, revised in 1561. *See* Cancel Calendars
Caly, Robert, printer (foren)
  1553–8
    managed Grafton printing house, 45, 59, 72
    used Grafton's materials, 50, 106
    productivity, 45, 88, 109, 198
Cancel Calendars (1561–2), 134–5, 196, 206–7
  commissioned by Elizabeth, 1561, 165
  began as a single quire B⁸, 175–7, 205
  bifolium A² subsequently prefixed, 175, 205
  errors, 194
  many additions to the miscellaneous column, 177–8, 205
  misprinted Psalm number perpetuated, 176
  new material in the Almanack, 176–7
  official holy days enumerated, 177
  the first edition, 178, 190, 232, *Plate 6*
  the second edition, 190–1, 194, 232
  the third edition, 191, 194–5, 233, *Plate 7*
  used to update 1552 BCPs, 195
cancel slips (paste-ons)
  1546, imprints, 147–8
  1549
    running titles, 11, 26
    the Lord's Prayer, 11
  1559
    imprints, 145, *146*

  misprinted initial corrected, 68, *69*
cancel leaves
  1552, Black Rubric, 33, 35
  1559, BCP1559JC1,
    leaf A1, 51, 62, 71–2, 87, 137, 200, 207
    leaf N3, 51, 62, 71–2, 80, 87, 137, 141, 200, 207
cancel sheets
  1549, BCP1549W1,
    sheet X3:4, 13, 27
    sheets A2–5, 19
  1559, BCP1559G
    sheet ᵖA1:12, 110–11, 202–3, 207
    sheet ᵖA4:9, 82, 88, 101, 109, 111
  1559, BCP1559JC1,
    sheet C2:7, 51, 62, 71, 87, 137
    sheet ᵖA1:12, 88, 110–11, 202–3, 207
    sheet ᵖA4:9, 82, 101, 111, 207
cancel quire K in BCP1549G1a, 10
canticles for Matins and Evensong
  titles only in BCP1549G1a, 12
  appended to second issue (BCP1549G1b), 12, 19, 197
capitulum (*plural* capitula)
  significance of use in signatures, 14, 40
  used by Grafton
    in 1552 title-pages, 109
    in BCP1559G, 105–7
  distinctive example used by Kingston, 109
casting off defined, 5
casting off in practice, 10–11, 15–16, 40, 53, 67, 100
Catherine of Alexandria, St, 178, 182
Cave, Sir Ambrose, Privy Councillor
  signature, 117, *118*
Cawood, John, Queen's Printer to Mary I and Elizabeth I, 65
  1553
    appointed Queen's Printer, 45
    acquired Mierdman's printing materials, 45
    productivity, 49–50, 86
  1559
    Jugge's partner (in office only), xiii, 49, 62–3
    address, 62
    great primer textura with w2+, 70
    printed 1st edition of statute 1 Eliz. I, 97, 216
    printed part of 2nd edition of statute 1 Eliz. I, 216
    printed part of BCP1559JC1, 72, 84, 201, 225
    printed parts of BCP1559JC2, 138, 203, 226
    printed parts of BCP1559JC3, 138–41, 203, 227
    printed part of BCP1559 4°.1, 153–4, 204, 229

Index

Cawood (cont.)
    included Black Rubric in BCP1559 4°.1, 153–4, 209
    psalter rights arbitrated (by Stationers?), 159–60
  1560
    shared BCP1560 4° with Jugge, 163
  1560–1
    printed his first Great Bible in quarto, 220
    calendar in quire ¶⁸ was printed by Jugge, 189
  1562
    shared BCP1562 4° with Jugge, 163
Cecil, Sir William, principal secretary, 46, 82–3
  employer and patron of William Seres, 157
  unable to deliver bills to the Lords, 48, 219, *Plate 1a*
  signature, 117, *118*
Cecilia, St, 178
Chad, St, 178, 182
Chair of Peter, The, 184
Cheke, Sir John, 83
Christ Church, Oxford
  imperfect copy of BCP1549G1c, 16, 26
  first edition, third issue, 21
  copy of BCP1552Graf.1, 35
church attendance made compulsory 1552, 38
Churching of Women, The, 14, 40
Clegg, Cyndia Susan, 2, 31, 39, 49, 53–4, 59, 65, 119, 125
  suggested date of BCP1559G, 117–19
Clement, St, 173
Clinton, Edward Fiennes de, Lord Admiral
  signature, 117, *118*
Cobbe, Richard
  former owner of Corpus Christi BCP1559G, 119
collation defined, 7
collational formulae
  explained, 7
  1549
    the earliest editions, 7, 9–10, 14
    the first edition, 17, 20–1
    the second edition, 21
    the later Whitchurch editions, 25
    the last two Grafton editions, 26
  1552
    the earliest editions, 40
    the latest editions, 43
  1559
    BCP1559G, 112, 224
    BCP1559JC1, 112, 225
    BCP1559JC2, 226
    BCP1559JC3, 227
    BCP1559 4°.1, 229

    BCP1559 8°.1, 230
    Grafton ordinal, 231
    Jugge ordinal, 125, 231
  1560
    Cawood bible, 220
  1561
    Cancel Calendars, 232
Collects
  in section 1b of the BCP, 9
colophon
  defined, 7
  of the 1550 ordinal, 115
  of the Grafton ordinal, 119–21, 147
colophons, dated, 109–10, 147–8, 189
  of 1549, 4, 7, 14–15, *18*, 19, 23
Commination, A, 14, 39
Communion service, 20, 27, 31, 41, 56, 58, 209
  section 1c of the BCP, 9, 11, 28
  See also words of administration
compressing the text to lower costs
  Grafton in 1549, 26
  Grafton in 1552, 40–2
  Whitchurch in 1549, 25
  Whitchurch in 1552, 41
  Whitchurch again in 1552, 42
  Mierdman in 1552, 42
Confirmation service
  in section 2a of the BCP, 14
contents list of 1559, the
  identifying the printer (John Kingston), 102
  printed before the title-page forme, 102
  printed from that of BCP1552Whit4, 104
  same setting in both first editions, 102
Cooke, Sir Anthony, MP, 48, 219
Copland, Robert, printer, 125
  an early pioneer of shared printing, 13
Copland, William, printer
  1559
    printed one sheet of the Jugge ordinal, 84, 87, 125, 203, 232
    printed part of psalter for Seres, 158–9, 204, 229
Corpus Christi College, Oxford
  copy of BCP1559G annotated by Privy Council, 117
  bound with unique copy of the Grafton ordinal, 117–19
Court of High Commission, the
  instructed to revise calendar, 165
Coverdale, Miles, 2
Cranmer, Margaret (later Whitchurch), 66, 200
Cranmer, Thomas, archbishop of Canterbury, 1, 40, 58, 93, 209
  English litany
    first published 1544, 3

revised version printed early 1559, 47
Eucharistic writings, 28, 32, 55
and the Black Rubric, 31–2
books banned by Mary I, 58–9
burned by Mary I, 66
his widow married Edward Whitchurch, 66
Crispin, St, 178, 182
Cromwell, Thomas, 1
Cummings, Brian, 32, 155, 178, 196
Cuthbert, St, 184 *See also* Cuthburga, St
Cuthburga, St (listed as 'Cuthbert'), 184
Cyprian, St, 178

D'Ewes, Sir Simonds, 214
David, St, 178, 182
Davis, E. Jeffries, cited, 48, 219
Dawson, Thomas, printer
  apprenticed to Richard Jugge in 1559, 133
  printed 1580 replacement sheet BB5:6 for Jugge ordinal, 129, *131*
Day, George, bishop of Chichester
  opposed the ordinal, 114
Day, John, printer, xv
  1549 improvisations
    V inverted for use as A, 74
  1552
    printed 15 sheets of BCP1552Graf.6a, 34, 42, 54, 197
    printed 5 sheets of BCP1552Graf.6b, 34, 42, 54
    sheets reissued in some copies of BCP1559G, 59, 61, 201
  1558
    printed books 'by' Richard Jugge, 46, 51, 63, 82
Denys, St, 178, 186
devices
  McKerrow 122 (Richard Grafton), *120*, 231
  McKerrow 123 (Richard Jugge), 142
  McKerrow 125 (Richard Jugge)
    1552–53 used by Steven Mierdman, 142
    used by Jugge himself in BCP1559JC1, JC3, 142, 225, 227
    used by Richard Payne in the Jugge ordinal, 125, 142, 231
    used by John Kingston in BCP1559JC2, *122*, 142, 226
Dickens, A. G., 32
Dominical letters
  in bible calendars from 1537, 185
  in the BCP calendars, 171–2
Dorothy, St, 183
Dreyfus, John, cited, 105
drop capitals. *See* ornamental initials
Dunstan, St, 178, 183

Durham Cathedral Library
  copy of BCP1549G1c, 16, 26
  first edition, third issue, 21
Dyson, Humphrey
  former owner of British Library BCP1549G1a, 16

edition-sheets as units of productivity, 49, 84–5
edition-size, usually only a guess, 49
Edmund of Abingdon, St, 182–4
Edmund, King and St, 178, 184
Edward the Confessor, St, 178, 182
Edward the Martyr, St, 178, 182–3, 188
Edward VI, King, 17, 47, 66, 116, 159, 204
  acceded January 1547, 3
  and the Black Rubric, 31–2, 209
  died July 1553, 33, 44
EEBO, 149
  digitized copy of STC 16269.5 misidentified, 26
Elizabeth I, Queen, 47, 66, 114, 204
  1558
    acceded 17 November, 46
    appointed Richard Jugge Queen's Printer, 46
  1559
    published revised form of Litany, 47, 56, 199
    appointed John Cawood (second) Queen's Printer, 49, 199
    became Supreme Governor of Church on 8 May, 48, 216
    probably unaware of conflict in Seres patent, 159
  1561
    her view of supremacy, 165–7
    required calendar to be revised and printed, 165, 205
    the revision to 'bee quietlie donne', 165, 175, 205
  See also lectionary, the, revisions of 1561
'Elizabethan Settlement', the, xiii, 47
Elton, G. R., 216–18
Ember days
  added to 1560 calendar by Jugge or Cawood, 189, 221
Emery, Edward, signature, 128
Enurcus. *See* Evurtius, St
Epistles, Gospels, in section 1b of the BCP, 9
Erasmus, Desiderius, *Paraphrases upon the New Testament*, 13–14
Erasmus, St, 184
ESTC, xxv, 29, 157
  statistics
    copies of the earliest 1549 editions, 15–16
    copies of 1549 Whitchurch editions, 25

ESTC (cont.)
   extant Edwardian BCPs, 179–80
   extant Elizabethan BCPs, 180
Etheldreda, St, 178, 186
'Euensong' in section 1a of 1549 BCP, 9
   renamed 'Euenyng prayer' in 1552, 39, 172
   'Euensong' again in 1559 table of proper lessons, 100
Evurtius, St, 178

Fabian, St, 178, 183
Fabyan, Robert, *The Chronicle*
   1559 edition contemporary with BCP1559G, 102, *108*, 109
Faith, St, 178, 182
Felix, St, 184
Fiennes de Clinton, Edward, Lord Admiral
   signature, 117, *118*
Floate, Sophie, help acknowledged, 21
foliation defined, 6
folio defined, 5
Forster, Anne (former owner of York Minster copy of BCP1559JC2), signature, 128
Fraktur. *See* type
frisket defined, 9, 78
Froschauer, Christoph, printer in Zurich, 188

Gardiner, Stephen, bishop of Winchester
   probably led the book-trade purge, 45
Gaskell, Philip, cited, 61
gathering defined, 5
Gaultier, Thomas, printer (immigrant)
   printed 1553 French translation of BCP1552W4°, 182
Gawyn, John, 66
genealogy of Joseph, the
   excluded from the lectionary, 193
George, St, 173
Gibbs, Kenneth, 26
Giles, St, 178, 183
'Godly Prayers'
   in psalters appended to BCP, 34, 155, 158
Golden numbers, 186
   in Bible calendars from 1537, 185
   in the BCP calendars in 1552, 172
   omitted by Kingston from BCP1559G, 173
   retained by Wolfe in BCP1559JC1, 174
Grafton ordinal, the. *See* ordinal, the 1559 Grafton edition
Grafton, Richard, King's Printer to Edward VI (Grocer), 185
   career before 1547, 1–3, 74, 81
   productivity, 50, 88
   1547
     appointed King's Printer, 3
     joint patent with Whitchurch for service books, 3
   1549
     the events of March, 23–4
     BCP1549G1a preliminaries, 7, 24, 26
     BCP1549G1a cancelled running tites, 10–11
     BCP1549G1a quire K, 10
     BCP1549G1a colophon dated 8 March, 4, 7, 17–19
     BCP1549G1b colophon dated 16 March, *18*
     BCP1549G1c part 2, 14–15
     printed abbreviated BCP with quarto psalter, 182
   1552
     BCP preliminaries, 35–9
     the events of April and May, 40
     3 editions complete by 27 Sept., 31
     printed Black Rubric cancels, 33–4
     listed Act of Uniformity among Contents, 39
   1553
     added miscellanea to BCP calendars, 179
     book misattributed to, 107–9
     fired as Royal Printer, 45
     octavo BCP has its own selection of miscellanea, 184, 206
     octavo BCP calls fasts 'Fish' days, 183
   1553–58, business managed by Robert Caly, 45
   1557, as Grocer, became ineligible to print, 50
   1558, evicted Robert Caly, 50
   1559
     commissioned to reprint a 1552 BCP, 51, 200
     great primer textura with w^{sc}, 70
     large headings in Bible Fraktur, 106
     five identifiable capitula used, 106–7
     printed most of BCP1559G, xv, 52–3, 59–61, 225
     recycled many 1552 sheets in printing the ordinal unaided, 119, 203
     BCP1559G, xv, 59–61, 200
     the ordinal colophon, 119–21, 203
     improper use of *Cum Priuilegio*, 110, 119–21, 147, 224, 231, *Plate 2*
     retirement, 145
     BCP1559G imprint cancelled, 145–7
Grant Ferguson, Meraud, 50
great primer textura
   range of sizes, 77
   varieties of w, 70–1
     w^{2+} described, 70
     w^{sc} described, 70
Greg, W. W., cited, xxiii–xxiv
Gregory, St, 178, 190
Griffiths, David N., errors in his *Bibliography*, xv, 3, 211, 224, 230

Index

Grindal, Edmund, bishop of London
　instructed to revise calendar, 165, 205

Haddon, Walter, ecclesiastical commissioner
　one of the revisers of the 1561 calendar, 190
　translated BCP1559 into Latin, 187
Harrison, Richard, printer, 96
headlines. *See* running titles
Heath, Nicholas, bishop of Worcester
　opposed the ordinal, 114
Helen, St, 182
Henry VIII, King, 41, 47, 114, 116, 185, 199
Herbert, William, bibliographer, cited, 50
Herbert, William (earl of Pembroke), signature, 117, *118*
Herford, John, printer (immigrant), 74–5
Herford, Katherine, printer (widow), 74
Herford, William, printer (Grocer), 74–5
Hester, Andrew, 188
Hetherington, John R., 154, 229
　cited by STC, 67, 147
Higgins, Ben, help acknowledged, 128
Hilary, St, 178, 182
Hill, Nicholas, printer (immigrant), xv, 107
　printed one sheet of BCP1549W1, xv
　1548–9, shared books with Whitchurch, 13, 65
　1549
　　printed one sheet of BCP1549W1, 13, 21
　　printed 12 sheets of BCP1549W2, 27, 197
　　printed 20 sheets of BCP1549W3, 27, 197
　　printed 15 sheets of BCP1549W5, 197
　1549
　　printed 15 sheets of BCP1549W5, 27
　1550–1
　　bible calendars included only BCP miscellanea, 185
　1552
　　printed 2 sheets of BCP1552Graf.6a, 34, 42, 54, 197
　　printed 2 sheets of BCP1552Graf.6b, 34, 42, 54
　　sheets reissued in some copies of BCP1559G, 59, 201
　1553
　　shared a quarto bible with Grafton, 106
　　returned to Europe, 45, 81
Hill, William, printer, 185
Hinman, Charlton, cited, 60
holy days (fixed)
　All Saints (1 November), 91, 170, 172
　Andrew (30 November), 169, 183
　　1549 collect rewritten 1552, 40
　Annunciation (25 March), 172, 182–3
　Barnabas (11 June), 48, 172
　　not listed as holy in 1561, 177

　Bartholomew (24 August), 169, 183
　Christmas Day (25 December), 91, 98, 164, 170, 172, 183
　　1st communion discontinued 1552, 40
　Circumcision (1 January), 91, 100, 169–70, 172
　Conversion of Paul (25 January), 100, 170, 172, 192
　　not listed as holy in 1561, 177
　Epiphany (6 January), 91, 99, 169–70, 172
　Innocents' Day (28 December), 91, 100, 168–9, 172
　James (25 July), 169, 183
　John the Baptist (24 June), 48, 91, 100, 170, 172, 183, 192
　John the Evangelist (27 December), 91, 169
　Luke (18 October), 169
　Mary Magdalene (22 July), 172
　　service eliminated 1552, 40, 172
　　in BCP1552W4° miscellanea, 182
　　not listed as holy in 1561, 177
　　reappears in 1561 miscellanea, 178
　Matthew (21 September), 169, 183
　Matthias (24 February), 170, 172, 221
　Michael (29 September), 169, 172
　Nativity of Mary (8 September), 178
　Nativity of Q. Elizabeth (7 September)
　　added to calendar in 1580, 178
　Peter (29 June), 169, 183–4
　See also Chair of Peter, The
　Philip & James the Less (1 May), 98, 172, 189
　Purification (2 February), 100, 170, 172
　Simon & Jude (28 October), 169, 172, 183
　Stephen (26 December), 169, 172
　Thomas (21 December), 169, 183
holy days (moveable)
　Ascension Day, 177, 192
　Ash Wednesday, 14
　Easter Day, 98–100, 168, 177
　　2nd communion discontinued 1552, 40
　Easter Monday, 10, 177, 197
　Easter Tuesday, 177
　Good Friday, 168
　Septuagesima, 98–100, 177
　Trinity Sunday, 98, 168
　Whit Sunday, 98
　Whit Monday, 177, 192
　Whit Tuesday, 177, 192
Holy Ghost, the sign of the, 62
Hooper, John, bishop of Gloucester, 114
hours of daylight
　recorded in calendars
　　1549–50 by Reyner Wolfe, 186–7
　　1550 by John Oswen, 187
　　1552–3 by Mierdman for Jugge, 187

hours of daylight (cont.)
  1559 by Reyner Wolfe, 96, 174
  1561 by Richard Jugge, 190
Howard, William, Lord Chamberlain
  in France in early 1559, 119
  signature, 117, *118*
Hugh, St, 178
Hughes, Lewis, 193

imprint defined, 7
in sixes defined, 5
inflation
  1549–52, 41
initials, ornamental. *See* ornamental initials
injunctions for religion
  of Henry VIII and Edward VI compared, 116–17
inner forme defined, 5
Introits in section 1b of 1549 BCP, 9
  omitted in and after 1552, 40
Isaac, Frank S., cited, 70, 105

Jaggard, William, printer, Z rotated for use as N, 73
Jerome, St, 178, 182
John of Beverley, St, 182
John, St, ante portam Latinam, 178, 183
Jones, Norman L. *Faith by Statute* cited, 47–8, 214–15, 218
Jones, William, fined for selling an Edwardian BCP in 1559, 88
Journals of the House of Commons cited, 4, 30, 38, 47–8, 114, 214, 217, 219
Journals of the House of Lords cited, 4, 30, 38, 48, 114, 214, 217–18
Jugge ordinal, the. *See* ordinal, the 1559 Jugge edition
Jugge, Richard, Queen's Printer to Elizabeth I
  early career as publisher, 46, 185, 187
  1558
    appointed Queen's Printer, 46, 199
    books printed for him by John Day, 46
  1559
    address, 62–3
    Cawood's partner (in office only), xiii, 62–3
    commissioned to oversee reprinting of a 1552 BCP, 50, 200
    had no printing house before May, 69
    first great primer textura with w^{sc}, *70*, 71, 80, 137
    ornament stock acquired from Edward Whitchurch, 65, 70, 83, 87, 196
    printed parts of BCP1559JC1, 62, 71, 83–4, 201, 226
    printed Black Rubric on N3^r of BCP1559JC1 before cancellation, 71, 209
    printed one sheet of the Jugge ordinal, 125, 203, 231
    printed title-page of BCP1559JC1 on recto of Kingston's cancel ^{π}A1^v, 104, 203
    second great primer textura with w^{2+}, *70*, 71, 81, 137
    initials acquired from late John Mychell, 70, 83
    initials acquired from Richard Grafton, 83, 143–5
    initials borrowed from John Kingston, 65, 83
    initials obtained from John Cawood, 83
    initials obtained from Reyner Wolfe, 83
    initials obtained from Richard Payne, 83
    printed parts of BCP1559JC2–3, 137, 140, 203, 226–7
    printed part of BCP1559 4°.1, 153, 204, 229
    printed all known of BCP1559 4°.2, 204, 229
    prime suspect to have printed BCP1559 8°.2, 163
    printed part of 2nd edition of statute 1 Eliz. I, 216
    psalter rights arbitrated (by Stationers?), 159–60
  1559 improvisations
    A inverted for use as V, *144*, 145
    F mutilated for use as E, *144*, 145
    uncial M inverted for use as T, *144*, 145
  1559–60, new initials imported, 83, 221
  1560
    added to the miscellaneous column, 188–9
    printed calendar quire for Cawood's 4° bible, 220–1
    shared BCP1560 4° with Cawood, 162
  1561
    probable source of miscellanea in the Cancel Calendars, 190, 206
  1562
    lent a title-page border to L. Askell, 160
    shared BCP1562 4° with Cawood, 162
  1570s, unaware of incomplete ordinals, 133

'Kanzlei' (Fraktur titling) capitals, 65
Keble College, Oxford
  editions misidentified in ESTC
    STC 16269, 16
    STC 16292a, 228
King, John, printer
  lent initials etc. to Owen Rogers, 73
  lent title-page border to Henry Sutton, 158
Kingston, Anthony
  Stationer, perhaps related to John, 82

Kingston, John, printer (Grocer)
  career before 1559, 78, 81–2
    acquired Nicholas Hill's printing materials, 81
    partnership with Henry Sutton, 81, 106–9
    productivity, 87
  1557, as Grocer, became ineligible to print, 82
  1558, printed pirated sermons for Marshe, 82
  1559
    great primer textura with w^{2+} and w^{sc} mixed, 71, 102
    corrected 1552 calendar errors, 94
    revised calendar layout, 93, 173, *Plate 4*
    printed calendar quire for BCP1559G, 93–4, 202, 225
    printed cancels for BCP1559G, 109, 203, 225
    printed contents list for BCP1559G *and* 1559JC1, 102–4, 202–3
    printed parts of BCP1559JC1, 81–2, 84, 201, 226
    printed parts of the Jugge ordinal, 125, 128, *130*, 203, 231
    printed parts of BCP1559JC2–3, 140, 142, 203, 226
    printed the preliminaries of BCP1559JC3, 142, 190, 227
    sole printer of BCP1559 8°.1, 160, 204, 230
kneeling. *See* Black Rubric
Knollys, Sir Francis, Privy Councillor
  absence from Council weakens Clegg's theory, 119
  signature, 117, *118*
Knox, John, and the Black Rubric, 31–2, 209

Lambert, St, 178
Lancaster, John, 34
large english textura. *See* type, textura
Laurence, St, 173, 183
law terms, dates of. *See* 'briefe declaration'
Le Roy, Loys, 76
leap year lessons
  1539–49
    February 24th repeats the 23rd, 182, 192–3
  1549–60
    February 26th repeats the 25th, 192
  in and after 1560,
    February 24th repeats the 23rd, 189, 193
lectionary, the
  explained, 90–1, 167–8
  books wholly or partly excluded, 91
  'lessons' assigned to Morning and Evening Prayer, 91, 167–8
  psalms assigned to days of the month, 90
  errors of 1552, 92–3

  essentially unchanged, 1549–60, 164
  revisions of 1561,
    what Elizabeth intended, 165, 167–8, 171
    what was done instead, 167, 169–71
legal-year dating, 107
Lennon and McCartney, 63
Leonard, St, 178, 182–3
Leviticus, little used in the 1549 lectionary, 91
Leviticus 26, sole addition to the 1561 lectionary, 167, 170–1
levity, uncalled for, xv, 5, 21, 55, 63, 79, 95, 171, 175, 193, 197, 214
Linus, St, 184
Litany, the
  1549
    not included in BCP1549G1a–b, 16–17, 20
    appended to BCP1549G1c, 20–1, 197
    inserted after part 1 in BCP1549W1, 20
  1552 and after
    follows Evening Prayer, 21
  1559
    revision required by Act of Uniformity, 56
    already revised before 7 February, 47, 51, 126
    BCPs not set from printed octavo, 67
    sheet B4:5 unrevised in BCP1559JC1, 66–8, 200
    additional changes made in ordinal, 126–8
Loach, Jennifer, 32
Lucian, St, 178
Lucrece, the sign of, 80
Lucy, St, 178, 182, 188–9

MacCulloch, Diarmaid, 31–3, 66
Machutus, St, 178, 188
McKerrow, R. B., cited, xxii
McKerrow and Ferguson, cited, 107
Magnificat. *See* canticles
Magnus, St, 184
Margaret, St, 178, 182
Marler, Anthony, 2
Marriage service
  in section 2a of the BCP, 14
Marshe, Thomas, printer, 77
  1555
    printed first book, 78
  1557
    apparently 'invented' press figures, 78, *79*
    ringleader in piracy of Wolfe patent, 78
  1558, published pirated reprint of sermons, 82
  1559
    great primer textura with w^{2+}, 70
    printed part of BCP1559JC1, 78–9, 84, 201, 225
    used press figures in BCP1559JC1, 78–9, 201

Martin of Tours, St, 178, 182, 184, 188, 194
Mary I, Queen, 46–7, 66, 85, 157, 159, 199, 204
  acceded July 1553, 44
  purged the London book trade, 45–6, 198
  had BCPs called in for burning, 49, 179, 209
  reimposed Catholicism, 44–6
  granted the Stationers a printing monopoly, 50
  died November 1558, 46
Mary Magdalene, St. *See under* holy days (fixed)
Mason, Sir John, Privy Councillor
  Council attendance weakens Clegg's theory, 119
'Mattyns' in section 1a of 1549 BCP, 9
  renamed 'Mornyng prayer' in 1552, 39, 172
  'Mattens' again in 1559 table of proper lessons, 100
Maunsell, Andrew, cited, 50
Mierdman, Steven, printer (immigrant), xv, 62, 77, 82–3, 188
  1549 improvisations
    A 'packed' and inverted for use as V, 76
    E 'packed' for use as F, 76
    V inverted for use as A, 74
  1552
    printed 22 sheets of BCP1552Whit.4. 34, 42–3, 197
    printed 22 sheets of BCP1552Whit.5. 34, 42–3
  1553
    Coverdale Bible for Jugge adds few miscellanea, 185
    returned to Europe, 45
Mildred, St, 182
miscellanea recorded in Cancel Calendars
  Beheading of John the Baptist, 178, 184
  Conception of Mary, 178, 182
  Elizabeth's accession, 177
  Exaltation of the Cross, 178, 188–9
  'Invention' of the Cross, 178, 182, 188
  Mary Magdalene, St, 178
  Name of Jesus, 178, 183
  Nativity of Mary, 178, 182, 189
  O sapientia, 178, 188
  Transfiguration, 178, 183
  Visitation of Mary, 178, 182, 194
  zodiac notes (usually red), 177
miscellanea recorded in small Edwardian BCPs
  Assumption of Mary, 182
  Seven Sleepers, 182
miscellaneous column, the
  in BCP calendars
    1549, 172–3
    1559, 174
    1561, 177–8

Moschella, Jay, help acknowledged, 68
Moxon, Joseph, 60, 76
Mychell, John, printer in Canterbury, 70, 83–4, 145

Nativity of Elizabeth I
  added to miscellanea in BCP1580, 195
Neale, J. E., 32
New College, Oxford, copy of BCP1549G1a
  mistaken for hybrid, 16
  really first edition, first issue, 20
Newcastle fragment, the (BCP1559 8°.2), 160–3
Nicholas, St, 178, 182
Nicomedes, St, 178, 183, 194
Nunc dimittis. See canticles

Oastler, C. L., cited, 95
oath of supremacy
  included in ordinal, 114
OED cited, 15, 113, 209
ordain, ordination
  Tudor ordinals use *order, ordering*, 113
ordinal
  original (Catholic) meaning, 113
  present (post-1658) Anglican meaning, 113
ordinal, the
  1550, commissioned and published, 114–15
  1552
    appended to all folio BCPs, 34–5, 104, 115, 126
    compressed to nine sheets, 41, 43
  1559 version
    oath of supremacy replaced by oath of sovereignty, 127–8
    officially detached from the BCP, 116–17, 123, 202, 207, 213, 216
  1559 Grafton edition, 117–25, 231
    perhaps suppressed, 116, 203
  1559 Jugge edition, *124*, 125, 231–2
    only sheet AA3:6 printed by Jugge, 125
    John Kingston printed AA1,2,4:5,7,8 and BB5: 6, 125
    Richard Payne printed sheets BB1–3:8–10, 125
    William Copland printed sheet BB4:7, 125
    most copies lack original BB5:6 201–2, 128–9
    York copy is made up with leaves from BCP1552Graf.4. 128
    two copies have a 1580 reprint by Thomas Dawson, 129
    one copy has a reprint by Thomas Purfoot, *c.* 1581. 129

ornament stock
  Mierdman's acquired by Cawood, 45, 220
  Whitchurch's, 65, 74, 86, 198, 200
    acquired by Jugge, 70, 87, 96, 103
  Whitchurch's and Wolfe's, combined, 68
ornamental initials, 8
  found more than once in a quire, 54
  of Edward Whitchurch, 65
  of John King, 73
  of John Kingston
    borrowed by Jugge, 65
    borrowed by Thomas Marshe, 107
  of Nicholas Hill, 12
  of Owen Rogers, 73–4
  See also Rogers, Owen, 1559 improvisations
  of Reyner Wolfe, *64*, 65
  of Richard Grafton, acquired by Jugge, 145
  of Thomas Dawson, datable to 1580, 129
  of Thomas Purfoot, datable to *c*. 1581, 129
  W misprinted as Y, 68
  Y corrected to W, 68
ornaments (printers'), 2, 52, 66, 94, 109, 140, 221
'ornaments' of the church, 166
  the 'ornaments' rubric, 56–7, 148
Osmund, St, 183
Oswen, John, printer in Worcester
  1549
    patent for church books for Wales, 4
    printed BCP1549Worcester, 4, 152
    printed BCP1549Worcester4°, 4, 152, 181
    exploited retail price limits, 20
  1550
    New Testament calendar includes hours of daylight, 187
  1552
    printed BCP1552Worcester, 31, 41
outer forme defined, 5
Oxford Dictionary of the Christian Church, The, 33

'packing' an initial to obscure parts of the letter, 75–6
Page, William, cited, 13
Pancras of Rome, St, 183
Pantzer, Katharine F., xiv, 84, 121, 207
Paris, 2
Parker, Matthew, archbishop of Canterbury
  instructed to revise calendar, 165, 205
Parliament, Acts of
  25 Hen. VIII, c. 20.
    repealed by Mary, 216
  2 & 3 Edw. VI, c. 1. See Acts of Uniformity, 1549
  3 & 4 Edw. VI, c. 10.
    abolishing Catholic liturgies, 113
  3 & 4 Edw. VI, c. 12.

  establishing the ordinal, 214
  5 & 6 Edw. VI, c. 1. *See* Acts of Uniformity, 1552
  1 Mar. I, st. 1, c. 1.
    defining *treason* and *praemunire*, 44
  1 Mar. I, st. 2, c. 2.
    repealing Edwardian acts, 44
  1 Eliz. I
    the printed statute, 97, 213
  1 Eliz. I, c. 1. *See* Act of Supremacy
  1 Eliz. I, c. 2. *See* Acts of Uniformity, 1559
  1 Eliz. I, c. 4+ (The Missing Act)
    'For Admitting and Consecrating Archbishops and Bishops', 213–16, Plate *1b*
  1 Eliz. I, c. μ 17,
    for spawn and fry of fish, 219
Parry, Sir Thomas, Privy Councillor
  signature, 117, *118*
Payne (formerly Berthelet), Margery, 80
Payne, Richard, printer (foren), 102
  1556, married Margery Berthelet, 80
  1557, as foren, became ineligible to print, 80
  1559
    great primer with w³, 70, 81
    printed part of BCP1559JC1, 80–1, 84, 201, 225
    printed part of Jugge ordinal, 125, 203, 232
    printed parts of BCP1559JC2, 141, 203, 226
    printed parts of BCP1559JC3, 203, 227
    productivity, 86
    Q mutilated for use as O, *144*, 145
Peele, James, 107
perfecting defined, 6
Perpetua, St, 178
Petronilla, St, 183
Petyt, Thomas, printer (Draper), 158
Pickering, William
  1844 reprints of key BCP editions, 181
pilcrows, 15, 106
piracy, 78, 82, 86
Plantin, Christopher, 76
Ponet, John, bishop of Rochester, 114
Powell, Humphrey, printer in Dublin, 4
Powell, Thomas, 80
preliminaries defined, 6
preliminaries
  of 1549, 7
  of 1552, 35–9, 41, 56
    not recyclable in 1559, 59
  of 1559, 43, 52, 90, 143
    collaboration summarized, 111
prices. *See* retail price limits
printers' devices. *See* devices
Prisca, St, 178

Privy Council, the, 117
  and the Black Rubric, 1552, 31–2
  1559
    detached the revised ordinal, 105
    set price limits for the BCP, 17, 61
    See also retail price limits
production costs, lowering. *See* compressing
productivity. *See under* the names of printers
proper lessons
  1549 specified in text with Introits etc., 98
  1552 tabulated in the preliminaries, 98
  1559
    Act of Uniformity requires many additions, 55, 97, 205
    annual number increased (from 72 to 227), 98
proper lessons, 1559 table of
  printed in BCP1559G by Grafton, 97
  printed in BCP1559JC1 by Kingston, 97–101
  six pages available in prelims, 98
  first two pages probably cancelled, 101
  only four pages used, 98, 100–1
Protestation of the Two and Twenty Divines, The, 193
Psalm 98,
  text omitted from Graf.1, Whit.1, 35
psalters
  1552
    appended to small-format BCPs, 34, 155, 204
  1559
    added to William Seres's patent for primers, 157–60, 204
    printed for Seres by Sutton and Copland, 158
Purfoot, Thomas the elder, printer
  c. 1581 printed replacement sheet BB5:6 for Jugge ordinal, 129, *132*
  unconnected with the BCP printers, 133
Purification of Women
  in section 2a of the 1549 BCP, 14
  renamed 'Churching' of Women in 1552, 14

quads defined, 9
Quaritch, Bernard, 26
quire defined, 5

Rastell, John, printer (foren)
  an early pioneer of shared printing, 13
Raynald, Thomas, printer (Draper), 158, 185
Real Presence (corporal)
  seemingly implied in 1549 BCP, 27, 58
Recorde, Robert, *The Castle of Knowledge*
  initial T commissioned by Wolfe for, 96

recycling of 1552 sheets in 1559, 59–61, 225
reducing the page-count. *See* compressing
Regnault, François, printer in Paris, 2, 13, 74
Remigius, St, 178, 183
reprinting page for page
  some advantages of, 25, 27
retail price limits set by Privy Council
  2s. unbound
    BCP1549G1b, 1549W 1, 17–19, 123
  2s. unbound without ordinal
    BCP1552Graf.2–6, Whit.2–5, 41, 115, 123
  2s. 2d. unbound
    BCP1549G1c–G5, 1549W2–5, 20, 123
    BCP1549Worcester4°, 20
  2s. 4d. unbound
    BCP1559G, 1559JC2–3, 121, *122*
  2s. 6d. unbound
    BCP1549Worcester, 20
    BCP1552Graf.2–6, Whit.2–5, 115, 123
    BCP1552Worcester, 41
  3s. 4d. bound
    BCP1549G1b, 1549W 1, 17
  3s. 4d. bound without ordinal
    BCP1552Graf.2–6, Whit.2–5, 115
  3s. 8d. bound
    BCP1549G1c–G3, 1549W 2–3, 20, 25
    BCP1549Worcester4°, 20
    BCP1559G, 1559JC2–3, 121, *122*
  4s. bound
    BCP1549W2–5, 25
    BCP1549Worcester, 20
    BCP1552Graf.2–6, Whit.2–5, 41, 115
    BCP1552Worcester, 41
Reynes, John, 45
Richard, St, 178
Ridley, Nicholas, bishop of Rochester, London, 114
Rishton, Edward, 178
Rogers, Owen, printer, 145
  1555
    freed, and printed first book, 73
    borrowed initials from John King, 73
    productivity, 86
  1555–59 ornamental initials acquired from
    Richard Grafton, 73
    Edward Whitchurch or Thomas Gaultier, 73
    William Herford, 74
  1559
    230 textura type, 140
    great primer textura with w⁷, 75, 71, 139
    large english textura, 75, 139
    owned only one ornamental I, 74, 201
    printed part of BCP1559JC1, 73–7, 84, 201, 225

new W commissioned, *139*, 140
  printed parts of BCP1559JC2–3, 138–40,
    203, 226–7
  1559 improvisations
    B inverted, 'packed', for use as I, *139*, 140
    E inverted, 'packed', for use as I, *139*, 140
    I borrowed from Whitchurch, 75, 76
    S borrowed from Cawood, 77
    T 'packed' for use as I, 75, 76, 139
    T inverted, 'packed', for use as I, *139*, 140
    T inverted, lowered, for use as I, 75, 74
    T simply inverted for use as I, *139*, 140
    V inverted for use as A, 75, 74, 76, 139
  18-mm initial T
    its history from 1539, 74–5
Roman (pre-Julian) calendar, the
  in the BCP calendars, 171–2
Rouen, 45
rubrics (Edwardian)
  never in red ink, 33
  typically in smaller type, 41
running titles
  in BCP1549G1a misprinted, 10
  cancelled, and sheets re-used, 11, 26
Russell, Francis (earl of Bedford), signature,
  117, *118*
Rypins, Stanley, cited, 208

St Clement Danes, parish of, 147
St Dunstan in the West, parish of, 147
St George, the sign of, 147
St Paul's Churchyard, 62–3
Sainty, John Christopher, 215
Sarum use, 1, 3
Sebastian, St, 183
Seres, William
  early career, 157
  1559
    psalters included in new patent, 157–60
    psalter rights arbitrated (by Stationers?),
      159–60, 204
    publisher (not printer) of the 4° psalter, *156*,
      158–9, 229
Seymour, John, clerk of the Commons, 216–18
shared printing
  early history of, 12–14
  of BCP1559JC1, reasons for, 72
signatures (autograph)
  Bacon, Sir Nicholas, 117, *118*, 226, *Plate 3*
  Cave, Sir Ambrose, 117, *118*
  Cecil, Sir William, 117, *118*
  Clinton, Edward Fiennes de, 117, *118*
  Dyson, Humphrey, 16
  Emery, Edward, 128
  Fiennes de Clinton, Edward, 117, *118*

Forster, Anne, 128
Herbert, William, 117, *118*
Howard, William, 117, *118*
Knollys, Sir Francis, 117, *118*
Parry, Sir Thomas, 117, *118*
Russell, Francis, 117, *118*
signatures (printed)
  defined, 6
  always cited in roman (letters) and arabic
    (numerals), xxii, 6
  in preliminaries, 6
  misprinted, 7, 17, 68–9
  curtailed alphabets, 15
  multiple alphabets, xxii, xxiv, 14–15
Skot, John, printer
  an early pioneer of shared printing, 13
Smith, Sir Thomas, Secretary of State, 4
SOLO (Search Oxford Libraries Online), 16, 228
Spilman, Francis, clerk of Parliaments, 40, 93
Stationers' Company, the
  1557 charter granted a printing monopoly,
    50, 80
Statutes of the Realm cited, 38, 44, 113–15
STC, xxv, 29, 34, 65
  annotations cited, 14, 67, 147
  errors, xv, 137
    collation and priority of Graf.1. 34–5
    description of BCP1559JC3, 134, 227–8
    nature of '16284.5', 30
    nature of 16287, 30
    order of 1559 quartos, 153, 157
    status of 16267, 21
Sunday letters. *See* Dominical letters
sunrise, sunset. *See* hours of daylight
Sutton, Henry
  1553–7 partnership with John Kingston, 81,
    106–9
  1559 printed part of psalter for Seres, 158,
    204, 229
Swithun, St, 178
Sylvester, St, 178

Table of Proper Lessons. *See* proper lessons, 1559
  table of
Te deum laudamus. *See* canticles
Ten Commandments, the
  'tables' of, to be displayed in churches, 165
textura. *See* type
Theodore, St, 183
Thirlby, Thomas, bishop of Westminster,
    Norwich, 114
  opposed the ordinal, 114
title-page borders
  McK & F 33 (John Kingston),
    used by him in BCP1559 8°.1, *161*, 230

title-page borders (cont.)
   McK & F 37 (John King)
      used by Henry Sutton in BCP1559 4°.1, *156*, 158, 228
   McK & F 38 (John Kingston), 101
   McK & F 46 etc. (Richard Grafton)
      used by Richard Tottell in 1553–8, 50
   McK & F 67 (Richard Grafton), 105, 107
      1548–53 used by Grafton himself, *22*, *36*, 107
      used by Kingston and Sutton in 1554, 107–9
      used by Richard Tottell in 1555–7, 107
      used by Thomas Marshe in 1557, 107
      used by John Kingston in 1559, *108*, 109, 142, 224, Plate 2
   McK & F 68 (Richard Jugge)
      1548–56 used by Edward Whitchurch, *37*, 142
      used by John Kingston in the Jugge ordinal, 103, 109, *124*, 125, 142, 231
      used by Jugge himself in BCP1559JC1, 103–4, 142, 225, Plate 3
      used by John Kingston in BCP1559JC3, *136*, 142, 227
   McK & F 110
      used by John Cawood in 1560, 220
   McK & F 111 (Richard Jugge)
      used by Leonard Askell in 1562, 160
   not in McK & F (Richard Jugge)
      used in 1559, 142
      used in BCP1559 4°.1, 228, Plate 8
Tottell, Richard, printer
   held monopoly of lawbooks, 50
   married Grafton's daughter in 1558, 50
   productivity, 49
Toy, Robert, 185
transubstantiation, 27, 58
Treveris, Peter, printer in Southwark
   an early pioneer of shared printing, 13
Trinity, the sign of the, 147
Tudor Royal Proclamations cited, 44, 49, 56, 58, 198
Tunstall, Cuthbert, bishop of Durham
   opposed the ordinal, 114
Tylley, William, printer (Barber-Surgeon)
   1548–9 New Testament calendars list many saints, 186
type
   Fraktur
      'Bible', *64*, 105–7
      'Wolfe', *64*, 95–6
   textura
      large english, 75, 77
      great primer, 70–1, 77
      230 mm, *64*, 77, 95, 105–10

Valentine, St, 178, 182
Veale, Abraham, 185
   1557, accomplice of Marshe in piracies, 78
   1558, published pirated reprint of sermons, 82
verso defined, 6
Vervliet, H. D. L., cited, 105
vestments, 56–7
Vincent, St, 178, 183
Visitation of the Sick
   in section 2a of the BCP, 14

Wales and the Marches
   church books to be printed for, 4
Ward, Thomas, 33
Wayland, John, printer (Scrivener), 107
   1553–6, managed Whitchurch printing house, 45–6, 65
Weston, Dr Hugh, 32
Whitchurch (formerly Cranmer), Margaret, 66, 200
Whitchurch, Edward, printer (Haberdasher), 8, 185
   career before 1547, 1–3, 74
   productivity, 50, 85
   1547 joint patent with Grafton for service books, 3
   1548–9 shared books with Nicholas Hill, 12–13
   1549
      no calendar in his Great Bible, 185
      the events of March, 23–4
      BCP1549G1a colophon dated 7 March, 4, 7, 14, *18*
      BCP1549G1a part 2, 14–15
      BCP1549W1 preliminaries, 7, 17
      BCP1549W2 preliminaries rearranged, 9
      printed abbreviated BCP with quarto psalter, 182
   1552
      BCP preliminaries, 35–9
      the events of April and May, 40
      3 editions complete by 27 Sept., 31
      printed Black Rubric cancels, 33–4
      quarto BCP adds many miscellanea to calendar, 179, 182, 206
   1553
      2nd quarto BCP adds different miscellanea to calendar, 183, 206
      octavo BCP revises miscellanea yet again, 183–4, 206
   1553–6, business managed by John Wayland, 45–6
   1556, closed printing house and moved out, 46, 198
   1556–8?
      married widow Margaret Cranmer, 66

1557, as Haberdasher, became ineligible to print, 50
1559
to participate in reprinting 1552 BCP, 50
his printing materials accessible, 50
ornamental initials, *64*, 65, 83
with Reyner Wolfe, printed part of BCP1559JC1, 65–6, 84, 200, 201, 225
1560
a book printed for him by Wolfe, 96
Wolfe, Reyner, printer
address, 66
productivity, 85–6
1547, appointed Royal Typographer in Latin, Greek, and Hebrew, 66, 78, 85
1549–50
New Testament calendars include hours of daylight, 186–7
1559
ornamental initials, *64*, 95–6
other ornaments, 94–6
with Edward Whitchurch, printed part of BCP1559JC1, 65–6, 84, 225
corrected most 1552 calendar errors, 94
revised calendar layout, 96, 173–4, *Plate 5*
probably printed calendar quire unaided, 94–6, 190, 201, 226
Woodhead, Abraham, 33, 211
Worcester, 4, 20, 152, 181
Worcester Cathedral
copy of BCP1552Worcester, 30, 33
Worde, Wynkyn de, printer
an early pioneer of shared printing, 13
words of administration
1549, 27–8
1552, 30
Wyer, Robert, printer (Salter), xv, 105, 125
an early pioneer of shared printing, 13
printed 6 sheets of BCP1549G3, 27, 197
printed 4 sheets of BCP1549G4, 27, 197
printed 12 sheets of BCP1549G5, 27, 197

Zion Research Library
copy of BCPGraf.1 untraced, 35